# ROCK GARDEN PLANTS

# ROCK GARDEN PLANTS

## A COLOR ENCYCLOPEDIA

## BALDASSARE MINEO

To Nancy!
Good rocks
Gardenning
Baldassare
Mineo
2/02

**WITH
PHOTOGRAPHIC ASSISTANCE
BY
FRITZ KUMMERT**

Timber Press
Portland, Oregon

Frontispiece
Crevice garden at Siskiyou Rare Plant Nursery

Published in 1999 by
Timber Press, Inc.
The Haseltine Building
133 S.W. Second Avenue, Suite 450
Portland, Oregon 97204, U.S.A.

Reprinted 2000

Designed by Susan Applegate

Printed in Hong Kong

Library of Congress Cataloging-in-Publication Data

Mineo, Baldassare.
    Rock garden plants : a color encyclopedia / Baldas-
sare Mineo ; with photographic assistance by Fritz Kummert.
        p.        cm.
    Includes index.
    ISBN 0-88192-432-6
    1. Rock plants—Encyclopedias. 2. Rock plants—Pic-
torial works. I. Title.
SB421.M55   1999                              99-20672
635.9'672—dc 21                               CIP

# CONTENTS

# PREFACE

Coincidentally, when I graduated from college, I also graduated into rock gardening. I lived in sunny, coastal California, halfway between San Francisco and Los Angeles. I had always gardened because I always had gardening mentors around me. Even the teacher laughed when I shared with the class on the first day back to school as a third-grade student, 8 years old, "My favorite summer activity was watching my plants grow." After college I began working in a retail nursery and filled my home garden with every plant that would grow, including a few rock garden plants. They were my favorites. They were neat and compact, and I could plant dozens of them in a small space. I knew there was something special about these lovable dwarf plants, and I felt I had graduated to a new level—the world of rock gardening.

I borrowed every book, newsletter, and bulletin I could from a friend who was the only rock gardener I had ever met. I pored over this literature, especially the illustrations. How fascinating these little plants looked —if only I could grow them in mild, sunny California. I needed a book that had hundreds of photographs and told me whether I could grow them in my climate zone.

In 1978 I purchased Siskiyou Rare Plant Nursery and moved to southern Oregon, to the town of Medford. Little did I know that along with my partner at the time, Jerry Cobb Colley, I was beginning the adventure of a lifetime. The nursery had been in existence for 16 years and was well known for growing and mail-ordering alpines and other rock garden plants, especially unusual native plants of southern Oregon and northern California, the home of the botanically rich Siskiyou Mountains.

From 1978 and well into the 1980s, the cofounders of the nursery, Lawrence Crocker and Boyd Kline, were our mentors. When they sold the nursery they were listing about 650 different species in their catalog, plants that few nurseries sold, half of them local natives. Jerry and I were fascinated and anxious to learn about all these "new" plants. Before that, our focus had been growing and wholesaling larger perennials and shrubs in California. Lawrence and Boyd taught us expertly. They wisely kept us focused on the plants that needed our attention at the moment, thus preventing us from becoming overwhelmed by the mammoth task of learning about the hundreds of plant species we had purchased and were now responsible for maintaining, propagating, and marketing through our small, annual catalog.

In spite of all their care, it was not possible for Lawrence and Boyd to protect us from the avalanche of new plant material that was soon to come our way. We joined the North American Rock Garden Society, the Alpine Garden Society of England, the Scottish Rock Garden Club, and the Alpine Garden Club of British Columbia. I encourage all rock gardeners to join these fine organizations. Each of these organizations conducted annual seed exchanges; thus we entered the world of seed sources. Through these groups we learned about and joined more specialized horticultural groups such as those devoted to primroses and conifers. We found other sources of seed such as collecting expeditions that sold shares in their collections, and seed businesses, and we became acquainted with individual home gardeners skilled at harvesting seed and anxious to trade with us.

We did not realize that a new age of plant exploration was flourishing in the 1970s, and we had hundreds of additional plants to learn about, cultivate, and list in our increasingly large and more frequently published catalogs. The number of our plant listings increased each year. Now my staff and I cultivate about 5000 different species and cultivars, half of them rock garden plants.

In 1992, after watching a slide presentation that I gave at the North American Rock Garden Society Winter Study Weekend, Richard Abel, then of Timber Press, asked if I would like to do a "picture book" on rock garden plants, fulfilling my earlier wish for just such a book. It is with great pleasure that after more than 20 years of being associated with Siskiyou Rare Plant Nursery and 7 years of research, I have finally completed this book. It is my intention that this book be used by those who wish to *grow* these wonderful plants as well as read about them.

## For Further Information

In addition to years of personal experience with the plants themselves, I was fortunate to have the benefit of books that make available the experience and knowledge of others with rock garden plants. These books remain useful sources of additional information and include H. Lincoln Foster's *Rock Gardening* (1968, reprinted by Timber Press), Will Ingwersen's *Manual of Alpine Plants* (1978), Wilhelm Schacht's *Rock Gardens* (1981), the Alpine Garden Society's *Encyclopaedia of Alpines* (1993–1994), and the Royal Horticultural Society's *Index of Garden Plants* (1994, Timber Press), edited by Mark Griffiths. In addition, there are many other fine reference books on rock garden plants, although none has such comprehensive color photographic coverage as the present book.

## Acknowledgments

My sincerest appreciation goes to the many friends who have helped make this book a reality, from the early years of guidance from Boyd Kline and Lawrence Crocker, through the growth years with Jerry Cobb Colley, to this final fruition. I thank the friends who helped provide photographs (unless otherwise credited, the photographs are mine), Sheila Gaquin, Armen Gevjan, Phyllis Gustafson, Franz Hadacek, Josef Halda, Reuben Hatch, Roy Herold, Panayoti Kelaidis, Ted Kipping, Kelley Leonard, Sigurd Lock, Mark McDonough, Paul Martin, Ernest O'Byrne, Phil Pearson, and especially, Fritz Kummert, who supplied nearly half of the photographs and who, together with E. M. Upward, recommended plants to include from a European rock gardening perspective. Last but certainly not least, the following friends and staff have generously given their time in assisting with the tedious work of organizing and proofing that is necessary in a project such as this book. These loyal helpers are Don Buckingham, Michele Register, John Robertson, and Debbie Berry.

# ROCK GARDEN PLANTS

Rock gardeners appreciate nature because in nature, rock garden plants are everywhere. What is a rock garden plant? The broad definition has been chosen here: A rock garden plant is a plant that looks good growing among rocks. Such plants can be found all over the world. They may be at the seashore, in the forest, in the desert, in the tundra, and of course, in the mountains. Another criterion that has been respected here is that the plant should mature to a height of usually less than 24 inches (60 cm). Most of the plants are actually well under that height; they should not grow out of scale with the rocks and engulf them. It is the appeal of compactly growing plants set among stone and rock that draws many to rock gardening. The re-creation of "natural" landscapes in the rock garden, large or small, is a source of contentment to many rock gardeners, as is the care and cultivation of the plants, including the challenges they sometimes present.

*Rock Garden Plants, A Color Encyclopedia,* presents most of the genera of rock garden plants. Although not every species and cultivar could be included, of course, the attempt has been made to provide a good representation of many genera. I regret the omission of any genus that a reader feels should have been included. In the process of gathering the plants treated here, the photographs of them, and the information about them, I have learned much but admit I am not a botanist in the strict sense of the word. I am, however, an enthusiastic gardener as well as a collector of the rare and unusual who wishes to share his love of these plants with other gardeners. Species and cultivars not yet grown or readily available in the United States are portrayed. In turn, many American natives and cultivars are shown that are rare in gardens elsewhere in the world, including Europe. An important feature of the present book is the provision of cultivation information, plant by plant, in the descriptions accompanying the photographs. The specialized terms involving cultivation, mentioned in passing below, are discussed further in the chapter, About the Descriptions.

## Alpine Plants

"Alpines" or alpine plants are usually rock garden plants; rock garden plants are not necessarily alpines. As mentioned before, plants judged appropriate for the rock garden may be native to various habitats, including desert, seashore, and forest as well as lofty mountaintops. An alpine, strictly defined, is a plant that is native to mountain heights above timberline, the upper limit of true tree growth. The origin of the word alpine is connected with the Alps, the grand mountain range extending from France, Switzerland, and Italy into the Balkan Peninsula. But every continent has alpine regions, even some areas near the equator usually thought of as tropical. Plants from above timberline in these other mountainous areas are also true alpines. Casual usage has led "alpine" to be used interchangeably with "rock garden plant," doubtless because plants from alpine regions, with their low, cushion habit and miniaturized proportions, epitomize the classic rock garden plant. Cushion plants are listed in the appendix, Rock Garden Plants for Specific Purposes and Locations.

Plants from alpine areas of tropical mountain ranges may not prove particularly hardy in most temperate gardens and often require special care and protection in a well-ventilated greenhouse, possibly with some supplementary heat. Such houses are called alpine houses. Cold frames and bulb frames are also devices frequently used to control climatic conditions in order to grow unusual, and often difficult, alpines. Plants for alpine houses and frames are listed in the appendix, Rock Garden Plants for Specific Purposes and Locations.

When giving tours of my nursery and garden, I often pause at a small area of calcareous tufa (porous limestone rock, a common medium for growing alpines), point out the saxifrages (*Saxifraga*) and other plants growing there, and refer to them as classic rock garden plants. I say that because these small, congested, dome-shaped plants present the classic picture of plants growing in alpine regions. When they are in flower, I add to the explanation that alpines usually have relatively large flowers compared to the diminutive overall size of the plant. Some say the plants are equipped with such conspicuous flowers in order to attract the wayward pollinating insect, which seems reasonable to me. When I sit on a rock outcrop at high elevations, admiring the alpine flora, I ponder what existence must be like for these precious plants. They may appear dainty and delicate but they have adapted to withstand poor, rocky soil and extremes of weather, including high winds, intense cold and blazing heat, and deep snow and summer drought. Their size and habit have been shaped by their environment.

The native plants of the Siskiyou Mountains that straddle the border of Oregon and California near my home have adjusted to extremely rocky, nutrient-deficient soil, and long periods of summer drought. *Lewisia cotyledon* is an endemic, a species found only in these mountains. It is grown by rock gardeners the world over. It is not difficult to grow if given a few conditions that reflect its native habitat such as perfect drainage, a collar of gritty rock around the crown of the plant, and a drying-off period in summer. It is an excellent plant for the semishady rock garden, the crevice garden, or for cultivation in a container in the alpine house. Many hybrids and selections have been made from this fine species, many of which have won horticultural awards in the United States and abroad.

*Lewisia cotyledon* is a good example of an alpine plant that has become a popular rock garden plant. It can be quite challenging to grow in climates that are very different from its own such as areas with heavy rainfall, high summer humidity and moisture, or alkaline soil. If those conditions exist, steps must be taken to grow the plant successfully. For many gardeners, meeting such challenges is part of the appeal of growing alpines. Other outstanding alpines from other mountain ranges that can be challenging, but quite growable, include *Asperula pontica* from the mountains of Iraq and Turkey, *Campanula raineri* from the Italian and Swiss Alps, *Daphne jasminea* from the mountains of Greece, and *Saxifraga oppositifolia*, whose native geographical distribution is circumpolar, extending into mountains further south.

But many true alpine plants are surprisingly easy to cultivate in rock gardens in a wide range of climatic zones, including favored species and cultivars of *Achillea, Androsace, Aurinia, Campanula, Draba, Gentiana, Sedum, Thymus,* and *Veronica*. Such examples prove to the beginning rock gardener that not all true alpines are difficult and should be left only to the experts. On the contrary, there are many alpines that are proven, hardy, easy-to-grow landscape plants whose only requirements are well-drained soil, water, and sunshine. Easy-to-grow rock garden plants are listed in the appendix, Rock Garden Plants for Specific Purposes and Locations. Also, the label "rock garden plant" includes many types of plants such as those for the peat bed, shady situations, the front of the perennial border, and the alpine house. They can be herbaceous perennials, dwarf shrubs and trees, ground covers, ferns, and "bulbs," bulbous, cormous, rhizomatous, and tuberous perennials.

## Mediterranean Plants

Plants from low elevations but native to harsh, extreme conditions have evolved into sizes and shapes that also make them perfect rock garden candidates. They come from many lands and usually from rocky, dryish conditions, from sea level to mountainous elevations. The lands in the vicinity of the Mediterranean Sea have a rich flora, as do other regions of the world with a winter-wet, summer-dry Mediterranean climate, for example, much of California. Hundreds of fine plants of alpine character are native to areas with a Mediterranean climate. The plants native to these regions are usually tolerant of heat and drought and thrive in the sun and on some level of neglect. They may be cultivated in a variety of soils but some require dry conditions in summer, others in winter, as listed in the appendix, Rock Garden Plants for Specific Purposes and Locations. Mediterranean plants for the rock garden include representatives from the genera *Andryala, Anthyllis, Cistus, Helianthemum, Lithodora, Origanum, Ptilotrichum, Sternbergia, Teucrium,* and *Thymus.*

## Dryland Plants

Dryland, even desert, regions have many plants to offer the rock gardener. Overlapping into other areas such as those with a Mediterranean climate, the dryland regions include plants that thrive in heat and sun, but to an even greater degree. Dryland plants are subject to prolonged spells with little or no rainfall. During these periods many dryland natives survive by entering a period of dormancy. The dryland gardener must reduce irrigation or risk overwatering the plants during dormancy. There are many useful and desirable plants in this category. Their usefulness includes their ability to thrive in harsh garden situations where little else will grow. They often require poor, dry, or sandy soil. Plants for sandy soil, and that tolerate heat and drought, are listed in the appendix, Rock Garden Plants for Specific Purposes and Locations. Once established, some plants need little water and usually no fertilizing. Some may need extra protection from moisture during summer or winter or both. Dryland plants include many with fascinating foliage and an abundance of beautiful flowers. Species and cultivars of the following genera fall into this interesting dryland group: *Acantholimon, Epilobium, Eriogonum, Penstemon, Salvia,* and *Talinum.*

## Woodland Plants

Shady situations are also home to many rock garden plants. Plants that would suffer in full sun can be accommodated where either dappled or heavy shade is cast by one tree or many. The narrow strip of a garden on the north side of a building can also provide space for plants that do well in shade. Such settings typically feature richer, usually acid soil, and cooler, often moister conditions that satisfy a wide range of plants native to

woodlands. In nature, humus-rich soil develops beneath many types of trees. Trees whose root systems do not deplete the soil of nutrients make the best companions to woodland plants. There, many shrubs will thrive such as *Rhododendron,* including azaleas, and dwarf conifers. Drifts of herbaceous plants are most attractive in the woodland, especially in spring, beginning with *Anemone, Hepatica,* and *Pulmonaria. Corydalis, Epimedium, Erythronium, Helleborus, Trillium,* and many more genera continue the display well into summer. The shady rock garden is a haven for a wide range of plants where shade or part shade is a critical requirement, and such plants are listed in the appendix, Rock Garden Plants for Specific Purposes and Locations.

## Peat Plants

Most rock gardens have areas devoted to plants growing in soil that consists of a deep bed of peaty, acid humus. Plants native to such habitats are often mountain plants that grow in pockets of this rich soil, or heaths and heathers such as *Calluna* and *Erica* that cover large areas of moorland. A wide range of species and cultivars is available, offering an array of foliage textures and colors in addition to flowers that bloom in every season of the year. Plants for the peat garden are listed in the appendix, Rock Garden Plants for Specific Purposes and Locations. The higher mountain inhabitants of acid peat regions include dwarf rock garden plants from the genera *Cassiope, Gaultheria, Primula,* and *Rhododendron* among many others.

## Plants for Special Areas of Cultivation

The rock garden can include specialized areas for successful cultivation of many different kinds of plants. Such areas may include a planted wall, a bog, a sand bed, troughs and containers, and even structures such as an alpine house, cold frame, or bulb frame. Some or all of these elements can be combined to enrich the tapestry of the rock garden, each area created to accommodate plants with particular needs. Plants for such areas are listed in the appendix, Rock Garden Plants for Specific Purposes and Locations. Each garden is an outgrowth of the rock gardener's attempt to cultivate an ever increasing number of genera and species.

# ABOUT THE DESCRIPTIONS

## Scientific Names

Plants in the Color Encyclopedia are arranged alphabetically by scientific name, genus and species, an arrangement that facilitates quick reference when the book is used in conjunction with another book, a seed list, or a plant catalog, for example. The application of scientific names of plants is governed by the *International Code of Botanical Nomenclature*. Individuals and populations of plants may be grouped into a species, and related species into a genus (plural, genera). Each species bears the name of a genus plus a species name, a combination called a binomial, for example, *Crocus sieberi*, distinguishing it from all other species. Groups of distinctive populations within a species may be recognized taxonomically by naming them at the ranks, in descending order, of subspecies, variety, and form, for example, *Crocus sieberi* subsp. *sublimis* f. *tricolor* and *Agave utahensis* var. *eborispina*. Groups of more closely related species within a genus may be recognized by naming them at the ranks, in descending order, of subgenus, section, and series, for example, *Iris* subgenus *Limniris* [the Beardless irises], section *Limniris*, series *Californicae* [the Pacific Coast irises].

Species that are known to be the result of hybridization, either in the wild or in gardens, are designated with a multiplication sign, such as *Anemone ×lesseri*, formed by the hybridization, *A. multifida × A. sylvestris*. Genera, too, may be known hybrids, such as ×*Halimiocistus*, formed by the hybridization, *Halimium × Cistus*. The multiplication sign is ignored in alphabetizing and is not pronounced.

Tentative identifications are indicated with the abbreviation cf. for confer, meaning compare, for example, *Delosperma* cf. *congestum*; the abbreviation is also ignored in alphabetizing.

No discussion of nomenclature would be complete without addressing the issue of name changes that seem to occur frequently in the world of botany. Such changes are usually the result of continuing research in an effort to understand ever more deeply the relationships of plants. Thus the same plant species may bear different names in different books, over a period of time. For the present book, when a choice had to be made between names, the longer established and thus more familiar name has been used, unless the newer name has become widely accepted in the gardening world. Synonymous names that are likely to be encountered, however, are given at the beginning of the description, for example, for *Androsace vandellii*, "synonym, *A. imbricata*," and synonyms are cross-referenced to the accepted name in the Index.

**FAMILIES.** Related genera of plants are grouped together into families, and the family for each genus (or for the species when only one species in a genus is represented) is given in the Color Encyclopedia. Some families, especially the larger ones, are sometimes divided into a number of smaller families. For genera so affected, the smaller family is given in parentheses following the larger family in the description, for example, for *Acorus gramineus*, Araceae (Acoraceae). Perhaps not surprisingly, genera within the same family often have many of the same gardening attributes so it is helpful to know what other genera belong to a family. All of the genera represented in the Color Encyclopedia are grouped by family in the appendix, Families of Rock Garden Plants.

## Cultivar Names

Just as scientific names are governed by a code, so too are cultivar names, by the *International Code of Nomenclature for Cultivated Plants*. A cultivar may be a selection made from naturally occurring, variable populations, such as a white-flowered plant from a species that usually has flowers of another color, for example, *Begonia grandis* 'Alba'. Or a cultivar may be the result of hybridization, usually done intentionally in a garden, for example, *Daphne* ×*mantensiana*, formed by the hybridization, *D.* ×*burkwoodii* [itself a hybrid, *D. caucasica* × *D. cneorum*] × *D. retusa*. Cultivars of particular species are mentioned under the species. Cultivars resulting from interspecific hybridization are listed alphabetically among the other species in the genus.

## Common Names

Common names or vernacular names are given when they are known to have some actual use. There is no code governing the application of common names, and not all such names are indeed common. The same common name may be used for more than one plant, or a plant may have more than one common name, or none. Thus common names can be misleading or ambiguous and, for that reason, the scientific name (in addition to the cultivar name for those plants) should be used. Yet some common names are useful in identifying plants, and they are often colorful or evocative and occasionally suggest something of the history of the interaction between plants and people and thus should not be ignored. Common names are cross-referenced to the accepted scientific names in the Index.

## Growth Habit

Growth habit, that is, the "kind" of plant each one is, is an important consideration in the cultivation of a plant. As mentioned in the chapter, Rock Garden Plants, true alpines and rock garden plants in general can be of different kinds. Descriptions in the Color Encyclopedia begin with a brief mention of the growth habit of the plant.

Perennials may be evergreen, in various degrees, or deciduous. Any plant living for more than a year is a perennial, but when the term is used by itself it is meant to refer to an herbaceous perennial. Additional terms used to describe perennials include the following: bulbous, cormous, rhizomatous, stoloniferous, tuberous, colony forming, cushion forming, hummock forming, mat forming, rosette forming, fibrous rooted, tap-rooted, suckering, insectivorous, woody, shrubby, succulent, self-sowing, and short-lived, sometimes annual or biennial or monocarpic, dying after flowering. Grasses and grass-like plants for rock gardens are perennial and may be evergreen or deciduous and are often tufted. Succulents, plants with thickened, water-storing tissues, may be evergreen or deciduous (or for example in cacti, a taxonomic category, members of the family Cactaceae, essentially leafless); they may be herbaceous or quite fibrous and tough, or even woody. Rock garden orchids (another taxonomic category, members of the family Orchidaceae) are all terrestrial rather than epiphytic, and may be rhizomatous or tuberous from the pseudobulbs characteristic of members of the family.

Woody plants such as shrubs, subshrubs, or shrublets may also be evergreen, in various degrees, or deciduous. They may be further described as upright, spreading, prostrate, hummock forming, mat forming, stoloniferous, or trailing, for example.

Ground covers may be herbaceous or woody and display the additional characteristics of those kinds of plants.

## Exposure

Good light is essential for most plants to grow well. This is especially true for rock garden plants, which more often than not are native to areas receiving full sun. The full-sun conditions in the typical lowland garden, or the garden farther from the poles, however, can be much too intense for many alpines or other rock garden plants. Some shading, or reduction in the daily duration of sun a plant receives, is usually the solution. With this in mind, the individual gardener will want to assess his or her climate, including sun intensity. This can be done by observing what grows well in gardens in the particular region, seeking out information from local gardening sources and organizations, and through individual trial and error. With such careful consideration given to the individual garden situation and local climatic conditions, follow the sun versus shade recommendation in each description: sun, part shade, or shade. Often a plant will grow well in more than one of these light exposures.

## Soil and Drainage

Success with most rock garden plants requires care in the choice of soil and rock. An adjective describing plants that grow among rocks is saxatile from the Latin *saxum,* rock. Some rock garden plants actually require the presence of rocks in order to grow successfully; they need the effects of rock to provide such things as shade, improved drainage, minerals, or a protected root run. The rocks can be entirely or partially below the soil surface. For many such plants, large rocks are not essential, only the appropriate, well-drained soil. A quick look through the cultivation recommendations in the descriptions in the Color Encyclopedia reveals that the majority of plants require some type of well-drained soil. Poorly draining soil that stays moist may be good for bog and wetland plants, but for the majority of plants drainage will have to be improved by amending the soil. Beware of amendments that act as sponges and hold water, such as peat moss; use such amendments only if drainage is too fast, as with sandy or gravelly soils. To improve drainage, add organic matter or rock. Research shows the best organic matter, for example, aged wood bark, has limited sponge action and will improve heavy soils such as clay or clay loam. Drainage is also improved by incorporating rocks, gravel, and small fragments of stone in the soil. Many alpines require rocky soil, also known as scree.

**SCREE.** Scree is rocky soil often associated with alpines in their native habitat where pockets of broken rock have naturally accumulated. The scree garden or scree bed is a planting area that provides excellent drainage, adequate moisture, and an unrestricted root run. A raised bed is a good way to achieve scree at least 6 inches (15 cm) deep, and deeper is usually better. If the site is flat or drains poorly, a deeper base of larger rock, even chunks of broken brick or concrete, will be necessary to prevent puddling directly below the scree. To prevent

the scree from sifting into the larger rubble below, it is necessary to provide an intermediate layer of leaves or hardware cloth that does not prevent water percolation.

The ingredients that make up the scree mixture can vary to suit the plants. A basic scree mixture that has proven most successful consists of equal parts coarse sand, grit, and leaf mold (or aged bark or peat). Grit is usually ¼- to 1-inch (0.5- to 1-cm) sharp gravel that is free of any fine dust or silt. Such a scree mixture produces good results if not allowed to dry out and if occasional fertilizing is done as nutrients are depleted. A "rich" or humus-rich scree may be made with the same basic ingredients with an increase in the proportion of organic matter. The scree mixture can be made "lean" by increasing the amount of sand or grit or both.

A sloping site at the base of larger rocks and boulders is recommended for the scree garden. Such pockets of broken rock naturally occur in the wild and thus appear natural in the garden. A rock garden scree slope most commonly begins at the top of a slope where a rocky outcrop of larger rock is visible, the scree then spreading down the slope and fanning out, ending at the edge of a path. The scree slope may face in any direction, but north- and east-facing slopes allow the greatest number of different species to be grown. Only those plants that thrive with a summer baking, intensified in low-elevation gardens, will do well in south- or west-facing scree.

Some demanding scree plants also require that their roots have access to a gentle flow of moving water during the growing season. Such an arrangement of scree and underground moisture is called a moraine, simulating the habitat of plants that grow in rocky deposits left by a glacier. The moisture must be well below the surface of the scree, about 12 inches (30 cm). This is usually accomplished with an underground pipe that has its own shut-off valve. This pipe brings water to the top of the moraine slope where it is connected to other pipes that branch out and continue down the slope. These branches, buried about 12 inches (30 cm) deep, are perforated with small holes and capped off or sealed at the bottom ends. Under pressure, the water is then forced to seep through all of the perforated holes and trickle through the entire moraine. During the growing season an ideal balance is achieved when the seepage of water, which is constantly provided, is either used by the plants or evaporated at the surface, preventing any puddling at the bottom.

**pH.** Most rock garden plants are indifferent to the pH of the soil, flourishing in lime-free, acid soil or in lime-rich, alkaline soil. A pH of 7 means the soil is neutral, neither acid nor alkaline. Plants described as requiring acid soil (lime-free soil) need soil with a pH value between 3.5 and 6.3. Those described as requiring lime-rich, limy, or alkaline soil need soil with a pH value above 7.5. Plants for acid, peaty soil and plants that tolerate, prefer, or require limy soil are listed in the appendix, Rock Garden Plants for Specific Purposes and Locations.

## Flowering

Not all rock garden plants produce showy flowers—fortunately most do. The combination of compact, saxatile plants smothered in abundant flowers is a frequent sight in the rock garden. This is one of the delights of rock gardening, and often the gardener's greatest reward for all of his or her labor. In the descriptions, the season of flowering is listed, followed by the color or range of colors of the flowers. When fruit is of particular value ornamentally, its color is also described. The season of fruiting usually follows shortly after the flowering season is complete. Rock garden plants that flower later in the year are listed in the appendix, Rock Garden Plants for Specific Purposes and Locations.

## Dimensions

The potential height and spread of a plant is a major concern for a plant to be considered a rock garden plant. As mentioned in the chapter, Rock Garden Plants, the plants should not be out of scale with the rocks. Neither should they be out of scale with each other. This is an area in which tradition may come into conflict with one's personal opinion and gardening style. In the present book and others on rock gardening, one may encounter plant descriptions that read "too large for the rock garden" or "appropriate only for the large rock garden." Customarily, rock garden plants are dwarf or miniature, compact plants. A plant that grows taller than 24 inches (60 cm) is too large for the average rock garden and would tower over the majority of other plants. Combining very large and smaller rock garden plants must be done carefully; there is the danger that eventually the larger will shade out or cover up the smaller. To

avoid that, research the habit (or traits) of the plants and place them accordingly. Generally, rock garden plants are mat-forming creepers barely 1 inch (2.5 cm) high, up to erect or spreading plants 12 inches (30 cm) high. Plants within this range of heights can be planted together in a rock garden with few problems of incompatibility due to size, provided there is sufficient spacing between them to prevent the taller ones overtaking the smaller. Often in a rock garden, a few taller plants can be carefully chosen and placed to add variety and interest; these are usually plants only up to 24 inches (60 cm) in height. A rock garden of exclusively large plants, 12–24 inches (30–60 cm) or even larger, up to 36 inches (90 cm), are best grouped and grown together, again with proper spacing.

In the descriptions in the Color Encyclopedia, measurements for height and width are given for a mature plant under ideal conditions at the time of flowering. Under normal conditions most perennials would attain these dimensions after 3 years of growth. Many dwarf shrubs, and other dwarf woody plants, would take 5 or more years to attain the given height and spread.

## Hardiness Zones

A hardiness zone rating is included in the description of each plant. Two United States Department of Agriculture (U.S.D.A.) zone numbers are given for each plant, for example, for *Xerophyllum tenax*, "Zones 3–8." The first zone designation is intended as an estimate of winter tolerance, that is, the coldest zone in which the plant should be expected to survive outdoors. The second zone number is an estimate of mild climate tolerance, that is, the warmest zone in which the plant should be expected to do well outdoors. (Rock garden plants for mild climates are listed in the appendix, Rock Garden Plants for Specific Purposes and Locations.) The zones for North America and Europe are mapped in the appendix, Hardiness Zone Maps. In my experience, European reference books that provide zone hardiness information frequently list plants as less hardy than in U.S. references. In other words, the European references are more conservative in their prediction of cold hardiness for many plants.

The zone guidelines are just that; they are not a guarantee of success. Use them to see which plants are recommended for your zone. If the zone in which you garden falls within the range given for a plant, that should be an encouragement. A plant recommended for Zones 3–8, for example, would not be recommended for Zones 1, 2, 9, 10, or 11. Using the zone recommendation is only one step in determining if a plant will grow in your garden, however. With the correct conditions and care, many plants are known to grow in zones colder or warmer than their ratings. Factors other than minimum winter temperature determine hardiness, such as soil, wind, winter sun exposure, the condition of plants when they enter winter, and the origin of the plants.

## Geographical Distribution

Descriptions in the Color Encyclopedia conclude with an indication of the natural distribution of the plants. For garden hybrids, the names of the parent plants are given when they are known.

# COLOR ENCYCLOPEDIA

 **A** 

## Abies balsamea
balsam fir
Pinaceae
A conifer for part shade and fertile, well-drained soil. The cultivar 'Nana', dwarf balsam fir, is an indestructibly hardy miniature conifer that forms a tidy, flat-topped cushion of dark, glossy green foliage, silvery beneath. It may be slow or sometimes difficult to establish. Grows 12 inches (30 cm) high, 24 inches (60 cm) wide. Zones 3–8. The species is from northeastern North America.

## Acaena microphylla
New Zealand burr
Rosaceae
In the garden, as in the wild, the showy red stick-tight fruits can be a nuisance when brushed by a passerby. As for all aggressive ground covers, use this perennial away from less vigorous plants. Cultivate in sun and any well-drained soil. Flowers (with white anthers) in summer to early fall, insignificant. Grows 3 inches (7.5 cm) high, 36 inches (90 cm) wide. Zones 6–9. New Zealand.

## Acantholimon
Plumbaginaceae

All of the species of *Acantholimon* have sharply pointed leaves, many rigid and painfully needle-like, and showy flowers followed by long-lasting papery bracts as striking as the flowers. The genus includes shrubs but the species treated here are cushion-forming perennials.

## Acantholimon araxanum
With especially nice, silvery foliage. Cultivate in sun and scree. Flowers in early summer, rose pink. Grows 6 inches (15 cm) high, 12 inches (30 cm) wide. Zones 5–9. Greece eastward.

*Acantholimon araxanum*

*Abies balsamea* 'Nana', courtesy of Ernest O'Byrne

*Acaena microphylla*, courtesy of Fritz Kummert

*Acantholimon araxanum* in seed

19

### Acantholimon armenum

Cultivate in sun and scree. Flowers in early summer, pink. Grows 8 inches (20 cm) high, 18 inches (45 cm) wide. Zones 5–9. Turkey, Syria, and Armenia.

### Acantholimon ulicinum

synonym, *A. androsaceum*
One of the most dwarfed species of the genus, forming a perfect pincushion of tiny gray-green needles. Cultivate in sun and scree. Flowers in early summer, pink. Grows 4 inches (10 cm) high, 8 inches (20 cm) wide. Zones 5–9. Crete.

### Acantholimon venustum

Cultivate in sun and scree. Flowers in early summer, pink. Grows 10 inches (25 cm) high, 18 inches (45 cm) wide. Zones 5–9. Turkey.

*Acantholimon armenum,* courtesy of Fritz Kummert

*Acantholimon ulicinum*

### Achillea

yarrow
Compositae

The dwarf yarrows are easily grown rock garden plants with handsome foliage texture as well as bright flowers. Individual flower heads are generally larger than those found on the taller, border plants and consist of perfectly formed daisies $1/2$–$3/4$ inch (1–2 cm) across in neat clusters.

### Achillea ageratifolia

Greek yarrow
Cultivate in sun and well-drained soil. Flowers in May to July, white. Grows 6 inches (15 cm) high, 12 inches (30 cm) wide. Zones 5–9. Balkan Peninsula.

### Achillea chrysocoma

Cultivate in sun and scree. Flowers in June to September, gold. Grows 6 inches

*Acantholimon venustum,* courtesy of Fritz Kummert

*Achillea ageratifolia*

(15 cm) high, 18 inches (45 cm) wide. Zones 6–10. Balkan Peninsula.

### Achillea clavennae

Cultivate in sun and well-drained soil. Flowers in summer, white. Grows 10 inches (25 cm) high, 18 inches (45 cm) wide. Zones 3–9. Eastern Alps to the Balkan Peninsula.

### Acinos alpinus

alpine calamint
Labiatae
A perennial for sun in limy, well-drained soil. Flowers in summer, violet. Grows 8 inches (20 cm) high, 12 inches (30 cm) wide. Zones 6–9. Mountains of central and southern Europe.

### Aciphylla squarrosa

bayonet plant, speargrass
Umbelliferae
*Aciphylla* is a genus of mountain perennials mostly from New Zealand, most

*Achillea chrysocoma*

*Achillea clavennae,* courtesy of Fritz Kummert

Acinos alpinus, courtesy of Fritz Kummert

grown for their evergreen, rosette-forming foliage, usually making dense clumps. Many are smaller than *A. squarrosa,* some larger. *Aciphylla squarrosa* needs sun and any good, sandy or sharply drained soil. Flowers in summer, cream. Grows 36 inches (90 cm) high and wide. Zones 5–9. New Zealand.

## Acorus gramineus

grassy-leaved sweet flag
Araceae (Acoraceae)

Although sweet flags are in the arum family, they create a grass-like effect. They are evergreen, rhizomatous perennials. If the foliage is bruised there is a lemon scent. Cultivate *A. gramineus* in sun or part shade in any good, moist soil. Flowers in summer in a yellowish spadix. Zones 5–10. China and Japan.

**Cultivars**. The dwarf cultivars mentioned here rarely produce flowers.

*Acorus gramineus* 'Ogon' (synonym, 'Wogon'), golden grassy-leaved sweet flag, grows 10 inches (25 cm) high, 18 inches (45 cm) wide.

*Acorus gramineus* 'Pusillus Aureus Minimus', golden miniature grassy-leaved sweet flag, grows 2 inches (5 cm) high, 8 inches (20 cm) wide.

*Acorus gramineus* 'Pusillus Variegatus', variegated grassy-leaved sweet flag, grows 4 inches (10 cm) high, 8 inches (20 cm) wide.

## Adiantum

maidenhair fern
Adiantaceae

All the maidenhair ferns have delicate, graceful foliage that seems to float in the air.

## Adiantum aleuticum

five-finger fern
synonym, *A. pedatum*

A perennial for shade or part shade in humus-rich, moist soil. Grows 12–18 inches (30–45 cm) high, 12 inches (30 cm) wide. Zones 3–8. North America.

**Subspecies**. *Adiantum aleuticum* subsp. *subpumilum* (synonym, *A. aleuticum* 'Subpumilum'), dwarf five-finger

Aciphylla squarrosa, courtesy of Fritz Kummert

Acorus gramineus 'Pusillus Aureus Minimus'

Acorus gramineus 'Ogon'

Acorus gramineus 'Pusillus Variegatus'

*Adiantum aleuticum*

*Adiantum aleuticum* subsp. *subpumilum*

*Adiantum venustum*

fern, grows 4–8 inches (10–20 cm) high, 12 inches (30 cm) wide. Northwestern Vancouver Island, British Columbia.

### Adiantum venustum
Himalayan maidenhair
Forming an attractive, near-evergreen colony, spreading by slender rhizomes, *A. venustum* is an excellent, hardy perennial fern for wall, woodland, and pan culture. Cultivate in shade or part shade in humus-rich, moist soil. Grows 10 inches (25 cm) high, 24 inches (60 cm) wide. Zones 4–8. China and the Himalayas.

## Adonis
Ranunculaceae

### Adonis amurensis
Amur adonis
A perennial for sun or part shade in any good, well-drained soil. Flowers in February to April, yellow. Grows 12 inches (30 cm) high and wide. Zones 4–8. Northeastern Asia.

### Adonis vernalis
pheasant's eye
A perennial for sun or part shade in any good, well-drained soil. Flowers in February to April, yellow. Grows 8 inches (20 cm) high, 12 inches (30 cm) wide. Zones 5–8. Europe.

## Aethionema
stone cress
Cruciferae

All of the aethionemas are valuable dwarf, shrubby plants that do well in hot, dry places and bring color to the

*Adonis amurensis,* courtesy of Fritz Kummert

*Adonis vernalis,* courtesy of Josef Halda

rock garden after the flush of spring bloom is over.

## Aethionema grandiflorum
Persian candytuft, Persian stone cress
A woody-based perennial for sun in any good, well-drained soil, preferably alkaline. Flowers in May and June, soft pink. Grows 8 inches (20 cm) high, 12 inches (30 cm) wide. Zones 4–9. Turkey, Iraq, and Iran.

## Aethionema oppositifolium
synonym, *Eunomia oppositifolia*
A cushion-forming perennial for sun in any good, well-drained soil, preferably alkaline. Flowers in May and June, pink-lilac. Grows 2 inches (5 cm) high, 6 inches (15 cm) wide. Zones 5–8. Lebanon and Turkey.

## Aethionema 'Warley Rose'
Persian candytuft
Sometimes listed as *A. armenum* 'Warley Rose', *Aethionema* 'Warley Rose' is a

Aethionema grandiflorum

*Aethionema oppositifolium,* courtesy of Franz Hadacek

woody-based perennial for sun in any good, well-drained soil, preferably alkaline. Flowers in May and June, rose pink. Grows 4 inches (10 cm) high, 12 inches (30 cm) wide. Zones 4–9. Origin uncertain.

## Agave
century plant
Agavaceae

Agaves are succulent perennials. Though the species treated here are relatively small and clump forming, they still make bold statements in the large, dryland rock garden.

## Agave parryi
Cultivate in sun in well-drained soil. Flowers in summer, yellow. Grows 24

Aethionema 'Warley Rose'

*Agave parryi,* courtesy of Fritz Kummert

inches (60 cm) high and wide, the inflorescence to 18 feet (5.5 m) high. Zones 8–10. Southwestern United States and adjacent Mexico.

## Agave utahensis var. eborispina
Cultivate in sun in well-drained soil. Flowers in summer, yellow. Grows 18 inches (45 cm) high and wide, the inflorescence to 12 feet (3.7 m) high. Zones 9–10. Southwestern United States.

## Ajuga pyramidalis
spinach ajuga
Labiatae
Most ajugas are too large and vigorously spreading to be used in the rock garden. The cultivar 'Metallica Crispa Purpurea' and its green-leaved counterpart, 'Metallica Crispa', are perennials that form congested cushions, slowly increasing in size without producing long runners. For sun or part shade in any good, moist soil. Flowers in spring, deep violet-blue. Grows 4 inches (10 cm) high, 6 inches (15 cm) wide. Zones 4–10. The species is from Europe.

Agave utahensis var. eborispina

*Ajuga pyramidalis* 'Metallica Crispa Purpurea'

### Albuca humilis

Liliaceae (Hyacinthaceae)

A bulbous perennial for sun in sharply drained soil, and for the bulb frame or alpine house. Flowers in spring, white with green and yellow markings. Grows 4 inches (10 cm) high, 2 inches (5 cm) wide. Zones 8–9. Drakensberg Mountains of Lesotho, southern Africa.

### Alchemilla alpina

mountain lady's mantle

Rosaceae

The very handsome, dark green foliage of *A. alpina* is edged and backed in silky, silvery hairs. Spreading by stolons, it is a perennial for sun or part shade in well-drained soil. Flowers in late spring, greenish yellow. Grows 6 inches (15 cm) high, 18 inches (45 cm) wide. Zones 4–8. European mountains.

### Alkanna

Boraginaceae

### Alkanna ancheriana

A perennial for sun in fertile, well-drained soil. Flowers in summer, blue or purple. Grows 6 inches (15 cm) high, 12 inches (30 cm) wide. Zones 6–9. Turkey.

### Alkanna graeca

A self-sowing perennial for sun in fertile, well-drained soil. Flowers in early summer, yellow. Grows 12 inches (30 cm) high, 24 inches (60 cm) wide. Zones 7–9. Southern Greece.

### Alkanna tinctoria

A perennial for sun in any well-drained soil. Flowers in summer, bright blue. Grows 12 inches (30 cm) high, 18 inches (45 cm) wide. Zones 7–9. Southern Europe.

### Allium

onion

Liliaceae (Alliaceae)

One of the largest genera of the lily family, *Allium* includes more than 600 species, with many desirable flowering onions for the rock garden. All are perennial bulbs. In most cases, locating alliums in full sun achieves the most dwarfed stature and the best flowering performance.

### Allium akaka

Cultivate in sun in well-drained soil. Flowers in early summer, off-white to lilac pink. Grows 6 inches (15 cm) high, 12 inches (30 cm) wide. Zones 8–9. Turkey, Armenia, and Iran.

### Allium carinatum subsp. pulchellum

keeled garlic

Cultivate in sun in well-drained soil. Flowers in summer, violet purple. The cultivar 'Nanum' grows 8 inches (20 cm) high, 12 inches (30 cm) wide. Zones 7–9. The subspecies is from southern Europe.

*Albuca humilis*, courtesy of Fritz Kummert

*Alkanna ancheriana*, courtesy of Fritz Kummert

*Alkanna tinctoria*, courtesy of Franz Hadacek

*Alchemilla alpina*, courtesy of Franz Hadacek

*Alkanna graeca*

*Allium akaka*, courtesy of Fritz Kummert

## Allium cernuum

lady's leek, nodding or wild onion
Cultivate in sun in well-drained soil.
Flowers in summer, rose purple, pink, or
sometimes white. Grows 12–18 inches
(30–45 cm) high and wide. Zones 3–9.
Canada to Mexico.

## Allium cyaneum

An invaluable dwarf plant with a long
season of late summer flowers. Cultivate
in sun in well-drained soil. Flowers in
July and August, violet and purplish
blue. Grows 9 inches (22 cm) high, 6
inches (15 cm) wide. Zones 4–8. China.

*Allium cyaneum*

## Allium cyathophorum var. farreri

Cultivate in sun in well-drained soil.
Flowers in spring, wine red. Grows 8–10
inches (20–25 cm) high. Zones 5–8.
China.

## Allium flavum

small yellow onion
Cultivate in sun in well-drained soil.
Flowers in summer, yellow. Grows 12
inches (30 cm) high and wide. Zones
4–8. Central and southern Europe to
western Asia.

*Allium carinatum* subsp. *pulchellum* 'Nanum',
courtesy of Fritz Kummert

*Allium cyathophorum* var. *farreri*, courtesy of Mark McDonough

*Allium flavum*, courtesy of Mark McDonough

*Allium cernuum*, various color forms, courtesy of Mark McDonough

*Allium karataviense*

### Allium karataviense

A very un-onion-like onion with broad, flat gray leaves that frame the short-stemmed, spherical flower heads. Cultivate in sun in well-drained soil. Flowers in spring, white to pinkish purple with a darker midrib. Grows 8 inches (20 cm) high, 12 inches (30 cm) wide. Zones 4–8. Central Asia.

### Allium moly

golden garlic, lily leek, yellow onion
Cultivate in sun or part shade in well-drained soil. Flowers in June, yellow. Grows 12 inches (30 cm) high, 18 inches (45 cm) wide. Zones 4–8. Southwestern Europe.

### Allium narcissiflorum

A very beautiful species that is not always easy to acquire as seeds are slow to germinate and the bulbs are slow to produce offsets, and available seed is frequently not true to the name. *Allium insubricum*, a fine, similar species from Italy with more pendant umbels, is often mistakenly grown as *A. narcissiflorum*. Cultivate *A. narcissiflorum* in sun in well-drained soil. Flowers in summer, pink. Grows 15 inches (38 cm) high, 8 inches (20 cm) wide. Zones 6–9. Northern Portugal and the southwestern Alps.

### Allium nutans

Cultivate in sun in well-drained soil. Flowers in summer, purplish pink to pale lilac. Grows 12–24 inches (30–60 cm) high. Zones 4–8. Siberia.

### Allium schoenoprasum

chives
Cultivate in sun or part shade in any soil. Flowers in early summer, pink, lilac purple, or white. Grows 10–24 inches (25–60 cm) high, 12 inches (30 cm) wide. Zones 1–8. Europe, Asia, and North America.

*Allium moly*, courtesy of Mark McDonough

*Allium narcissiflorum*, courtesy of Fritz Kummert

*Allium nutans*, various color forms, courtesy of Mark McDonough

## Allium sikkimense

Cultivate in sun in well-drained soil. Flowers in summer, pale purple-blue. Grows 8–12 inches (20–30 cm) high. Zones 5–8. China and Tibet.

## Allium siskiyouense

A fine alpine species deserving a warm and sunny spot with only minimal summer irrigation. A similar species found only in California is *A. falcifolium.* Cultivate *A. siskiyouense* in sun in well-drained soil. Flowers in summer, deep pink. Grows 6 inches (15 cm) high, 12 inches (30 cm) wide. Zones 7–9. Siskiyou Mountains of Oregon.

## Alopecurus lanatus

foxtail grass
Gramineae
A perennial tufted grass for sun in dryish, well-drained soil. Flowers in mid- to late summer in woolly white clusters. Grows 12 inches (30 cm) high, 24 inches (60 cm) wide. Zones 6–9. Eastern Mediterranean.

## Alstroemeria pygmaea

Peruvian lily
Alstroemeriaceae
synonym, *Schickendantzia pygmaea*
A perennial for sun in fertile, well-drained soil. Flowers in summer, deep yellow with dark red spots. Grows 6 inches (15 cm) high, 12 inches (30 cm) wide. Zones 7–9. Andes of Argentina, Bolivia, and Peru.

## Alyssum

madwort
Cruciferae

The many miniature alyssums bring sunshine-yellow flowers to the rock garden. Some bloom early in spring, many later in spring, some not until summer. They are good candidates for troughs. The alyssums treated here are perennials; other species include annuals or subshrubs.

## Alyssum ovirense

Cultivate in sun in any good, well-drained soil, preferably alkaline. Flowers in spring, yellow. Grows 4 inches (10 cm) high, 18 inches (45 cm) wide. Zones 4–10. Central Europe.

## Alyssum propinquum

Cultivate in sun in any good, well-drained soil, preferably alkaline. Flowers in summer, yellow. Grows 3 inches (7.5 cm) high, 12 inches (30 cm) wide. Zones 7–10. Turkey.

*Allium schoenoprasum,* dwarf form from Corsica, courtesy of Mark McDonough

*Allium sikkimense,* courtesy of Mark McDonough

*Allium siskiyouense,* courtesy of Kelley Leonard

*Alopecurus lanatus,* courtesy of Franz Hadacek

*Alstroemeria pygmaea,* courtesy of Fritz Kummert

*Alyssum ovirense*

### Alyssum tortuosum

Cultivate in sun in any good, well-drained soil, preferably alkaline. Flowers in spring, yellow. Grows 3 inches (7.5 cm) high, 12 inches (30 cm) wide. Zones 4–10. Eastern Europe.

### Alyssum wulfenianum

Cultivate in sun in any good, well-drained soil, preferably alkaline. Flowers in late spring, sulfur yellow. Grows 8 inches (20 cm) high, 16 inches (40 cm) wide. Zones 5–10. Southeastern Alps.

### Amitostigma kieskii

Orchidaceae
A rare miniature, tuberous, terrestrial orchid native to moist vertical surfaces and suited to walls, *A. kieskii* can also be grown in a container of humus-rich soil with a moss collar. A top layer of moss helps to maintain a humid microclimate. Any type of moss will suffice. Cultivate in part shade. Flowers in May and June, pink. Grows 6 inches (15 cm) high. Zones 6–10. Japan.

### Anacyclus pyrethrum var. depressus

Atlas daisy
Compositae
synonym, *A. depressus*
A perennial for sun in scree. Flowers in April to June, white, red on reverse. Grows 4 inches (10 cm) high, 12 inches (30 cm) wide. Zones 6–10. Morocco.

### Anagallis monellii

blue pimpernel
Primulaceae
Sometimes a short-lived evergreen perennial, often blooming itself to exhaustion. It is easily perpetuated by seeds or cuttings. Cultivate in sun or part shade in any good, well-drained soil, and in the alpine house. Flowers in summer, blue, red, and paler shades of both colors. Grows 12 inches (30 cm) high, 18 inches (45 cm) wide. Zones 7–10. Southwestern Europe.

### Anaphalis triplinervis

pearly everlasting
Compositae
A perennial for sun in any good, well-drained soil. Flowers in summer and fall, shining white. Grows 12–24 inches

*Anacyclus pyrethrum* var. *depressus*

*Alyssum propinquum*

*Alyssum wulfenianum*

*Anagallis monellii*, courtesy of Fritz Kummert

*Alyssum tortuosum*

*Amitostigma kieskii*

*Anaphalis triplinervis*, courtesy of Fritz Kummert

(30–60 cm) high, 24 inches (60 cm) wide. Zones 5–9. Afghanistan to southwestern China.

## Anchusa caespitosa
bugloss
Boraginaceae
An outstanding perennial with a woody rootstock that must be kept dry during its winter dormancy. It is challenging to keep but worth the effort. Cultivate in sun or part shade in fertile, gritty scree with protection from winter wetness, or in the alpine house. Flowers in late spring to early summer, deep bright blue with a white eye. Grows 6 inches (15 cm) high, 10 inches (25 cm) wide. Zones 5–9. Crete.

## Andromeda polifolia
bog rosemary
Ericaceae
Cultivate in sun or part shade in moist, acid soil or in the peat bed. Flowers in late spring; 'Nana Alba' is white, the species and other forms are in shades of pink. The cultivar 'Nana Alba', white dwarf bog rosemary, is an evergreen shrublet that grows 8 inches (20 cm) high, 24 inches (60 cm) wide. Zones 3–8. The species is circumpolar in the northern hemisphere.

## Androsace
rock jasmine
Primulaceae

*Androsace* is one of the largest genera of refined and desirable alpine plants. Different species are widely distributed throughout Asia, Europe, and North America. Many are easy to grow, though most of the smaller ones are more easily cared for and better enjoyed in an alpine house.

## Androsace alpina
A cushion-forming perennial for sun or part shade in fertile, well-drained, lime-free soil. Flowers in spring and early summer, pink or white with a yellow eye. Grows 2 inches (5 cm) high, 8 inches (20 cm) wide. Zones 5–8. Switzerland.

## Androsace brevis
A short-lived, cushion-forming perennial for sun or part shade in fertile, well-drained, lime-free soil. Flowers in spring and early summer, pink with a yellow eye. Grows 1 inch (2.5 cm) high, 3 inches (7.5 cm) wide. Zones 5–8. Northern Italy.

## Androsace carnea subsp. rosea
synonym, *A. carnea* var. *halleri*
Delightful and one of the easiest rock jasmines to grow, *A. carnea* is widespread in distribution and many fine subspecies and cultivars exist. They are perennials of tufted habit for sun or part shade in fertile, well-drained soil. *Androsace carnea* subsp. *rosea* flowers in spring and early summer, pink. Grows 6 inches (15 cm) high, 8 inches (20 cm) wide. Zones 5–8. Alps.

## Androsace chamaejasme
A perennial that forms mats by stolons, cultivate in sun or part shade in fertile, well-drained soil. Flowers in spring and

*Anchusa caespitosa,* courtesy of Fritz Kummert

*Andromeda polifolia* 'Nana Alba'

*Androsace alpina,* courtesy of Fritz Kummert

*Androsace brevis,* courtesy of Fritz Kummert

*Androsace carnea* subsp. *rosea,* courtesy of Fritz Kummert

*Androsace chamaejasme,* courtesy of Fritz Kummert

early summer, white, aging to pink with a yellow eye. Grows 3 inches (7.5 cm) high, 12 inches (30 cm) wide. Zones 5–8. Siberia, central Asia, China, and North America.

## Androsace ciliata

A cushion-forming perennial prone to aphid infestation, cultivate in sun or part shade in fertile, well-drained soil. Flowers in early summer, pink to rose red with an orange or yellow throat. Grows 2 inches (5 cm) high, 6 inches (15 cm) wide. Zones 5–8. Western central Pyrenees.

## Androsace delavayi

A high-elevation perennial that will eventually form wide-spreading mats with age, cultivate in sun or part shade in fertile, well-drained soil. Flowers in spring, white, pale or deep pink, with a yellowish eye, and fragrant. Grows 2 inches (5 cm) high, 8 inches (20 cm) wide. Zones 3–8. Himalayas to Tibet, southwestern China, and northern Myanmar (Burma).

*Androsace ciliata*, courtesy of Fritz Kummert

*Androsace delavayi*, courtesy of Fritz Kummert

## Androsace globifera

A perennial, cushion forming at first, then maturing into wide mats, cultivate in sun or part shade in fertile, well-drained soil with protection from winter wetness. Flowers in early summer, lilac pink or white with a yellow eye. Grows 3 inches (7.5 cm) high, 12 inches (30 cm) wide. Zones 4–8. Himalayas.

## Androsace hausmannii

A short-lived cushion-forming perennial, cultivate in sun or part shade in scree in a crevice, preferably alkaline. Flowers in spring and early summer, white to pure pink with a yellow eye. Grows 1 inch (2.5 cm) high, 2 inches (5 cm) wide. Zones 6–8. Dolomites of the eastern Alps and other nearby limestone mountains.

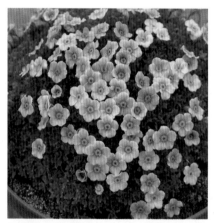

*Androsace globifera*, courtesy of Fritz Kummert

*Androsace hirtella*, courtesy of Fritz Kummert

## Androsace hirtella

One of the easiest cushion-forming perennials to grow, cultivate in sun or part shade in fertile, well-drained soil. Flowers in spring and early summer, white and fragrant. Grows 1 inch (2.5 cm) high, 6 inches (15 cm) wide. Zones 6–8. Northern Pyrenees.

## Androsace lanuginosa

A vigorous, easy-to-grow, loosely mat-forming perennial with silvery trailing stems ending in flower clusters all summer long. Cultivate in sun in any good, well-drained soil. Flowers in summer, lavender-pink with white eyes. Grows 6 inches (15 cm) high, 18 inches (45 cm) wide. Zones 4–8. Himalayas.

## Androsace mucronifolia

A mat- or hummock-forming perennial, cultivate in sun or part shade in fertile,

*Androsace hausmannii*, courtesy of Fritz Kummert

well-drained soil. Flowers in spring, white to deep pink and fragrant. Grows 4 inches (10 cm) high, 15 inches (38 cm) wide. Zones 5–8. Northwestern Pakistan, Kashmir in India, and western Tibet.

## Androsace muscoidea

A densely mat-forming perennial, cultivate in sun or part shade in fertile, well-drained soil with protection from winter wetness. Flowers in spring and early

*Androsace lanuginosa*

*Androsace mucronifolia,* courtesy of Fritz Kummert

*Androsace muscoidea,* courtesy of Fritz Kummert

summer, white with a greenish eye. Grows 2 inches (5 cm) high, 8 inches (20 cm) wide. Zones 5–8. Himalayas.

## Androsace pyrenaica

No doubt the easiest to grow of the choice cushion-forming perennial androsaces, *A. pyrenaica* is still deserving of extra care in an alpine house. Cultivate in sun or part shade in fertile, well-drained, lime-free soil. Flowers in spring and early summer, white. Grows 1 inch (2.5 cm) high, 4 inches (10 cm) wide. Zones 6–8. Pyrenees.

## Androsace sarmentosa

synonym, *A. primuloides*
A mat-forming and stoloniferous perennial, cultivate in sun or part shade in fertile, well-drained soil. Flowers in April and May, pink with a greenish yellow eye. Some forms of this variable species are sometimes found classified as *A. primuloides.* From the gardener's standpoint these two species are the same. Grows 6 inches (15 cm) high, 18 inches

*Androsace pyrenaica,* courtesy of Fritz Kummert

*Androsace sarmentosa*

(45 cm) wide. Zones 3–8. Kashmir to western China.

**Cultivars**. *Androsace sarmentosa* 'Brilliant' has deep carmine-pink flowers.

*Androsace sarmentosa* 'Sherriffii' has pale pink flowers.

## Androsace sempervivoides

A perennial forming mats by red stolons, cultivate in sun or part shade in fertile, well-drained soil. Flowers in late spring, bright pink with a yellow eye,

*Androsace sarmentosa* 'Brilliant', courtesy of Fritz Kummert

*Androsace sarmentosa* 'Sherriffii'

*Androsace sempervivoides,* courtesy of Fritz Kummert

aging red. Grows 3 inches (7.5 cm) high, 8 inches (20 cm) wide. Zones 4–8. Kashmir and Tibet.

## *Androsace vandellii*

synonym, *A. imbricata*

A bit more demanding than *A. pyrenaica,* the tight cushion-forming perennial *A. vandellii* is not too difficult to grow in the alpine house. Cultivate in sun or part shade in scree with no overhead watering, and in the alpine house.

*Androsace vandellii,* courtesy of Fritz Kummert

*Androsace wulfeniana,* courtesy of Fritz Kummert

*Andryala aghardii,* courtesy of Franz Hadacek

Flowers in spring, white with a yellow eye. Grows 2 inches (5 cm) high, 4 inches (10 cm) wide. Zones 6–8. Alps, Apennines, Pyrenees, Sierra Nevada of Spain, and Atlas Mountains.

## *Androsace wulfeniana*

A densely cushion-forming perennial, cultivate in sun or part shade in fertile, well-drained, lime-free soil. Flowers in spring, glowing pink with a yellow or orange-yellow eye, shy to flower in cultivation. Grows 3 inches (7.5 cm) high, 6 inches (15 cm) wide. Zones 5–8. Eastern Alps.

## *Andryala aghardii*

Compositae

A first-class foliage plant for troughs or the crevice garden, where it must have

dry winter conditions, *A. aghardii* is a perennial with a woody root stock. Cultivate in sun in scree, and in the alpine house. Flowers in summer, lemon yellow. Grows 6 inches (15 cm) high, 8 inches (20 cm) wide. Zones 6–9. Mountains of southern Spain.

## *Anemone*

windflower
Ranunculaceae

Most tuberous-rooted perennial anemones spread by creeping rhizomes and form dense colonies, carpeting the woodland garden.

## *Anemone apennina*

Cultivate in cool part shade in any good, well-drained soil. Flowers in early spring, bright blue. Grows 8 inches (20

*Anemone apennina* with *Euphorbia amygdaloides* var. *robbiae,* courtesy of Fritz Kummert

*Anemone blanda*

cm) high, 18 inches (45 cm) wide. Zones 5–9. Southern Europe.

## Anemone blanda

Cultivate in cool part shade in any good, well-drained soil. Flowers in early spring in shades of blue and pink or white. Grows 8 inches (20 cm) high, 18 inches (45 cm) wide. Zones 5–9. Southeastern Europe, Cyprus, western Turkey, and the Caucasus Mountains.

## Anemone crinita

Cultivate in sun or part shade in any good, well-drained soil. Flowers in late spring, white. Grows 18 inches (45 cm) high, 12 inches (30 cm) wide. Zones 3–8. Siberia.

## Anemone ×lesseri

A somewhat taller anemone with sizable flowers, good in the large rock garden or

*Anemone crinita*

*Anemone ×lesseri, courtesy of Armen Gevjan*

even the border foreground. Cultivate in sun or part shade in fertile, well-drained soil. Flowers in early summer, rose red. Grows 12 inches (30 cm) high, 8 inches (20 cm) wide. Zones 3–8. A garden hybrid, *A. multifida* × *A. sylvestris*.

## Anemone narcissiflora

*Anemone narcissiflora* has a woody rootstock. Cultivate in sun in scree. Flowers in summer, white flushed with pink without. Grows 10–18 inches (25–45 cm) high, 10 inches (25 cm) wide. Zones 3–8. Central and southern Europe, Turkey, Russia, Japan, and Alaska.

## Anemone nemorosa

European wood anemone

A species so variable in the wild that there are numerous named cultivars selected for size and color of blossom. Cultivate in part shade in any good, well-drained soil. Flowers in April and May, white, occasionally flushed blue, pink, or purple. Grows 5 inches (12.5 cm) high, 12 inches (30 cm) wide, eventually forming a wide, dense carpet. Zones 3–8. Northern Europe and northwestern Asia.

**Cultivars**. *Anemone nemorosa* 'Alba Plena' has flowers that are white with a white pompom center.

Flowers of *Anemone nemorosa*

*Anemone narcissiflora, courtesy of Fritz Kummert*

*Anemone nemorosa*

*Anemone nemorosa* 'Alba Plena'

*Anemone nemorosa* 'Bracteata'

*Anemone nemorosa* 'Lychette'

'Bracteata' are white flushed with blue, with a collar of green and white bracts.

Flowers of *Anemone nemorosa* 'Lychette' are white and single petaled.

### Anemone ranunculoides
European wood anemone
The plant illustrated here is sometimes listed as subspecies *ranunculoides*. A less vigorous form native to northern central Europe has been named subspecies *wockeana*. Cultivate in part shade in any good, well-drained soil. Flowers in April and May, golden yellow. Grows 6–10 inches (15–25 cm) high, 18 inches (45 cm) wide. Zones 4–8. Europe except the Mediterranean region.

**Cultivar**. *Anemone ranunculoides* 'Flore Pleno' has doubled, yellow flowers.

### Anemone ×seemannii
synonym, *A. ×lipsiensis*
Cultivate in part shade in any good, well-drained soil. Flowers in April and May, pale sulfur yellow. Grows 6 inches (15

cm) high, 12 inches (30 cm) wide. Zones 3–8. A hybrid, *A. nemorosa* × *A. ranunculoides*.

### Anemone sylvestris
snowdrop windflower
In humus-rich soil and considerable sun the lovely *A. sylvestris* spreads fast by a running woody rootstock to form a ground cover with scalloped foliage. Cultivate in sun or part shade in any good, well-drained soil. Flowers in April and May, white. Grows 12–15 inches (30–38 cm) high, 24 inches (60 cm) wide. Zones 3–8. Central and eastern Europe to the Caucasus Mountains. See under *Pinellia ternata* for another photograph.

### Anemonella thalictroides
rue anemone
Ranunculaceae
Differences in the flowers, including the style and seed, separate *Anemonella*

from *Anemone*. Like anemones, the rue anemones are perennials from tuberous roots. Cultivate *Anemonella thalictroides* in part shade in humus-rich, well-drained, moist soil. Flowers in spring, white. Grows 6 inches (15 cm) high, 8 inches (20 cm) wide. Zones 3–8. Eastern North America.

**Cultivars**. Doubled forms, such as the double white one illustrated, are longer blooming, often extending the season well into summer.

*Anemonella thalictroides* 'Rosea' has single pink flowers in spring.

*Anemonella thalictroides* 'Schoaff's Double Pink' also has pink flowers in spring and may be a bit shorter, growing 5 inches (12.5 cm) high.

### Anisotome imbricata
Umbelliferae
A perennial for sun in fertile, well-drained soil. Flowers in late spring and

Anemone ×seemannii

Anemonella thalictroides

Anemone ranunculoides

Anemone sylvestris

Anemonella thalictroides, double white

Anemone ranunculoides 'Flore Pleno'

summer, creamy yellow. Grows 6 inches (15 cm) high, 18 inches (45 cm) wide. Zones 7–9. South Island, New Zealand.

## Anomatheca laxa
Iridaceae
synonyms, *A. cruenta, Lapeirousia laxa*
Though not completely hardy, a charming cormous perennial that is valuable for its wiry stems with up to 10 flowers for 2 months in summer. Cultivate in

*Anemonella thalictroides* 'Rosea'

*Anemonella thalictroides* 'Schoaff's Double Pink'

*Anisotome imbricata*, courtesy of Franz Hadacek

sun or part shade in any well-drained soil. Flowers in June and July, coral red, sometimes rich pink to bluish, or white, all with red or purple markings at the base of the petals; *A. laxa* var. *alba* has pure white flowers. Grows 8–12 inches (20–30 cm) high, 12 inches (30 cm) wide. Zones 7–10. Eastern South Africa.

## Antennaria dioica
pussy toes
Compositae
A dwarf, carpeting evergreen perennial native to mountains and easy to grow in full sun and well-drained soil. Zones 3–8. The species is from Europe, North America, and northern Asia.

   **Cultivars**. *Antennaria dioica* 'Minima Rubra' grows 2 inches (5 cm) high, 6 inches (15 cm) wide. Flowers in spring, dark rose pink.

   *Antennaria dioica* 'Rotraut', similar to 'Nyewood Variety', grows 3 inches (7.5 cm) high, 12 inches (30 cm) wide. It may be cultivated in sun or part shade in

*Anomatheca laxa*

*Antennaria dioica* 'Minima Rubra', courtesy of Fritz Kummert

well-drained soil. Flowers in spring, cherry red.

## Anthemis
dog fennel
Compositae

## Anthemis carpatica
synonym, *A. cretica* subsp. *carpatica*
A woody-based perennial for sun in well-drained soil. Flowers in summer, white. Grows 6–15 inches (15–38 cm) high, 24 inches (60 cm) wide. Zones 6–9. Pyrenees, eastern Alps, Carpathians, and mountains of the Balkan Peninsula.

## Anthemis marschalliana
synonym, *A. biebersteiniana*
The flowers of *A. marschalliana* are a nice bonus but the intensely silver, filigreed foliage is the perennial's best quality. Cultivate in sun or part shade in

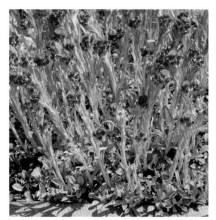
*Antennaria dioica* 'Rotraut', courtesy of Fritz Kummert

*Anthemis carpatica*, courtesy of Fritz Kummert

well-drained soil. Flowers in summer, golden yellow. Grows 12 inches (30 cm) high, 8 inches (20 cm) wide. Zones 4–10. Caucasus Mountains.

### Anthemis punctata subsp. cupaniana

A woody-based perennial for sun in well-drained soil. Flowers in spring through fall, white. Grows 10 inches (25 cm) high, 30 inches (75 cm) wide. Zones 7–10. Sicily.

### Anthericum liliago

St. Bernard's lily
Liliaceae
A perennial for sun or part shade in any good, well-drained soil. Flowers in late spring and early summer, white. Grows 24–36 inches (60–90 cm) high. Zones 5–8. Europe.

### Anthyllis

Leguminosae

Plants of this genus of meadow flowers

may be too large and, in some cases, self-sow too enthusiastically for the rock garden, but they are worth accommodating for their stunning flowers.

### Anthyllis hermanniae

A perennial for sun in well-drained soil. Flowers in summer, yellow. Grows 16 inches (40 cm) high, 36 inches (90 cm) wide. Zones 7–10. Mediterranean region and Turkey.

### Anthyllis montana

A woody-based perennial for sun in well-drained soil. The cultivar 'Rubra' flowers in summer, rose red. Grows 12 inches (30 cm) high, 18 inches (45 cm) wide. Zones 7–9. The species is from the mountains of southern Europe.

### Anthyllis vulneraria subsp. pulchella

*Anthyllis vulneraria*, kidney vetch, is a perennial. Cultivate in sun in well-drained soil. Subspecies *pulchella* flowers in May and June, white topped with orange and gold. Grows 12 inches (30 cm) high, 18 inches (45 cm) wide. Zones 4–9. Subspecies *pulchella* is from the Balkan Mountains, central Bulgaria.

### Antirrhinum

Scrophulariaceae

### Antirrhinum molle

perennial snapdragon
Quite hardy especially in dryish soil in winter. The charming flowers continue

Anthemis marschalliana

Anthericum liliago, courtesy of Fritz Kummert

Anthyllis montana 'Rubra', courtesy of Fritz Kummert

Anthemis punctata subsp. *cupaniana*

Anthyllis hermanniae, courtesy of Fritz Kummert

Anthyllis vulneraria subsp. *pulchella*

all summer when the plants are lightly sheared. Cultivate in sun in well-drained soil. Flowers in spring and summer, pink or cream with a yellow throat. Grows 12 inches (30 cm) high, 18 inches (45 cm) wide. Zones 7–10. Pyrenees.

### *Antirrhinum sempervirens*
perennial snapdragon
Cultivate in sun in well-drained soil. Flowers in spring and summer, cream with a yellow throat. Grows 8 inches (20 cm) high, 12 inches (30 cm) wide. Zones 7–10. Pyrenees and eastern central Spain.

### *Aphyllanthes monspeliensis*
Liliaceae (Aphyllanthaceae)
A fibrous-rooted, evergreen perennial for sun in any soil with protection from winter wetness. Flowers in early summer, blue with a darker midvein. Grows 12 inches (30 cm) high and wide. Zones

*Antirrhinum molle,* courtesy of Fritz Kummert

*Antirrhinum sempervirens*

8–10. Southwestern Europe and Morocco.

### *Aquilegia*
columbine
Ranunculaceae

Perennials that are often challenging to keep and grow to perfection, all of the dwarf and alpine columbines are worth cultivating for their exceedingly lovely flowers as well as their delicate, lacy foliage.

### *Aquilegia alpina*
Cultivate in sun or part shade in fertile, well-drained soil. Flowers in late spring, bright blue. Grows 6–30 inches (15–75

*Aphyllanthes monspeliensis* with *Helianthemum canum,* courtesy of Fritz Kummert

*Aquilegia alpina,* courtesy of Fritz Kummert

cm) high, 12 inches (30 cm) wide. Zones 2–8. Alps and the northern Apennines.

### *Aquilegia bertolonii*
One of the smallest and finest species of *Aquilegia,* the relatively large flowers of *A. bertolonii* are upturned, with a prominent, hooked spur. Cultivate in sun or part shade in fertile, well-drained soil. Flowers in late spring, blue to blue-violet. Grows 4–12 inches (10–30 cm) high, 8 inches (20 cm) wide. Zones 4–8. Eastern Alps.

### *Aquilegia caerulea*
Cultivate in sun or part shade in fertile, well-drained soil. Flowers in summer with blue, pink, or white sepals and white or cream petals. Grows 8–24 inches (20–60 cm) high, 12 inches (30 cm) wide. Zones 2–8. Rocky Mountains.

*Aquilegia bertolonii*

*Aquilegia caerulea,* courtesy of Fritz Kummert

## Aquilegia discolor

Cultivate in sun or part shade in fertile, well-drained soil. Flowers in late spring, soft blue and creamy white. Grows 6 inches (15 cm) high and wide. Zones 4–10. Northern Spain.

## Aquilegia einseleana

Cultivate in sun or part shade in fertile, well-drained soil. Flowers in spring and summer, violet-blue. Grows 8–18 inches (20–45 cm) high, 8 inches (20 cm) wide. Zones 5–8. Alps, especially the Dolomites.

Aquilegia discolor

Aquilegia einseleana, courtesy of Fritz Kummert

## Aquilegia flabellata

The cultivar 'Nana Alba' is a wonderful perennial for the rock garden or even the border, with short-spurred, nodding flowers and a short, stocky habit. Cultivate in sun or part shade in fertile, well-drained soil. Flowers in spring and summer, white. Grows 8 inches (20 cm) high and wide. Zones 3–9. The species is from Japan and eastern Asia.

## Aquilegia fragrans

Cultivate in part shade in fertile, well-drained soil. Flowers in summer, white or pale purple and sweetly fragrant.

Aquilegia flabellata 'Nana Alba'

Aquilegia fragrans, courtesy of Fritz Kummert

Grows 8–32 inches (20–80 cm) high, 12 inches (30 cm) wide. Zones 7–9. Himalayas.

## Aquilegia jonesii

Cultivate in sun in gritty scree, and in the alpine house. Flowers in summer, blue. Grows 1–4 inches (2.5–10 cm) high, 4 inches (10 cm) wide. Zones 2–8. Rocky Mountains, especially Wyoming.

## Aquilegia saximontana

An exceptionally hardy plant with the most dainty, hanging, lantern-like flowers. Cultivate in sun or part shade in scree. Flowers in late spring and early summer, blue and white. Grows 4 inches (10 cm) high, 6 inches (15 cm) wide. Zones 3–8. Rocky Mountains.

## Aquilegia scopulorum

Easier to cultivate and like a slightly larger version of *A. jonesii*, *A. scopulorum* needs spartan treatment in a stony scree. Cultivate in sun. Flowers in spring and summer, lavender to violet-blue

Aquilegia jonesii

Aquilegia saximontana

with a white to yellowish center. Grows 4–8 inches (10–20 cm) high, 6 inches (15 cm) wide. Zones 3–8. Western United States.

## *Arabis*
rock cress
Cruciferae

For the rock gardener there are two classes of *Arabis*: the extensively spreading, familiar, easy-to-grow types, and the smaller, choicer ones for scree, crevice, or alpine house. Of the latter, most

*Aquilegia scopulorum*, courtesy of Fritz Kummert

are true alpines and include frequently grown species such as *A. androsacea* and *A. bryoides*.

## *Arabis* ×*arendsii*
A mat-forming perennial for sun or part shade in well-drained soil. *Arabis* ×*arendsii* 'Monte Rosa' (synonym, *A. caucasica* 'Monte Rosa') flowers in spring and early summer, maroon and pink. Grows 6–10 inches (15–25 cm) high, 24 inches (60 cm) wide. Zones 5–9. *Arabis* ×*arendsii* is a hybrid, *A. aubrietoides* × *A. caucasica*.

## *Arabis blepharophylla*
A perennial for sun or part shade in well-drained soil. The cultivar 'Spring

*Arabis blepharophylla* 'Spring Charm'

Charm' flowers in spring, rosy purple. Grows 6 inches (15 cm) high, 12 inches (30 cm) wide. Zones 5–9. The species is from California.

## *Arabis caucasica*
A perennial for sun or part shade in well-drained soil. Grows 12 inches (30 cm) high, 24 inches (60 cm) wide. Zones 3–9. Southeastern Europe, Caucasia, and Iran.

**Cultivars.** *Arabis caucasica* 'Flore Pleno' flowers in spring and early summer, white, doubled.

*Arabis caucasica* 'Variegata' flowers in midspring, white.

## *Arabis ferdinandi-coburgii*
A perennial for sun or part shade in well-drained soil. The cultivar 'Variegata', with cream and green leaves, flowers in spring, white; 'Old Gold' has leaves

*Arabis caucasica* 'Flore Pleno'

*Arabis caucasica* 'Variegata'

*Arabis* ×*arendsii* 'Monte Rosa', courtesy of Fritz Kummert colored gold with green down the middle. Grow 4 inches (10 cm) high, 12 inches (30 cm) wide. Zones 5–9. The species is from southeastern Europe.

## Arabis sturii

A perennial for sun or part shade in well-drained soil. Flowers in spring, white. Grows 6 inches (15 cm) high, 12 inches (30 cm) wide. Zones 4–10. Origin and name uncertain, possibly a garden hybrid.

## Arctostaphylos
Ericaceae

Arabis ferdinandi-coburgii 'Variegata'

Arabis sturii, courtesy of Armen Gevjan

Arctostaphylos alpina with fall color foliage, courtesy of Fritz Kummert

## Arctostaphylos alpina
alpine bearberry, black bearberry
synonym, Arctous alpina

A choice little mat-forming, deciduous, ground-cover shrub that needs a cool climate in which to thrive. Cultivate in sun or part shade in fertile, well-drained, lime-free soil. It needs cool summers. Flowers in spring and early summer, white, followed by black berries in summer and autumn. Grows 1–2 inches (2.5–5 cm) high, 24 inches (60 cm) wide. Zones 1–7. Circumpolar, northern hemisphere.

## Arctostaphylos uva-ursi
common bearberry, kinnikinnick

A mat-forming, evergreen, ground-cover shrub for sun or part shade in any good, well-drained, acid soil. Flowers in

Arctostaphylos uva-ursi, courtesy of Fritz Kummert

Arenaria balearica

May and June, white or pink, followed by scarlet summer fruit. Grows 4–8 inches (10–20 cm) high, 48 inches (120 cm) wide. Zones 4–9. Circumpolar, northern hemisphere.

## Arenaria
sandwort
Caryophyllaceae

## Arenaria balearica

A mat-forming perennial with a mere film of tiny, bright green leaves, making an excellent ground cover for any shady spot. Cultivate in part shade in humus-rich, moist soil. Flowers in June, white. Grows 1 inch (2.5 cm) high, 12 inches (30 cm) wide. Zones 5–10. Balearic Islands, Spain

Arenaria montana

## Arenaria montana

Easy to grow and beautiful, producing clouds of large, pure white flowers that smother the plant, and also with attractive dark green foliage. Cultivate in sun in well-drained soil. Flowers in early summer, white. Grows 8 inches (20 cm) high, 24 inches (60 cm) wide. Zones 5–9. Southwestern Europe.

## Arenaria tetraquetra

A perennial for sun in scree. Flowers in June, white. Grows 3 inches (7.5 cm) high, 12 inches (30 cm) wide. Zones 5–8. Pyrenees and the Sierra Nevada of Spain.

**Cultivar**. *Arenaria tetraquetra* 'Granatensis', like the species, is a favorite cushion plant for the sunny scree. Flowers, though rarely, in June, white. Grows 4 inches (10 cm) high, 8 inches (20 cm) wide.

## Arisaema

cobra lily, Jack-in-the-pulpit
Araceae

All the arisaemas make wonderful plants for the woodland garden, for a shady pocket in the rock garden, or for the alpine house. They are deciduous, cormous perennials.

## Arisaema candidissimum

Cultivate in sun or part shade in fertile, well-drained soil. Flowers in early summer, white, pink, and green, and fragrant. Grows 16 inches (40 cm) high. Zones 6–9. Western China.

## Arisaema griffithii

Cultivate in part shade in fertile, well-drained soil. Flowers in late spring, brownish purple. Grows 16–24 inches (40–60 cm) high. Zones 6–9. Eastern Himalayas.

## Arisaema japonicum

synonym, *A. serratum*
Cultivate in part shade in fertile, well-drained soil. Flowers in spring, green to purple, sometimes striped white. Grows 24–36 inches (60–90 cm) high. Zones 5–9. Northeastern Asia and Japan.

## Arisaema ringens

A robustly growing species with heavily textured, tropical-looking leaves. Cultivate in part shade in fertile, well-drained soil. Flowers in April and May, green and black. Grows 18 inches (45 cm) high. Zones 5–10. Japan, China, and Korea.

*Arisaema japonicum*, courtesy of Fritz Kummert

*Arenaria tetraquetra*, courtesy of Fritz Kummert

*Arisaema candidissimum*, courtesy of Fritz Kummert

*Arenaria tetraquetra* 'Granatensis'

*Arisaema griffithii*, courtesy of Fritz Kummert

*Arisaema ringens*

## Arisaema sikokianum

Cultivate in part shade in fertile, well-drained soil. Flowers in early summer, spathe deep purple striped with green and white, spadix large, white, and club-shaped. Grows 12–18 inches (30–45 cm) high. Zones 5–9. Japan.

## Armeria
sea pink, thrift
Plumbaginaceae

The cushions of grassy foliage that characterize most species of *Armeria* are neat additions to the rock garden. The spherical heads of spring flowers will bloom again in summer if spent blooms are sheared.

## Armeria caespitosa
synonym, *A. juniperifolia*
A perennial for sun in well-drained soil. Flowers in spring and summer, pink. Grows 3 inches (7.5 cm) high, 12 inches (30 cm) wide. Zones 3–9. Central Spain.

*Arisaema sikokianum*, courtesy of Fritz Kummert

*Armeria caespitosa*, courtesy of Fritz Kummert

## Armeria maritima

A perennial for sun in well-drained soil. Grows 8 inches (20 cm) high, 12 inches (30 cm) wide. Zones 3–9. Northern hemisphere and southern South America.

**Cultivars**. *Armeria maritima* 'Dusseldorf Stolz' (synonym, 'Dusseldorfer Pride') flowers in spring and summer, dark pink.

*Armeria maritima* 'Rubrifolia', a cultivar that has become well distributed more recently, has strikingly colored foliage that is rich purplish red most of the year. It flowers in spring and summer, rosy pink.

*Armeria maritima* 'Dusseldorf Stolz', courtesy of Fritz Kummert

*Armeria maritima* 'Rubrifolia'

## Arnebia pulchra
prophet flower
Boraginaceae
synonym, *A. echioides*
A perennial for sun or part shade in fertile, well-drained soil. Flowers in late spring, yellow. Grows 12 inches (30 cm) high, 18 inches (45 cm) wide. Zones 7–9. Caucasia, the Republic of Georgia, Turkey, and Iran.

## Arnica
Compositae

## Arnica angustifolia

A rhizomatous perennial for sun in fertile, well-drained moist soil. Flowers in summer, yellow. Grows 20 inches (50

*Arnebia pulchra*, courtesy of Fritz Kummert

*Arnica angustifolia*, courtesy of Fritz Kummert

cm) high, 12 inches (30 cm) wide. Zones 2–8. Arctic areas of North America and northern Eurasia.

### Arnica chamissonis

A rhizomatous perennial for sun in fertile, well-drained moist soil. Flowers in summer, yellow. Grows 12–24 inches (30–60 cm) high, 18 inches (45 cm) wide. Zones 2–8. Alaska to New Mexico.

### Artemisia
mugwort, sage brush, wormwood
Compositae

Mats of congested, silver filigreed foliage characterize the aromatic perennial herbaceous species of *Artemisia* treated here.

### Artemisia pedemontana
synonyms, *A. assoana, A. caucasica*
Cultivate in sun in well-drained soil. Flowers in summer, greenish yellow. Grows 4 inches (10 cm) high, 12 inches (30 cm) wide. Zones 5–9. Southern Europe from central Spain to the Ukraine.

### Artemisia schmidtiana
Cultivate in sun in well-drained soil. Flowers in summer, yellowish. The cultivar 'Nana' grows 8 inches (20 cm) high, 18 inches (45 cm) wide. Zones 5–9. The completely deciduous perennial species is from Japan.

### Arum
Araceae

### Arum creticum
A tuberous-rooted perennial for sun or part shade in fertile, well-drained soil. Flowers in spring, bright yellow, greenish, or green-white. Grows 18 inches (45 cm) high and wide. Zones 7–9. Crete and other islands of Greece and islands of Turkey.

### Arum maculatum
cuckoo-pint, Jack-in-the-pulpit, lords-and-ladies
A tuberous-rooted perennial for sun or part shade in fertile, well-drained soil. Flowers in spring, pale green, often spotted, flushed, or margined purple, followed by orange fruits in summer. Grows 12 inches (30 cm) high, 18 inches (45 cm) wide. Zones 6–9. Europe east to Ukraine.

*Arnica chamissonis*, courtesy of Fritz Kummert

*Artemisia schmidtiana* 'Nana'

*Arum creticum*, courtesy of Fritz Kummert

*Artemisia pedemontana*

*Arum maculatum*, leafless with fruiting stems growing above another perennial, courtesy of Fritz Kummert

## Aruncus aethusifolius

dwarf goat's beard
Rosaceae
A rhizomatous perennial for sun or part shade in fertile, well-drained soil. Flowers in summer, cream white. Grows 10–18 inches (25–45 cm) high, 18 inches (45 cm) wide. Zones 5–9. Korea.

## Asarina procumbens

Scrophulariaceae
synonym, *Antirrhinum asarina*
One of the twining snapdragons, *A. procumbens* is a versatile perennial that will self-sow itself into sun or shade, staying much condensed in sun. Cultivate in sun or shade in well-drained soil. Flowers in spring and summer, cream. Grows 3 inches (7.5 cm) high, 24 inches (60 cm) wide. Zones 5–10. Eastern Pyrenees.

## Asarum

wild ginger
Aristolochiaceae

All of the wild gingers are handsome foliage plants for colonizing in the shade of trees and shrubs. Leaves are often ginger scented. A few species have fairly large, exotic flowers; most flowers are brownish jugs hidden beneath the leaves. In addition to the garden-worthy species discussed here, there is a large group of less virgorous and less hardy Asian species that are best grown in an alpine house.

## Asarum caudatum

western wild ginger
An evergreen perennial for part shade in humus-rich, well-drained soil. Flowers in spring, reddish brown. Grows 6 inches (15 cm) high, 24 inches (60 cm) wide. Zones 4–10. British Columbia to northern California.

## Asarum caulescens

A deciduous perennial for part shade in humus-rich, well-drained soil. Flowers in spring, pinkish brown and white-striped maroon inside. Grows 8 inches (20 cm) high, 18 inches (45 cm) wide. Zones 6–9. Honshu, Shikoku, and Kyushu, Japan.

## Asarum europaeum

asarabacca, European ginger
An absolutely evergreen perennial with dark, glossy green, kidney-shaped leaves year-round. Cultivate in part shade in humus-rich, well-drained soil. Flowers in spring, purple. Grows 5 inches (12.5 cm) high, 12 inches (30 cm) wide. Zones 4–8. Europe.

## Asarum hartwegii

cyclamen-leaved ginger
An evergreen perennial for part shade in humus-rich, well-drained soil. Flowers in spring, reddish brown. Grows 4 inches (10 cm) high, 12 inches (30 cm) wide. Zones 6–8. Oregon and California.

*Aruncus aethusifolius*, courtesy of Fritz Kummert

*Asarum caudatum*, courtesy of Fritz Kummert

*Asarum europaeum*

*Asarina procumbens*

*Asarum caulescens*

*Asarum hartwegii*

## Asarum maximum
panda-face ginger
An evergreen perennial for part shade in humus-rich, well-drained soil. Flowers in spring, black with white interior. Grows 10 inches (25 cm) high, 12 inches (30 cm) wide. Zones 7–9. China.

## Asarum shuttleworthii
An evergreen perennial for part shade in humus-rich, well-drained soil. The cultivar 'Callaway', Callaway's wild ginger, flowers in spring, brown. Grows 3 inches (7.5 cm) high, 24 inches (60 cm) wide. Zones 6–9. The species is from the southeastern United States.

## Asarum sieboldii
An evergreen perennial for part shade in humus-rich, well-drained soil. Flowers in spring, reddish brown. Grows 8 inches (20 cm) high, 12 inches (30 cm) wide. Zones 6–9. Japan.

Asarum maximum

Asarum shuttleworthii 'Callaway'

## Asperula
woodruff
Rubiaceae

There are several good, mat-forming perennial species of Asperula for the rock garden and the trough that are well known, and more recently introduced ones, especially from Turkey, are slowly coming into cultivation.

## Asperula lilaciflora
Cultivate in sun or part shade, bright but not hot or dry, in fertile, well-drained soil. Flowers in spring and early summer, pink. Grows 4 inches (10 cm) high, 12 inches (30 cm) wide. Zones 5–8. Western to central Asia.

## Asperula nitida
Cultivate in sun or part shade, bright but not hot or dry, in fertile, well-drained soil. Flowers in summer, pale pink. Grows 2 inches (5 cm) high, 8 inches (20 cm) wide. Zones 7–9. Greece and Turkey.

Asarum sieboldii, courtesy of Fritz Kummert

Asperula lilaciflora, courtesy of Fritz Kummert

## Asperula pontica
Cultivate in sun or part shade, bright but not hot or dry, in fertile, well-drained soil. Flowers in summer, pink. Grows 3 inches (7.5 cm) high, 10 inches (25 cm) wide. Zones 5–8. Mountains of Iraq and Turkey.

## Asperula sintenisii
Cultivate in sun or part shade, bright but not hot or dry, in fertile, well-drained

Asperula nitida, courtesy of Fritz Kummert

Asperula pontica

Asperula sintenisii

soil. Flowers in summer, pink. Grows 1 inch (2.5 cm) high, 6 inches (15 cm) wide. Zones 5–8. Turkey.

## Asperula suberosa

Cultivate in sun or part shade, bright but not hot or dry, in fertile, well-drained soil. Protect it from winter wetness. Flowers in late spring, pink. Grows 2 inches (5 cm) high, 10 inches (25 cm) wide. Zones 7–9. Greece and southwestern Bulgaria.

## Asphodelus acaulis

asphodel

Liliaceae (Asphodelaceae)

A rhizomatous perennial for sun or part shade in scree, and in the alpine house. Flowers in spring and early summer, flesh pink. Grows 4 inches (10 cm) high, 12 inches (30 cm) wide. Zones 8–10. Algeria and Morocco.

## Asplenium

Aspleniaceae

The aspleniums are a diverse group of small-growing ferns well suited to the shadier parts of the rock garden, wall garden, or alpine house.

## Asplenium ceterach

rusty back fern

synonym, *Ceterach officinarum*

A perennial for part shade in fertile, well-drained, limy soil. Grows 6 inches (15 cm) high, 12 inches (30 cm) wide. Zones 6–8. Europe east to the Caucasus Mountains and south to northern Africa.

## Asplenium platyneuron

ebony spleenwort

A perennial fern for part shade in fertile, well-drained, rocky soil. Grows 6 inches (15 cm) high, 12–18 inches (30–45 cm) wide. Zones 5–8. Eastern North America.

## Asplenium rhizophyllum

walking fern

synonym, *Camptosorus rhizophyllus*

With long, attenuate frond tips that root and produce plantlets when they touch the soil, a perennial fern that can form colonies when situated away from drying winds in cool, rocky soil and among mossy rocks. Cultivate in cool shade in fertile, well-drained soil. Grows 6 inches (15 cm) high, 18–24 inches (45–60 cm) wide. Zones 6–8. Eastern North America.

## Asplenium scolopendrium

hart's tongue fern

An evergreen perennial for cool shade in fertile, well-drained moist soil, preferably alkaline. Zones 5–9. North America, Europe, and Asia.

**Cultivars**. *Asplenium scolopendrium* 'Kaye's Variety', Kaye's hart's tongue fern, grows 10 inches (25 cm) high, 12 inches (30 cm) wide,

*Asplenium scolopendrium* 'Marginatum', margined hart's tongue fern, grows

*Asperula suberosa*, courtesy of Fritz Kummert

*Asplenium ceterach*

*Asplenium rhizophyllum*, courtesy of Armen Gevjan

*Asphodelus acaulis*, courtesy of Fritz Kummert

*Asplenium platyneuron*, courtesy of Armen Gevjan

*Asplenium scolopendrium* 'Kaye's Variety'

12–18 inches (30–45 cm) high, 12 inches (30 cm) wide.

## Asplenium trichomanes
maidenhair spleenwort
An evergreen perennial fern for shade or part shade in fertile, well-drained soil or rock crevices, preferably alkaline. Grows 6–8 inches (15–20 cm) high, 8 inches (20 cm) wide. Zones 2–9. Northern temperate regions.

## Aster
Compositae

## Aster alpinus
Worthy of its long history as a popular rock garden staple, *A. alpinus* is a perennial somewhat variable in size and length of flowering stem; the miniature forms with large flowers are best. Cultivate in sun or part shade in any good, well-drained soil. Flowers in May and June, violet-blue. Grows 4–6 inches (10–15 cm) high, 12 inches (30 cm) wide. Zones 2–9. Alps and Pyrenees.
**Cultivars**. White, pale pink, and dark-flowered forms are available. *Aster alpinus* 'Albus' grows 8 inches (20 cm) high, 12 inches (30 cm) wide. Flowers in May and June, white.

## Aster coloradoensis
synonym, *Machaeranthera coloradoensis*
A perennial for sun in fertile, well-drained soil. Flowers in early summer, rose pink. Grows 6 inches (15 cm) high, 12 inches (30 cm) wide. Zones 3–8. Colorado.

Aster alpinus

Aster alpinus 'Albus'

## Aster novi-belgii
Michaelmas daisy
A perennial for sun in fertile, well-drained soil. Zones 3–9. Northeastern United States and adjacent Canada.
**Cultivars**. *Aster novi-belgii* 'Alice Haslam' flowers in late summer and fall, deep rose pink. Grows 10 inches (25 cm) high, 18 inches (45 cm) wide.
*Aster novi-belgii* 'Niobe' flowers in late summer and fall, white. Grows 6 inches (15 cm) high, 12 inches (30 cm) wide.
*Aster novi-belgii* 'Violet Carpet' flowers in late summer and fall, violet-blue. Grows 8 inches (20 cm) high, 24 inches (60 cm) wide.

Aster novi-belgii 'Alice Haslam'

Aster novi-belgii 'Niobe'

Asplenium scolopendrium 'Marginatum'

Asplenium trichomanes

Aster coloradoensis

Aster novi-belgii 'Violet Carpet'

## Astilbe
perennial spiraea
Saxifragaceae

Most versatile plants, all astilbes will grow in sun provided the soil stays wet to moist. They make ideal woodland or peat garden plants in any good soil, and they perform well as container plants in the alpine house. They are rhizomatous perennials.

### Astilbe chinensis
Cultivate in sun or part shade in humus-rich soil, and in the alpine house. The cultivar 'Pumila' flowers in August to October, pink. Grows 9 inches (22 cm) high, 18 inches (45 cm) wide. Zones 4–8. The species is from China and Japan.

### Astilbe glaberrima
Cultivate in sun or part shade in humus-rich soil, and in the alpine house. *Astilbe glaberrima* 'Saxatilis' (synonym, *A. japonica* var. *terrestris*) flowers in early summer, pale pink. Grows 6 inches (15 cm) high, 12 inches (30 cm) wide. Zones 6–9. Kyushu Island, Japan.

### Astilbe simplicifolia
Cultivate in sun or part shade in humus-rich soil, and in the alpine house. The cultivar 'Sprite' flowers in summer, shell pink. Grows 12 inches (30 cm) high, 18 inches (45 cm) wide. Zones 4–9. The species is from Honshu, Japan.

## Astragalus
milk vetch
Leguminosae

These deeply rooted plants do not do well if disturbed, thus transplanting must be done carefully and when plants are young.

### Astragalus angustifolius
A softly spiny, hummock-forming shrub for sun in scree. Flowers in summer, dull white, sometimes tinted purple. Grows 8–12 inches (20–30 cm) high, 18 inches (45 cm) wide. Zones 7–9. Greece and Turkey.

*Astragalus angustifolius,* courtesy of Fritz Kummert

*Astilbe glaberrima* 'Saxatilis', courtesy of Fritz Kummert

*Astilbe chinensis* 'Pumila', courtesy of Fritz Kummert

*Astilbe simplicifolia* 'Sprite'

## Astragalus exscapus

A woody-based perennial for sun in scree. Flowers in summer, bright yellow. Grows 3 inches (7.5 cm) high, 12 inches (30 cm) wide. Zones 5–9. Central Europe to southeastern Spain and northern Greece.

## Athamanta cretensis

candy carrot
Umbelliferae
A perennial for sun or part shade in any good, well-drained soil. Flowers in summer, white. Grows 16–24 inches (40–60 cm) high, 24 inches (60 cm) wide. Zones 6–9. Southeastern Spain and eastern France to the western Balkan Peninsula.

## Athyrium

Woodsiaceae

## Athyrium filix-femina

lady fern
Taking many forms, with a wide range in size, habit, and delicacy of the fronds, a perennial for part shade in fertile,

Astragalus exscapus, courtesy of Fritz Kummert

Athamanta cretensis, courtesy of Fritz Kummert

well-drained, moist soil. Zones 3–8. Northern temperate zone, and tropical mountains and southern South America.

**Cultivars**. *Athyrium filix-femina* 'Fieldii' grows 24–36 inches (60–90 cm) high, 24 inches (60 cm) wide.

*Athyrium filix-femina* 'Frizelliae Cristatum', crested tatting fern, grows 12–16 inches (30–40 cm) high, 18 inches (45 cm) wide.

## Athyrium nipponicum

A perennial for part shade in fertile, well-drained, moist soil. The cultivar 'Pictum', Japanese painted fern, grows 12 inches (30 cm) high, 36 inches (90 cm) wide. Zones 3–8. The species is from Japan, China, Korea, and Taiwan.

## Aubrieta

aubretia, rock cress
Cruciferae

The commonly grown aubretias are classic, easy-to-grow plants for the rock

Athyrium filix-femina 'Fieldii'

Athyrium filix-femina 'Frizelliae Cristatum'

garden, along with *Arabis, Aurinia, Iberis,* and *Phlox.*

## Aubrieta ✕cultorum

An evergreen perennial for sun in any well-drained soil, preferably alkaline. Flowers in spring in a range of pinks, reds, and purples. They may be single (four-petaled), semidouble, or fully double. Grows 6–12 inches (15–30 cm) high, 24 inches (60 cm) wide. Zones 4–9. An example of one of many garden hybrids often of obscure parentage, usu-

Athyrium nipponicum 'Pictum'

Aubrieta ✕cultorum, courtesy of Fritz Kummert

Aubrieta ✕cultorum 'Variegata'

ally involving *A. deltoidea,* a native of the Aegean, naturalized in southwestern Europe.

**Cultivar.** *Aubrieta ×cultorum* 'Variegata', variegated aubretia or rock cress, flowers in spring, lavender-blue.

### Aubrieta gracilis

An evergreen perennial for sun in any well-drained soil, preferably alkaline. Flowers in late spring and early summer, purplish. Grows 3–5 inches (7.5–12.5 cm) high, 12 inches (30 cm) wide. Zones 7–9. Southern Balkan Peninsula.

### Aurinia saxatilis

basket-of-gold
Cruciferae
synonym, *Alyssum saxatile*
Sometimes misspelled *saxatile, Aurinia saxatilis* is a perennial for sun in any good, well-drained soil, preferably alkaline. Grows 8 inches (20 cm) high, 24 inches (60 cm) wide. Zones 4–10. Central and southeastern Europe.

**Cultivars.** There are several cultivars of this easy-to-grow and traditional rock garden plant. They benefit from heavy shearing after flowering.

*Aurinia saxatilis* 'Dudley Neville Variegated', variegated basket-of-gold, flowers in spring, yellow.

*Aurinia saxatilis* 'Sunny Border Apricot' flowers in spring, pale apricot gold.

Aubrieta gracilis

Aurinia saxatilis 'Sunny Border Apricot'

Aurinia saxatilis 'Dudley Neville Variegated'

 **B**

### Balsamorhiza hookeri

balsam root
Compositae
A perennial for sun in any good, well-drained soil. Flowers in spring and early summer, yellow. Grows 4–12 inches (10–30 cm) high, 12 inches (30 cm) wide. Zones 6–9. California north to Washington and east to Utah.

### Begonia
Begoniaceae

### Begonia grandis

hardy begonia
synonym, *B. evansiana*
A tuberous perennial for part shade in humus-rich, well-drained soil. Flowers in summer, pink. Grows 18 inches (45 cm) high, 12 inches (30 cm) wide. Zones 6–10. China and Japan. There is also a good white-flowered cultivar, 'Alba'.

*Balsamorhiza hookeri,* courtesy of Fritz Kummert

Begonia grandis

## Begonia sutherlandii

A tuberous perennial for part shade in humus-rich, well-drained soil and in the alpine house. Flowers in July through October, tangerine orange. Grows 8 inches (20 cm) high, 18 inches (45 cm) wide. Zones 8–10. KwaZulu-Natal, South Africa, to Tasmania.

## Bellis perennis
English daisy
Compositae

A perennial for sun or part shade in any good, well-drained soil. The cultivar 'Pompomette' flowers in spring and early summer, rose red, maturing whitish. Cultivars require regular division in fall to keep them healthy and vigorous.

Grow 4 inches (10 cm) high, 10 inches (25 cm) wide. Zones 4–10. The species is from Europe and western Asia.

## Bellium bellidioides
Compositae

Often incorrectly called *B. minutum*, which is an annual with tiny ray florets, *B. bellidioides* is a small, stoloniferous perennial that makes prostrate pads of tiny round leaves. It is especially effective in troughs and between paving stones. Cultivate in sun or part shade in fertile, well-drained soil. Flowers in summer, white. Grows 2 inches (5 cm) high, 6 inches (15 cm) wide. Zones 5–9. Greece and Turkey.

## Berardia subacaulis
Compositae

A perennial for sun in gritty scree, and in the alpine house. Flowers in late summer, white tinted with bluish mauve. Grows 3 inches (7.5 cm) high, 10 inches (25 cm) wide. Zones 5–9. Southwestern Alps.

## Berberis ×stenophylla
Berberidaceae

An evergreen shrub for sun or part shade in any good soil. The cultivar 'Corallina Compacta', coral barberry, flowers in May, orange. Grows 18 inches (45 cm) high and wide. Zones 5–10. *Berberis ×stenophylla* is a hybrid, *B. darwinii* × *B. empetrifolia*.

## Bergenia 'Bressingham White'
Saxifragaceae

The dwarfer species and hybrids of *Bergenia* look good with other large rock

Begonia sutherlandii

Bellis perennis 'Pompomette'

Berardia subacaulis, courtesy of Fritz Kummert

Bellium bellidioides, courtesy of Fritz Kummert

Berberis ×stenophylla 'Corallina Compacta'

garden plants. Flower colors range from white as shown to shades of pink. Very tough and adaptable evergreen perennials, they take sun or shade and look best given a fairly humus-rich, well-drained soil. Cultivate in sun or part shade to shade. Flowers in early spring, pure white. Grows 12 inches (30 cm) high, 18 inches (45 cm) wide. Zones 5–9.

## Betula
birch
Betulaceae

Birches for the rock garden are deciduous shrubs of small stature.

## Betula humilis
Cultivate in sun or part shade in fertile, well-drained soil. Flowers in summer in

*Bergenia* 'Bressingham White'

*Betula humilis*, courtesy of Fritz Kummert

catkins. Grows 18–72 inches (45–180 cm) high, 36 inches (90 cm) wide. Zones 1–8. Asia and Europe.

## Betula nana
arctic or dwarf birch
Cultivate in sun or part shade in fertile, well-drained soil. Flowers in summer in catkins. Grows 18 inches (45 cm) high and wide. Zones 4–8. Arctic alpine regions.

## Betula pendula
European white birch
Cultivate in sun or part shade in fertile, well-drained soil. Flowers in summer in catkins. The cultivar 'Trost's Dwarf', dwarf lace-leaved European white birch, is a more recent introduction but has become popular due to its finely dissected foliage, white bark, and dwarf habit. Grows 60 inches (150 cm) high, 36 inches (90 cm) wide. Zones 5–10. The species is from Europe and Turkey.

## Biarum
Araceae

## Biarum davisii
A tuberous perennial for part shade in fertile, well-drained soil. Flowers in fall,

*Betula nana*, courtesy of Franz Hadacek

pinkish brown. Grows 3 inches (7.5 cm) high, 6 inches (15 cm) wide. Zones 8–9. Crete and southwestern Turkey.

## Biarum tenuifolium
A tuberous perennial for part shade in fertile, well-drained soil. Flowers in spring, purple and green. Grows 12 inches (30 cm) high, 8 inches (20 cm) wide. Zones 8–9. Portugal to Turkey.

*Betula pendula* 'Trost's Dwarf'

*Biarum davisii*, courtesy of Fritz Kummert

*Biarum tenuifolium*, courtesy of Fritz Kummert

## Biscutella laevigata
buckler mustard
Cruciferae
A perennial for sun in any well-drained soil. Flowers in spring early summer, yellow. Grows 12–24 inches (30–60 cm) high, 12 inches (30 cm) wide. Zones 8–10. Central and southern Europe.

## Blechnum
hard fern
Blechnaceae

The blechnums are rhizomatous, perennial, evergreen ferns, beautiful in the shady rock garden. In colder climates they make decorative alpine house or greenhouse plants.

Biscutella laevigata, courtesy of Franz Hadacek

Blechnum penna-marina

## Blechnum penna-marina
Cultivate in part shade in any good, well-drained soil. Grows 4 inches (10 cm) high, 18 inches (45 cm) wide. Zones 6–9. New Zealand.

## Blechnum spicant
deer fern, hard fern
Cultivate in part shade in any good, well-drained soil. The cultivar 'Redwood Giant' grows 24–30 inches (60–75 cm) high, 24 inches (60 cm) wide. Zones

Blechnum spicant 'Redwood Giant', courtesy of Fritz Kummert

5–9. The species is from North America, Europe, Asia, and Japan.

## Bletilla striata
Orchidaceae
A tuberous terrestrial orchid for part shade in fertile, well-drained soil. Flowers in June and July, purple-pink and white. Grows 18–24 inches (45–60 cm) high, 18 inches (45 cm) wide. Zones 6–10. Eastern Asia. Smaller growing species, including B. ochracea with golden yellow flowers, from Yunnan Province, China, are less available but worth acquiring.

## Bloomeria crocea
Liliaceae (Alliaceae)
A bulbous perennial for sun in well-drained soil. Flowers in early summer,

Bletilla striata close up, courtesy of Fritz Kummert

Bletilla striata

orange-yellow. Grows 18 inches (45 cm) high, 12 inches (30 cm) wide. Zones 8–10. California.

## Bolax gummifera
Umbelliferae

The leathery glossy green leaf rosettes of the perennial species *B. gummifera*, sometimes called *B. glebaria* 'Nana' in the nursery trade, make an intriguing, armor-like pad. Cultivate in sun or part shade in fertile, well-drained soil. Flowers in summer, yellow. Grows 1 inch (2.5

*Bloomeria crocea*, courtesy of Fritz Kummert

*Bolax gummifera*, courtesy of Fritz Kummert

*Brachycome nivalis*, courtesy of Fritz Kummert

cm) high, 6 inches (15 cm) wide. Zones 4–8. Southern tip of Chile and Argentina, and the Falkland Islands.

## Brachycome nivalis
Swan River daisy
Compositae

A perennial for any good, well-drained soil. Flowers in summer, white. Grows 8 inches (20 cm) high, 12 inches (30 cm) wide. Zones 8–9. Australian Alps, southeastern Australia.

## Bruckenthalia spiculifolia
spike heath
Ericaceae

An evergreen shrub for sun or part shade in humus-rich, acid soil. Flowers in June, rose pink. Grows 8 inches (20 cm) high, 12 inches (30 cm) wide. Zones 5–8. Southern Europe and Turkey.

## Brunnera macrophylla
Boraginaceae

A perennial for part shade in humus-rich, moist soil. The cultivar 'Dawson's

*Bruckenthalia spiculifolia*

*Brunnera macrophylla* 'Dawson's White'

White' (synonym, 'Variegata'), variegated Siberian bugloss, flowers in spring, blue. Grows 12–18 inches (30–45 cm) high, 36 inches (90 cm) wide. Zones 4–10. The species is from the Caucasus Mountains and western Siberia.

## Buglossoides purpureocaeruleum
Boraginaceae

synonym, *Lithospermum purpureocaeruleum*
A perennial that is a reliable ground cover, competing well for root space. Other good, tough companion ground covers include *Anemone nemorosa*, *A. ranunculoides*, and *Euphorbia*. Cultivate *B. purpureocaeruleum* in sun or part shade in fertile, well-drained soil. Flowers in summer, red-purple, becoming bright blue. Grows 28 inches (70 cm) high, 36 inches (90 cm) wide. Zones 6–9. Western Europe to Iran.

## Bulbocodium vernum
spring meadow saffron
Liliaceae (Colchicaceae)

A cormous perennial for sun in fertile, well-drained soil. Flowers in spring, rose

*Buglossoides purpureocaeruleum*, courtesy of Fritz Kummert

*Bulbocodium vernum*, courtesy of Fritz Kummert

purple. Grows 4–6 inches (10–15 cm) high. Zones 4–9. Southwestern Alps to southern Russia.

## *Bupleurum*
thoroughwax, thorow-wax
Umbelliferae

### *Bupleurum ranunculoides*
A perennial for sun in any good, well-drained soil. Flowers in summer, yellow. Grows 12–18 inches (30–45 cm) high, 18 inches (45 cm) wide. Zones 6–9. Central and southern Europe.

*Bupleurum ranunculoides,* courtesy of Fritz Kummert

*Bupleurum stellatum,* courtesy of Fritz Kummert

### *Bupleurum stellatum*
A perennial for sun in any good, well-drained soil. Flowers in summer, greenish yellow. Grows 8–16 inches (20–40 cm) high, 18 inches (45 cm) wide. Zones 7–9. Alps and Corsica.

### *Buxus microphylla*
dwarf boxwood
Buxaceae
In addition to their most common use as edging plants, boxwoods, like conifers, lend a good evergreen permanence to the trough and rock garden. Cultivate in sun or part shade in any good, well-drained soil. The cultivar 'Kingsville' flowers in spring, petalless and inconspicuous. Grows 5 inches (12.5 cm) high, 6 inches (15 cm) wide. Zones 5–10. The species is from China, Japan, Korea, and Taiwan.

*Buxus microphylla* 'Kingsville'

*Calamintha cretica*

## *Calamintha*
calamint
Labiatae

### *Calamintha cretica*
A woody-based perennial for sun in any well-drained soil. Flowers in summer, pink. Grows 4 inches (10 cm) high, 12 inches (30 cm) wide. Zones 6–10. Mediterranean.

### *Calamintha grandiflora*
A perennial for sun or part shade in any well-drained soil, preferably alkaline. The cultivar 'Variegata', variegated large-flowered calamint, flowers in summer, pink. Grows 12 inches (30 cm) high, 18 inches (45 cm) wide. Zones 5–9. The

*Calamintha grandiflora* 'Variegata'

species is from northeastern Spain to European Turkey.

## Calandrinia umbellata
rock purslane
Portulacaceae
A short-lived perennial for sun in fertile, gritty scree. It does well in the alpine house. Flowers in early summer, brilliant crimson-magenta. Grows 6–8 inches (15–20 cm) high, 8 inches (20 cm) wide. Zones 8–9. Chile and Andean Argentina.

## Calanthe
Orchidaceae

## Calanthe discolor
A perennial orchid from pseudobulbs for light to part shade in leaf-mold-rich, well-drained soil, and in the alpine house. Flowers in spring, maroon, bronze, purple, or white, all with a pale pink lip. Grows 12–18 inches (30–45 cm) high, 12 inches (30 cm) wide. Zones 7–9. Japan, Korea, and China.

*Calandrinia umbellata*, courtesy of Panayoti Kelaidis

*Calanthe discolor*

## Calanthe striata
synonyms, *C. discolor* f. *sieboldii, C. sieboldii*
A perennial orchid from pseudobulbs for light to part shade in leaf-mold-rich, well-drained soil, and in the alpine house. Flowers in spring, yellow, petals often tinged reddish brown. Grows 12–18 inches (30–45 cm) high, 12 inches (30 cm) wide. Zones 7–9. Japan.

## Calceolaria
pocketbook flower, pouch flower, slipper flower, slipperwort
Scrophulariaceae

Calceolarias are enchanting South American pouch-flowered perennials that include many species that are hardy if given a cool position in summer, a dry one in winter.

*Calanthe striata*

*Calceolaria* 'John Innes'

## Calceolaria falklandica
A spreading, herbaceous perennial that requires regular dividing to maintain vigor. Cultivate in part shade in fertile, well-drained, moderately moist soil. Flowers in summer, yellow with purple spots. Grows 6 inches (15 cm) high, 12 inches (30 cm) wide. Zones 6–9. Falkland Islands.

## Calceolaria 'John Innes'
A spreading, herbaceous perennial that requires regular dividing to maintain vigor. Cultivate in part shade in fertile, well-drained, moderately moist soil. Flowers in late spring and early summer, yellow freckled with red. Grows 6 inches (15 cm) high, 8 inches (20 cm) wide. Zones 6–9. A hybrid, *C. biflora* × (proba-

*Calceolaria falklandica*

bly) *C. lanceolata*, both from Chile and Argentina.

## Calceolaria uniflora
synonym, *C. darwinii*
A woody-based perennial for part shade in fertile, well-drained, moderately moist soil, and doing best in an alpine house. Flowers in summer, yellow-brown with garnet red and a band of pure white. Grows 4 inches (10 cm) high, 8 inches (20 cm) wide. Zones 6–9. Southern Patagonia, Tierra del Fuego.

## Callianthemum anemonoides
Ranunculaceae
A rhizomatous perennial for sun or part shade in fertile, well-drained soil. Flowers in spring, white to pink. Grows 4–8 inches (10–20 cm) high, 10 inches (25 cm) wide. Zones 5–8. Austria.

## Callirhoe involucrata
purple poppy mallow, wine cups
Malvaceae
With brilliantly colored flowers that are quite a sensation for a long season, give

*Calceolaria uniflora*, courtesy of Fritz Kummert

*Callianthemum anemonoides*, courtesy of Fritz Kummert

this perennial room to spread among other plants of similar size and sunny, poorish soil requirements. Cultivate in sun in any well-drained soil. Flowers in June through fall, crimson-magenta. Grows 6 inches (15 cm) high, 36 inches (90 cm) wide. Zones 4–10. Wyoming to Texas.

## Calluna vulgaris
ling, Scots heather
Ericaceae
An evergreen shrub, *C. vulgaris* is the most variable of the hardy heaths and includes a wide selection of cultivars for the rock garden and peat bed. Callunas bring summer flowers and brilliant winter foliage color. A sunny location and humus-rich, acid soil that is moist but not wet will result in compact, healthy plants. Zones 5–8. *Calluna vulgaris* is

*Callirhoe involucrata*

from Siberia, Turkey, many parts of northern Europe, and the Azores.

**Cultivars.** *Calluna vulgaris* 'Corbett's Red' grows 6 inches (15 cm) high, 12 inches (30 cm) wide. Flowers in August and September, rosy red.

*Calluna vulgaris* 'Dainty Bess' grows 4 inches (10 cm) high, 24 inches (60 cm) wide. Flowers in August and September, mauve.

*Calluna vulgaris* 'John F. Letts' is a stunning, low, spreading cultivar with foliage of chartreuse and yellow, turning orange and red in winter. Grows 4 inches (10 cm) high, 18 inches (45 cm) wide. Flowers in August and September, lavender.

The colorful foliage of *Calluna vulgaris* 'Robert Chapman' is gold to orange turning reddish in the winter and spring. Grows 12 inches (30 cm) high, 24 inches

*Calluna vulgaris* 'Corbett's Red'

*Calluna vulgaris* 'Dainty Bess'

*Calluna vulgaris* 'John F. Letts'

(60 cm) wide. Flowers in August and September, lavender.

*Calluna vulgaris* 'Silver Queen' grows 8 inches (20 cm) high, 18 inches (45 cm) wide. Flowers in August and September, lavender.

*Calluna vulgaris* 'White Lawn' is a neat, compact cultivar with an attractive flat, spreading habit and fresh, bright green foliage. Grows 3 inches (7.5 cm) high, 12 inches (30 cm) wide. Flowers in August and September, white.

## *Calochortus*
Mariposa lily
Liliaceae (Calochortaceae)

Bulbous perennials, most calochortuses are difficult to grow in the open garden, but most can be grown in a bulb frame or in pots in the alpine house or cold greenhouse. All require a dormant period after flowering when water should be withheld until late fall.

## *Calochortus luteus*
Cultivate in sun in fertile scree. Flowers in spring, deep yellow with blotch and markings deep brown. Grows 8–16 inches (20–40 cm) high. Zones 7–9. California Coast Ranges and the interior.

## *Calochortus monophyllus*
cat's ears
Cultivate in sun in fertile scree. Flowers in spring, deep yellow with reddish basal markings. Grows 6–10 inches (15–

*Calluna vulgaris* 'Robert Chapman'

*Calochortus luteus*, courtesy of Fritz Kummert

*Calluna vulgaris* 'Silver Queen'

*Calluna vulgaris* 'White Lawn'

*Calochortus monophyllus*

25 cm) high. Zones 6–9. Western foothills of the Sierra Nevada, California.

## Calochortus tolmiei

cat's ears, pussy ears
Cultivate in sun in fertile scree. Flowers in spring, pale lavender. Grows 4–8 inches (10–20 cm) high. Zones 6–9. Mountains of Oregon and northern California. Very similar and sometimes considered synonymous are *C. coeruleus* and *C. maweanus.*

## Calochortus uniflorus

star tulip
Cultivate in sun in fertile scree. Flowers in spring, pale lilac. Grows 3–8 inches (7.5–20 cm) high. Zones 6–9. Coast Ranges of northern California and southern Oregon.

*Calochortus tolmiei,* courtesy of Fritz Kummert

*Calochortus uniflorus,* courtesy of Fritz Kummert

## Caltha

marsh marigold
Ranunculaceae
All of the calthas look at home in moist areas near a rock garden pond.

## Caltha introloba

A perennial for sun or part shade in any good, well-drained, moist soil. Flowers in late winter and spring, white or cream, sometimes with purple base or veining. Grows 4 inches (10 cm) high, 6 inches (15 cm) wide. Zones 6–8. Australian Alps, southeastern Australia.

## Caltha leptosepala

A perennial for sun or part shade in fertile soil, from moist to bog conditions. Flowers in spring to summer, white often tinted greenish or bluish. Grows 8 inches (20 cm) high, 12 inches (30 cm) wide. Zones 3–8. Northwestern North America in alpine zones.

## Caltha palustris

Cultivate in sun or part shade in fertile soil, from moist to bog conditions. The

*Caltha introloba,* courtesy of Fritz Kummert

*Caltha leptosepala*

cultivar 'Plena' (synonym, 'Multiplex'), double marsh marigold, flowers in March through June, golden yellow. Grows 12 inches (30 cm) high, 18 inches (45 cm) wide. Zones 3–10. The species is from northern temperate regions of Asia, North America, and Europe.

## Calylophus drummondii

Texas primrose
Onagraceae
*Calylophus* is a small genus of shrubby perennial evening primroses that bring continuous flowers to the hot rock garden and border. Cultivate *C. drummondii* in sun in well-drained soil. Flowers in summer and fall, yellow. Grows 8 inches (20 cm) high, 18 inches (45 cm) wide. Zones 5–9. Texas and Oklahoma.

*Caltha palustris* 'Plena'

*Calylophus drummondii,* shown with the silver foliage of *Santolina*

## Calyptridium umbellatum

pussy paws

Portulacaceae

synonym, *Spraguea umbellata*

A native of open forest and volcanic pumice screes ranging in elevation from 2500 to 11,000 feet (750–3300 m), *C. umbellatum* is a taprooted perennial. Grow in an alpine house or raised bed with sharply draining soil and protection from winter wet. Cultivate in sun in scree. Flowers in summer, pink or white. Grows 4–8 inches (10–20 cm) high, 8 inches (20 cm) wide. Zones 6–8. British Columbia to California and the Rocky Mountains.

## Campanula

bellflower

Campanulaceae

## Campanula alpestris

synonym, *C. allionii*

A beautiful perennial species, slowly forming a dense mat of small-foliage

Calyptridium umbellatum

Campanula alpestris

rosettes. It tends to be short-lived and difficult in cultivation, requiring scree conditions and control of rust in summer. Cultivate in sun or part shade in fertile scree. Flowers in summer, mid-blue to purple. Grows 3 inches (7.5 cm) high, 12 inches (30 cm) wide. Zones 5–8. Southwestern Alps.

## Campanula barbata

bearded bellflower

A biennial or short-lived perennial that comes readily from seed. Cultivate in sun or part shade in any good, well-drained soil. Flowers in summer, lavender-blue. Grows 6–10 inches (15–25 cm) high, 6 inches (15 cm) wide. Zones 4–8. Alps and mountains of Norway.

## Campanula betulifolia

synonym, *C. finitima*

Sometimes misspelled *betulaefolia*, *C. betulifolia* has beautiful loose clusters

Campanula barbata, courtesy of Fritz Kummert

Campanula betulifolia

of flowers, pink to red in bud, hanging from mostly decumbent stems, a perennial that makes an elegant show when planted in a wall or container. Cultivate in sun or part shade in any good, well-drained soil. Flowers in summer, white, sometimes pale pink. Grows 4 inches (10 cm) high, 12 inches (30 cm) wide. Zones 6–8. Armenia.

## Campanula 'Blue Gown'

A perennial for sun or part shade in any good, well-drained soil. Flowers in summer, lavender-blue with a prominent white eye. Grows 6 inches (15 cm) high, 24 inches (60 cm) wide. Zones 6–9.

## Campanula caespitosa

A perennial similar in appearance to *C. cochlearifolia* but forming clumps rather

Campanula 'Blue Gown'

Campanula caespitosa, courtesy of Fritz Kummert

than a mat of running roots. Cultivate *C. caespitosa* in sun or part shade in any good, well-drained soil. Flowers in summer, blue. Grows 6 inches (15 cm) high, 12 inches (30 cm) wide. Zones 4–8. Alps of eastern Europe.

## Campanula carpatica
tussock bellflower
A perennial for sun or part shade in any good, well-drained soil. Flowers in summer in shades of violet, purple, blue, or white. Grows 8–18 inches (20–45 cm) high, 24 inches (60 cm) wide. Zones 4–8. Carpathians, eastern Europe.

*Campanula carpatica*, courtesy of Fritz Kummert

*Campanula cenisia*, courtesy of Fritz Kummert

## Campanula cenisia
A perennial for sun or part shade in acid scree with protection from winter wetness, or in the alpine house. Flowers in summer, slate blue. Grows 4 inches (10 cm) high, 12 inches (30 cm) wide. Zones 5–8. Western Alps.

## Campanula chamissonis
synonyms, *C. dasyantha, C. pilosa var. dasyantha*
A perennial, spreading by short stolons, for sun or part shade in any good, well-drained soil. Flowers in May and June in shades of blue, some with white markings inside. Grows 4 inches (10 cm) high, 12 inches (30 cm) wide. Zones 4–8. Siberia to Japan, the Aleutians and Alaska. There are several named clones in circulation, many which are not distinctively different. An outstanding one well worth growing is 'Oyobenii' with solid blue flowers.

*Campanula chamissonis*, courtesy of Fritz Kummert

*Campanula cochlearifolia*, courtesy of Fritz Kummert

## Campanula cochlearifolia
fairy thimbles
synonyms, *C. bellardii, C. pumila, C. pusilla*
An ever-popular perennial, spreading by slender rhizomes and forming a mat-like colony of tiny, shining green leaves. Cultivate in sun or part shade in any good, well-drained soil. Flowers in July, lavender-blue but also in shades of lilac, lavender, blue, and white. Grows 3 inches (7.5 cm) high, 12 inches (30 cm) wide, and can eventually spread much more. Zones 4–8. Mountains of Europe, often on limestone. Many cultivars have been selected and are enjoyed, including 'Alba' with white flowers, and 'Miranda' with pale, icy blue flowers.

## Campanula elatines var. fenestrellata
Adriatic bellflower
*Campanula elatines* belongs to a group of perennial campanulas that includes the well-known *C. garganica*. All have attractive heart-shaped leaves, delicately toothed, and produce an abundance of star-shaped flowers. Cultivate in sun or part shade in any good, well-drained soil. *Campanula elatines* var. *fenestrellata* flowers in June and July, blue with silver markings. Grows 6 inches (15 cm) high, 18 inches (45 cm) wide. Zones 4–8. The variety is from mountains of northwestern Italy, on cliff faces.

## Campanula excisa
A delicate looking perennial with wiry stems; tiny, narrow leaves; and dainty,

*Campanula elatines* var. *fenestrellata*

pendant flowers with a rounded hole between petals from which the species derives its name. Not always easy to cultivate, it needs deep, acid scree soil in which it can spread and colonize new areas, or requires frequent division and replanting in fresh soil. Cultivate in part shade. Flowers in June and July, blue to violet. Grows 6 inches (15 cm) high, 12 inches (30 cm) wide. Zones 5–8. Southwestern and Swiss Alps, not common.

### Campanula formanekiana

Primarily a biennial that can be easily regrown from seed after it has flowered. Its gray, downy leaves require dryness in winter, making cultivation easiest on a dry wall or in an alpine house. Cultivate in sun or part shade in any good, well-

drained soil. Flowers in summer, white, often tinted bluish lilac. Grows 12–18 inches (30–45 cm) high, 12 inches (30 cm) wide. Zones 6–8. Balkan Peninsula.

### Campanula garganica

More robustly growing than *C. elatines*, cultivate *C. garganica* in sun or part shade in any good, well-drained soil. Flowers in summer, blue with a white center. Grows 4–6 inches (10–15 cm) high, 24 inches (60 cm) wide. Zones 4–9. Western Balkan Peninsula, eastern Italy. This long-popular, near-evergreen rock garden perennial is grown in many different forms, all excellent wall or crevice plants with low, spreading stems carrying many star-shaped flowers. Some favorites include 'W. H. Paine' with rich

blue, white-centered flowers, and 'Dickson's Gold' with golden yellow foliage.

### Campanula glomerata
clustered bellflower

A perennial for sun or part shade in any good, well-drained soil. The cultivars 'Acaulis' and 'Alba Nana', dwarf clustered bellflowers, grow 6–8 inches (15–20 cm) high, 18 inches (45 cm) wide. Zones 4–9. Flower in summer in shades of violet-blue, or white. The species is from Europe and Asia.

### Campanula hawkinsiana

A perennial from a central rootstock for sun or part shade in scree with protection from winter wetness. Flowers in summer, deep purple with darker vein-

*Campanula excisa*, courtesy of Fritz Kummert

*Campanula formanekiana*, courtesy of Fritz Kummert

*Campanula garganica*, courtesy of Fritz Kummert

*Campanula glomerata* 'Alba Nana'

Campanula glomerata 'Acaulis'

ing. Grows 4–8 inches (10–20 cm) high, 8 inches (20 cm) wide. Zones 6–8. Greece and Albania.

## Campanula incurva
synonym, *C. leutweinii*
A beauty that is like a compactly growing Canterbury bell, *C. medium*. Though basically monocarpic and a biennial, *C. incurva* is well worth growing for its large, soft and hairy foliage and for its chubby, inflated flowers, displayed over a long season. Cultivate in sun or part shade in any good, well-drained soil. Flowers in summer, pastel lavender-blue. Grows 12 inches (30 cm) high, 18 inches (45 cm) wide. Zones 6–9. Greece.

## Campanula 'Joe Elliott'
A perennial for sun or part shade in scree with protection from winter wetness, or in the alpine house. Flowers in July, violet-blue. Grows 3 inches (7.5 cm) high, 6 inches (15 cm) wide. Zones 6–8. A garden hybrid, *C. morettiana* × *C. raineri*.

## Campanula mirabilis
A most showy species, first creating wide rosettes of flat, fleshy, oval leaves. It takes several years to mature and produce the central stems of flowers that spring from each leaf axil. After flowering and dying, it is easily raised again from seed. Cultivate in sun or part shade in fertile scree

with protection from winter wetness, or, most easily, in the alpine house. Flowers in summer, soft lilac blue. Grows 12 inches (30 cm) high, 24 inches (60 cm) wide. Zones 6–8. Caucasus Mountains.

## Campanula morettiana
One of the finest alpine campanulas, a perennial deserving the reputation of being difficult to cultivate. It requires full alpine house conditions, including protection from excess moisture at all times. Cultivate in sun or part shade in tufa or limestone scree. Flowers in summer, violet-blue, rarely white or pink. Grows 3 inches (7.5 cm) high, 6 inches (15 cm) wide. Zones 6–8. Dolomites of northern Italy, and western Austria and Croatia.

## Campanula persicifolia
peach-leaved bluebell
A perennial for sun or part shade in any good, well-drained soil. The cultivar

*Campanula hawkinsiana*, courtesy of Fritz Kummert

*Campanula mirabilis*, courtesy of Fritz Kummert

*Campanula incurva*, courtesy of Fritz Kummert

*Campanula* 'Joe Elliott'

*Campanula morettiana*, courtesy of Fritz Kummert

'Planiflora' is a Mendelian recessive form. This microform is desirable to rock gardeners because of its dark, leathery leaves and short, erect stems of large, showy flowers in summer, blue in 'Planiflora', white in 'Planiflora Alba'. The dwarf peach-leaved bluebells grow 12 inches (30 cm) high, 10 inches (25 cm) wide. Zones 3–9. The species is from Europe, northern Africa, and western Asia.

### *Campanula piperi*

A perennial that does best in the alpine house, where it still may flower only poorly. Cultivate in sun or part shade in acid scree. Flowers in summer, blue with red anthers. Grows 2 inches (5 cm)

high, 6 inches (15 cm) wide. Zones 5–8. Olympic Mountains of Washington.

### *Campanula portenschlagiana*

A popular rock garden plant for hundreds of years. The species and cultivars can be invasive in humus-rich garden soil. They are near-evergreen perennials particularly suited to a wall or the crevice garden in part shade. Cultivate in any good, well-drained soil. The cultivar 'Resholt Variety' flowers in summer, deep violet-blue. Grows 6 inches (15 cm) high, 18 inches (45 cm) wide. Zones 4–8. The species is from western Croatia, on alpine cliffs.

### *Campanula ×pulloides*

A perennial for sun or part shade in any good, well-drained soil. Flowers in June and July, blue. Grows 4 inches (10 cm) high, 8 inches (20 cm) wide. Zones 5–8. A garden hybrid, *C. carpatica* var. *turbinata* × *C. pulla*.

### *Campanula punctata*

A perennial, spreading by slender rhizomes. Opinions of its garden worthiness vary. In some gardens it spreads rapidly and becomes a weed; in others it dies for no apparent reason. When growing well, the plant freely produces impressive, 2-inch- (5-cm-) long, hang-

*Campanula persicifolia* 'Planiflora Alba'

*Campanula portenschlagiana* 'Resholt Variety'

*Campanula piperi,* courtesy of Fritz Kummert

*Campanula ×pulloides*

ing bells. Cultivate in sun or part shade in sandy or peaty, well-drained soil. Flowers in May and June, rose purple, freckled darker inside. Grows 12 inches (30 cm) high, 36 inches (90 cm) wide. Zones 5–9. Japan and Siberia.

**Cultivars.** There seems to be some confusion in the naming of different selections of this variable species. *Campanula punctata* 'Nana Alba' is a dwarf white cultivar, 'Rosea' a dwarf dusty rose pink one.

## Campanula raineri

A cherished perennial alpine campanula for pot culture in the alpine house or in a sunny rock garden protected from winter wetness. Cultivate in sun or part shade in limestone scree. Flowers in summer, china blue. Grows 3 inches (7.5 cm) high, 10 inches (25 cm) wide. Zones 5–9. Italian and Swiss Alps among limestone rocks.

Campanula punctata 'Rosea'

Campanula raineri, courtesy of Fritz Kummert

## Campanula thyrsoides

A unique campanula in every respect and though unfortunately a biennial or short-lived, monocarpic perennial, it is easily raised from seed. Cultivate in sun in any good, well-drained soil. Flowers in summer, pale yellow. Grows 18 inches (45 cm) high, 12 inches (30 cm) wide. Zones 5–8. Alps, the Jura, and mountains of the Balkan Peninsula.

## Campanula tommasiniana

A perennial for sun or part shade in any good, well-drained soil. Flowers in July and August, lavender-blue. Grows 6 inches (15 cm) high, 12 inches (30 cm) wide. Zones 6–8. Mountains of the Istrian Peninsula, western Slovenia and Croatia.

Campanula thyrsoides, courtesy of Fritz Kummert

Campanula tommasiniana, courtesy of Fritz Kummert

## Campanula ×tymonsii

A perennial for sun or part shade in any good, well-drained soil. Flowers in July and August, purple-blue. Grows 4 inches (10 cm) high, 12 inches (30 cm) wide. Zones 4–8. A hybrid, *C. carpatica × C. pyramidalis.*

## Campanula zoysii

An irresistible little perennial with curious, bottle-shaped flowers, it is worthy of all the trouble it takes to grow it even though it is often short-lived due to flowering itself to death and is subject to slug damage. Cultivate in part shade in limestone scree, and in the alpine house. Flowers in summer in varying shades of blue. Grows 4 inches (10 cm) high, 6 inches (15 cm) wide. Zones 6–8. Eastern Alps.

## Cardamine
bittercress
Cruciferae

Excluding *C. hirsutus,* one of the worst weeds of rock gardens, there are several

Campanula ×tymonsii

Campanula zoysii, courtesy of Fritz Kummert

fine bittercresses for the cool, shady rock garden.

## Cardamine pentaphyllos

synonyms, *Dentaria digitata, D. pentaphyllos*
A perennial with scaly rhizomes for part shade in any fertile soil, not dry. Flowers in early spring, nodding pink. Grows 12–16 inches (30–40 cm) high, 12 inches (30 cm) wide. Zones 6–9. Central and western Europe.

## Cardamine trifolia

A perennial with surface-creeping, rooting rhizomes for part shade in any fertile soil, not dry. Flowers in spring, white, sometimes pink. Grows 6 inches (15 cm) high, 18 inches (45 cm) wide. Zones 6–9. Alps of central and southern Europe.

## Carduncellus
Compositae

## Carduncellus mitissimus
A perennial for sun in well-drained soil, preferably limy, and in the alpine house.

*Cardamine pentaphyllos*, courtesy of Fritz Kummert

*Cardamine trifolia*, courtesy of Fritz Kummert

Flowers in June through August, lavender-blue. Grows 4 inches (10 cm) high, 12 inches (30 cm) wide. Zones 6–9. France and Italy.

## Carduncellus rhaponticoides
A perennial for sun in well-drained soil, preferably limy, and in the alpine house. Flowers in late spring and summer, mauve-blue. Grows 4 inches (10 cm) high, 10 inches (25 cm) wide. Zones 7–9. Morocco, Atlas Mountains.

## Carex
sedge
Cyperaceae

## Carex conica
An evergreen perennial sedge for sun or part shade in any good, well-drained soil. The cultivar 'Variegata' (synonym, 'Marginata') flowers in spring in an inconspicuous panicle of green-white, aging brown. Grows 6 inches (15 cm) high, 10 inches (25 cm) wide. Zones 5–9. The species is from Japan and South Korea.

*Carduncellus mitissimus*

*Carduncellus rhaponticoides*, courtesy of Fritz Kummert

## Carex firma
dwarf pillow sedge
An evergreen perennial for sun or part shade in fertile, neutral to alkaline scree, and in the alpine house. Flowers in spring in a greenish spike. Grows 2 inches (5 cm) high, 4 inches (10 cm) wide. Zones 5–8. Mountains of central Europe.

**Cultivar.** One of the choicest sedges for rock garden or trough, *Carex firma* 'Variegata' is a variegated form that is very slow growing. It does best with its head in the sun and its roots shaded and growing in humus-rich, limestone scree.

## Carex flagellifera
bronze hair sedge
An evergreen perennial for sun or part shade in any good, well-drained soil. Flowers in spring in reddish brown to straw-colored spikes. Grows 12 inches (30 cm) high, 36 inches (90 cm) wide. Zones 7–10. New Zealand.

*Carex conica* 'Variegata'

*Carex firma* 'Variegata'

## Carex fraseri

Fraser's sedge

synonym, *Cymophyllus fraseri*

An evergreen perennial for part shade in moist, fertile soil, preferably acid. Flowers in early spring, white. Grows 12 inches (30 cm) high, 18 inches (45 cm) wide. Zones 4–9. Pennsylvania to South Carolina.

## Carex ornithopoda

bird's-foot sedge

An evergreen perennial for sun or part shade in any good, well-drained soil. The cultivar 'Variegata' flowers in summer in slender tan spikes, becoming brownish. Grows 4 inches (10 cm) high, 12 inches (30 cm) wide. Zones 7–9. The species is from northwestern Europe.

## Carex oshimensis

A very versatile sedge, similar to *C. morrowii* but more finely bladed and compact. Cultivate *C. oshimensis* in sun or part shade in any good, well-drained soil. Flowers in late spring in yellow-green spikes. Grows 12 inches (30 cm) high and wide. Zones 5–9. Honshu, Japan.

**Cultivar.** *Carex oshimensis* 'Evergold', Japanese variegated sedge, is an evergreen perennial that takes any garden soil and even bog conditions. This colorful cultivar has foliage striped with creamy yellow and green.

## Carex siderosticha

A rhizomatous, deciduous perennial for sun or part shade in any good, fertile soil. Flowers in spring, small, green, insignificant. Grows 12 inches (30 cm) high, 18 inches (45 cm) wide. Zones 6–8. The species is from Japan, Korea, and China.

*Carex flagellifera*

*Carex fraseri*

*Carex ornithopoda* 'Variegata'

*Carex oshimensis* 'Evergold'

*Carex siderosticha* 'Variegata'

## *Carlina acaulis*

stemless carline thistle
Compositae
A short-lived or monocarpic perennial for sun in any well-drained soil. Flowers in summer, silvery white to pale pink. Grows 4 inches (10 cm) high, 18 inches (45 cm) wide. Zones 4–8. Southern and eastern Europe.

## *Carmichaelia enysii*

Leguminosae
A mat-forming shrub for sun in any well-drained soil. Flowers in summer, purplish with darker veins. Grows 4 inches (10 cm) high, 10 inches (25 cm) wide. Zones 8–10. South Island, New Zealand.

## *Cassiope lycopodioides*

Ericaceae
Species of *Cassiope*, a genus of heath-like shrublets, are best grown in bright light but not hot sunshine. Humus-rich, well-drained, acid soil with grit added for good drainage can, in time, be enhanced with general fertilizing to maintain vigor. *Cassiope lycopodioides* flowers in spring and summer, white to creamy white. Grows 4 inches (10 cm) high, 12 inches (30 cm) wide. Zones 3–8. Japan, northeastern Asia, and Alaska.

## *Catananche caespitosa*

Cupid's dart
Compositae
A rare little beauty introduced by E. K. Balls and more recently reintroduced to cultivation, it is a perennial best grown in alpine house conditions. Cultivate in sun in any good, well-drained soil, preferably alkaline. Flowers in summer, deep yellow. Grows 4 inches (10 cm) high, 10 inches (25 cm) wide. Zones 7–9. Morocco, Atlas Mountains.

## *Ceanothus*

Rhamnaceae

## *Ceanothus prostratus*

Mahala mat, squaw carpet
A mat-forming, evergreen shrub for sun or part shade in any good, well-drained soil, avoiding overhead watering and excessive water in summer. Flowers in May and June, deep to light lavender-blue. Grows 2 inches (5 cm) high, 36 inches (90 cm) wide. Zones 5–8. Mountains of the northwestern United States.

## *Ceanothus pumilus*

Siskiyou mat
A mat-forming, evergreen shrub for sun or part shade in any good, well-drained soil. Avoid overhead watering and excessive water in summer. Flowers in spring, pale blue, lavender, or white. Grows 2–6 inches (5–15 cm) high, 24 inches (60 cm) wide. Zones 7–9. Northern California and southwestern Oregon.

*Carlina acaulis,* courtesy of Fritz Kummert

*Cassiope lycopodioides*

*Ceanothus prostratus*

*Catananche caespitosa,* courtesy of Fritz Kummert

*Ceanothus pumilus*

*Carmichaelia enysii,* courtesy of Fritz Kummert

## *Cedrus deodara*

Himalayan cedar

Pinaceae

Blue needled and incredibly tiny, the cultivar 'Pygmaea', miniature Himalayan cedar, is a condensed sport usually grafted onto more vigorous *C. deodara* rootstock. 'Pygmaea' is a coniferous gem for the rock garden and trough. Cultivate in sun or part shade in any good, well-drained soil. Grows 6 inches (15 cm) high and wide. Zones 6–10. The species is from Afghanistan to western Nepal.

## *Celmisia*

Compositae

*Celmisia* is a large genus of white-flowered alpine daisies, mostly from New Zealand and quite hardy and tolerant of humidity. Depending on climate, they take soil varying from peat or leaf mold to scree. They tolerate some heat but must never dry out.

Cedrus deodara 'Pygmaea'

Celmisia semicordata, courtesy of Franz Hadacek

## *Celmisia semicordata*

synonym, *C. coriacea*

A stoloniferous perennial for sun or part shade in any fertile, well-drained soil. Flowers in summer, white. Grows 18 inches (45 cm) high, 24 inches (60 cm) wide. Zones 7–9. South Island, New Zealand.

## *Celmisia spectabilis*

A perennial for sun or part shade in any fertile, well-drained soil. Flowers in summer, white. Grows 18 inches (45 cm) high, 24 inches (60 cm) wide. Zones 7–9. North and South Islands, New Zealand.

## *Centaurea uniflora*

knapweed

Compositae

A perennial for sun in any good soil. Flowers in summer, violet. Grows 12–18 inches (30–45 cm) high, 18 inches (45 cm) wide. Zones 4–9. Mountains of central and southeastern Europe.

Celmisia spectabilis, courtesy of Franz Hadacek

Centaurea uniflora, courtesy of Fritz Kummert

## *Cerastium*

Caryophyllaceae

## *Cerastium alpinum* subsp. *lanatum*

alpine mouse ear

A mat-forming perennial for sun in any well-drained soil. Flowers in summer, white. Grows 4 inches (10 cm) high, 12 inches (30 cm) wide. Zones 3–8. Circumpolar Arctic and mountains farther south.

## *Cerastium tomentosum* var. *columnae*

snow-in-summer

Whereas the species, *C. tomentosum*, is much too invasive for the rock garden, spreading by underground stems, the variety *columnae* is a slowly creeping perennial. The silver-haired rosette foliage is compressed into a tight carpet. Cultivate in sun in any well-drained soil. Flowers in summer, white. Grows 4

Cerastium alpinum subsp. *lanatum*, courtesy of Fritz Kummert

Cerastium tomentosum var. *columnae*

inches (10 cm) high, 18 inches (45 cm) wide. Zones 4–10. The species is from mountains of Europe and western Asia.

## *Chaenorrhinum origanifolium*
dwarf snapdragon
Scrophulariaceae
A perennial for sun in well-drained soil, preferably alkaline. Flowers in summer, blue-lilac, palette yellow. Grows 12 inches (30 cm) high and wide. Zones 7–9. Southwestern Europe.

## *Chamaecyparis*
Cupressaceae

There are many fine dwarf conifers to collect and grow in the rock garden. In addition to *Chamaecyparis,* there are other genera such as *Abies* (fir), *Juniperus* (juniper), *Picea* (spruce), *Thuja* (arborvitae), and *Tsuga* (hemlock). These conifers are some of the hardiest plants that can grow in the rock garden, but in

*Chaenorrhinum origanifolium*, courtesy of Fritz Kummert

*Chamaecyparis lawsoniana* 'Minima Aurea'

severe climates shade them from drying winter sun if snow cover is lacking.

## *Chamaecyparis lawsoniana*
Port Orford cedar
The cultivar 'Minima Aurea', dwarf golden Port Orford cedar, is an evergreen shrub for sun or part shade in humus-rich, well-drained soil. Grows 24 inches (60 cm) high, 18 inches (45 cm) wide. Zones 5–8. The species is from northwestern California and southwestern Oregon.

## *Chamaecyparis nootkatensis*
Alaskan cedar
The cultivar 'Compacta Glauca', dwarf Alaskan cedar, is an evergreen shrub with blue-green foliage for sun or part shade in humus-rich, well-drained soil. Grows 36 inches (90 cm) high, 24 inches

*Chamaecyparis nootkatensis* 'Compacta Glauca'

*Chamaecyparis obtusa* 'Golden Sprite'

(60 cm) wide. Zones 4–8. The species is from Oregon to Alaska.

## *Chamaecyparis obtusa*
Hinoki cypress
The species is from Japan.
   **Cultivars**. There are a number of dwarf Hinoki cypresses, all evergreen shrubs, for the rock garden. Cultivate in part shade in humus-rich, well-drained soil.
   *Chamaecyparis obtusa* 'Golden Sprite', golden golf ball, grows 4 inches (10 cm) high and wide. Zones 5–9.
   *Chamaecyparis obtusa* 'Kosteri' grows 30 inches (75 cm) high and wide. Zones 4–8.
   *Chamaecyparis obtusa* 'Nana' grows 8 inches (20 cm) high, 12 inches (30 cm) wide. Zones 5–8.
   *Chamaecyparis obtusa* 'Nana Lutea', golden dwarf Hinoki cypress, grows 12 inches (30 cm) high, 10 inches (25 cm) wide. Zones 5–8.
   The erect but gracefully twisted

*Chamaecyparis obtusa* 'Kosteri'

*Chamaecyparis obtusa* 'Nana'

trunk of *Chamaecyparis obtusa* 'Reis Dwarf' carries soft green, mounding foliage with silvery highlights. It is a beautiful selection. Grows 24 inches (60 cm) high, 12 inches (30 cm) wide. Zones 4–8.

## Chamaecyparis pisifera

Sawara cypress
The species is from Japan.

**Cultivars.** There are a number of dwarf Sawara cypresses, all evergreen shrubs. Cultivate in sun or part shade in humus-rich, well-drained soil.

*Chamaecyparis pisifera* 'Filifera Nana', dwarf thread cypress, grows 18 inches (45 cm) high, 36 inches (90 cm) wide. Zones 4–8.

*Chamaecyparis pisifera* 'Gold Dust', dwarf variegated Sawara cypress, grows 12 inches (30 cm) high, 18 inches (45 cm) wide. Zones 5–8.

*Chamaecyparis pisifera* 'Plumosa Compressa' grows 18 inches (45 cm) high, 8 inches (20 cm) wide. Zones 5–8.

*Chamaecyparis pisifera* 'Tsukumo' grows 10 inches (25 cm) high, 12 inches (30 cm) wide. Zones 3–8.

*Chamaecyparis pisifera* 'Plumosa Compressa'

*Chamaecyparis obtusa* 'Nana Lutea'

*Chamaecyparis pisifera* 'Filifera Nana'

*Chamaecyparis obtusa* 'Reis Dwarf'

*Chamaecyparis pisifera* 'Gold Dust'

*Chamaecyparis pisifera* 'Tsukumo'

### Chamaecyparis thyoides

Atlantic white cedar

The cultivar 'Andelyensis Conica' is a neat dwarf evergreen shrub with a pointed conical shape, adorned in blue-green juvenile foliage. Cultivate in sun or part shade in humus-rich, moist soil. Grows 36 inches (90 cm) high, 12 inches (30 cm) wide. Zones 4–8. The species is from the Atlantic and Gulf states of the United States.

### Chamaecytisus eriocarpus

Leguminosae

synonym, *C. absinthoides*

A shrub for sun in any well-drained soil. Flowers in summer, yellow. Grows 18–30 inches (45–75 cm) high, 36

Chamaecyparis thyoides 'Andelyensis Conica'

*Chamaecytisus eriocarpus*, courtesy of Fritz Kummert

inches (90 cm) wide. Zones 6–9. Balkan Peninsula.

### Chamaemelum nobile

double-flowered chamomile

Compositae

A perennial for sun in any good, well-drained soil. Flowers in summer, a white daisy, yellow-eyed. The cultivar 'Plenum' has fully double white flowers. Grows 6 inches (15 cm) high, 30 inches (75 cm) wide. Zones 4–10. The species is from western Europe and North Africa.

### Cheilanthes

lip fern

Adiantaceae

The lip ferns are decorative foliage plants from dry, rocky situations. They require the protection from excessive

*Chamaemelum nobile* 'Plenum', courtesy of Fritz Kummert

*Cheilanthes fendleri* with *Antennaria* in the foreground

winter wetness provided by properly well-drained, rocky soil, by proper placement in a rock crevice or on a dry wall, or by an alpine house. Good, bright light, but not a southern exposure, is best for these evergreen perennials.

### Cheilanthes fendleri

A fern for sun or part shade in any good, well-drained soil, preferably alkaline. Grows 8 inches (20 cm) high, 12 inches (30 cm) wide. Zones 4–8. Rocky Mountains from Colorado to Texas and Arizona.

### Cheilanthes gracillima

A fern for part shade in humus-rich scree. Grows 8 inches (20 cm) high, 12 inches (30 cm) wide. Zones 6–8. California to British Columbia and Montana.

### Cheilanthes lanosa

A fern for sun or part shade in any good, well-drained, neutral to acid soil. Grows 6–10 inches (15–25 cm) high, 12 inches

Cheilanthes gracillima

Cheilanthes lanosa

(30 cm) wide. Zones 6–9. Eastern coast of the United States to Mexico.

## Cheilanthes siliquosa
Indian's dream
synonyms, *Onychium densum, Pellaea densa*
A fern for sun or part shade in humus-rich scree in rock crevices, preferably limestone or serpentine. Grows 6–10 inches (15–25 cm) high, 12 inches (30 cm) wide. Zones 6–8. California to British Columbia, Montana, and Quebec.

## Chiastophyllum oppositifolium
Crassulaceae
An evergreen perennial for part shade in any good, well-drained soil. Flowers in late spring and early summer, yellow.

*Cheilanthes siliquosa*

Grows 6 inches (15 cm) high, 24 inches (60 cm) wide. Zones 6–9. Caucasus Mountains. The neat, rounded, fleshy leaves are normally green but a variegated cultivar is available, 'Jim's Pride'.

## Chionodoxa forbesii
glory of the snow
Liliaceae (Hyacinthaceae)
A bulb for sun or part shade and any good, well-drained soil. The cultivar 'Pink Giant' flowers in early spring, pink with a white center. Grows 10 inches (25 cm) high, 18 inches (45 cm) wide. Zones 4–9. The species is from western Turkey.

## Chionohebe pulvinaris
Scrophulariaceae
synonym, *Pygmaea pulvinaris*
The six species of *Chionohebe*, all alpine cushion plants, are a challenge to grow and are best attempted in the alpine house. *Chionohebe pulvinaris* is a perennial for sun or part shade in humus-rich scree that never dries out. Flowers in spring, white. Grows 1–2 inches (2.5–5 cm) high, 5 inches (12.5 cm) wide. Zones 7–8. South Island, New Zealand.

## Chrysanthemum
Compositae
The large genus *Chrysanthemum* previously included annuals, perennials, and shrubs. It has been split into several smaller genera and technically includes only annuals. Here the old familiar genus is retained with the synonyms indicating the more recent classification.

## Chrysanthemum alpinum
synonym, *Leucanthemopsis alpina*
A perennial, often short-lived in cultivation. Cultivate in sun in humus-rich scree. Flowers in summer, white or pink.

*Chionodoxa forbesii* 'Pink Giant'

*Chionohebe pulvinaris*, courtesy of Franz Hadacek

*Chrysanthemum alpinum*, courtesy of Fritz Kummert

*Chiastophyllum oppositifolium*

Grows 6 inches (15 cm) high, 12 inches (30 cm) wide. Zones 5–8. European mountains.

**Subspecies.** *Chrysanthemum alpinum* subsp. *tomentosum* flowers in summer, white. Grows 2 inches (5 cm) high, 6 inches (15 cm) wide.

## Chrysanthemum arcticum

synonyms, *C. sibiricum, Arctanthemum arcticum, Dendranthema arcticum*
A perennial for sun in any good, well-drained soil. Flowers in June and July, white or tinged with pink. Grows 10–12 inches (25–30 cm) high, 18 inches (45 cm) wide. Zones 2–8. Japan and Alaska.

## Chrysanthemum atratum

synonym, *Leucanthemum atratum*
A perennial for sun in any good, well-drained soil. Flowers in summer, white. Grows 8 inches (20 cm) high, 18 inches (45 cm) wide. Zones 6–9. Alps and mountains of southeastern Europe.

*Chrysanthemum alpinum* subsp. *tomentosum,* courtesy of Fritz Kummert

*Chrysanthemum arcticum,* courtesy of Fritz Kummert

## Chrysanthemum hosmariense

synonyms, *Chrysanthemopsis hosmariensis, Leucanthemopsis hosmariensis*
A perennial for sun in scree. Flowers in August and September, white. Grows 12 inches (30 cm) high, 18 inches (45 cm) wide. Zones 7–10. Morocco.

*Chrysanthemum atratum,* courtesy of Fritz Kummert

*Chrysanthemum hosmariense*

## Chrysanthemum weyrichii

synonym, *Leucanthemum weyrichii*
A neat evergreen perennial mat of cut, shining green leaves, it is attractive running through rocky crevices. Cultivate in sun in humus-rich scree. Flowers in summer, pink. Grows 8 inches (20 cm) high, 18 inches (45 cm) wide. Zones 4–9. Japan and Sakhalin.

## Chrysogonum virginianum

golden knee, green and gold
Compositae
A perennial for sun or part shade in any good, well-drained soil. Flowers in spring, gold. Grows 6–12 inches (15–30 cm) high, 18 inches (45 cm) wide. Zones 3–9. Eastern United States.

*Chrysogonum virginianum*

*Chrysanthemum weyrichii*

## *Cirsium acaule*

plume thistle
Compositae
A perennial for sun in any good, well-drained soil. Flowers in summer, purple. Grows 18 inches (45 cm) high, 18 inches (45 cm) wide. Zones 4–8. Europe to central Asia.

## *Cistus*

rock or sun rose
Cistaceae

Cistuses are evergreen shrubs that thrive in well-drained, nutrient-lacking soil, preferably alkaline.

## *Cistus albidus*

white-leaved rock rose
Cultivate in sun in any poorish, well-drained soil. Flowers in spring, often repeating in fall, rosy pink to lilac. Grows 40 inches (100 cm) high, 48 inches (120 cm) wide, but usually lower. Zones 7–10. Southwestern Europe, including Portugal.

## *Cistus crispus*

Cultivate in sun in any poorish, well-drained soil. Flowers in spring, purple-pink. Grows 36 inches (90 cm) high, 60 inches (150 cm) wide. Zones 7–10. Western Mediterranean and Portugal.

## *Cistus ladanifer*

common gum cistus, crimson-spot rock rose
Cultivate in sun in any poorish, well-drained soil. Flowers in June and July, white with a dark crimson spot at the base of each petal. Grows 36–60 inches (90–150 cm) high, 60 inches (150 cm) wide. Zones 7–10. Southwestern Europe and North Africa.

## *Cistus ×purpureus*

orchid rock rose
Cultivate in sun in any poorish, well-drained soil. Flowers in June and July, reddish purple with a dark red spot at the base of each petal. Grows 30–48 inches (75–120 cm) high, 48 inches (120 cm) wide. Zones 7–10. A hybrid, *C. incanus* subsp. *creticus* × *C. ladanifer*.

## *Claytonia megarhiza*

spring beauty
Portulacaceae
A perennial succulent that is the finest of the genus and not terribly difficult to grow. It does best in a deep pot in the alpine house with dryish summer and fall conditions. Cultivate in sun in fertile scree or in a crevice, with dry conditions during winter. Flowers in spring, white to light or dark pink. Grows 4 inches (10 cm) high, 8 inches (20 cm) wide. Zones 4–8. Washington south to New Mexico.

*Cistus crispus,* courtesy of Fritz Kummert

*Cistus ×purpureus,* courtesy of Fritz Kummert

*Cirsium acaule,* courtesy of Franz Hadacek

*Cistus ladanifer,* courtesy of Fritz Kummert

*Claytonia megarhiza*

*Cistus albidus,* courtesy of Fritz Kummert

## Clematis
Ranunculaceae

### Clematis alpina
A deciduous climber for sun or part shade with roots in a shaded position in fertile moist soil. Flowers in spring, blue, violet, or purple, and many cultivars are available in a wider range of colors, including pink and white. Climbs 8–12 feet (2.4–3.7 m). Zones 4–9. Mountains of Europe and northern Asia.

### Clematis ×cartmanii
The cultivar 'Joe' is a delightful, nonclimbing evergreen shrub with arching stems of finely dissected, purple tinted leaves and large panicles of up to 30 flowers. Long growth can be trimmed for compactness. It makes a fine rock garden and container plant. Cultivate in part shade in fertile, moist soil. Flowers in spring, white. Grows 8 inches (20 cm) high, 18 inches (45 cm) wide. Zones 7–9. Clematis ×cartmanii is a hybrid, C. marmoraria × C. paniculata.

### Clematis douglasii var. scottii
old maid's bonnet
synonym, *C. hirsutissima* var. *scottii*
A nonclimbing perennial for sun or part shade with roots in a shaded position in fertile moist soil. Flowers in spring and summer, lavender to pale magenta. Grows 36 inches (90 cm) high and wide. Zones 5–8. British Columbia and Washington east to Montana and Wyoming.

### Clematis integrifolia
The erect perennial stems rise from a resting bud in spring. They remain somewhat upright in sun but tend to flop and weave among neighboring plants in less sunny conditions. Cultivate in sun or part shade in any good, well-drained soil. Flowers in summer, blue, dark violet, or rarely white, 'Alba', as shown. Grows 24 inches (60 cm) high and wide. Zones 2–9. The species is from central Europe and southwestern Russia.

### Clematis tenuiloba
A deciduous, procumbent vine for sun in humus-rich, limestone scree. Flowers in March and April, purple-pink. Grows 10 inches (25 cm) high, 18 inches (45 cm) wide. Zones 4–8. Rocky Mountains.

### Clematis texensis
scarlet clematis
A deciduous vine for sun with the roots shaded, in any good, well-drained soil. Flowers in summer through autumn, scarlet-red or carmine. Climbs 8–12 feet

*Clematis alpina,* courtesy of Fritz Kummert

*Clematis* ×*cartmanii* 'Joe', courtesy of Fritz Kummert

*Clematis douglasii* var. *scottii,* courtesy of Fritz Kummert

*Clematis integrifolia* 'Alba'

*Clematis tenuiloba,* courtesy of Fritz Kummert

*Clematis texensis,* courtesy of Fritz Kummert

(2.4–3.7 m). Zones 5–9. Southwestern United States, primarily Texas.

## Clintonia andrewsiana
Liliaceae (Convallariaceae)
A rhizomatous perennial for part to full shade in humus-rich soil. Flowers in summer, pink to rose purple, followed by dark blue fruit. Grows 10–18 inches (25–45 cm) high, 12 inches (30 cm) wide. Zones 8–9. Coastal woods of northern California.

## Codonopsis
bonnet bellflower
Campanulaceae

*Clintonia andrewsiana*

*Codonopsis bulleyana,* courtesy of Fritz Kummert

## Codonopsis bulleyana
A perennial for sun or part shade in any good, well-drained soil. It does best in cooler conditions. Flowers in summer, pale, grayish blue. Grows 12 inches (30 cm) high and wide. Zones 4–8. Southern China and Tibet.

## Codonopsis ovata
A perennial often misrepresented in cultivation by the inferior *C. clematidea,* which has similar flowers on lax, climbing stems, and a pungent, skunky odor. Cultivate in sun or part shade in any good, well-drained soil. It does best in

*Codonopsis ovata,* courtesy of Fritz Kummert

*Colchicum autumnale,* courtesy of Fritz Kummert

cooler conditions. Flowers in summer, pale blue, purple veined within. Grows 18 inches (45 cm) high, 12 inches (30 cm) wide. Zones 4–8. Western Himalayas and Kashmir.

## Colchicum
Liliaceae (Colchicaceae)

## Colchicum autumnale
autumn crocus
A cormous perennial for sun or part shade in any good, well-drained soil. Flowers in late summer and fall, purplepink to white. Grows 12 inches (30 cm) high and wide. Zones 3–8. Central and western Europe.

    **Cultivar**. *Colchicum autumnale* 'Album Plenum', double white autumn crocus, flowers in October, white.

## Colchicum hungaricum
Smaller growing species of *Colchicum* that flower with partially developed leaves, such as the cormous perennial *C. hungaricum,* are best grown in the bulb frame or alpine house. Cultivate in sun or part shade in any good, welldrained soil. Flowers in late winter to early spring, purplish pink to white.

*Colchicum autumnale* 'Album Plenum'

*Colchicum hungaricum,* courtesy of Fritz Kummert

Grows 6–10 inches (15–25 cm) high, 12 inches (30 cm) wide. Zones 6–9. Hungary and the Balkan Peninsula.

### Colchicum kesselringii

synonyms, *C. crociflorum, C. regelii*
A charming miniature cormous perennial with two to seven leaves that begin to expand at flowering time. Cultivate in sun or part shade in any good, well-drained soil; does best in the bulb frame or alpine house. Flowers in early spring, petals white with a red-purple central stripe. Grows 4 inches (10 cm) high, 10 inches (25 cm) wide. Zones 6–8. Central Asia and northern Afghanistan.

### Colchicum luteum

A cormous perennial with leaves partially expanding at flowering time and

*Colchicum kesselringii,* courtesy of Fritz Kummert

*Colchicum luteum,* courtesy of Fritz Kummert

considered difficult to grow in the garden, thus recommended for the bulb frame or alpine house. Cultivate in sun or part shade in any good, well-drained soil. Flowers in spring, pale to deep yellow. Grows 6–12 inches (15–30 cm) high, 12 inches (30 cm) wide. Zones 6–8. Central Asia, northern India, and southwestern China.

### Colchicum speciosum

One of the easiest species to grow but a cormous perennial with postflowering foliage that often grows too large for the rock garden. Cultivate in sun or part shade in any good, well-drained soil. Flowers in fall in shades of pale to deep rose purple, often white at the base within. The cultivar 'Album', white autumn crocus, has white flowers. Grows 12–15 inches (30–38 cm) high, 12 inches (30 cm) wide. Zones 4–8. The species is from eastern Turkey and Iran.

*Colchicum speciosum* 'Album'

*Colchicum szovitsii,* courtesy of Fritz Kummert

### Colchicum szovitsii

A cormous perennial for sun or part shade in fertile, well-drained soil. Flowers in early spring, light purple-pink or white. Grows 6–10 inches (15–25 cm) high, 12 inches (30 cm) wide. Zones 6–8. Iran, Turkey, and the Caucasus Mountains.

### Colchicum 'Waterlily'

A cormous perennial for sun or part shade in any good, well-drained soil. Flowers in September and October, lavender-pink, doubled. Grows 12 inches (30 cm) high, 18 inches (45 cm) wide. Zones 3–8.

### Collomia debilis

alpine collomia
Polemoniaceae
A perennial for sun in any good, well-drained soil. Flowers in summer to early fall, pink or violet to white, drying purple. Grows 4–8 inches (10–20 cm) high, 8 inches (20 cm) wide. Zones 6–8. Mountains of Washington, Oregon, Montana, and Utah.

*Colchicum* 'Waterlily'

*Collomia debilis,* courtesy of Fritz Kummert

## Commelina dianthifolia

dayflower
Commelinaceae
A tuberous-rooted perennial for sun or part shade in any good, well-drained soil. Flowers in summer, purplish to clear blue. Grows 12–18 inches (30–45 cm) high, 12 inches (30 cm) wide. Zones 7–9. Southwestern United States and adjacent Mexico.

## Conandron ramondioides

Gesneriaceae
With glossy chartreuse leaves attractively toothed and crinkled, an evergreen perennial that is dormant in winter and does best in a moist, rocky crevice or in the alpine house in full shade. Cultivate in humus-rich, well-drained soil. Flowers June to August, lavender, rarely white. Grows 4–8 inches (10–20 cm) high, 8 inches (20 cm) wide. Zones 6–9. Japan.

*Commelina dianthifolia*, courtesy of Fritz Kummert

*Conandron ramondioides*, courtesy of Franz Hadacek

## Convolvulus

bindweed
Convolvulaceae

## Convolvulus boissieri

Woody-based perennials for sun in scree and in the alpine house. Flower in summer, white. Grow 3 inches (7.5 cm) high, 8–18 inches (20–45 cm) wide. Zones 6–9.
**Subspecies**. *Convolvulus boissieri* subsp. *boissieri* is from Spain.
*Convolvulus boissieri* subsp. *compactus* is from Turkey.

## Convolvulus lineatus

A woody-based perennial for sun in any well-drained soil. Flowers in summer, pink. Grows 6–8 inches (15–20 cm)

*Convolvulus boissieri* subsp. *boissieri*, courtesy of Panayoti Kelaidis

high, 12 inches (30 cm) wide. Zones 7–10. Southern central Russia and Greece.

## Coptis japonica

gold thread
Ranunculaceae
The gold threads are evergreen perennials named for the golden, running, underground stolons that allow them to

*Convolvulus lineatus*, courtesy of Fritz Kummert

*Coptis japonica*

*Convolvulus boissieri* subsp. *compactus*, courtesy of Panayoti Kelaidis

spread into large mats of shining foliage. Cultivate *C. japonica* in part shade in well-drained, acid, peaty soil. Flowers in spring, white. Grows 10 inches (25 cm) high, 18 inches (45 cm) wide, eventually much wider. Zones 6–9. Japan.

## Coreopsis rosea
tickseed
Compositae
A perennial, spreading by slender rhizomes, for sun in any good soil, preferably moist. Flowers in late summer, pink. Grows 12 inches (30 cm) high, 24 inches (60 cm) wide. Zones 4–10. Nova Scotia to Maryland.

## Cornus canadensis
bunchberry, creeping dogwood
Cornaceae
synonym, *Chamaepericlymenum canadense*
A superb woodland perennial ground cover with creeping rhizomes, particularly suited to the peat garden. The red berries are as spectacular as the white-bracted flowering clusters. Cultivate in part shade in moist, acid, well-drained soil. Flowers in summer, bracts white, followed by bright red fruit. Grows 4 inches (10 cm) high, 24 inches (60 cm) wide. Zones 2–8. North America and eastern Asia, including Japan and Korea.

## Coronilla valentina
Leguminosae
An evergreen shrublet for sun in any well-drained soil. Flowers in late spring and summer, yellow and fragrant. Grows 36 inches (90 cm) high and wide.

*Cornus canadensis*, courtesy of Armen Gevjan

*Cornus canadensis* with berries

Zones 8–10. Mediterranean region and southern Portugal. A dwarf form, *C. valentina* subsp. *glauca* 'Pygmaea', is only 10 inches (25 cm) tall and somewhat hardier.

## Cortusa matthioli
Primulaceae
A perennial for part shade in humus-rich, moist soil. Flowers in late spring and summer, purple-violet to magenta. Grows 12 inches (30 cm) high, 8 inches (20 cm) wide. Zones 6–9. Southeastern and southern central Europe, Russia, and Japan.

## Corydalis
Papaveraceae

Corydalises are ferny-leaved perennials with hooded and spurred flowers available in a wide range of colors.

*Coronilla valentina*

*Coreopsis rosea*, courtesy of Fritz Kummert

*Cortusa matthioli*, courtesy of Fritz Kummert

## Corydalis ambigua

synonym, *C. fumariifolia*

A tuberous-rooted perennial for part shade in humus-rich, well-drained, acid soil. Flowers in spring and summer, blue, lavender, to muddy pink. Grows 8 inches (20 cm) high and wide. Zones 6–9. Japan.

## Corydalis cashmeriana

A tuberous-rooted perennial for part shade in humus-rich, well-drained, acid soil. Flowers in summer in shades of blue that vary with temperature. Grows 10 inches (25 cm) high, 12 inches (30 cm) wide. Zones 5–8. Kashmir to south-eastern Tibet.

## Corydalis caucasica var. alba

synonym, *C. malkensis*

A tuberous-rooted perennial for part shade in humus-rich, well-drained soil. Flowers in late spring or early summer, creamy white. Grows 6 inches (15 cm) high, 12 inches (30 cm) wide. Zones 6–9. Caucasus Mountains.

## Corydalis lutea

*Corydalis lutea* and *C. ochroleuca* spread easily by self-sowing and are too inva-

*Corydalis ambigua*

*Corydalis cashmeriana*, courtesy of Fritz Kummert

sive for the rock garden but are excellent garden plants given enough room. They are useful when allowed to naturalize under heavily rooted trees or in difficult limestone conditions. *Corydalis lutea* is a taprooted perennial for sun or part shade in any good soil. Flowers in late spring through summer, yellow. Grows 12–16 inches (30–40 cm) high, 24 inches (60 cm) wide. Zones 5–9. Europe.

*Corydalis caucasica var. alba*

*Corydalis lutea*, courtesy of Fritz Kummert

*Corydalis ochroleuca*

## Corydalis ochroleuca

A taprooted perennial for sun or part shade in any good soil (note the caveat under *C. lutea*). Flowers in summer to late fall, white to pale cream with a green or yellow tip. Grows 12–16 inches (30–40 cm) high, 18 inches (45 cm) wide. Zones 5–9. Italy and the western Balkan Peninsula.

## Corydalis popovii

The largest-flowered species of *Corydalis* with blossoms almost 2 inches (5 cm) long, *C. popovii* is a tuberous-rooted perennial that requires a drying period in summer and is recommended for alpine house culture. Cultivate in sun or part shade in humus-rich scree. Flowers in spring, rose to deep purple, tipped maroon. Grows 4–6 inches (10–15 cm) high, 10 inches (25 cm) wide. Zones 7–9. Mountainous areas of central Asia.

## Corydalis solida

fumewort

A tuberous-rooted perennial for part shade in humus-rich, well-drained soil. Flowers in spring in shades of pink, red,

*Corydalis popovii*, courtesy of Fritz Kummert

*Corydalis solida*

and purple, occasionally white. Grows 10 inches (25 cm) high, 16 inches (40 cm) wide. Zones 6–9. Northern Europe and Asia

## Corydalis wilsonii

Often considered tender, *C. wilsonii* has proven to be a fairly hardy garden plant. It may be short-lived but it self-sows somewhat. A taprooted perennial for part shade in humus-rich, well-drained soil. Flowers in spring, bright yellow, tinged green. Grows 12 inches (30 cm) high and wide. Zones 7–9. Central China.

## Cotoneaster apiculatus

Rosaceae
A deciduous shrub for sun or part shade in any good soil. The cultivar 'Tom Thumb' is nonflowering. Grows 4 inches

*Corydalis wilsonii*, courtesy of Armen Gevjan

*Cotoneaster apiculatus* 'Tom Thumb'

(10 cm) high, 10 inches (25 cm) wide. Zones 4–10. The species is from China.

## Cotula pyrethrifolia

brass buttons
Compositae
synonym, *Leptinella pyrethrifolia*
A mat-forming perennial for sun or part shade in any good, well-drained soil. Flowers in summer, white. Grows 4 inches (10 cm) high, 24 inches (60 cm) wide. Zones 7–10. New Zealand

## Craspedia minor

billy buttons, drumsticks
Compositae
An evergreen perennial for sun in any good, well-drained soil, and in the alpine house. Flowers in summer, yellow or white. Grows 4–8 inches (10–20 cm) high, 12 inches (30 cm) wide. Zones 8–10. New Zealand.

*Cotula pyrethrifolia*, courtesy of Fritz Kummert

*Craspedia minor*, courtesy of Fritz Kummert

## Crepis aurea

hawk's beard
Compositae
A perennial for sun in any good soil. Flowers in summer, orange-bronze, often red in bud. Grows 12 inches (30 cm) high, 18 inches (45 cm) wide. Zones 6–9. Alps and mountains of Italy and the Balkan Peninsula.

## Crocus

Iridaceae

Unless otherwise mentioned, the crocuses mentioned here are primarily easy-to-grow cormous perennials for the sunny garden, particularly the simulated alpine meadow where they can be planted among ground covers.

*Crepis aurea*, courtesy of Franz Hadacek

*Crocus alatavicus*, courtesy of Fritz Kummert

## Crocus alatavicus

Cultivate in sun or part shade in fertile, well-drained soil. Flowers in spring, white suffused with violet, throat yellow. Grows 4 inches (10 cm) high. Zones 4–9. Central Asia and northern Iran.

## Crocus biflorus subsp. crewei

Cultivate in sun or part shade in fertile, well-drained soil. Flowers in spring, white with brownish stripes, throat yellow. Grows 3 inches (7.5 cm) high. Zones 4–9. Western Turkey.

## Crocus dalmaticus

Cultivate in sun or part shade in fertile, well-drained soil. Flowers in late winter and spring, pale or deep lilac to purple with a buff exterior. Grows 2–4 inches (5–10 cm) high. Zones 6–9. Southwestern Balkan Mountains of Bulgaria, and northern Albania.

Crocus biflorus subsp. crewei, courtesy of Fritz Kummert

Crocus dalmaticus, courtesy of Fritz Kummert

## Crocus etruscus

Cultivate in sun or part shade in fertile, well-drained soil. Flowers in late winter and spring, lilac with a pale yellow throat. Grows 4 inches (10 cm) high. Zones 6–9. Northwestern Italy.

## Crocus fleischeri

Cultivate in sun or part shade in fertile, well-drained soil. Flowers in late winter and spring, white, sometimes flushed maroon or mauve at the base. Grows 2–4 inches (5–10 cm) high. Zones 6–9. Southern and western Turkey and the eastern Aegean Islands.

## Crocus imperati

Cultivate in sun or part shade in fertile, well-drained soil. Flowers in late winter and spring, deep lilac with a buff exterior that is striped purple. Grows 3–5 inches (7.5–12.5 cm) high. Zones 7–9. Western Italy.

## Crocus malyi

Cultivate in sun or part shade in fertile, well-drained soil. Flowers in spring,

Crocus etruscus, courtesy of Fritz Kummert

Crocus fleischeri, courtesy of Fritz Kummert

white with a yellow throat. Grows 4–6 inches (10–15 cm) high. Zones 6–9. Western Balkan Mountains of Bulgaria and eastern Yugoslavia.

## Crocus medius

Cultivate in sun or part shade in fertile, well-drained soil. Flowers in fall, lilac or purple with internal basal purple stripes or blotch. Grows 5 inches (12.5 cm) high. Zones 6–9. Northwestern Italy and southern France.

## Crocus michelsonii

A desirable species rare in cultivation and not easy to maintain even with bulb

Crocus imperati, courtesy of Fritz Kummert

Crocus malyi, courtesy of Fritz Kummert

Crocus medius, courtesy of Fritz Kummert

frame protection. Cultivate in sun or part shade in fertile, well-drained soil in the bulb frame. Flowers in spring, white suffused with lilac, throat white-lilac. Grows 3–4 inches (7.5–10 cm) high. Zones 6–9. Russia and Iran.

### Crocus minimus

Cultivate in sun or part shade in fertile, well-drained soil. Flowers in midspring, lilac or purple with a buff exterior that is striped and blotched with purple. Grows 8–10 inches (20–25 cm) high. Zones 5–9. Corsica and Sardinia.

### Crocus olivieri

Cultivate in sun or part shade in fertile, well-drained soil. Flowers in late winter

Crocus michelsonii, courtesy of Fritz Kummert

Crocus minimus, courtesy of Armen Gevjan

and spring, yellow or maroon with a yellow throat. Grows 2–3 inches (5–7.5 cm) high. Zones 6–9. Balkan Peninsula and Turkey.

### Crocus pestalozzae

A miniature plant best appreciated in the bulb frame. Cultivate in sun or part shade in fertile, well-drained soil. Flowers in late winter and early spring, white to blue-mauve, marked black at the base. Grows 2–3 inches (5–7.5 cm) high. Zones 7–9. Northwestern Turkey.

### Crocus reticulatus

synonym, *C. variegatus*

Cultivate in sun or part shade in fertile, well-drained soil in the alpine house or cold frame. Subspecies *reticulatus* flow-

Crocus olivieri, courtesy of Fritz Kummert

Crocus pestalozzae, courtesy of Fritz Kummert

ers in spring, lilac with variable darker bands and feathering on the exterior. Grows 3 inches (7.5 cm) high. Zones 7–9. Italy to Turkey and Caucasia.

### Crocus serotinus subsp. *clusii*

Cultivate in sun or part shade in fertile, well-drained soil; probably best in a bulb frame in cold, wet climates. Flowers in fall, pale or deep lilac. Grows 8–9 inches (20–22 cm) high. Zones 6–9. Portugal and Spain.

Crocus reticulatus subsp. *reticulatus*, courtesy of Fritz Kummert

Crocus serotinus subsp. *clusii*, courtesy of Fritz Kummert

Crocus sieberi subsp. *sublimis* f. *tricolor*, courtesy of Fritz Kummert

### Crocus sieberi subsp. sublimis f. tricolor

Cultivate in sun or part shade in fertile, well-drained soil. Flowers in late winter and early spring with three bands of lilac, white, and golden yellow. Grows 3–4 inches (7.5–10 cm) high. Zones 5–9. Greece and southern Albania.

### Crocus tommasinianus

A popular crocus, easy to grow and naturalize in the garden. Its increase by seed and offsets in light soils can be so prolific as to make it a nuisance. Cultivate in sun or part shade in fertile, well-drained soil. Flowers in late winter and early spring, pale or deep lilac with a white throat and an often silvery white or cream exterior. Grows 3–6 inches (7.5–15 cm) high. Zones 4–9. Hungary to Bulgaria.

### Crocus vernus

The subspecies *vernus* is very easily grown and is a parent to the large-flowered hybrid Dutch crocuses. Cultivate in sun or part shade in fertile, well-drained soil. Flowers in spring and early summer, mauve, purple, or white. Grows 3–5 inches (7.5–12.5 cm) high. Zones 4–9.

Mountains of central and western Europe.

### Crocus versicolor

Cultivate in sun or part shade in fertile, well-drained soil. The cultivar 'Picturatus' flowers in late winter and spring, white or lilac with distinct purple stripes externally. Grows 4–5 inches (10–12.5 cm) high. Zones 5–9. The species is from southern France and western Italy.

### Cryptogramma crispa

European or mountain parsley fern
Pteridaceae (Cryptogrammataceae)
For the similar and somewhat more easily grown North American version of this fern, one must look for *C. acrostichoides* (synonym, *C. crispa* var. *acrosti-*

Crocus tommasinianus

Crocus versicolor 'Picturatus', courtesy of Fritz Kummert

Crocus vernus subsp. vernus, courtesy of Fritz Kummert

Cryptogramma crispa, courtesy of Fritz Kummert

*choides*), the American rock brake or American parsley fern. *Cryptogramma crispa* is a deciduous perennial for part shade in humus-rich, gritty, acid soil. Grows 6–10 inches (15–25 cm) high, 12 inches (30 cm) wide. Zones 6–9. Europe and Asia.

### *Cryptomeria japonica*
Japanese cryptomeria
Cupressaceae (Taxodiaceae)
The cultivar 'Compressa' is a dwarf evergreen coniferous shrub for sun or part shade in humus-rich, well-drained, moist soil. Grows 18 inches (45 cm) high, 12 inches (30 cm) wide. Zones 6–9. The species is from China and Japan.

### *Cyananthus microphyllus*
Campanulaceae
synonym, *C. integer*
A perennial for sun or part shade in humus-rich scree. Flowers in fall, violet-

Cryptomeria japonica 'Compressa'

*Cyananthus microphyllus,* courtesy of Fritz Kummert

blue. Grows 4 inches (10 cm) high, 12 inches (30 cm) wide. Zones 4–8. Northern India, and Nepal to southwestern Tibet.

### *Cyclamen*
alpine violet, Persian violet, sowbread
Primulaceae

Cyclamens are tuberous perennials that make excellent container plants for the alpine house or cold frame. The many hardy species are delightful garden plants for a variety of situations, including the rock garden and woodland, where they will often naturalize.

*Cyclamen cilicium,* courtesy of Fritz Kummert

*Cyclamen coum,* marbled leaf with light pink flowers

### *Cyclamen cilicium*
Cultivate in part shade in fertile, well-drained, gritty soil. Flowers in fall, pale to mid-pink with a crimson blotch at base of each lobe, and fragrant. Grows 2–4 inches (5–10 cm) high, 6 inches (15 cm) wide. Zones 5–9. Southwestern Turkey.

### *Cyclamen coum*
Cultivate in part shade in fertile, well-drained, gritty soil. Flowers in winter to early spring, white, pale pink to dark magenta, or almost red. Leaves solid green or marbled. Grows 2–4 inches (5–10 cm) high, 6 inches (15 cm) wide. Zones 5–9. Bulgaria, Turkey, Caucasia, Lebanon, and Israel.

### *Cyclamen graecum*
Similar in many ways to *C. hederifolium* but generally not hardy in most temper-

*Cyclamen coum,* solid green leaf with dark pink flowers

ate gardens, *C. graecum* is easily grown in a sunny alpine house or frame, and with proper care it may succeed in a protected, sunny location given a summer rest with only minimal moisture. Cultivate in sun or part shade in fertile, well-drained, gritty soil. Flowers in fall to early winter, pale pink to deep carmine with magenta streaks at the base of each lobe. Grows 3 inches (7.5 cm) high, 6 inches (15 cm) wide. Zones 8–9. Southern Greece, Aegean Islands, southern Turkey, and Cyprus.

*Cyclamen graecum,* courtesy of Fritz Kummert

*Cyclamen hederifolium,* courtesy of Fritz Kummert

*Cyclamen libanoticum,* courtesy of Fritz Kummert

## Cyclamen hederifolium

synonym, *C. neapolitanum*

Cultivate in sun or part shade in fertile, well-drained, gritty soil. Flowers in September through November, pale to deep pink with a purple blotch at the base of each lobe. Grows 4 inches (10 cm) high, 6 inches (15 cm) wide. Zones 5–9. Southern Europe to Turkey. The popular garden white form, forma *album* (synonym, 'Album'), is common in cultivation but rare in the wild.

## Cyclamen libanoticum

A dainty species that is proving itself hardier than first believed, a good alpine house subject that is also good in a sunny, raised bed given protection from excessive winter wetness. Cultivate in

*Cyclamen mirabile,* courtesy of Fritz Kummert

sun or part shade in fertile, well-drained, gritty soil. Flowers in winter to early spring, white turning pale pink, each lobe with a maroon basal blotch, and pepper scented. Grows 3 inches (7.5 cm) high, 6 inches (15 cm) wide. Zones 7–9. Lebanon and Syria.

## Cyclamen mirabile

Very similar in appearance to *C. cilicium*, the best forms of *C. mirabile* have foliage that is marbled with red or pink on the upper surface of the leaves. Cultivate in part shade in fertile, well-drained, gritty soil. Flowers in fall, pale pink with a crimson blotch at the base. Grows 2–4 inches (5–10 cm) high, 6 inches (15 cm) wide. Zones 6–9. Southwestern Turkey.

## Cyclamen pseudibericum

One of the finest species of *Cyclamen* though not as hardy as some of the others, *C. pseudibericum* is often grown as a container subject under protection but can be successful outdoors in a sheltered location when provided with somewhat dryish conditions in the winter. This can be accomplished by planting it beneath shrubs. Cultivate in sun or part shade in fertile, well-drained, gritty soil kept somewhat dry during the winter. Large flowers in early spring, lilac or magenta

*Cyclamen pseudibericum,* courtesy of Fritz Kummert

Cyclamen purpurascens, "fatrense" form, courtesy of Josef Halda

Cyclamen repandum

Cymbalaria aequitriloba

with a dark crimson blotch at the base of each petal, and fragrant. Grows 4–6 inches (10–15 cm) high, 12 inches (30 cm) wide. Zones 7–9. Turkey.

## Cyclamen purpurascens
synonym, *C. europaeum*
Cultivate in part shade in fertile, well-drained, gritty soil. Flowers in summer, deep pink. Grows 3 inches (7.5 cm) high, 6 inches (15 cm) wide. Zones 4–9. Central and eastern Europe. A form from the Czech Republic is shown that according to some authorities should be given a specific name, *"fatrense."* It is distinctive, having plain green leaves and larger flowers.

## Cyclamen repandum
Cultivate in part shade in fertile, well-drained, gritty soil. Flowers in March and April, pale to deep pink to carmine-magenta. Grows 4 inches (10 cm) high, 8 inches (20 cm) wide. Zones 5–9. Central and eastern Mediterranean.

## Cymbalaria
Scrophulariaceae

## Cymbalaria aequitriloba
synonym, *Linaria aequitriloba*
A ground- and rock-hugging perennial creeper that can be rampant but is so flat and colorful that it is a delight to have on walls, in crevices, or creeping over porous rock. It can even be used as a moss substitute. Cultivate in part shade in any good, well-drained soil. Flowers in June through August, purple-pink. Grows 1 inch (2.5 cm) high and wide, spreading to 36 inches (90 cm) or more. Zones 5–10. Southern Europe.

## Cymbalaria muralis
Kenilworth ivy, ivy-leaved toadflax
A perennial for sun or part shade in any good, well-drained soil. The cultivar 'Nana Alba' is a dwarf that flowers in June through August, white with a yellow throat. Grows 5 inches (12.5 cm) high, 12 inches (30 cm) wide. Zones 6–10. The species is from the southern Alps and is naturalized in Europe and Britain.

Cymbalaria muralis 'Nana Alba'

## *Cypripedium*
Orchidaceae

### *Cypripedium calceolus*
lady's slipper
Broadly defined, *C. calceolus* is the most widespread species of the genus, includ-ing distinct varieties in North America known as *parviflorum* and *pubescens* (both considered as varieties of *C. parviflorum* in some classifications). *Cypripedium calceolus* is a rhizomatous terrestrial orchid for sun or part shade in humus-rich, well-drained soil. Flowers in midspring to late summer, light to deep yellow lip, sepals and petals purple-brown. Grows 12–24 inches (30–60 cm) high, 12 inches (30 cm) wide. Zones 5–8. Europe and Asia.

### *Cypripedium macranthum* var. *atsumoreanum*
A rhizomatous terrestrial orchid for sun or part shade in humus-rich, well-drained, gritty soil. Flowers in early summer, pink to purple. Grows 12–18 inches (30–45 cm) high, 12 inches (30 cm) wide. Zones 6–8. The species is from European Russia to Japan; the variety shown has an unverified name and is from Japan.

### *Cypripedium reginae*
showy lady's slipper
synonym, *C. spectabile*
Rated as one of the most beautiful of all the hardy cypripediums, a rhizomatous terrestrial orchid that is often grown successfully in a humus-rich pocket in the rock garden or in a raised peat bed. Cultivate in sun or part shade. Flowers in late spring and summer, pink lip with white sepals and petals. Grows 18–36 inches (45–90 cm) high, 18 inches (45 cm) wide. Zones 4–9. Eastern North America.

*Cypripedium calceolus*, courtesy of Fritz Kummert

*Cypripedium macranthum* var. *atsumoreanum,* courtesy of Fritz Kummert

*Cypripedium reginae,* courtesy of Fritz Kummert

## *Cytisus*
broom
Leguminosae

### *Cytisus ×beanii*
A deciduous, mat- to hummock-forming shrub for sun in any well-drained soil. Flowers in spring, rich yellow. Grows 12–16 inches (30–40 cm) high, 36 inches (90 cm) wide. Zones 5–8. A garden hybrid, *C. ardoinii* × *C. purgans*.

### *Cytisus pygmaeus*
A shrub for sun in any well-drained soil. Flowers in spring, yellow. Grows 6 inches (15 cm) high, 18 inches (45 cm) wide.

*Cytisus ×beanii*, courtesy of Fritz Kummert

*Cytisus pygmaeus*

*Daboecia cantabrica* 'Alba'

Zones 6–9. Eastern Balkan Peninsula to Turkey.

## *Daboecia*
Ericaceae

### *Daboecia cantabrica*
Connemara heath, Irish heath, St. Daboec's heath
The cultivar 'Alba' (synonym, *D. cantabrica* f. *alba*) is a prostrate evergreen shrublet that is sometimes offered in the nursery trade as *D. cantabrica* 'Creeping White'. Cultivate in sun or part shade in well-drained, moist, acid soil. Flowers in

*Daboecia ×scotica* 'William Buchanan', courtesy of Fritz Kummert

*Dactylorhiza maculata*, courtesy of Fritz Kummert

summer to early fall, white. Grows 6 inches (15 cm) high, 30 inches (76 cm) wide. Zones 6–9. The species is from western Europe.

### *Daboecia ×scotica*
The cultivar 'William Buchanan' is an evergreen shrublet for sun or part shade in well-drained, moist, acid soil. Flowers in summer to early fall, rosy purple. Grows 10 inches (25 cm) high, 24 inches (60 cm) wide. Zones 6–9. *Daboecia ×scotica* is a garden hybrid, *D. azorica* × *D. cantabrica*.

### *Dactylorhiza maculata*
Orchidaceae
A tuberous terrestrial orchid for sun or part shade in humus-rich soil, preferably alkaline. Flowers in late spring and early summer, white, rose pink, red, or mauve. Grows 12–24 inches (30–60 cm) high. Zones 6–9. Most of Europe.

## *Daphne*
Thymelaeaceae

All daphnes except *D. genkwa* produce deliciously fragrant flowers of varying degree and type of scent. A humus-rich, loamy soil with good drainage is required for cultivation, preferably neutral to moderately alkaline.

### *Daphne arbuscula*
An evergreen shrublet for sun or part shade in fertile, well-drained soil. Flowers in spring and early summer, deep rose pink to white. Grows 6 inches (15 cm) high, 12 inches (30 cm) wide. Zones 5–8. Carpathians, eastern Europe.

*Daphne arbuscula*

## Daphne ×burkwoodii

A deciduous to semi-evergreen shrub for sun or part shade in fertile, well-drained soil. A garden hybrid, *D. caucasica × D. cneorum*.

**Cultivars**. *Daphne ×burkwoodii* 'Carol Mackie' is variegated. Flowers in spring, pinkish white. Grows 36 inches (90 cm) high and wide. Zones 4–8.

*Daphne ×burkwoodii* 'Lavenirii' flowers in spring, pink. Grows 36 inches (90 cm) high and wide. Zones 5–8.

*Daphne ×burkwoodii* 'Carol Mackie'

*Daphne ×burkwoodii* 'Lavenirii'

*Daphne caucasica*

## Daphne caucasica

An easy-to-grow and attractive, deciduous to semi-evergreen shrub with rich green foliage and glistening white, very fragrant flowers for a good part of the year. Cultivate in sun or part shade in fertile, well-drained soil. Flowers in late spring and summer with a later flush. Grows 36–48 inches (90–120 cm) high, 24 inches (60 cm) wide. Zones 5–8. Caucasia and Turkey.

## Daphne cneorum

garland flower

All forms of garland flower will grow equally well in gritty or sandy, acid or alkaline soil. For health and longevity after bloom, top-dress with a mixture of peat and sand to keep roots cool and to promote rooting of trailing stems. A low-growing evergreen shrub for sun or part shade in fertile, well-drained soil. Zones 4–9. Central and southern Europe and Russia.

**Cultivars**. *Daphne cneorum* 'Eximia'

*Daphne cneorum* 'Eximia' in bud

*Daphne cneorum* 'Eximia'

is the most popular and vigorously growing form of garland flower, often simply listed as *D. cneorum* in nursery catalogs. Flowers in April and May with a repeat bloom in fall, rose pink. Grows 4–6 inches (10–15 cm) high, 24 inches (60 cm) wide.

*Daphne cneorum* 'Lela Haines' is the most miniature of all the cultivars and perfect for the trough and crevice gar-

*Daphne cneorum* 'Lela Haines'

*Daphne cneorum* 'Pygmaea Alba'

*Daphne cneorum* 'Ruby Glow'

*Daphne collina*

den. Flowers in spring, pink. Grows 2 inches (5 cm) high, 12 inches (30 cm) wide.

*Daphne cneorum* 'Pygmaea Alba', miniature white garland flower, flowers in spring, white. Grows 3 inches (7.5 cm) high, 12 inches (30 cm) wide.

*Daphne cneorum* 'Ruby Glow' flowers in spring, rich pink. Grows 8 inches (20 cm) high, 24 inches (60 cm) wide.

## Daphne collina

A beautiful, hardy, evergreen shrublet that is sometimes confused with *D. sericea*, which is comparatively widespread, being native from Italy through Turkey. *Daphne sericea* is more tender than *D. collina* and grows more loosely and open with age. Cultivate *D. collina* in sun or part shade in fertile, well-drained soil. Flowers in June through August, deep lilac pink, followed by fleshy orange-red fruit. Grows 12–18 inches (30–45 cm) high, 18 inches (45 cm) wide. Zones 6–9. Southern Italy in the area of Naples.

## Daphne genkwa

lilac daphne

A deciduous shrub that thrives better than other daphnes in hot, sunny locations and in drier conditions. The two forms shown are those distributed in the United States. It has been suggested that the smaller-flowered one is actually *D. championii* and the larger-flowered one the true *D. genkwa*. Cultivate in sun or light shade in any good, well-drained

*Daphne genkwa*, large-flowered form

soil with minimal watering. Scentless flowers in March and April, usually lilac but can be rose purple, or white. Grows 36 inches (90 cm) high and wide. Zones 5–9. China.

### Daphne giraldii

A deciduous shrub for sun or part shade in fertile, well-drained soil. Flowers in early to midsummer, yellow, followed by red fruit. Grows 24 inches (60 cm) high, 18 inches (45 cm) wide, and in the wild, 48 inches (120 cm) high, 24 inches (60 cm) wide. Zones 3–8. China.

### Daphne ×hendersonii

An evergreen shrub for sun or part shade in fertile, well-drained soil. Flow-

ers in late spring, soft pink. Grows 4 inches (10 cm) high, 18 inches (45 cm) wide. Zones 6–9. A naturally occurring hybrid, *D. cneorum* × *D. petraea*.

### Daphne jasminea

Two distinct forms of the evergreen *D. jasminea* are known, one a very dwarf, semiprostrate, hummock-forming plant from Delphi, Greece, described here, and one with erect stems 12–18 inches (30–45 cm) long, found elsewhere in Greece and also in Libya. Cultivate in sun or light shade in fertile, well-drained soil with grit added. It does well in the alpine house. Flowers in late spring and intermittently through summer, white or cream, reddish outside. Grows 6

inches (15 cm) high, 18 inches (45 cm) wide. Zones 6–9. Delphi, Greece.

### Daphne 'Lawrence Crocker'

A petite, long-blooming evergreen shrublet found in the garden of Lawrence Crocker, one of the two founders of Siskiyou Rare Plant Nursery, Med-

*Daphne ×hendersonii,* courtesy of Fritz Kummert

*Daphne jasminea,* Delphi form, courtesy of Fritz Kummert

*Daphne genkwa*

*Daphne giraldii*

*Daphne 'Lawrence Crocker'*

ford, Oregon. Cultivate in sun or part shade in fertile, well-drained soil. Flowers in spring and early summer, deep pink. Grows 12 inches (30 cm) high and wide. Zones 6–9. A garden hybrid, *D. arbuscula* × *D. collina*. There are other hybrids of the same parentage, for example, *Daphne* 'Cheriton', which may prove to be identical or nearly so with 'Lawrence Crocker'.

### Daphne ×mantensiana

An evergreen shrub for part shade in fertile, well-drained soil. Flushes of flowers in spring, summer, and fall, orchid purple. Grows 24 inches (60 cm)

high and wide. Zones 6–9. A garden hybrid, *D.* ×*burkwoodii* × *D. retusa*.

### Daphne mezereum

February daphne, mezereon
A deciduous shrub for sun or part shade in fertile, well-drained soil. Flowers in midwinter to spring, red-purple to almost pink on bare stems, followed by bright red fruit. Grows 24–48 inches (60–120 cm) high, 24 inches (60 cm) wide. Zones 3–9. Europe, Turkey, Caucasia, central Asia, and Siberia. The equally garden-worthy white form, *D. mezereum* f. *alba* (synonyms, f. *albida*, f. *albiflora*), and other white clones have

more compact growth than the pinker form and produce yellow fruit.

### Daphne ×napolitana

synonym, *D. collina* var. *neapolitana*
An evergreen shrub for sun or part shade in fertile, well-drained soil. Flowers in spring with later flushes in summer and fall, rose pink from rose purple buds. Grows 24 inches (60 cm) high and wide. Zones 7–9. A hybrid of uncertain origin, *D. collina* × *D. cneorum* or *D. oleoides*.

### Daphne petraea

An evergreen shrublet for sun or part shade in fertile, well-drained soil. Flowers in late spring and summer, bright pink. Grows 4–6 inches (10–15 cm) high, 12 inches (30 cm) wide. Zones 6–8. Limestone mountains of northern Italy.

*Daphne* ×*mantensiana*

*Daphne mezereum* with *Arum italicum* 'Pictum' at the base, courtesy of Fritz Kummert

*Daphne* ×*napolitana*

*Daphne petraea*, courtesy of Fritz Kummert

## Daphne ×rosettii

synonym, *Daphne* 'Rosettii'

An evergreen shrublet for part shade in fertile, well-drained soil. Flowers in spring, cream to green-yellow. Grows 12 inches (30 cm) high and wide. Zones 6–9. A naturally occurring hybrid from the Pyrenees, *D. cneorum* × *D. laureola* subsp. *philippii*.

## Degenia velebitica

Cruciferae

A perennial for sun in humus-rich, gritty scree. Flowers in spring, yellow. Grows 4 inches (10 cm) high and wide. Zones 5–8. Velebit, mountains of western Croatia.

## Delosperma

ice plant
Aizoaceae

Exciting and hardy species of *Delosperma* from higher elevations in southern Africa continue to be introduced.

Daphne ×rosettii, courtesy of Fritz Kummert

Degenia velebitica, courtesy of Fritz Kummert

## Delosperma ashtonii

A deciduous perennial for sun in fertile scree. Flowers in April and May, pink with a white center. Grows 4 inches (10 cm) high, 12 inches (30 cm) wide. Zones 6–9. Higher Drakensberg Mountains, South Africa.

## Delosperma cf. congestum

gold nugget ice plant

A perennial for sun in fertile scree and best kept dry in winter. Flowers in summer, yellow. Grows 1 inch (2.5 cm) high, 12 inches (30 cm) wide. Zones 4–8. Drakensberg Mountains, South Africa.

## Delosperma cooperi

A perennial for sun in fertile scree. Flowers in June through August, purple. Grows 5 inches (12.5 cm) high, 24 inches (60 cm) wide. Zones 6–9. Free State (Orange Free State), South Africa.

Delosperma ashton

## Delosperma cf. nubigenum

A spreading, deeply rooted, succulent perennial for banks and sunny areas of the large rockery. Cold temperature turns the leaves red. This well-distributed plant has been given the cultivar name 'Lesotho' and may actually be a sterile hybrid, and the true *D. nubigenum*, which has orange-red flowers,

Delosperma cf. congestum, courtesy of Paul Martin

Delosperma cooperi, courtesy of Fritz Kummert

Delosperma cf. nubigenum 'Lesotho'

may have yet to be introduced. Cultivate in sun in fertile scree. Flowers in April and May, yellow. Grows 1 inch (2.5 cm) high, 36 inches (90 cm) wide. Zones 5–10. South Africa.

## Delphinium
larkspur
Ranunculaceae

### Delphinium decorum
A perennial for sun or part shade in fertile, well-drained soil. Flowers in spring, blue-purple to purple-violet. Grows 12–16 inches (30–40 cm) high, 8 inches (20 cm) wide. Zones 7–9. California and southern Oregon.

*Delphinium decorum*

*Delphinium grandiflorum* 'Blue Butterfly'

### Delphinium grandiflorum
A perennial often treated as an annual. Cultivate in sun or part shade in fertile, well-drained soil. The cultivar 'Blue Butterfly' flowers in summer, blue. Grows 12–18 inches (30–45 cm) high, 12 inches (30 cm) wide. Zones 3–9. The species is from Siberia and eastern Asia.

### Delphinium nudicaule
Though a short-lived perennial with a tuber-like root, it is a dainty, brightly colored species easily raised from seed in the spring. Cultivate in sun or part shade in fertile, well-drained soil in rocky crevices. Flowers in spring and summer, yellow to bright red. Grows 12–24 inches (30–60 cm) high, 12 inches (30 cm) wide. Zones 6–9. Southern Oregon and northern California.

### Delphinium oxysepalum
A perennial for sun or part shade in fertile, well-drained soil. Flowers in summer, deep blue to violet. Grows 4–18

*Delphinium nudicaule,* courtesy of Fritz Kummert

*Delphinium oxysepalum,* courtesy of Fritz Kummert

inches (10–45 cm) high, 8 inches (20 cm) wide. Zones 6–9. Western Carpathians.

### Delphinium uliginosum
A perennial for sun or part shade in fertile, well-drained soil. Flowers in summer, white and violet. Grows 12–24 inches (30–60 cm) high, 12 inches (30 cm) wide. Zones 6–9. Northern California.

### Deschampsia flexuosa
hair grass
Gramineae
A perennial for sun or part shade in any fertile soil. The cultivar 'Aura', golden hair grass, flowers in summer, golden,

*Delphinium uliginosum* with *Phlox nana* in the foreground, courtesy of Fritz Kummert

*Deschampsia flexuosa* 'Aura'

fading brown. This excellent, colorful cultivar's name honors a person named Aura and is not a misspelling of the word *aurea*. Grows 18 inches (45 cm) high and wide. Zones 5–9. The species is from Europe, Asia, northeastern North America, and South America.

## Deutzia crenata
Hydrangeaceae
A shrub for sun or part shade in any good, well-drained soil. *Deutzia crenata* 'Nakaiana' (often listed as *D. gracilis* 'Nakaiana') is single rather than double flowered, May and June, white. Grows 8–12 inches (20–30 cm) high, 48 inches (120 cm) wide. Zones 5–8. The species is from Japan and southeastern China.

## Dianthus
pink
Caryophyllaceae

The dianthuses are well-known and important perennials for the rock garden and alpine house.

## Dianthus alpinus
alpine pink
A classic alpine and one of the best species of the genus. Cultivate in sun or part shade in any good, well-drained soil, preferably alkaline. Flowers in June through August in many shades of pink to cerise with crimson-purple spots on a white eye. Grows 3–6 inches (7.5–15 cm) high, 8 inches (20 cm) wide. Zones 3–8. Austria and the eastern Alps.

**Cultivar**. *Dianthus alpinus* 'Albus'. Flowers white.

## Dianthus 'Blue Hills'
Cultivate in sun in any good, well-drained soil, preferably alkaline. Flowers in June through August, crimson-

*Dianthus alpinus,* courtesy of Fritz Kummert

*Dianthus alpinus* 'Albus'

magenta. Grows 4 inches (10 cm) high, 12 inches (30 cm) wide. Zones 4–9.

## Dianthus callizonus
Cultivate in sun or part shade in fertile, limestone scree. Flowers in summer, pink to carmine with a central ring of flecked crimson and white. Grows 3–4 inches (7.5–10 cm) high, 6 inches (15 cm) wide. Zones 5–9. Romania and the southern Carpathians.

## Dianthus deltoides
maiden pink
Cultivate in sun in any good, well-drained soil. Flowers in summer, pale to

*Dianthus* 'Blue Hills', courtesy of Phyllis Gustafson

*Dianthus callizonus,* courtesy of Fritz Kummert

*Dianthus deltoides,* courtesy of Fritz Kummert

*Deutzia crenata* 'Nakaiana'

deep pink with pale spots in a dark eye. Grows 6 inches (15 cm) high, 18 inches (45 cm) wide. Zones 3–9. Europe and Asia. Several clones with deep red or crimson flowers and dark green foliage have been selected and named.

### Dianthus erinaceus

A distinctive species, forming prickly, *Acantholimon*-like cushions and little, fringed flowers on short, stubby stems. Cultivate in sun in scree, preferably alkaline. Flowers in June through August, pink to rose red. Grows 3–6 inches (7.5–15 cm) high, 12 inches (30 cm) wide. Zones 6–9. Turkey.

### Dianthus freynii

Cultivate in sun in limestone scree. Flowers in June and July, pink. Grows 4 inches (10 cm) high, 6 inches (15 cm) wide. Zones 5–9. Central Balkan Peninsula.

### Dianthus 'Goblin'

Cultivate in sun in any good, well-drained soil, preferably alkaline. Flowers in June through August, pink. Grows 10 inches (25 cm) high, 12 inches (30 cm) wide. Zones 3–8.

### Dianthus hamaetocalyx subsp. pindicola

Cultivate in sun in scree, preferably alkaline. Flowers in summer into fall, reddish pink tinged with yellow beneath. Grows 3 inches (7.5 cm) high, 8 inches (20 cm) wide. Zones 5–9. Balkan Peninsula.

### Dianthus 'Inshriach Dazzler'

Cultivate in sun in fertile, well-drained, neutral to acid soil. Flowers in summer, vivid carmine pink, backs of petals buff. Grows 4 inches (10 cm) high, 6 inches (15 cm) wide. Zones 4–9. A garden hybrid involving *D. pavonius* as one of the parents.

### Dianthus 'La Bourboule'

Frequently misspelled 'La Bourbille', *Dianthus* 'La Bourboule' is a deservedly popular miniature pink, equally charming in the white form. It is a good plant for the rock garden, among paving, or a wall plant that blooms heavily. Cultivate in sun or part shade in fertile, well-drained soil. Flowers in June through August, pink. Grows 3 inches (7.5 cm) high, 6 inches (15 cm) wide. Zones 4–8. A garden hybrid involving *D. gratianopolitanus* as one of the parents.

*Dianthus hamaetocalyx* subsp. *pindicola*

*Dianthus erinaceus*

*Dianthus* 'Inshriach Dazzler'

*Dianthus freynii,* courtesy of Fritz Kummert

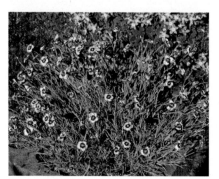
*Dianthus* 'Goblin'

*Dianthus* 'La Bourboule', courtesy of Fritz Kummert

### Dianthus myrtinervius

Cultivate in sun in scree. Flowers in summer, bright pink. Grows 3 inches (7.5 cm) high, 8 inches (20 cm) wide. Zones 4–9. Mountains of the Balkan Peninsula.

### Dianthus nardiformis

A somewhat neglected, though delightful, species for the rock garden, with woody stems and needle-like leaves that are hard and pointed. Cultivate in sun in fertile, well-drained soil. Flowers in

Dianthus myrtinervius

Dianthus nardiformis

summer, pink. Grows 10 inches (25 cm) high, 16 inches (40 cm) wide. Zones 4–9. Romania and eastern Bulgaria.

### Dianthus pavonius

synonym, *D. neglectus*

Cultivate in sun in fertile, well-drained soil, preferably lime-free. Flowers in summer, pale to deep pink, backs of petals buff. Grows 6 inches (15 cm) high, 12 inches (30 cm) wide. Zones 4–9. Southwestern Alps, including Italy, Switzerland, and France.

### Dianthus petraeus subsp. noeanus

synonym, *D. noeanus*

Cultivate in sun or part shade in fertile, well-drained soil. Flowers in summer, white. Grows 10 inches (25 cm) high, 12 inches (30 cm) wide. Zones 4–8. Balkan Mountains of central Bulgaria.

Dianthus petraeus subsp. noeanus

### Dianthus 'Pike's Pink'

Cultivate in sun or part shade in fertile, well-drained soil. Flowers in spring and summer, pink, semidoubled, clove scented. Grows 6 inches (15 cm) high, 18 inches (45 cm) wide. Zones 4–9.

### Dianthus simulans

The congested gray, spiny leaves form a smooth, undulating cushion that is quite impressive with or without flowers. Cultivate in sun in scree. Flowers in summer, rosy pink with a paler center. Grows 3 inches (7.5 cm) high, 5 inches (12.5 cm) wide. Zones 4–8. Mountains bordering Greece and Bulgaria.

### Dianthus sylvestris

Cultivate in sun in fertile, well-drained soil. Flowers in summer in various shades of pink. Grows 4–8 inches (10–20 cm) high, 12 inches (30 cm)

Dianthus pavonius, courtesy of Fritz Kummert

Dianthus 'Pike's Pink'

Dianthus simulans

wide. Zones 4–9. Central and southern Europe.

### Dianthus 'Tiny Rubies'

Cultivate in sun or part shade in fertile scree. Flowers in spring, rosy red. Grows 2 inches (5 cm) high, 12 inches (30 cm) wide. Zones 3–8. A cultivar involving *D. gratianopolitanus*.

### Diascia
Scrophulariaceae

### Diascia anastrepta

A perennial for sun or light shade in fertile, well-drained soil. Flowers in summer and fall, medium to rich pink. Grows 12–16 inches (30–40 cm) high, 18 inches (45 cm) wide. Zones 8–10. Drakensberg Mountains, South Africa.

### Diascia barberae

A perennial for sun or light shade in fertile, well-drained soil. The cultivar 'Ruby Field', a seedling selection, flowers in spring through fall, salmon pink. Grows 10 inches (25 cm) high, 18 inches (45

*Dianthus sylvestris,* courtesy of Fritz Kummert

*Dianthus* 'Tiny Rubies'

cm) wide. Zones 8–10. The species is from southern Africa.

### Diascia fetcaniensis

A perennial that is easy to grow and hardy, with a very long blooming season. Cultivate in sun or part shade in fertile, well-drained soil. Flowers in summer and fall, salmon pink. Grows 18

*Diascia anastrepta,* courtesy of Fritz Kummert

*Diascia barberae* 'Ruby Field'

*Diascia fetcaniensis,* courtesy of Fritz Kummert

inches (45 cm) high, 24 inches (60 cm) wide. Zones 7–10. Lesotho and Drakensberg Mountains, South Africa.

### Dicentra
bleeding heart
Fumariaceae

### Dicentra canadensis
squirrel corn

A perennial for part shade in moist, humus-rich soil with a drier summer dormancy. Flowers in March through May, white, tinged pink. Grows 6 inches (15 cm) high and wide. Zones 4–8. Eastern North America, Canada south to North Carolina and Tennessee.

### Dicentra cucullaria
Dutchman's breeches

A perennial with a bulb-like rootstock of small white tubers for part shade in moist, humus-rich soil with a drier

*Dicentra canadensis,* courtesy of Panayoti Kelaidis

*Dicentra cucullaria*

summer dormancy. Flowers in early spring, white, occasionally yellow or flushed with pink. Grows 6–10 inches (15–25 cm) high, 12 inches (30 cm) wide. Zones 4–8. Eastern North America, Nova Scotia to North Carolina and west to Kansas. There is a western form of the species that is sometimes called *D. occidentalis*; it is native to Idaho, eastern Washington, and northeastern Oregon. From the gardener's standpoint the western form is taller and more robust.

## Dicentra eximia
staggerweed, turkey corn, wild bleeding heart

A rhizomatous perennial for part shade in humus-rich, well-drained soil. Flowers in spring to late summer or early fall, pink to rose red. Grows 12–18 inches (30–45 cm) high, 18 inches (45 cm) wide. Zones 3–10. Mountains of the eastern United States, New York to Georgia. The cultivar 'Alba' is a white-flowered selection, as is 'Snowdrift' in addition to several other cultivars that may actually be hybrids with *D. formosa*, 'Bountiful', 'Luxuriant', and 'Zestful'.

## Dicentra formosa
wild bleeding heart

A rhizomatous perennial. California to British Columbia.

**Subspecies and Cultivar**. *Dicentra formosa* subsp. *oregana* (synonym, *D. oregana*), Oregon dicentra. Cultivate in sun or part shade in scree. Flowers in May to August, cream and pink. Grows 8 inches (20 cm) high, 12 inches (30 cm) wide. Zones 4–9. Siskiyou Mountains of northern California and southern Oregon.

*Dicentra formosa* 'Sweetheart' is a superb form, ranking high as a most satisfactory, long-blooming plant for woodland gardens. Tolerant of considerable sun but not hot summer conditions. It has light green foliage and beautiful white flowers. Cultivate in part shade in humus-rich, well-drained soil. Flowers in May to October. Grows 12 inches (30 cm) high, 24 inches (60 cm) wide. Zones 4–9.

*Dicentra formosa* subsp. *oregana*, courtesy of Fritz Kummert

## Dicentra peregrina
A beautiful and difficult rhizomatous perennial best attempted in the alpine house. Cultivate in part shade in humus-rich, gritty scree. Flowers in early summer, white or pink to purple with paler tips and darker veining. Grows 4 inches (10 cm) high, 10 inches (25 cm) wide. Zones 5–9. Japan, China, and eastern Siberia.

## Dionysia
Primulaceae

The species of cushion-forming perennials treated here are relatively easy to cultivate although the alpine house is the best place to provide the necessary protection from winter wetness.

*Dicentra formosa* 'Sweetheart'

*Dicentra eximia* 'Alba'

*Dicentra peregrina*, courtesy of Franz Hadacek

## Dionysia aretioides

Cultivate in sun or part shade in humus-rich scree. Flowers in spring, yellow. Grows 1 inch (2.5 cm) high, 6–8 inches (15–20 cm) wide. Zones 6–8. Northern Iran.

## Dionysia involucrata

Cultivate in sun or part shade in humus-rich scree. Flowers in early summer, lilac to violet purple with a white eye when young and reddening with age; there is also a rare white-flowered form in culti-

Dionysia aretioides, courtesy of Armen Gevjan

Dionysia involucrata, courtesy of Fritz Kummert

Dionysia tapetodes, courtesy of Fritz Kummert

vation. Grows 1 inch (2.5 cm) high, 6 inches (15 cm) wide. Zones 6–8. Russia.

## Dionysia tapetodes

Cultivate in sun or part shade in humus-rich scree. Flowers in late spring and early summer, yellow. Grows 1 inch (2.5 cm) high, 10 inches (25 cm) wide. Zones 6–8. Southern Russia, northeastern Iran, Afghanistan and western Pakistan.

## Diplarrhena moraea
Iridaceae

A very pretty rhizomatous, evergreen perennial for the large rock garden, or protected in an alpine house. Cultivate in sun in peaty, well-drained soil. Flowers in summer, white suffused or veined with mauve or blue. Grows 12–24 inches (30–60 cm) high, 12 inches (30 cm)

Diplarrhena moraea, courtesy of Fritz Kummert

Disporum flavens, courtesy of Armen Gevjan

wide. Zones 7–9. Tasmania and southeastern Australia.

## Disporum
Liliaceae (Colchicaceae)

## Disporum flavens
fairy bells

A rhizomatous perennial for part shade in humus-rich, well-drained soil. Flowers in late spring, yellow. Grows 18–24 inches (45–60 cm) high, 12 inches (30 cm) wide. Zones 6–9. Korea.

## Disporum sessile
fairy bells

A rhizomatous perennial for part shade in humus-rich, well-drained soil. Flowers in spring, white with greenish tips. Grows 12–24 inches (30–60 cm) high, 12 inches (30 cm) wide. Zones 6–9. Japan.

Disporum sessile

Disporum smithii, courtesy of Fritz Kummert

## *Disporum smithii*

fairy lantern

A perennial for part shade in humus-rich, well-drained soil. Flowers in spring, white to cream. Grows 12–18 inches (30–45 cm) high, 12 inches (30 cm) wide. Zones 5–9. Coast Ranges of California and Oregon.

## *Dodecatheon*

American cowslip, bird bill, shooting star
Primulaceae

The pretty spring *Cyclamen*-like blossoms can be white, pink to purplish, or almost red in color. These perennials require plenty of moisture in spring but do best if allowed to dry out somewhat in summer when they go dormant after flowering.

## *Dodecatheon alpinum*

alpine shooting star

Cultivate in sun or part shade in humus-rich, moist soil. Flowers in late spring and early summer, magenta to lavender. Grows 6–12 inches (15–30 cm) high, 6 inches (15 cm) wide. Zones 3–8. Alpine areas of California, southern Oregon, Arizona, and Utah.

## *Dodecatheon hendersonii*

Cultivate in part shade in humus-rich, moist soil, keeping it quite dry in summer. Flowers in spring, red-purple. Grows 8–10 inches (20–25 cm) high. Zones 4–9. Vancouver Island, British Columbia, to California.

*Dodecatheon alpinum*, courtesy of Fritz Kummert

**Cultivar**. *Dodecatheon hendersonii* 'Sooke', dwarf shooting star. Cultivate in part shade in humus-rich, moist soil, keeping it dryish in summer. Flowers in late spring, cherry red. Grows 6–8 inches (15–20 cm) high. Zones 4–9. Vancouver Island, British Columbia.

## *Dodecatheon meadia*

American cowslip, shooting star
Cultivate in part shade in humus-rich, moist soil. Flowers in late spring, purple, pink, or white. Grows 18 inches (45 cm)

*Dodecatheon hendersonii*, courtesy of Fritz Kummert

*Dodecatheon hendersonii* 'Sooke'

high, 12 inches (30 cm) wide. Zones 3–8. Midwestern to eastern United States.

## *Doronicum columnae*

leopard's bane
Compositae
synonym, *D. cordatum*
A perennial for sun or part shade in any fertile soil. Flowers in early spring, yellow. Grows 12–20 inches (30–50 cm) high, 12 inches (30 cm) wide. Zones 4–9. Southern Europe and western Asia.

*Dodecatheon meadia*

*Doronicum columnae*, courtesy of Fritz Kummert

### Dorycnium hirsutum
Leguminosae

A perennial for sun in any well-drained soil, preferably poor and alkaline. Flowers in June through September, white flushed with pink. Grows 18 inches (45 cm) high, 30 inches (75 cm) wide. Zones 6–10. Portugal to Turkey.

### Douglasia
Primulaceae

Some authorities have moved all of the American douglasias to the genus *Androsace*. Wherever they may be placed, they are excellent alpines, challenging and beautiful.

### Douglasia laevigata

A densely mat-forming perennial for sun or part shade in cool scree. Flowers in late spring, rose pink with a darker eye. Grows 3 inches (7.5 cm) high, 12 inches (30 cm) wide. Zones 6–8. Cascade Ranges of Oregon and Washington and the Olympic Mountains.

### Douglasia montana

A perennial for sun or part shade in fertile, gritty scree. Grows 2 inches (5 cm) high, 6 inches (15 cm) wide. Zones 4–8. British Columbia to Idaho and Wyoming. *Douglasia montana* var. *biflora*, from the Rocky Mountains, is more robust and easier to grow.

### Draba
Cruciferae

All drabas perform well as alpine house subjects. Most can be grown well outside in a raised bed, but most require protection from winter wetness, especially those with woolly leaves.

### Draba bruniifolia

A cushion- to mat-forming perennial for sun in any good, well-drained soil. Flowers in early spring, yellow. Grows 3 inches (7.5 cm) high, 12 inches (30 cm) wide. Zones 5–9. Caucasia, Armenia, and Turkey. *Draba bruniifolia* subsp. *olympica* (synonym, *D. olympica*) is similar to subspecies *bruniifolia* and most rewarding, considered one of the easiest drabas to grow.

### Draba cappadocica

A cushion-forming perennial for sun in any good, well-drained soil. Flowers in early spring, yellow. Grows 3 inches (7.5 cm) high, 8 inches (20 cm) wide. Zones 5–9. Turkey and Kurdistan

### Draba incerta

A cushion- to mat-forming perennial for sun in any good, well-drained, gritty soil. Flowers in spring, yellow. Grows 3 inches (7.5 cm) high, 8 inches (20 cm)

*Dorycnium hirsutum*

*Douglasia montana*

*Draba bruniifolia* subsp. *bruniifolia*, courtesy of Fritz Kummert

*Douglasia laevigata*

*Draba cappadocica*, courtesy of Fritz Kummert

wide. Zones 4–8. Northwestern contiguous United States, Canada, and Alaska.

## Draba mollissima

A hummock-forming perennial that is often considered the gem of the genus with its furry foliage of very tiny rosettes that are sensitive to moisture, as are those of *D. polytricha*. Cultivate *D. mollissima* in sun in any good, well-drained, gritty soil in the alpine house. Flowers in April and May, yellow. Grows 2 inches (5 cm) high, 6 inches (15 cm) wide. Zones 5–7. Caucasus Mountains.

## Draba polytricha

A cushion-forming perennial (note also the discussion under *D. mollissima*) for

*Draba incerta*

*Draba mollissima*

*Draba polytricha,* courtesy of Fritz Kummert

sun in any good, well-drained, gritty soil in the alpine house. Flowers in spring, yellow. Grows 2 inches (5 cm) high, 6 inches (15 cm) wide. Zones 5–7. Caucasus Mountains.

## Draba rigida

A cushion-forming perennial for sun in any good, well-drained soil. Flowers in early spring, yellow. Grows 3 inches (7.5 cm) high, 5 inches (12.5 cm) wide. Zones 4–8. Armenia and Turkey.

**Subspecies**. *Draba rigida* var. *bryoides* (synonym, *D. bryoides*) is one of the finest drabas, making a hard cushion of moss-like foliage. Cultivate in sun in any good, well-drained, gritty soil. Flowers in March and April, yellow. Grows 2 inches (5 cm) high, 3 inches (7.5 cm) wide. Zones 5–8. Armenia and the Caucasus Mountains.

## Draba ussuriensis

A loosely mat-forming perennial for sun in any good, well-drained soil. Flowers

*Draba rigida*

*Draba rigida* var. *bryoides,* courtesy of Fritz Kummert

in spring, white. Grows 8 inches (20 cm) high, 12 inches (30 cm) wide. Zones 5–9. Northeastern Asia.

## Dracocephalum austriacum

dragon head
Labiatae

A perennial for sun or part shade in fertile, well-drained, moist soil. Flowers in summer, blue-violet. Grows 10–18 inches (25–45 cm) high, 18 inches (45 cm) wide. Zones 4–9. Southeastern France to central Ukraine.

## Dryas

mountain avens
Rosaceae

Dryases are popular and easy-to-grow plants, best in the sunny rock garden where they eventually make dense, evergreen mats of scalloped leaves. The shrublets tend to be short-lived in acid soils. *Anemone*-like flowers are followed by long-lasting, attractive, silky seed heads.

*Draba ussuriensis*

*Dracocephalum austriacum,* courtesy of Fritz Kummert

### Dryas drummondii
Cultivate in sun in any good, well-drained, alkaline to neutral soil. Flowers in late spring, creamy yellow. Grows 3 inches (7.5 cm) high, 18 inches (45 cm) wide. Zones 1–7. Arctic and alpine regions of Canada and northwestern contiguous United States.

### Dryas octopetala
Cultivate in sun in any good, well-drained, alkaline to neutral soil. Flowers in late spring, white. Grows 3 inches (7.5 cm) high, 24 inches (60 cm) wide. Zones 1–7. Arctic and alpine regions of the northern hemisphere.

### Dryopteris
male or shield fern
Dryopteridaceae

Dryas drummondii, courtesy of Fritz Kummert

Dryas octopetala

### Dryopteris affinis
golden-scaled male fern
A semi-evergreen to deciduous perennial for full to part shade in humus-rich, well-drained, moist soil. Dryopteris affinis subsp. affinis 'Crispa Gracilis', crisped dwarf golden-scaled male fern, is an outstanding dwarf fern for the shady rock garden that is often confused with D. affinis 'Crispa Congesta', another fine dwarf selection; 'Crispa Gracilis' grows 4–8 inches (10–20 cm) high, 8 inches (20 cm) wide. Zones 4–9. The species is from Caucasia to Europe, including Norway and the British Isles.

Dryopteris affinis subsp. affinis 'Crispa Gracilis'

Dryopteris erythrosora var. prolifica, courtesy of Fritz Kummert

### Dryopteris erythrosora var. prolifica
proliferous autumn fern, proliferous copper shield fern
A semi-evergreen to deciduous perennial for full to part shade in humus-rich, well-drained, moist soil. Grows 12–18 inches (30–45 cm) high, 24 inches (60 cm) wide. Zones 5–9. Japan.

 **E**

### Echinocereus
hedgehog cactus
Cactaceae

### Echinocereus fendleri
A perennial, low-growing, shrubby cactus for sun in any well-drained soil. Variety fendleri flowers in spring into summer, purple-magenta to white. Grows 12–18 inches (30–45 cm) high, 24 inches (60 cm) wide. Zones 7–9. Southwestern United States and northwestern Mexico.

Echinocereus fendleri var. fendleri, courtesy of Fritz Kummert

Echinocereus triglochidiatus var. mojavensis, courtesy of Fritz Kummert

### Echinocereus triglochidiatus var. *mojavensis*
claret cup

A perennial, low-growing, shrubby cactus for sun in any well-drained soil. Flowers in spring, orange to scarlet, rarely pink. Grows 12 inches (30 cm) high, 18 inches (45 cm) wide. Zones 6–9. Southwestern United States and northern Mexico.

### Echinocereus viridiflorus

A perennial, low-growing, shrubby cactus for sun in any well-drained soil. Flowers in spring, green to yellow-green and lemon scented. Grows 8 inches (20 cm) high, 12 inches (30 cm) wide. Zones 6–9. Southern central United States.

### Edraianthus
grassy bells
Campanulaceae

The edraianthuses are splendid, early-summer-blooming perennial campanulads with up-facing bells at the growth tips.

*Echinocereus viridiflorus,* courtesy of Fritz Kummert

*Edraianthus dinaricus,* courtesy of Fritz Kummert

### Edraianthus dinaricus

Cultivate in sun or light shade in scree. Flowers in early summer, blue to violet. Grows 3 inches (7.5 cm) high, 10 inches (25 cm) wide. Zones 5–8. Central and western Balkan Peninsula.

### Edraianthus pumilio

Probably the most outstanding species of *Edraianthus,* a miniature tuft of silver-gray grassy leaves. Cultivate in sun or light shade in scree. Flowers in early summer, violet. Grows 3 inches (7.5 cm) high, 5 inches (12.5 cm) wide. Zones 5–8. Mediterranean.

### Ephedra
joint fir
Ephedraceae

*Ephedra* is a genus of curious shrubs, making a link in the plant kingdom between flowering plants and conifers. They are very drought tolerant.

### Ephedra distachya

An evergreen shrub for sun in any fertile, well-drained soil. Flowers in spring,

*Edraianthus pumilio*

*Ephedra distachya,* courtesy of Fritz Kummert

small and yellow, followed by red "fruit" in summer. Grows 18 inches (45 cm) high, 36 inches (90 cm) wide. Zones 4–10. Mediterranean to Siberia.

### Ephedra minima

An evergreen shrublet for sun in scree. Flowers in spring, small and yellow, followed by bright red "fruit." Grows 4 inches (10 cm) high, 12 inches (30 cm) wide. Zones 4–10. Tibet.

### Epilobium
Onagraceae

### Epilobium rigidum
willowherb

A perennial for sun in sandy or gritty scree. Flowers in summer, pink. Grows 6–8 inches (15–20 cm) high, 12 inches (30 cm) wide. Zones 6–8. Siskiyou Mountains of northern California and southern Oregon.

### Epimedium
bishop's hat or mitre
Berberidaceae

*Ephedra minima*

*Epilobium rigidum*

Considered the aristocrats of ground covers for shade, epimediums spread into dense colonies and have dainty flowers that appear before the new foliage unfurls in spring. The handsome, heart-shaped foliage is tinged bronze when new.

### Epimedium acuminatum

A rhizomatous evergreen perennial for part shade in humus-rich soil. Flowers in spring, usually dull purple and pink, also white and yellow. Grows 12–18 inches (30–45 cm) high, 24 inches (60 cm) wide. Zones 5–9. Central and western China.

### Epimedium diphyllum

A deciduous perennial for part shade in humus-rich soil. Flowers in spring, white. Grows 12 inches (30 cm) high, 18 inches (45 cm) wide. Zones 5–9. Japan.

### Epimedium grandiflorum

synonym, *E. macranthum*
A deciduous perennial for part shade in humus-rich soil. Flowers in spring,

*Epimedium acuminatum,* courtesy of Fritz Kummert

*Epimedium diphyllum,* courtesy of Fritz Kummert

white, yellow, pink, or purple. Grows 12 inches (30 cm) high, 18 inches (45 cm) wide. Zones 5–9. Central and southern Japan.

*Epimedium grandiflorum,* courtesy of Fritz Kummert

*Epimedium pinnatum* subsp. *colchicum,* courtesy of Fritz Kummert

*Epimedium ×versicolor* 'Sulphureum' with *Muscari armeniacum* 'Blue Spike', courtesy of Fritz Kummert

### Epimedium pinnatum subsp. colchicum

A near-evergreen perennial for part shade in humus-rich soil. Flowers in March to May, yellow. Grows 12 inches (30 cm) high, 36 inches (90 cm) wide. Zones 5–9. Western Asia.

### Epimedium ×rubrum

A low, compact deciduous perennial that is a rapid spreader. Cultivate in part shade in humus-rich soil. Flowers in March to May, crimson and white. Grows 6 inches (15 cm) high, 24 inches (60 cm) wide. Zones 5–9. A garden hybrid, *E. alpinum × E. grandiflorum.*

### Epimedium ×versicolor

A deciduous perennial for part shade in humus-rich soil. The cultivar 'Sulphur-

*Epimedium ×rubrum*

eum' flowers in spring, pale yellow to creamy white and deeper yellow. Grows 24 inches (60 cm) high, 36 inches (90 cm) wide. Zones 5–9. *Epimedium ×versicolor* is a garden hybrid, *E. grandiflorum × E. pinnatum* subsp. *colchicum*.

## Epimedium ×warleyense

A near-evergreen perennial for part shade in humus-rich soil. Flowers in spring, yellow and red, fading to orange. Grows 12–18 inches (30–45 cm) high, 24 inches (60 cm) wide. Zones 5–9. A garden hybrid, *E. alpinum × E. pinnatum* subsp. *colchicum*.

## Epimedium ×youngianum

A deciduous perennial for part shade in humus-rich soil. The cultivar 'Niveum' flowers in spring, white. Grows 6 inches (15 cm) high, 18 inches (45 cm) wide. Zones 5–9. *Epimedium ×youngianum* is a garden hybrid, *E. diphyllum × E. grandiflorum*.

## Epipactus
Orchidaceae

## Epipactus gigantea

chatterbox orchid, stream orchid
A rhizomatous terrestrial orchid for moisture-retentive soil or streamside, where plants form slowly spreading colonies. Cultivate in sun or part shade in humus-rich, moist soil. Flowers in summer, purple-green. Grows 24 inches (60 cm) high and wide. Zones 4–9. Western North America.

## Epipactus palustris

marsh helleborine
A rhizomatous terrestrial orchid for sun or part shade in humus-rich, moist soil. Flowers in mid- to late summer, tepals brown to purplish green, lip white with red veins and yellow dots. Grows 12–18 inches (30–45 cm) high, 24 inches (60 cm) wide. Zones 4–8. Europe.

## Eranthis hyemalis

winter aconite
Ranunculaceae
A rhizomatous, tuberous perennial for sun or part shade in humus-rich, well-drained soil. Flowers in winter, yellow.

*Epipactus palustris*, courtesy of Fritz Kummert

*Epimedium ×warleyense*

*Epimedium ×youngianum* 'Niveum'

*Epipactus gigantea*, courtesy of Fritz Kummert

Grows 4–6 inches (10–15 cm) high, 12 inches (30 cm) wide. Zones 5–9. Southern Europe, naturalized in western Europe and Britain.

## Erica
heather
Ericaceae

The many dwarf shrubby forms of *Erica* are useful rock garden and peat garden plants, having an exceptionally long season of bloom and evergreen foliage that is neat and fresh looking year-round. Sandy soil with peat moss, oak leaf mold, or compost is ideal. Roots should never go completely dry nor ever be soggy.

### Erica carnea
alpine or winter heather
Cultivate in sun or part shade in humus-rich, sandy soil. It is tolerant of lime. Flowers in shades of pink, reddish, and purple, and in white. Zones 4–10. Central European Alps, northwestern Italy, and the northwestern Balkan Peninsula.

**Cultivars**. *Erica carnea* 'Springwood White' flowers in January to May, white. Grows 6 inches (15 cm) high, 24 inches (60 cm) wide.

*Erica carnea* 'Vivellii' flowers in January through March, crimson. Grows 8 inches (20 cm) high, 16 inches (40 cm) wide.

### Erica cinerea
bell heather, fine-leaved heath
Cultivate in sun or part shade in humus-rich, sandy, acid soil. Flowers in June through August, bright red-purple to white. The cultivar 'Alba Minor' has finely textured, light green foliage and white flowers. Grows 4 inches (10 cm) high, 12 inches (30 cm) wide. Zones 5–8. The species is from Britain and northern Europe.

### Erica erigena
Irish heather
Cultivate in sun or part shade in humus-rich, sandy soil. It is tolerant of lime. The cultivar 'Golden Lady', golden Irish heather, flowers in May, white with golden foliage as shown; other cultivars may be in shades of pink. Grows 12 inches (30 cm) high and wide. Zones 7–9. The species is from southwestern Europe and western Ireland.

### Erica tetralix
cross-leaved heath
Cultivate in sun or part shade in humus-rich, sandy, lime-free soil. Flowers in summer in shades of purple, pink, and white. Grows 6–8 inches (15–20 cm) high, 12–24 inches (30–60 cm) wide. The cultivar 'Pink Glow' has vivid magenta flowers, June through September, and neat, gray-green foliage. Grows 8 inches (20 cm) high, 24 inches (60 cm) wide. Zones 3–9. The species is from Europe.

### Erica vagans
Cornish heather
Cultivate in sun or part shade in humus-rich, sandy, acid soil. The cultivar 'Birch

*Eranthis hyemalis,* courtesy of Fritz Kummert

*Erica carnea* 'Vivellii', courtesy of Panayoti Kelaidis

*Erica erigena* 'Golden Lady'

*Erica carnea* 'Springwood White'

*Erica cinerea* 'Alba Minor'

*Erica tetralix* 'Pink Glow'

Glow' has rich, dark green foliage and brightly colored flowers in dense, erect, pointed clusters. Flowers in July through October, rose pink. Grows 10 inches (25 cm) high, 18 inches (45 cm) wide. Zones 5–8. The species is from western Europe, including southwestern England and Ireland.

## *Erigeron*
fleabane
Compositae

### *Erigeron aureus*
A perennial for sun or part shade in humus-rich, acid scree. Flowers in spring to fall, rich yellow. Grows 4 inches (10 cm) high, 8 inches (20 cm) wide. Zones 5–8. Mountains of western Canada and Washington.

**Cultivar**. *Erigeron aureus* 'Canary Bird' flowers in spring to fall, creamy yellow.

Erica vagans 'Birch Glow'

*Erigeron aureus,* courtesy of Fritz Kummert

### *Erigeron chrysopsidis*
The cultivar 'Grand Ridge' is a miniature gem from the Wallowa Mountains of Oregon and was found by Phil Pearson and Steve Doonan of Grand Ridge Nursery, Issaquah, Washington. In spite of its long flowering season, it seems to be a long-lived perennial. Cultivate in sun in humus-rich scree. Flowers in spring to fall, bright yellow. Grows 4 inches (10 cm) high, 8 inches (20 cm) wide. Zones 5–8. The species is from California, Nevada, Oregon, and Washington.

Erigeron aureus 'Canary Bird'

Erigeron chrysopsidis 'Grand Ridge'

*Erigeron compositus*

### *Erigeron compositus*
A perennial for sun in fertile scree. Flowers in summer, white, pink, or bluish. Grows 6 inches (15 cm) high, 8 inches (20 cm) wide. Zones 3–8. Western United States and Canada to Greenland.

### *Erigeron glaucus*
beach aster, seaside daisy
The cultivar 'Olga' is an introduction by the Siskiyou Rare Plant Nursery and is a perennial with a particularly low-growing habit. Cultivate in sun or part shade in any good, well-drained soil. Flowers in April through August, lilac with a yellow eye. Grows 6 inches (15 cm) high, 18 inches (45 cm) wide. Zones 5–10. The species is from the California and Oregon coast.

### *Erigeron linearis*
A perennial for sun or part shade in scree. Flowers in early summer, yellow. Grows 6 inches (15 cm) high, 12 inches

Erigeron glaucus 'Olga'

*Erigeron linearis,* courtesy of Fritz Kummert

(30 cm) wide. Zones 5–8. Mountains of western North America.

## Erigeron scopulinus

A perennial for sun or part shade in any good, well-drained soil. Flowers in spring, white. Grows 2 inches (5 cm) high, 10 inches (25 cm) wide. Zones 5–7. Arizona.

## Erinacea anthyllis

Leguminosae
synonym, *E. pungens*
blue broom, branch thorn, hedgehog
   broom

Given a truly hot location, a dome-shaped, spiky, evergreen shrublet that is sure to please when smothered in near-stemless flowers. Cultivate in sun in well-drained gritty soil, preferably alkaline. Flowers in summer, violet-blue. Grows 6–12 inches (15–30 cm) high, 12 inches (30 cm) wide. Zones 5–8. Morocco, Spain, and southern France.

## Erinus alpinus

alpine balsam, fairy foxglove
Scrophulariaceae

A tiny, short-lived, evergreen mountain perennial that is easy to grow, colorful, and reseeds nicely onto mossy rocks or into crevices without becoming a nuisance. Cultivate in sun or part shade in any good, well-drained soil. Flowers usually rose purple in the wild. Grows 3–6 inches (7.5–15 cm) high, 8 inches (20 cm) wide. Zones 4–10. Mountains of Europe.

**Cultivars**. *Erinus alpinus* 'Albus' flowers in May and June, white.
*Erinus alpinus* 'Carmineus' flowers in May and June, carmine-pink.

## Eriogonum

St. Catherine's lace, umbrella plant, wild
   buckwheat
Polygonaceae

The alpine buckwheats are natives of western North America and make ideal additions to the dry rock garden.

## Eriogonum caespitosum subsp. douglasii

A mat-forming perennial or subshrub for sun in any gritty, well-drained soil. Flowers in summer, yellow, aging to reddish. Grows 6 inches (15 cm) high, 12 inches (30 cm) wide. Zones 5–9. Washington to California and Nevada.

## Eriogonum ovalifolium

A mat-forming perennial for sun in any gritty, well-drained soil. Flowers in summer, cream or rose to purple. Grows 4–8 inches (10–20 cm) high, 12 inches (30 cm) wide. Zones 5–9. Oregon, California, and Nevada.

## Eriogonum umbellatum

sulfur flower

A mat-forming perennial or subshrub for sun in any gritty, well-drained soil.

*Erigeron scopulinus*, courtesy of Panayoti Kelaidis

*Erinus alpinus* 'Albus'

*Eriogonum caespitosum* subsp. *douglasii*, courtesy of Fritz Kummert

*Erinacea anthyllis*, courtesy of Fritz Kummert

*Erinus alpinus* 'Carmineus'

*Eriogonum ovalifolium*

Flowers in summer in all shades of yellow to cream. The dwarf form illustrated grows 4–12 inches (10–30 cm) high, 12–18 inches (30–45 cm) wide. Zones 4–9. The species is from British Columbia to California, Montana, Wyoming, and Arizona.

**Cultivars.** *Eriogonum umbellatum* 'Alturas Red' is a Siskiyou Rare Plant Nursery color selection from wild plants in northern California, displaying a superior combination of coin-like foliage tinged red in winter, and stocky stems of colorful flowers most of the summer. Flowers in summer, gold, changing to russet red. Grows 10 inches (25 cm) high, 18 inches (45 cm) wide. Zones 5–9.

*Eriogonum umbellatum* 'Siskiyou Gold' flowers in summer, yellow, turning gold. Grows 12 inches (30 cm) high, 18 inches (45 cm) wide. Zones 5–9.

## Eriophorum vaginatum
cotton grass, hare's tail
Cyperaceae
A perennial grass-like plant for sun or part shade in humus-rich, moist soil. Flowers in July and August, white. The dwarf form shown grows 10 inches (25 cm) high, 6 inches (15 cm) wide. Zones 2–8. The species is from Arctic regions.

## Eriophyllum lanatum
Oregon sunshine, woolly sunflower
Compositae
A perennial for sun in any well-drained soil, even poor soil. Flowers in midsummer, golden yellow. Grows 8–24 inches (20–60 cm) high, 12–36 inches (30–90 cm) wide. A variable species in the wild, regarding size and habit. Zones 5–9. British Columbia to California, through the Rocky Mountains to Montana. The cultivar 'Siskiyou' is a Siskiyou Rare Plant Nursery selection that is a vigorous, low, spreading clone, 10 inches (25

cm) high, 36 inches (90 cm) wide, adapting easily to garden conditions.

## Eritrichium
alpine forget-me-not
Boraginaceae

Eritrichiums are outstanding alpine plants that the best cultivators attempt to grow at some point in their careers, usually with only temporary success.

## Eritrichium howardii
A mat-forming perennial for sun or part shade in humus-rich, gritty scree. Flowers in summer, blue. Grows 4 inches (10 cm) high, 12 inches (30 cm) wide. Zones 3–8. Montana and Wyoming.

## Eritrichium nanum
A cushion-forming perennial for sun or part shade in humus-rich, gritty scree. Flowers in summer, deep blue to white. Grows 2 inches (5 cm) high, 8 inches (20 cm) wide. Zones 3–8. Circumpolar in

*Eriogonum umbellatum*, dwarf form

*Eriogonum umbellatum* 'Siskiyou Gold'

*Eriophyllum lanatum* 'Siskiyou'

*Eriogonum umbellatum* 'Alturas Red'

*Eriophorum vaginatum*, dwarf form

*Eritrichium howardii*, courtesy of Fritz Kummert

the northern hemisphere and south through mountains.

## Erodium
crane's, heron's, or stork's bill
Geraniaceae

Erodiums are very showy, summer-flowering *Geranium* relatives from the Mediterranean. They thrive in climates similar to that region's, but many are quite hardy and adaptable.

## Erodium cheilanthifolium
synonym, *E. petraeum* subsp. *crispum*
A perennial for sun in well-drained soil, preferably limy. Flowers in summer,

Eritrichium nanum

*Erodium cheilanthifolium*

*Erodium cheilanthifolium* 'David Crocker'

white with cerise veining and a purple-black blotch. Grows 8 inches (20 cm) high, 18 inches (45 cm) wide. Zones 6–9. Spain and Morocco.

   **Cultivar.** *Erodium cheilanthifolium* 'David Crocker' flowers in summer, white with no veining and a raspberry pink blotch.

## Erodium chrysanthum
A perennial for sun in well-drained soil, preferably limy. Flowers in summer, pale to sulfur yellow. Grows 6 inches (15 cm) high, 12 inches (30 cm) wide. Zones 5–9. Central and southern Greece.

## Erodium glandulosum
synonym, *E. macradenum*
A perennial for sun in well-drained soil, preferably limy. The cultivar 'Roseum' flowers in summer, deep pink, blotched

*Erodium chrysanthum*

*Erodium glandulosum* 'Roseum'

purple. Grows 8 inches (20 cm) high, 18 inches (45 cm) wide. Zones 6–9. The species is from the Pyrenees.

## Erodium reichardii
synonym, *E. chamaedryoides*
A perennial for sun or part shade in any good, well-drained soil. The cultivar 'Roseum' flowers in June through August, pink. Grows 2 inches (5 cm) high, 8 inches (20 cm) wide. Zones 7–10. The species is from the Balearic Islands, Spain.

## Eryngium
eryngo, sea holly
Umbelliferae

Eryngiums are perennials with bold, bluish leaves. A few species are small enough for the rock garden. They brighten up the sunny summer garden.

*Erodium reichardii* 'Roseum'

## Eryngium bourgatti

Cultivate in sun in fertile, well-drained soil. Flowers in summer, bluish. Grows 12–18 inches (30–45 cm) high, 12 inches (30 cm) wide. Zones 6–10. Pyrenees.

## Eryngium maritimum

sea eryngium, sea holly, sea holm
Cultivate in sun in sandy, well-drained soil. Flowers in summer and early fall, blue. Grows 12–24 inches (30–60 cm) high, 12 inches (30 cm) wide. Zones 5–10. Coastal Europe and naturalized on the eastern coast of the United States.

## Erysimum helveticum

Cruciferae
A perennial wallflower for sun in any good soil. Flowers in spring, yellow from purple tinted buds. Grows 3 inches (7.5

cm) high, 12 inches (30 cm) wide. Zones 4–9. Alps.

## Erythronium

fawn or trout lily
Liliaceae

All erythroniums are excellent wildflowers for shade, and are bulbous perennials that are basically easy to grow and permanent. They do not do well when disturbed and may make a poor show for a few years after being transplanted.

## Erythronium citrinum

Cultivate in shade or part shade in humus-rich, well-drained soil. Flowers in March and April, cream to pale yellow. Grows 12 inches (30 cm) high and wide. Zones 3–8. Siskiyou Mountains of northern California and southern Oregon.

## Erythronium dens-canis

dog-tooth violet
Cultivate in shade or part shade in humus-rich, well-drained soil. Flowers in early spring in shades of rose to mauve, rarely white, with a yellow throat with a brown or rusty red spot. Grows 8 inches (20 cm) high, 12 inches (30 cm) wide. Zones 3–8. Europe and Asia.

## Erythronium hendersonii

Cultivate in shade or part shade in humus-rich, well-drained soil. Flowers

*Erythronium citrinum*

*Erythronium dens-canis,* courtesy of Fritz Kummert

*Eryngium bourgatti*

*Eryngium maritimum,* courtesy of Fritz Kummert

*Erysimum helveticum*

*Erythronium hendersonii*

in April, soft to deep lilac with dark accents. Grows 8 inches (20 cm) high, 6 inches (15 cm) wide. Zones 3–8. Foothills of the Siskiyou Mountains of northern California and southern Oregon.

### *Erythronium howellii*
Cultivate in shade or part shade in humus-rich, well-drained soil. Flowers in spring, cream with a yellow center. Grows 6 inches (15 cm) high and wide. Zones 3–8. Siskiyou Mountains of northern California and southern Oregon.

### *Erythronium* 'Pagoda'
A popular and well-tested plant, probably the best and most vigorous erythronium of all. Cultivate in shade or part shade in humus-rich, well-drained soil. Flowers in spring, yellow. Grows 12 inches (30 cm) high and wide. Zones 3–8. A garden hybrid involving *E. tuolumnense*.

### *Erythronium tuolumnense*
Cultivate in shade or part shade in humus-rich, well-drained soil. Flowers in spring, golden yellow with a green eye. Grows 12–15 inches (30–38 cm) high, 12 inches (30 cm) wide. Zones 3–8. Sierra Nevada of California.

### *Escobaria*
Cactaceae

### *Escobaria missouriensis*
synonym, *Neobesseya missouriensis*
A perennial, low-growing cactus for sun in any well-drained soil. Flowers in spring, cream with pinkish midstripe or yellow or pink, often tinged green. Grows 8 inches (20 cm) high, 10 inches (25 cm) wide. Zones 7–9. United States and northeastern Mexico.

### *Escobaria vivipara*
synonym, *Coryphantha vivipara*
A perennial, low-growing cactus for sun in any well-drained soil. Flowers in spring, pink to purple, yellow, or rarely white, and tinged green, orange, or brown. Grows 6–12 inches (15–30 cm) high, 12 inches (30 cm) wide. Zones 7–9. Southern Canada, the United States, south into Mexico.

### *Euonymus fortunei*
Celastraceae
An evergreen shrub for sun or part shade in any well-drained soil. The cultivar 'Harlequin' flowers in spring, small, yellow-green, insignificant. Grows 6 inches (15 cm) high, 24 inches (60 cm) wide. Zones 4–9. The species is from China, Korea, and Japan.

### *Euphorbia*
spurge
Euphorbiaceae

*Euphorbia* is a genus of hardy, succulent plants with striking foliage and colorful bracts that substitute as "flowers." Avoid the milky sap, which flows from any broken stem or leaf; it is an irritant.

*Erythronium howellii*

*Erythronium* 'Pagoda'

*Erythronium tuolumnense*

*Escobaria missouriensis,* courtesy of Fritz Kummert

*Escobaria vivipara,* courtesy of Fritz Kummert

*Euonymus fortunei* 'Harlequin'

## Euphorbia myrsinites

An evergreen perennial for sun or part shade in any well-drained soil. Flowers in spring, electric yellow. Grows 6 inches (15 cm) high, 24 inches (60 cm) wide. Zones 4–10. Southern Europe.

## Euphorbia polychroma

synonym, *E. epithymoides*
A perennial for sun or part shade in any well-drained soil. Flowers in spring, chartreuse. Grows 18 inches (45 cm) high and wide. Zones 4–9. Central and southeastern Europe to Turkey.

## Euphorbia seguieriana subsp. niciciana

A woody-based perennial for sun or part shade in any well-drained soil. Flowers in summer, bright yellow. Grows 12 inches (30 cm) high, 18 inches (45 cm) wide. Zones 5–10. The species is from central and western Europe, east to Caucasia and Siberia.

## Euryops acraeus

Compositae
An evergreen shrublet for sun or part shade in any good, well-drained soil. Flowers in spring and summer, yellow. Grows 12–18 inches (30–45 cm) high, 18 inches (45 cm) wide. Zones 7–9. Drakensberg Mountains of South Africa.

## Festuca ovina

sheep's fescue
Gramineae
An evergreen perennial grass for sun in sandy, well-drained soil. Flowers in summer in a narrow panicle tinged with purple. Grows 12–24 inches (30–60 cm) high, 18 inches (45 cm) wide. Zones 5–10. Northern temperate regions. Clumps of fine, blue grass add greatly to the texture of the rock garden. Such is the effect from *F. ovina* 'Glauca' and many other

fescue species and cultivars that are readily available.

## Frankenia thymifolia

sea heath
Frankeniaceae
A mat-forming perennial for sun or part shade in sandy, well-drained soil. Flowers in June through August, rose pink. Grows 2 inches (5 cm) high, 12 inches (30 cm) wide. Zones 7–10. Spain and North Africa.

## Fritillaria

fritillary
Liliaceae

## Fritillaria acmopetala

Cultivate in sun or part shade in fertile, well-drained soil. This species and other tall, sturdy fritillaries such as *F. affinis*, *F. gentneri*, and *F. recurva*, can be successfully cultivated under shrubs where the root competition keeps the bulbous perennials comfortably dry in summer.

*Euphorbia myrsinites*

*Euphorbia seguieriana* subsp. *niciciana*

*Festuca ovina* 'Glauca'

*Euphorbia polychroma*

*Euryops acraeus*, courtesy of Ted Kipping

*Frankenia thymifolia*

*Fritillaria acmopetala* flowers in spring, green with tips and base marked reddish brown. Grows 10–18 inches (25–45 cm) high, 12 inches (30 cm) wide. Zones 6–9. Eastern Asia and the western Mediterranean.

## Fritillaria affinis

checker lily, mission bell, narrow-leaved or rice-grain fritillary

synonym, *F. lanceolata*

Cultivate in sun or part shade in humus-rich, well-drained soil. Flowers in spring, green, heavily checkered with brown. Grows 6–40 inches (15–100 cm) high, 6

*Fritillaria acmopetala,* courtesy of Fritz Kummert

*Fritillaria affinis*

inches (15 cm) wide. Zones 5–9. Western North America from British Columbia to central California, east to Idaho.

## Fritillaria bucharica

Cultivate in sun or part shade in fertile, well-drained soil. Flowers in spring, white or off-white with green veins. Grows 6–12 inches (15–30 cm) high, 6 inches (15 cm) wide. Zones 5–8. Central Asia and northern Afghanistan.

## Fritillaria camschatcensis

Kamchatka lily

Cultivate in part shade in fertile, well-drained soil. Flowers in March to May, nearly black, brown, or yellowish green. Grows 12–30 inches (30–75 cm) high, 12 inches (30 cm) wide. Zones 3–8. Asia, Alaska south to Washington.

## Fritillaria crassifolia

synonym, *F. ophioglossifolia*

Cultivate in sun or part shade in humus-rich, limestone scree. Subspecies *crassi-*

*Fritillaria bucharica,* courtesy of Fritz Kummert

*Fritillaria camschatcensis,* courtesy of Fritz Kummert

*folia* flowers in spring, yellowish or greenish with brown tessellations. Grows 6–8 inches (15–20 cm) high, 6 inches (15 cm) wide. Zones 6–9. Southwestern to northeastern Turkey.

## Fritillaria eduardii

Cultivate in sun or part shade in humus-rich, well-drained soil. Flowers in spring, pale orange, rarely reddish or yellow. Grows 24–40 inches (60–100 cm) high, 12 inches (30 cm) wide, sometimes taller. Zones 6–9. Central Asia, Tajikistan, and southern Kashmir.

## Fritillaria gentneri

Gentner's red bell

Rare and like a larger flowering form of *F. recurva* with nonrecurving petals. *Fritillaria gentneri* has rice-grain bulbils. Cultivate in sun or light shade in any good, sandy or gritty, well-drained soil. Keep it dryish in summer. Flowers in spring, orange-red to scarlet, tessellated with yellow. Grows 12–36 inches (30–90 cm) high. Zones 5–9. Jackson

*Fritillaria crassifolia* subsp. *crassifolia,* courtesy of Fritz Kummert

*Fritillaria eduardii,* courtesy of Fritz Kummert

and Josephine Counties of southern Oregon.

### Fritillaria graeca

synonym, *F. guicciardii*

Cultivate in sun in humus-rich, limestone scree. Flowers in spring, green with brown striping. Grows 3–8 inches (7.5–20 cm) high, 6 inches (15 cm) wide. Zones 7–9. Balkan Peninsula, mainly Greece.

### Fritillaria involucrata

Cultivate in sun or part shade in fertile, well-drained soil. Flowers in spring, green marked with purple-brown. Grows 6–10 inches (15–25 cm) high, 6 inches (15 cm) wide. Zones 7–9. Southeastern France and northwestern Italy.

### Fritillaria latifolia

Cultivate in sun in humus-rich scree. Flowers in spring, dark purplish. Grows 6–10 inches (15–25 cm) high, 4 inches (10 cm) wide. Zones 5–8. Northeastern Turkey, Caucasia, and northwestern Iran.

### Fritillaria meleagris

checkered lily, guinea hen flower, guinea hen tulip, snake's head fritillary

Cultivate in sun or part shade in humus-rich, well-drained soil. Flowers in spring, purplish to pink, heavily checkered, occasionally white and veined with green. Grows 6–18 inches (15–45 cm) high, 6 inches (15 cm) wide. Zones 4–9. Nor-

way, England, east through the middle of Europe to Caucasia.

### Fritillaria michailovskyi

Cultivate in sun in humus-rich, well-drained soil. Flowers in April and May, maroon-brown or greenish, yellow tipped. Grows 4–8 inches (10–20 cm) high, 4 inches (10 cm) wide. Zones 5–8. Northeastern Turkey.

### Fritillaria pallidiflora

Cultivate in sun in humus-rich, well-drained soil. Flowers in spring and early

*Fritillaria gentneri*

*Fritillaria graeca*, courtesy of Fritz Kummert

*Fritillaria involucrata*, courtesy of Fritz Kummert

*Fritillaria latifolia*, courtesy of Fritz Kummert

*Fritillaria meleagris*, courtesy of Fritz Kummert

*Fritillaria michailovskyi*

*Fritillaria pallidiflora*, courtesy of Fritz Kummert

summer, pale yellow, tinged green with light reddish brown markings. Grows 6–30 inches (15–75 cm) high, 8 inches (20 cm) wide. Zones 3–8. Central Asia, especially the mountains of the Russian-Chinese border, the Dzungarian Ala Tau or Alataw Shan, and the Tian Shan or Tyan' Shan'.

## Fritillaria pinardii

Cultivate in sun in humus-rich, well-drained soil. Flowers in spring, gray or purplish, yellow-green to orange inside. Grows 6–12 inches (15–30 cm) high, 6 inches (15 cm) wide. Zones 5–8. Turkey and western Iran.

## Fritillaria pudica

yellow bell, yellow fritillary
Cultivate in sun in any good, sandy or gritty, well-drained soil, keeping it dry-

Fritillaria pinardii, courtesy of Fritz Kummert

Fritillaria pudica

ish in summer. Flowers in spring, yellow to orange-yellow. Grows 4–8 inches (10–20 cm) high, 4 inches (10 cm) wide. Zones 3–8. Western North America.

## Fritillaria raddeana

Cultivate in sun in humus-rich, well-drained soil. Flowers in spring, pale yellow. Grows 18–30 inches (45–75 cm) high, 6 inches (15 cm) wide. Zones 4–8. Northeastern Iran and foothills east of the Caspian Sea.

## Fritillaria recurva

red bells, scarlet fritillary
With rice-grain bulbils. Cultivate in sun or light shade in any good, sandy or gritty, well-drained soil. Keep it dryish in summer. Flowers in spring, red to orange, tessellated with yellow. Grows 12–36 inches (30–90 cm) high. Zones 5–9. Northern California and southern Oregon.

Fritillaria raddeana, courtesy of Fritz Kummert

Fritillaria recurva

## Fritillaria uva-vulpis

Cultivate in sun in humus-rich, well-drained soil. Flowers in spring, gray-purple, yellow tipped and yellow within. Grows 6–15 inches (15–38 cm) high, 6 inches (15 cm) wide. Zones 6–8. Northern Iraq, western Iran, and southeastern Turkey.

## Galanthus reginae-olgae

snowdrop
Amaryllidaceae
All the snowdrops, whether fall, winter, or spring blooming, are excellent small bulbous perennials for naturalizing in the woodland and partially shaded rock garden. Cultivate G. reginae-olgae in part shade in moist, fertile, well-drained soil. Flowers in fall, white with apical green markings. Grows 6 inches (15 cm) high, 6 inches (15 cm) wide. Zones 6–9. Sicily, Greece, and southwestern Turkey.

## Gaultheria

Ericaceae

The dwarfer gaultherias, both shrubby or carpeting types, provide lush, ever-green foliage in the cool, moister parts

Fritillaria uva-vulpis, courtesy of Fritz Kummert

of the rock garden. Delicate pendant, waxy bells are followed by berry-like fruits colored white, pink, red, or glowing shades of blue or violet.

## Gaultheria miqueliana

Cultivate in sun or part shade in humus-rich, acid soil. Flowers in late spring, white, followed by white, wintergreen-flavored fruit. Grows 8–12 inches (20–30 cm) high, 18 inches (45 cm) wide. Zones 5–9. Japan, Kuriles, and Aleutians.

## Gaultheria nummularioides

A prostrate shrublet for sun or part shade in humus-rich, acid soil. Flowers in summer, pinkish white, followed by blue-black berries. Grows 4 inches (10 cm) high, 24 inches (60 cm) wide. Zones 6–9. Himalayas and China.

Galanthus reginae-olgae, courtesy of Fritz Kummert

Gaultheria miqueliana

## Gaultheria procumbens

wintergreen, checkerberry, teaberry

A stoloniferous shrublet for part shade in humus-rich, acid soil. Flowers in summer, pinkish white, followed by scarlet fruit. Grows 3–6 inches (7.5–15 cm) high, 24 inches (60 cm) wide. Zones 4–9. Northeastern North America.

## Gaura lindheimeri

Onagraceae

A perennial for sun in any well-drained soil, keeping it dryish in winter. The cultivar 'Siskiyou Pink' flowers in July through October, rose pink. This clone was discovered growing in the garden at Siskiyou Rare Plant Nursery, Medford, Oregon. It was propagated from a single pink-flowering stem, a mutation on a typical white-flowered G. lindheimeri plant. It is dwarfer and more compactly growing than the species. Grows 30 inches (75 cm) high, 36 inches (90 cm) wide. Zones 5–10. The species is from

Gaultheria nummularioides

Gaultheria procumbens

the southern central United States and adjacent Mexico.

## Genista

broom

Leguminosae

## Genista delphinensis

It is generally accepted that this fine, miniature species is a small version of G. sagittalis. Genista delphinensis is a prostrate and mat-forming shrublet for sun in any soil with good drainage. Flowers in late spring, yellow. Grows 3 inches (7.5 cm) high, 12 inches (30 cm) wide. Zones 4–9. Southern France.

## Genista lydia

A wide-spreading shrub for the large rock garden that looks good throughout the year. Though deciduous, the light green, arching stems with pendulous branch tips are most attractive in winter.

Gaura lindheimeri 'Siskiyou Pink'

Genista delphinensis, courtesy of Panayoti Kelaidis

Cultivate in sun in any soil with good drainage. Flowers in late spring, yellow. Grows 12 inches (30 cm) high, 36 inches (90 cm) wide. Zones 5–9. Eastern Balkan Peninsula and Syria.

### Genista pilosa

A deciduous shrub for sun in any soil with good drainage. The cultivar 'Vancouver Gold', an introduction by the University of British Columbia Botanical Garden, flowers in late spring and early summer, yellow. Grows 2–4 inches (5–10 cm) high, 36 inches (90 cm) wide. Zones 5–8. The species is from central and western Europe.

### Genista tinctoria
dyer's greenweed
A deciduous shrub for sun in any soil with good drainage. The cultivar 'Plena' flowers in summer, yellow, doubled. Grows 12 inches (30 cm) high, 24 inches (60 cm) wide. Zones 3–10. The species is from Europe and Turkey to Ukraine.

### Genista villarsii
synonym, *G. pulchella*
A shrublet for sun in any soil with good drainage. Flowers in late spring and early summer, yellow. Grows 2 inches (5 cm) high, 12 inches (30 cm) wide. Zones 6–8. Southeastern France and Croatia.

### Gentiana
gentian
Gentianaceae

Gentians are some of the most admired and sought-after plants for the rock garden and woodland landscape.

### Gentiana acaulis
stemless gentian
Like some other gentians, forms small mats of shiny, evergreen leaves from which rise gorgeous, trumpet-shaped flowers. A perennial for sun or part

Genista pilosa 'Vancouver Gold'

Genista lydia in flower

Genista tinctoria 'Plena'

Genista lydia in winter

Genista villarsii

shade in fertile, well-drained soil. Flowers in spring and early summer, deep blue, spotted green inside. Grows 3 inches (7.5 cm) high, 12 inches (30 cm) wide. Zones 3–9. Alps, Carpathians, northern Spain, Italy, and Croatia.

## Gentiana algida
A perennial for sun or part shade in fertile, well-drained, acid soil with grit added. Flowers in summer to fall, white speckled with purple-blue. Grows 4 inches (10 cm) high, 8 inches (20 cm) wide. Zones 2–8. Northeastern Asia and western North America.

## Gentiana asclepiadea
willow gentian
A tall, elegant perennial, only for the largest rock garden or background. Makes an eye-catching, late-season display, especially when the blue-flowered form is massed with the white *G. asclepiadea* 'Alba'. Cultivate *G. asclepiadea* in sun or part shade in fertile, well-drained soil. Flowers in July to fall, blue to purple-blue, or white. Grows 18–30 inches (45–75 cm) high, 24 inches (60 cm)

Gentiana acaulis

Gentiana algida

wide. Zones 5–9. The species is from central Europe, Turkey, and Caucasia.

## Gentiana calycosa
explorer's gentian
A perennial for sun or part shade in fertile, well-drained, moist soil. Flowers in summer, pale to deep blue, spotted green inside. Grows 8–12 inches (20–30 cm) high, 12–18 inches (30–45 cm) wide. Zones 4–8. British Columbia to California and Montana.

## Gentiana cruciata
A perennial for sun or part shade in fertile, well-drained soil. Flowers in summer, blue to purple, marked green. Grows 6–12 inches (15–30 cm) high, 12 inches (30 cm) wide. Zones 5–8. Europe, central and western Asia.

## Gentiana frigida
A perennial for sun or part shade in fertile, well-drained soil. Flowers in sum-

Gentiana asclepiadea, courtesy of Fritz Kummert

Gentiana asclepiadea 'Alba'

mer to early fall, yellowish white, spotted and veined blue. Grows 3–4 inches (7.5–10 cm) high, 8 inches (20 cm) wide. Zones 5–8. Carpathians, southwestern Bulgaria, and the Alps of central Austria.

## Gentiana newberryi
alpine gentian
A perennial for sun or part shade in fertile, well-drained soil. Keep it moist at all times. Flowers in August, deep blue, interior white with green spots. Grows 4

Gentiana calycosa, courtesy of Panayoti Kelaidis

Gentiana cruciata, courtesy of Fritz Kummert

Gentiana frigida, courtesy of Fritz Kummert

inches (10 cm) high, 8 inches (20 cm) wide. Zones 4–8. Southern Oregon, northern California to northwestern Nevada.

## Gentiana paradoxa

A perennial for sun or part shade in fertile, well-drained soil. Flowers in late summer, blue with white and green markings. Grows 4–6 inches (10–15 cm) high, 12 inches (30 cm) wide. Zones 5–8. Caucasus Mountains.

Gentiana newberryi

Gentiana paradoxa, courtesy of Fritz Kummert

Gentiana scabra

## Gentiana scabra

A perennial for sun or part shade in fertile, well-drained soil. Flowers in fall, blue to purple-blue. Grows 8–12 inches (20–30 cm) high, 12 inches (30 cm) wide. Zones 5–9. China, Korea, and Japan.

## Gentiana septemfida
crested gentian

An easy-to-grow and reliable, long-lived perennial for the rock garden. Cultivate in sun or part shade in fertile, well-drained soil. Flowers in August, dark blue. Grows 4 inches (10 cm) high, 12–18 inches (30–45 cm) wide. Zones 2–8. Turkey, Caucasia, and Iran. *Gentiana septemfida* var. *lagodechiana* (synonym, *G. lagodechiana*) is more prostrate, less robust, and has fewer flowers in each cluster.

Gentiana septemfida

Gentiana sino-ornata, courtesy of Roy Herold

## Gentiana sino-ornata

A perennial for sun or part shade in moist, fertile, acid soil. Flowers in fall, rich blue with some variation to purple-pink. Grows 8 inches (20 cm) high, 12–18 inches (30–45 cm) wide. Zones 5–8. China.

## Gentiana verna
spring gentian

A perennial for sun or part shade in moist, fertile, well-drained soil. Flowers in spring, blue. Grows 3 inches (7.5 cm) high, 6 inches (15 cm) wide. Zones 4–8. Europe and Asia.

**Subspecies**. *Gentiana verna* subsp. *tergestina* (synonym, *G. angulosa*) flowers in spring, sky blue. Grows 3 inches (7.5 cm) high, 12 inches (30 cm) wide. Apennines, Bulgaria, and Turkey.

Gentiana verna, courtesy of Panayoti Kelaidis

Gentiana verna subsp. *tergestina*, courtesy of Fritz Kummert

## Geranium
crane's bill
Geraniaceae

The mountain geraniums mentioned here are all excellent and easy-to-grow plants for the rock garden, tolerant of nearly any good, well-drained soil, even alkaline.

## Geranium cinereum

Cultivate in sun or part shade in any good, well-drained soil. Flowers in late spring and early summer, white or in shades of pink, with purple or white veining. Grows 6 inches (15 cm) high, 12–18 inches (30–45 cm) wide. Zones 4–10. Pyrenees.

**Cultivars and Subspecies**. *Geranium cinereum* 'Ballerina' flowers in May and June and intermittently to fall, lilac pink with a purple-red center and veining. Grows 4 inches (10 cm) high, 12 inches (30 cm) wide.

*Geranium cinereum* subsp. *subcaulescens* flowers in late spring and early summer, magenta-red with a black center. Grows 6 inches (15 cm) high, 12–18 inches (30–45 cm) wide. Italy, the Balkan Peninsula, and Turkey.

*Geranium cinereum* subsp. *subcaulescens* 'Splendens' flowers in late spring and early summer, bright red-pink with a black-red basal blotch with a white margin. Grows 6 inches (15 cm) high, 12–18 inches (30–45 cm) wide.

## Geranium dalmaticum

A perennial, trailing by underground rhizomes, for sun or part shade in any good, well-drained soil. Flowers in early summer, clear pink. Grows 6 inches (15 cm) high, 18 inches (45 cm) wide. Zones 3–9. Southwestern Balkan Peninsula.

## Geranium farreri
synonym, *G. napuligerum*
A perennial for sun or part shade in humus-rich scree. Flowers in early summer, light pink. Grows 4–8 inches (10–20 cm) high, 16 inches (40 cm) wide. Zones 4–8. Western China.

## Geranium himalayense
synonym, *G. grandiflorum*
A long-blooming perennial that is usually too large and spreading (by seed and underground rhizomes) for most rock gardens but well worth positioning in the background or nearby. Cultivate

*Geranium dalmaticum*, courtesy of Fritz Kummert

*Geranium cinereum*

*Geranium cinereum* subsp. *subcaulescens*

*Geranium farreri*, courtesy of Fritz Kummert

*Geranium cinereum* 'Ballerina'

*Geranium cinereum* subsp. *subcaulescens* 'Splendens'

*Geranium himalayense*

in sun in humus-rich, well-drained, moist soil. Flowers in May through July, violet-blue. Grows 16 inches (40 cm) high, 24 inches (60 cm) wide. Zones 3–8. Himalayas. Two more appropriately sized cultivars are *G. himalayense* 'Gravetye' and 'Plenum' (synonym, 'Birch Double'), the latter with purplish blue flowers, doubled.

## Geranium renardii

A perennial for sun or part shade in any good, well-drained soil. Flowers in sum-

*Geranium renardii*

*Geranium sanguineum* 'Alpenglow'

mer, white, veined with purple. Grows 12 inches (30 cm) high and wide. Zones 5–8. Caucasus Mountains.

## Geranium sanguineum
bloody crane's bill

A perennial for sun or part shade in any good, well-drained soil. Zones 3–9. Europe, northern Turkey, and Caucasia.

**Cultivars and Variety.** *Geranium sanguineum* 'Alpenglow' flowers in May through August, rich rose red. Grows 6 inches (15 cm) high, 24 inches (60 cm) wide.

*Geranium sanguineum* 'Nanum', dwarf bloody crane's bill, flowers in May through August, rose red. Grows 4 inches (10 cm) high, 18 inches (45 cm) wide.

*Geranium sanguineum* 'Nanum', courtesy of Armen Gevjan

*Geranium sanguineum* var. *striatum* (synonyms, *G. sanguineum* var. *lancastriense*, *G. sanguineum* var. *prostratum*) flowers in May through August, pale flesh pink, veined crimson. Grows 6 inches (15 cm) high, 24 inches (60 cm) wide. Zones 3–8. Walney, an island off the northwestern coast of England.

## Geranium sessiliflorum subsp. novaezelandiae 'Nigricans' × G. traversii

A perennial for sun or part shade in any good, well-drained soil. Flowers in summer, pinkish, fading white. Grows 6 inches (15 cm) high, 12 inches (30 cm) wide. Zones 7–10. *Geranium sessiliflorum* is a native of New Zealand, *G. traversii* of the Chatham Islands, New Zealand. See *Pimelea prostrata* for a photograph of the foliage of the parent, *G. sessiliflorum* subsp. *novaezelandiae* 'Nigricans'.

*Geranium sanguineum* var. *striatum*

*Geranium sessiliflorum* subsp. *novaezelandiae* 'Nigricans' × *G. traversii*

## Geranium stapfianum
synonym, *G. forrestii*
With cheerful flowers and foliage, a deciduous perennial with underground stolons and with silver-marbled, bright green leaves that look good in spring and summer. Cultivate in sun or part shade, for best flowering, in fertile scree. Flowers in early summer, pink with a white eye. Grows 6 inches (15 cm) high, 18 inches (45 cm) wide. Zones 6–8. China and Tibet.

## Geum
avens
Rosaceae

## Geum montanum
alpine avens
synonym, *Sieversia montana*
A perennial with creeping rhizomes for sun or part shade in fertile, well-drained soil. Flowers in early summer, golden yellow. Grows 6–12 inches (15–30 cm) high, 12 inches (30 cm) wide. Zones 6–9. Mountains of central and southern Europe.

## Geum reptans
creeping avens
A mat-forming perennial, spreading by long, red, strawberry-like runners, for sun or part shade in humus-rich scree.

Flowers in early summer, yellow. Grows 6–10 inches (15–25 cm) high, 24 inches (60 cm) wide. Zones 5–8. Alps, Carpathians, and mountains of the Balkan Peninsula.

## Gladiolus
corn flag, sword lily
Iridaceae

*Geum montanum,* courtesy of Fritz Kummert

*Geum reptans,* courtesy of Fritz Kummert

## Gladiolus illyricus
A cormous perennial for sun in fertile, well-drained soil. Flowers in summer, red to red-purple. Grows 12–20 inches (30–50 cm) high. Zones 6–9. Southern and western Europe, including southern England, and Turkey and Caucasia.

## Gladiolus imbricatus
A cormous perennial for sun in fertile, well-drained soil. Flowers in summer,

*Gladiolus illyricus,* courtesy of Fritz Kummert

*Gladiolus imbricatus,* courtesy of Fritz Kummert

*Geranium stapfianum*

reddish to violet-purple. Grows 18–30 inches (45–75 cm) high. Zones 6–9. Central and southern Europe.

### *Glaucidium palmatum*
Ranunculaceae

Looking like a large *Anemone*, a most desirable rhizomatous perennial for deep, humus-rich, acid soil and shade that is best increased by seed, although it is said that root cuttings are possible. Flowers in spring and early summer, mauve to pinkish lilac, occasionally white. Cultivate in shade or part shade in well-drained soil, keeping it always moist. Grows 12–18 inches (30–45 cm) high, 12 inches (30 cm) wide. Zones 6–9. Mountains of Honshu and Hokkaido, Japan.

### *Globularia*
globe daisy
Globulariaceae

### *Globularia repens*
synonyms, *G. cordifolia* 'Nana', *G. nana*

An evergreen subshrub for sun in any good, well-drained soil. It flowers best in limy scree. Flowers in early summer, lavender-blue. Grows 3 inches (7.5 cm) high, 8 inches (20 cm) wide. Zones 5–10. Mountains of southwestern Europe.

### *Globularia trichosantha*
An evergreen woody perennial. Cultivate in sun in any good, well-drained soil. Flowers in late spring, blue. Grows 8 inches (20 cm) high, 18 inches (45 cm)

*Glaucidium palmatum,* courtesy of Fritz Kummert

wide. Zones 5–10. Eastern Balkan Peninsula and Turkey.

### *Goodyera oblongifolia*
giant rattlesnake plantain
Orchidaceae

A most attractive evergreen terrestrial woodland orchid with big, 4-inch (10-cm) leaves that are dark green, veined white. Cultivate in shade or part shade in humus-rich, acid soil. Flowers in summer, white. Flower spikes 18 inches (45 cm) tall. Zones 4–10. Western Canada south to New Mexico, Arizona, and California.

### *Gymnocarpium*
Woodsiaceae

### *Gymnocarpium dryopteris*
oak fern

A rhizomatous perennial for shade or part shade in humus-rich, well-drained, moist soil. Grows 8–12 inches (20–30 cm) high, 24 inches (60 cm) wide. Zones 3–8. Northern temperate regions and mountains farther south.

*Globularia repens*

*Globularia trichosantha*

### *Gymnocarpium robertianum*
limestone or northern oak fern

A rhizomatous perennial for shade or part shade in humus-rich, well-drained, moist soil. Grows 8–18 inches (20–45 cm) high, 24 inches (60 cm) wide. Zones 4–8. Northern temperate regions and mountains farther south but usually in limestone areas.

### *Gymnospermium albertii*
Berberidaceae

*Gymnospermium* is a small genus of unusual members of the barberry family, usually cultivated in an alpine house or cold frame. *Gymnospermium albertii* is a rhizomatous, deciduous perennial for sun in well-drained, gritty or sandy soil. Flowers in early spring, yellow, veined red-brown on the back. Grows 8–10 inches (20–25 cm) high, 8 inches (20 cm) wide. Zones 4–8. Central Asia.

*Goodyera oblongifolia*

*Gymnocarpium dryopteris*

## Gypsophila
Caryophyllaceae

### Gypsophila aretioides

A hummock-forming perennial for sun in humus-rich, limestone scree with protection from winter wetness, or in the alpine house. Flowers in early summer, white. Grows 1/2 inch (1 cm) high, 5 inches (12.5 cm) wide. Zones 4–7. High mountains of Iran and Caucasia.

### Gypsophila briquetiana

A cushion-forming perennial for sun in humus-rich, limestone scree. Flowers in early summer, pinkish white with a maroon eye. Grows 4 inches (10 cm) high, 8 inches (20 cm) wide. Zones 4–8. Turkey.

### Gypsophila cerastioides

A tufted to mat-forming perennial for sun or part shade in humus-rich, well-drained soil. Flowers in June to August, white with purple lines. Grows 4 inches (10 cm) high, 12 inches (30 cm) wide. Zones 4–8. Kashmir.

### Gypsophila repens

A mat-forming perennial for sun in any good, well-drained soil. The cultivar 'Rosea' flowers in June through August, rose pink. Grows 6 inches (15 cm) high, 18 inches (45 cm) wide. Zones 4–8. The species is from mountains of central and southern Europe.

*Gypsophila briquetiana*

*Gypsophila cerastioides*

*Gymnocarpium robertianum*

*Gypsophila repens* 'Rosea'

*Gymnospermium albertii*, courtesy of Fritz Kummert

*Gypsophila aretioides*, courtesy of Panayoti Kelaidis

 **H** 

## Haberlea ferdinandi-coburgii
Gesneriaceae

synonym, *H. rhodopensis var. ferdinandi-coburgii*

A perennial for part shade in humus-rich, well-drained soil. Flowers in spring and early summer, white flecked with golden inside, lavender outside. Grows 4 inches (10 cm) high, 12 inches (30 cm) wide. Zones 4–8. Bulgaria.

## Hacquetia epipactus
Umbelliferae

A perennial for part shade in humus-rich, acid sand or heavy, alkaline loam. Gold spring flowers, green bracts. Grows 6 inches (15 cm) high, 10 inches (25 cm) wide. Zones 5–8. Alps.

*Haberlea ferdinandi-coburgii*

## Hakonechloa macra
Gramineae

The cultivar 'Aureola', variegated Japanese forest grass, is a slowly growing, deciduous perennial, spreading by underground runners, beautiful in the rock garden and containers. With predominantly golden foliage, red highlights occur in full sun, which it tolerates with sufficient moisture. 'Albo Striata' is another variegated cultivar, having thin lines of creamy white on green foliage. Cultivate in shade or part shade in humus-rich soil. Flowers in late summer in yellow-green spikes, fading light brown. Grows 10 inches (25 cm) high, 18 inches (45 cm) wide. Zones 5–9. The species is from Japan.

*Hacquetia epipactus*

## ×Halimiocistus wintonensis
Cistaceae

An evergreen shrub for sun in any good, well-drained soil, preferably dry, especially in winter. Flowers in summer, white with a purple spot at each petal base. Grows 18 inches (45 cm) high, 36 inches (90 cm) wide. Zones 7–10. A garden hybrid, *Halimium ocymoides × Cistus salviifolius.*

## Halimium ocymoides
Cistaceae

An evergreen shrub for sun in any good, well-drained soil. Flowers in spring and early summer, yellow with a black and purple eye. Grows 24 inches (60 cm) high, 48 inches (120 cm) wide. Zones 8–10. Spain and Portugal.

## Haplocarpha rueppellii
Compositae

A perennial, forming mats by stolons, for sun in well-drained, poor soil. Flowers in late spring and summer, golden yellow. Grows 6 inches (15 cm) high, 36 inches (90 cm) wide. Zones 8–10. Mountains of East Africa and Ethiopia.

*×Halimiocistus wintonensis,* courtesy of Fritz Kummert

*Halimium ocymoides,* courtesy of Fritz Kummert

*Hakonechloa macra* 'Aureola'

## Haplopappus glutinosus

Compositae

synonym, *H. coronopifolius*

A wide, mat-forming perennial for sun in any good, well-drained soil. Flowers in summer, yellow. Grows 6 inches (15 cm) high, 30 inches (75 cm) wide. Zones 6–9. Chile and Argentina.

## Hebe

Scrophulariaceae

The hebes are a group of shrubby, *Veronica*-like plants, all from New Zealand. They do best in moderate and mild winter climates. Many have showy flowers, but all have intriguing foliage that varies tremendously from one species to another.

## Hebe buchananii

A shrub for sun or part shade in any good, well-drained soil. The cultivar 'Minor' flowers in late spring, white, but rarely produced. Grows 4 inches (10 cm) high, 12 inches (30 cm) wide. Zones 7–10. The species is from New Zealand.

Haplocarpha rueppellii, courtesy of Fritz Kummert

*Haplopappus glutinosus*

## Hebe cupressoides

An evergreen shrub for sun or part shade in any good, well-drained soil. The cultivar 'Boughton Dome' rarely flowers. Grows 12–18 inches (30–45 cm) high, 18 inches (45 cm) wide. Zones 7–10. The species is from alpine areas of South Island, New Zealand.

## Hebe ochracea

The cultivar 'James Sterling' is a flat-topped, evergreen shrublet for sun or part shade in any good, well-drained soil. Flowers in late spring, white. Grows 10 inches (25 cm) high, 16 inches (40 cm) wide. Zones 7–10. The species is from mountains of West Nelson, South Island, New Zealand.

## Hebe pinguifolia

An evergreen shrub for sun or part shade in any good, well-drained soil. *Hebe pinguifolia* 'Pagei' (synonym, *Hebe* 'Pagei') flowers in summer, white. Grows 8 inches (20 cm) high, 24 inches (60 cm) wide. Zones 7–10. The species is from alpine areas of South Island, New Zealand.

Hebe buchananii 'Minor'

Hebe cupressoides 'Boughton Dome'

## Hebe 'Youngii'

An evergreen shrub for sun or part shade in any good, well-drained soil. Flowers in summer, violet. Grows 10 inches (25 cm) high, 18 inches (45 cm) wide. Zones 8–10. A garden hybrid, *H. elliptica* × *H. pimeleoides*.

## Hedera helix

English ivy

Araliaceae

Ivies are easy-to-grow, hardy, handsome, evergreen foliage plants, provid-

Hebe ochracea 'James Sterling'

Hebe pinguifolia 'Pagei'

Hebe 'Youngii'

ing an outstanding range of leaf color and texture. In time, even the dwarfest will begin spreading beyond the allotted bounds, usually due to a gradual reversion to more normal foliage and vigor. Cultivate in sun or part shade in any good soil. Zones 5–10. The species is from Europe, Scandinavia, and Russia.

**Cultivars**. *Hedera helix* 'Erecta', cathedral ivy, is an evergreen shrub. Flowers in spring, greenish white. Grows 30 inches (75 cm) high, 24 inches (60 cm) wide.

*Hedera helix* 'Spetchley' is an evergreen creeping shrub. Nonflowering. Grows 6 inches (15 cm) high, 30 inches (75 cm) wide.

## Helianthemum
rock or sun rose
Cistaceae

The sun roses require annual shearing after they flower to maintain their vigor and longevity. Sometimes this results in a second flowering. All are heat-tolerant plants for the drier rock garden.

*Hedera helix* 'Erecta'

*Hedera helix* 'Spetchley'

## Helianthemum appeninum
An evergreen shrublet for sun in any good, well-drained soil. Flowers in late spring to midsummer, white, yellow at base. Grows 12–18 inches (30–45 cm) high, 18 inches (45 cm) wide. Zones 5–10. Western and southern Europe.

*Helianthemum appeninum,* courtesy of Fritz Kummert

*Helianthemum canum*

*Helianthemum nummularium* 'Bright Spot'

## Helianthemum canum
An evergreen shrublet for sun in any good, well-drained soil. Flowers in mid-spring and summer, yellow. Grows 6–12 inches (15–30 cm) high, 12 inches (30 cm) wide. Zones 5–10. Central and southern Europe. See under *Aphyllanthes monspeliensis* for another photograph.

## Helianthemum nummularium
An evergreen shrub for sun in any good, well-drained soil. Grows 6 inches (15 cm) high, 24 inches (60 cm) wide. Zones 5–10. Europe.

**Cultivars**. *Helianthemum nummularium* 'Bright Spot' flowers in May to July, coppery red.

*Helianthemum nummularium* 'Eloise' flowers in May and June, yellow with an orange eye.

*Helianthemum nummularium* 'Eloise'

## Helichrysum

everlasting flower
Compositae
Helichrysums are known for their foliage, sometimes beautiful, often a bit bizarre, and for their flower heads, which are often "everlasting straw flowers."

## Helichrysum frigidum

A subshrub for sun in gritty, well-drained soil. It does best in the alpine house. Flowers in summer, white. Grows 6 inches (15 cm) high, 8 inches (20 cm) wide. Zones 8–10. Corsica and Sardinia.

## Helichrysum italicum subsp. serotinum

curry plant
A perennial for sun in any good, well-drained soil. Flowers in summer, golden yellow. Grows 16 inches (40 cm) high, 24 inches (60 cm) wide. Zones 7–10. Southwestern Europe.

## Helichrysum milfordiae

A mat-forming, stoloniferous subshrub for sun in gritty, well-drained soil with

*Helichrysum frigidum*

*Helichrysum italicum* subsp. *serotinum*

protection from winter wet, or in the alpine house. Flowers in spring, white. Grows 2 inches (5 cm) high, 12 inches (30 cm) wide. Zones 7–9. Mountains of Lesotho and KwaZulu-Natal, South Africa.

## Helichrysum 'Mo's Gold'

A woody-based perennial for sun in any good, well-drained soil. Flowers in September and October, golden yellow. Grows 4 inches (10 cm) high, 18 inches (45 cm) wide. Zones 8–10. Possibly a hybrid, the parental species unknown.

## Helichrysum scapiforme

A woody-based perennial for sun in any good, well-drained soil. Flowers in summer, white. Grows 6 inches (15 cm) high, 18 inches (45 cm) wide. Zones 4–9. Mountains of Lesotho, southern Africa.

*Helichrysum milfordiae* in crimson-colored bud, courtesy of Fritz Kummert

*Helichrysum* 'Mo's Gold', courtesy of Ted Kipping

## Helichrysum selago

synonym, *Ozothamnus selago*
A shrub for sun in any good, well-drained soil. Flowers in summer, creamy white. Grows 8–12 inches (20–30 cm) high, 12 inches (30 cm) wide. Zones 6–9. South Island, New Zealand.

## Helichrysum thianschanicum

A perennial for sun in any good, well-drained soil. The cultivar 'Golden Baby'

*Helichrysum scapiforme*

*Helichrysum selago*

*Helichrysum thianschanicum* 'Golden Baby'

(synonym, 'Goldkind') flowers in summer, gold. Grows 12 inches (30 cm) high, 18 inches (45 cm) wide. Zones 6–9. The species is from Turkistan.

## Helleborus
hellebore
Ranunculaceae

Hellebore species and cultivars feature big, bold foliage for the woodland or rock garden background. Most have early-season flowers that brighten the winter and early spring landscape.

### Helleborus argutifolius
synonyms, *H. corsicus, H. lividus* subsp. *corsicus*
A perennial for sun or part shade in humus-rich, well-drained soil. Flowers in winter and early spring, yellow-green. Grows 24–36 inches (60–90 cm) high, 36 inches (90 cm) wide. Zones 5–9. Corsica and Sardinia.

### Helleborus foetidus
A perennial for sun or part shade in humus-rich, well-drained soil. Flowers in February to April, pale green. Grows 18 inches (45 cm) high and wide. Zones 5–9. Western Europe.

### Helleborus niger
Christmas rose
A perennial for sun or part shade in humus-rich, well-drained soil. Flowers in winter and spring, white, aging to pinkish. Grows 12 inches (30 cm) high,

18 inches (45 cm) wide. Zones 3–9. Central Europe.

### Helleborus orientalis
Lenten rose
An often evergreen perennial for sun or part shade in humus-rich, well-drained soil. Flowers in late winter and spring, white, cream, green, or pinkish mauve to purple. Grows 18 inches (45 cm) high, 24 inches (60 cm) wide. Zones 3–8. Greece and western Turkey.

*Helleborus foetidus*

*Helleborus niger*

**Cultivars**. *Helleborus orientalis* 'Purple Strain' flowers in late winter and spring, blackish maroon.

*Helleborus orientalis* 'Medallion' is a Siskiyou Rare Plant Nursery selection of the *H. orientalis* subsp. *guttatus* type, with substantial flowers of white with a contrasting center of dark purple spotting. Flowers in late winter and spring.

*Helleborus orientalis* 'Purple Strain'

*Helleborus orientalis* 'Medallion'

*Helleborus argutifolius*

*Helleborus orientalis*

*Helleborus torquatus*, courtesy of Fritz Kummert

## *Helleborus torquatus*

A deciduous perennial for sun or part shade in humus-rich, well-drained soil. Flowers in late winter and spring, dark purple. Grows 18 inches (45 cm) high and wide. Zones 6–9. Balkan Peninsula.

## *Helleborus viridis*

A deciduous perennial for sun or part shade in humus-rich, well-drained soil. Flowers in late winter and spring, lime green. Grows 8–10 inches (20–25 cm) high, 18 inches (45 cm) wide. Zones 6–9. Central and southern Europe.

## *Hepatica*
liverleaf
Ranunculaceae

Liverleafs never fail to charm with their very early spring flowers and attractive foliage, neatly variegated in some.

## *Hepatica acutiloba*

A perennial for part shade in humus-rich, well-drained soil. Flowers in March and April, pink or white. Grows 6 inches

*Helleborus viridis*

*Hepatica acutiloba*, courtesy of Armen Gevjan

(15 cm) high, 9 inches (22 cm) wide. Zones 4–7. Eastern North America.

## *Hepatica americana*

A perennial for part shade in humus-rich, well-drained soil. Flowers in March and April, blue. Grows 5 inches (12.5 cm) high, 6 inches (15 cm) wide. Zones 3–7. Eastern North America.

## *Hepatica* 'Millstream Merlin'

A perennial for part shade in humus-rich, well-drained soil. Flowers in March and April, deep purple-blue, semidoubled. Grows 6 inches (15 cm) high and wide. Zones 4–8. A garden hybrid, *H. americana* × *H. transsilvanica*, originated by H. Lincoln Foster, Connecticut.

## *Hepatica nobilis*

synonyms, *H. triloba, Anemone hepatica*
A perennial for part shade in humus-rich, well-drained soil. Flowers in early spring, blue-purple to white or pink.

*Hepatica americana*, courtesy of Armen Gevjan

*Hepatica* 'Millstream Merlin'

Grows 6 inches (15 cm) high and wide. Zones 4–8. Europe but not the extreme north or south.

## *Hermodactylus tuberosus*
snake's head or widow iris
Iridaceae
A tuberous perennial, a close *Iris* relative, that goes dormant shortly after flowering and is best given a warm, dry

*Hepatica nobilis*

*Hepatica nobilis*, pink form, courtesy of Fritz Kummert

*Hermodactylus tuberosus*, courtesy of Franz Hadacek

summer interval. Cultivate in sun in any good, well-drained soil. Flowers in early spring, light green with brownish violet shading. Grows 12–18 inches (30–45 cm) high. Zones 7–9. Southern Europe.

## *Hesperochiron*
Hydrophyllaceae

### *Hesperochiron californicus*

A perennial for sun in any good, well-drained soil. Keep it moist in spring and use minimal moisture during the dormant summer season. Flowers in late spring, white to bluish white. Grows 2 inches (5 cm) high, 4 inches (10 cm) wide. Zones 6–9. California, Oregon, Montana, and Utah.

### *Hesperochiron pumilus*

A perennial for sun in any good, well-drained soil. Keep it moist in spring and use minimal moisture during the dormant summer season. Flowers in late spring, white veined with lavender and

*Hesperochiron californicus,* courtesy of Fritz Kummert

*Hesperochiron pumilus*

yellow at the base. Grows 2 inches (5 cm) high, 4 inches (10 cm) wide. Zones 6–9. Washington to Idaho, California, Nevada, and Arizona.

## *Heuchera*
alumroot, coral bells
Saxifragaceae

Heucheras have spectacular, variegated foliage in many shades of green, gray, and purple with contrasting veining and markings of silver. All but a few of the newer cultivars grow too large for the rock garden and are better reserved for the border; a good exception is *Heuchera* 'Can Can'.

### *Heuchera* 'Can Can'

One of the dwarfer hybrids, small enough for the rock garden. A perennial for sun or part shade in any good, well-drained soil. Flowers in early summer, greenish and white. Grows 8 inches (20 cm) high, 18 inches (15 cm) wide, and in flower, 18 inches (45 cm) high. Zones 4–9.

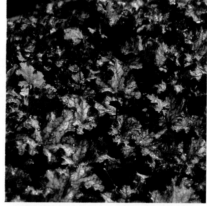

*Heuchera* 'Can Can'

*Heuchera* 'Chiqui'

### *Heuchera* 'Chiqui'

A perennial for sun or part shade in fertile, well-drained soil. Flowers in early summer, shrimp pink. Grows 24 inches (60 cm) high, 18 inches (45 cm) wide. Zones 4–9. A garden hybrid, *H. cylindrica* × *H. sanguinea*.

### *Heuchera cylindrica*

A perennial for sun or part shade in fertile, well-drained soil. Flowers in spring, cream white. The dwarf alpine form illustrated grows 8 inches (20 cm) high and wide. Zones 4–8. The species is from northwestern North America.

*Heuchera cylindrica,* dwarf alpine form, courtesy of Fritz Kummert

*Heuchera rubescens* var. *alpicola*

## *Heuchera rubescens* var. *alpicola*

reddish heuchera

A perennial for sun or part shade in fertile, well-drained soil. Flowers in spring, pink and white. Grows 18 inches (45 cm) high, 12 inches (30 cm) wide. Zones 4–8. Oregon and California.

## *Hippocrepis comosa*

horseshoe vetch
Leguminosae

A woody-based perennial for sun in well-drained soil, preferably alkaline. Flowers in spring and summer, yellow. Grows 3 inches (7.5 cm) high, 24 inches (60 cm) wide. Zones 7–9. Central and southern Europe to northern Africa.

## *Horminum pyrenaicum*

dragon mouth, Pyrenean dead nettle
Labiatae

A perennial for sun or part shade in any good, well-drained soil. Flowers in mid-summer, violet-blue. Grows 12 inches (30 cm) high and wide. Zones 5–9. Alps and Pyrenees.

## *Hosta*

plantain lily
Liliaceae

In the ever-growing world of hosta hybrids there are many dwarf forms from which to choose for the rock garden. These are mainly foliage plants and are usually for partly shaded to fully shaded areas, or for sun given humus-rich, moist soil.

## *Hosta* 'Golden Tiara'

A perennial for part shade in humus-rich, well-drained, moist soil. Flowers in June to August, purple. Grows 8 inches (20 cm) high, 12 inches (30 cm) wide. Zones 4–9.

## *Hosta tardiflora*

A perennial for part shade in humus-rich, well-drained, moist soil. Flowers in fall, mauve to mauve-purple. Grows 10 inches (25 cm) high, 6 inches (15 cm) wide. Zones 4–9. Japan, but does not occur in the wild.

## *Houstonia caerulea*

bluets, innocence, Quaker ladies
Rubiaceae
synonym, *Hedyotis caerulea*

A perennial for sun or part shade in humus-rich, moist soil. Flowers in spring, light blue. Grows 3–6 inches (7.5–15 cm) high, 6 inches (15 cm) wide. Zones 5–8. Eastern North America.

## *Hutchinsia alpina*

chamois cress
Cruciferae
synonym, *Pritzelago alpina*

An evergreen perennial for sun or part shade in any well-drained soil, preferably alkaline. Flowers in late spring and summer, white. Grows 4 inches (10 cm) high, 8 inches (20 cm) wide. Zones 5–9. Mountains of Europe.

*Hippocrepis comosa,* courtesy of Fritz Kummert

*Hosta* 'Golden Tiara'

*Houstonia caerulea*

*Horminum pyrenaicum,* courtesy of Franz Hadacek

*Hosta tardiflora,* courtesy of Fritz Kummert

*Hutchinsia alpina*

### Hydrangea macrophylla
Hydrangeaceae
A shrub for part shade in humus-rich, well-drained soil. The cultivar 'Pia', miniature bigleaf hydrangea, flowers in June through August, pink. With annual fall removal of the stems of spent flowers it is easy to keep this dwarf cultivar 18 inches (45 cm) high and wide. Zones 6–9. The species is from Japan.

### Hylomecon japonicum
Papaveraceae
A perennial for part shade in humus-rich, well-drained, moist soil. Flowers in late spring, yellow. Grows 12 inches (30 cm) high and wide. Zones 6–9. Japan, Korea, and China.

### Hymenoxys
Compositae

### Hymenoxys grandiflora
synonyms, *Rydbergia grandiflora*, *Tetraneuris grandiflora*
A perennial, or monocarpic, for sun in scree. Flowers in summer, deep yellow.

Grows 6–12 inches (15–30 cm) high, 12 inches (30 cm) wide. Zones 4–8. Idaho, Montana, Utah, and Colorado.

### Hymenoxys scaposa
synonyms, *Actinella scaposa, Tetraneuris scaposa*
A perennial for sun in scree. Flowers in late spring and summer, yellow. Grows 12 inches (30 cm) high, 18 inches (45 cm) wide. Zones 5–8. Utah, Colorado, and Kansas.

### Hypericum
Hypericaceae

Hypericums are reliable, summer-flowering plants. All feature five-petaled flowers in shades of yellow, centered with a prominent sunburst of long, exaggerated stamens.

### Hypericum ericoides
An evergreen shrublet for sun in any good, well-drained soil. Flowers in summer, yellow. Grows 3–6 inches (7.5–15 cm) high, 8 inches (20 cm) wide. Zones 7–9. Spain and North Africa.

### Hypericum olympicum
A woody-based perennial for sun in any good, well-drained soil. The cultivar 'Citrinum' flowers in summer, lemon yellow. Grows 12 inches (30 cm) high, 18 inches (45 cm) wide. Zones 6–9. The species is from the Balkan Peninsula to western and southern Turkey.

### Hypoxis hirsuta
stargrass
Hypoxidaceae
A cormous perennial for sun or part shade in any good, well-drained soil. Flowers in April through August, yellow. Grows 8–12 inches (20–30 cm) high, 6 inches (15 cm) wide. Zones 3–8. Eastern North America.

### Iberis
candytuft
Cruciferae

Candytufts are easy to grow and fill the early rock garden with color, along with *Arabis, Aubrieta, Aurinia,* and *Phlox*.

Hydrangea macrophylla 'Pia'

Hymenoxys grandiflora, courtesy of Fritz Kummert

Hypericum ericoides

Hylomecon japonicum

Hymenoxys scaposa, courtesy of Fritz Kummert

Hypericum olympicum 'Citrinum', courtesy of Fritz Kummert

## Iberis saxatilis

An evergreen subshrub for sun or part shade in any good, well-drained soil, preferably alkaline. Flowers in spring, white. Grows 3–6 inches (7.5–15 cm) high, 18 inches (45 cm) wide. Zones 5–9. Pyrenees to Sicily.

## Iberis sempervirens

An evergreen subshrub for sun or part shade in any good, well-drained soil, preferably alkaline. The cultivar 'Autumn Snow' flowers in spring with a repeat in fall, white. Grows 10 inches (25 cm) high, 24 inches (60 cm) wide. Zones 4–9. The species is from southern Europe.

## Imperata cylindrica

Japanese blood grass
Gramineae
A deciduous perennial for sun or part shade in any good, well-drained soil. The cultivar 'Red Baron' is nonflowering

and thus never becomes a self-sowing pest as does the species. Grows 12 inches (30 cm) high, 18 inches (45 cm) wide. Zones 5–10. The species is from Japan.

## Incarvillea
Bignoniaceae

## Incarvillea emodii

A perennial for sun or part shade in any good, well-drained soil. Flowers in late

*Incarvillea emodii*

*Hypoxis hirsuta,* courtesy of Panayoti Kelaidis

*Iberis saxatilis,* courtesy of Fritz Kummert

*Iberis sempervirens* 'Autumn Snow'

*Imperata cylindrica* 'Red Baron'

spring and early summer, rosy purple with a yellow throat. Grows 24 inches (60 cm) high and wide. Zones 6–9. Western Nepal to Afghanistan.

*Incarvillea mairei* 'Frank Ludlow', courtesy of Fritz Kummert

### Incarvillea mairei

A member of the acaulescent group of incarvilleas, which means it rises from dormancy as a tuft of foliage from a long, deep root. All incarvilleas in this group require dryish conditions in winter, otherwise roots will rot in water-logged soil. A perennial for sun or part shade in humus-rich, well-drained soil, keeping it moist in spring. The cultivar 'Frank Ludlow' flowers in early summer, crimson tinged with pink. Grows 4 inches (10 cm) high, 10 inches (25 cm) wide. Zones 4–9. The species is from southwestern China, and Tibet to western Nepal.

### Indigofera decora

indigo
Leguminosae
synonym, *I. incarnata*
A deciduous shrubby perennial for sun or part shade in any good, well-drained soil. The cultivar 'Alba' flowers in June to August, white. Grows 24 inches (60 cm) high and wide. Zones 6–8. The species is from Japan and China.

### Inula

Compositae

### Inula ensifolia

A perennial for sun in any good, well-drained soil. Flowers in June through August, golden yellow. Grows 12 inches (30 cm) high and wide. Zones 3–9. Caucasus Mountains and southern Europe.

### Inula rhizocephala

A perennial, forming a flat rosette with sessile flower heads, for sun in fertile scree with added grit, *I. rhizocephala* is a distinctive species that requires dry winter conditions. Flowers in summer, yellow. Grows 8 inches (20 cm) high, 12 inches (30 cm) wide. Zones 6–9. Pakistan to Kashmir in India.

### Ipheion uniflorum

spring starflower
Liliaceae (Alliaceae)
An excellent bulbous perennial for naturalizing, even under trees and shrubs where little else grows well. Cultivate in sun or part shade in any well-drained soil. The cultivar 'Rolf Fiedler' flowers in

*Indigofera decora* 'Alba'

*Inula ensifolia*

*Inula rhizocephala*, courtesy of Fritz Kummert

February to June, sky blue with a white throat. Other cultivars come in purple, violet, and white. Grow 8 inches (20 cm) high, 12 inches (30 cm) wide. Zones 5–10. The species is from Uruguay and northern Argentina.

## Ipomopsis congesta
Polemoniaceae
synonym, *Gilia congesta*
A perennial for sun in any well-drained soil. Flowers in spring, white. Grows 4–10 inches (10–25 cm) high, 4 inches (10 cm) wide. Zones 6–9. Sierra Nevada of California.

## Iris
flag, fleur-de-lis
Iridaceae

*Iris* is a genus with many dwarf species for the rock garden, woodland, and bog. All are perennial and either rhizomatous or bulbous. Because of the large size and complexity of the genus, species are grouped together in (descending order

*Ipheion uniflorum* 'Rolf Fiedler'

*Ipomopsis congesta*, courtesy of Fritz Kummert

of rank) subgenera, sections, and series. The irises treated here may be grouped as follows:

Subgenus *Iris*, Bearded irises
  Section *Iris*—I. attica, I. pumila, I. suaveolens
  Section *Psammiris*—I. humilis
  Section *Onocyclus*—I. acutiloba, I. iberica
  Section *Pseudoregelia*—I. kamaonensis
Subgenus *Limniris*, Beardless irises
  Section *Lophiris*, Evansia irises—I. cristata, I. gracilipes, I. lacustris
  Section *Limniris*
    Series *Ruthenicae*—I. ruthenica
    Series *Californicae*, Pacific Coast irises—I.chrysophylla,I. douglasiana, I. innominata
    Series *Spuriae*—I. graminea, I. sintenisii
    Series *Unguiculares*—I. unguicularis
Subgenus *Scorpiris*, Juno irises—I. bucharica, I. nicolai, I. persica
Subgenus *Hermodactyloides*, Reticulata irises—Iris 'Clairette', I. histrio, I. histrioides, Iris 'Katherine Hodgkin', I. kolpakowskyana, I. reticulata, I. winogradowii

## Iris acutiloba subsp. *lineolata*
Section *Onocyclus*, rhizomatous. Cultivate in sun in any good, well-drained soil. It does best in the alpine house. Flowers in late spring, whitish and boldly veined brownish, each fall with a blackish patch. Grows 8–10 inches (20–25 cm) high. Zones 6–8. The species is from Transcaucasia.

*Iris acutiloba* subsp. *lineolata*, courtesy of Fritz Kummert

## Iris attica
synonym, *I. pumila* subsp. *attica*
Section *Iris*, rhizomatous. *Iris attica* may not do well in winters that are wet and cold. Cultivate in sun in any good, well-drained soil. Flowers in spring in shades of yellow or purple, may be bicolored. Grows 4 inches (10 cm) high, 6 inches (15 cm) wide. Zones 6–9. Greece, the southern Balkan Peninsula, and western Turkey.

## Iris bucharica
Subgenus *Scorpiris*, bulbous. Cultivate in sun or part shade in any good, well-drained soil. Flowers in late spring, white with yellow on falls or completely

*Iris attica*, courtesy of Fritz Kummert

*Iris bucharica*, courtesy of Fritz Kummert

yellow. Grows 8–14 inches (20–35 cm) high. Zones 5–8. Central Asia and northeastern Afghanistan.

### Iris chrysophylla

Series *Californicae*, fibrous rooted. *Iris chrysophylla* is a dwarf with remarkable flowers that are large and flat. Cultivate in sun or part shade in any good, well-drained soil. Keep it dryish in summer. Flowers in spring, white to yellow, finely veined blue or brown. Grows 6–8 inches (15–20 cm) high, 18 inches (45 cm) wide. Zones 6–9. Southern and western Oregon and northern California.

### Iris 'Clairette'

A garden hybrid, *I. reticulata* × *I. bakeriana*, both subgenus *Hermodactyloides*, bulbous. Cultivate in sun or part shade in any good, well-drained soil. The hybrid flowers in early spring, white to shades of lilac, blue, or purple with yellow crest on falls. Grows 4–6 inches (10–15 cm) high when in flower, leaves

*Iris chrysophylla*

*Iris* 'Clairette', courtesy of Fritz Kummert

maturing to 12 to 16 inches (30–40 cm). Zones 4–9. *Iris reticulata* is from Turkey, Iran, Iraq, and Russia, and *I. bakeriana* is from Turkey, Iran, and Iraq.

### Iris cristata

dwarf crested iris

Section *Lophiris*, rhizomatous. Cultivate in part shade in humus-rich, well-drained soil. Flowers in April and May, light blue and pale lilac to purple. Grows 6 inches (15 cm) high, 18 inches (45 cm) wide. Zones 3–8. Eastern United States. There is a lovely white cultivar, 'Alba'.

### Iris douglasiana

Series *Californicae*, rhizomatous. Cultivate in sun or part shade in any well-drained soil. The cultivar 'Cape Sebastian' is a Siskiyou Rare Plant Nursery

*Iris cristata*, courtesy of Fritz Kummert

*Iris douglasiana* 'Cape Sebastian'

selection chosen for its large, showy flowers. Flowers in spring, white with a purple center. Grows 18 inches (45 cm) high, 24 inches (60 cm) wide. Zones 6–10. The species is from southern Oregon to California.

### Iris gracilipes

Section *Lophiris*, rhizomatous. Cultivate in part shade in humus-rich, well-drained soil. Flowers in early summer, pink to blue-lilac. Grows 6 inches (15 cm) high, 18 inches (45 cm) wide. Zones 6–9. China and Japan.

### Iris graminea

plum tart iris

Series *Spuriae*, rhizomatous. The sweet, plum scented flowers are nestled amid the grassy foliage. Easy to establish in open woods and meadow gardens. Cultivate in sun or part shade in humus-rich, well-drained soil. Flowers in May and June, red-purple. Grows 12 inches (30 cm) high and wide. Zones 5–9. Caucasia and western Russia to southern Europe.

### Iris histrio var. aintabensis

Subgenus *Hermodactyloides*, bulbous. Cultivate in sun or part shade in any good, well-drained soil. Flowers in winter and early spring, pale blue. Grows

3–4 inches (7.5–10 cm) high. Zones 6–9. Southern Turkey.

## Iris histrioides

Subgenus *Hermodactyloides,* bulbous. Cultivate in sun or part shade in any good, well-drained soil. The cultivar 'Major' flowers in winter and early spring, violet-blue. The plant illustrated may not be the true cultivar, but it has been commonly distributed as such. Grows 4 inches (10 cm) high in flower; foliage matures to 18 inches (45 cm). Zones 5–9. The species is from northern Turkey.

## Iris humilis

synonyms, *I. arenaria, I. flavissima*
Section *Psammiris,* rhizomatous. Cultivate in sun in any good, well-drained soil. Flowers in late spring, yellow, veined purple. Grows 8–10 inches (20–25 cm) high, 6 inches (15 cm) wide. Zones 6–8. Eastern Europe and Russia.

## Iris iberica subsp. *elegantissima*

Section *Onocyclus,* rhizomatous. Cultivate in sun in any good, well-drained soil. Flowers in spring with falls ivory, spotted maroon, and standards white, veined brown at the base. Grows 8–12 inches (20–30 cm) high. Zones 6–8. Caucasia to northeastern Turkey, Iraq, Iran, and Russia.

## Iris innominata

Series *Californicae,* rhizomatous, evergreen. *Iris innominata* requires minimal summer watering to keep it floriferous, long-lived, and healthy. It provides at-

*Iris histrioides* 'Major', courtesy of Fritz Kummert

*Iris humilis,* courtesy of Fritz Kummert

*Iris iberica* subsp. *elegantissima,* courtesy of Fritz Kummert

*Iris gracilipes*

*Iris graminea,* courtesy of Fritz Kummert

*Iris histrio* var. *aintabensis,* courtesy of Fritz Kummert

*Iris innominata*

tractive tufts of thin, evergreen leaves. Cultivate in sun or part shade in any good, well-drained soil. Flowers in spring, blue, lavender, cream, yellow, gold, or copper, and solid or veined. Grows 8 inches (20 cm) high, 12 inches (30 cm) wide. Zones 6–10. Northern California and southern Oregon.

### Iris kamaonensis

Section *Pseudoregelia,* rhizomatous. Cultivate in sun or part shade in any good, well-drained soil. Flowers in early summer, pale purple with dark mottling. Grows 8–10 inches (20–25 cm) high with young, shorter foliage; leaves mature to 12 to 18 inches (30–45 cm). Zones 6–8. Pakistan to China.

### Iris 'Katherine Hodgkin'

A garden hybrid, *I. histrioides* × *I. winogradowii,* both subgenus *Hermodacty-* *loides,* bulbous. Cultivars arise from tiny bulbs that multiply to form attractive carpets in the garden. They also make good subjects for pan culture. Cultivate in sun or part shade in any good, well-drained soil. Flowers in February and March. 'Katherine Hodgkin' has yellow flowers suffused with pale blue, veined blue. Grows 6 inches (15 cm) high when in flower. Zones 5–8. *Iris histrioides* is from northern Turkey, and *I. winogradowii* is from the Caucasus Mountains.

### Iris kolpakowskyana

Subgenus *Hermodactyloides,* bulbous. Cultivate in sun or part shade in any good, well-drained soil in the alpine house. Flowers in late winter, pale purple to lilac blue. Grows 4 inches (10 cm) high when in flower. Zones 5–8. Russian Asia.

### Iris lacustris

Section *Lophiris,* rhizomatous. *Iris lacustris* is one of the smallest species and looks like a miniature *I. cristata.* Cultivate in part shade in humus-rich, well-drained soil. Flowers in late spring, sky blue to pale lilac. Grows 4 inches (10 cm) high, 12 inches (30 cm) wide. Zones 3–8. Great Lakes region of North America.

### Iris nicolai

Subgenus *Scorpiris,* bulbous. Cultivate in sun or part shade in any good, well-drained soil in the alpine house, keeping water off the foliage. Flowers in spring, off-white to pale lilac, with falls blotched dark purple with a golden crest and a dark violet vein on each side. Grows 6 inches (15 cm) high when in flower; leaves mature to 10 inches (25 cm).

*Iris kamaonensis,* courtesy of Fritz Kummert

*Iris kolpakowskyana,* courtesy of Fritz Kummert

*Iris nicolai,* courtesy of Fritz Kummert

*Iris* 'Katherine Hodgkin'

*Iris lacustris,* courtesy of Fritz Kummert

*Iris persica,* courtesy of Fritz Kummert

Zones 5–8. Central Asia and northeastern Afghanistan.

## Iris persica

Subgenus *Scorpiris*, bulbous. Cultivate in sun or part shade in any good, well-drained soil. Flowers in spring, green-blue, silver-gray, yellow, or brown, with blades of falls deeper purple. Grows 4 inches (10 cm) high. Zones 6–9. Turkey, Iraq, and Syria.

## Iris pumila

Section *Iris*, rhizomatous, deciduous. *Iris pumila* is a dwarf bearded iris from which has come many forms. It is easily grown and produces dense mats and abundant flowers. Cultivate in sun in any good, well-drained soil. Flowers in spring, mostly purple-violet but also in shades of white, yellow, blue, or purple, all with blue or yellow beards. Grows 4–6 inches (10–15 cm) high, 12 inches (30 cm) wide. Zones 4–9. Eastern central Europe to the Urals.

## Iris ruthenica

Series *Ruthenicae*, deciduous. Cultivate in sun or part shade in any good, well-drained soil. Flowers in May and June, purple. Grows 10 inches (25 cm) high, 12 inches (30 cm) wide. Zones 5–8. China to eastern Europe.

## Iris sintenisii

Series *Spuriae*, rhizomatous. Cultivate in sun or part shade in any good, well-drained soil. Flowers in summer with falls white, heavily veined purple, and standards blue-violet. Grows 14 inches (35 cm) high, 6 inches (15 cm) wide. Zones 6–8. Southeastern Europe to Russia and Turkey.

## Iris suaveolens

synonym, *I. mellita*

Section *Iris*, rhizomatous. *Iris suaveolens* is similar in appearance to *I. pumila*. Cultivate in sun or part shade in any good, well-drained soil. Flowers in spring, yellow to purple, and bicolored.

Grows 4–6 inches (10–15 cm) high, 8 inches (20 cm) wide. Zones 6–9. Southeastern Europe to northwestern Turkey. Leaves are red margined in *I. suaveolens* var. *rubromarginata*.

## Iris unguicularis

Algerian iris, winter iris

Series *Unguiculares*, rhizomatous. Cultivate in sun or part shade in any good, well-drained soil. Flowers in late fall to early spring, lavender-blue with a yellow zone and dark veining on falls. Grows up to 18 inches (45 cm) high. Zones 6–9. Greece, southern and western Turkey, and northern Africa.

## Iris winogradowii

Subgenus *Hermodactyloides*, bulbous. Cultivate in sun or part shade in any good, well-drained soil. Flowers in late winter and early spring, primrose yellow. Grows 6 inches (15 cm) tall when in flower. Zones 5–9. Caucasus Mountains.

*Iris pumila*, courtesy of Armen Gevjan

*Iris sintenisii*, courtesy of Fritz Kummert

*Iris unguicularis*, courtesy of Fritz Kummert

*Iris ruthenica*, courtesy of Fritz Kummert

*Iris suaveolens*, courtesy of Fritz Kummert

*Iris winogradowii*, courtesy of Fritz Kummert

## Isopyrum thalictrioides

false rue anemone
Ranunculaceae
A perennial for shade or part shade in humus-rich, moist soil. Flowers in March and April, white. Grows 6 inches (15 cm) high, 12 inches (30 cm) wide. Zones 4–9. Central Europe to Afghanistan.

## J

## Jankaea heldreichii

Gesneriaceae
A lovely but difficult evergreen perennial from rocky areas in Greece, doing best in an alpine house that is kept quite dry in winter, but the plant should be kept well watered during the time of spring growth yet avoiding getting moisture on the foliage. Cultivate in part shade in a crevice of humus-rich soil with crushed limestone added, and in the alpine house. Flowers in spring, crystalline lilac blue. Grows 2–3 inches (5–7.5 cm) high, 3 inches (7.5 cm) wide. Zones 6–8. Mountains of Greece, especially Mount Olympus.

## Jasione laevis

shepherd's scabious, sheep's bit
Campanulaceae
synonyms, *J. perennis, J. pyrenaica*
A perennial for sun in any dryish soil, even poor soil. Flowers in summer, blue. Grows 8–12 inches (20–30 cm) high, 12 inches (30 cm) wide. Zones 5–9. Southern and western Europe.

## Jasminum parkeri

jasmine, jessamine
Oleaceae
An evergreen shrub for sun or part shade in any good, well-drained soil. Flowers in June through August, yellow. Grows 12 inches (30 cm) high, 18–24 inches (45–60 cm) wide. Zones 7–10. Northwestern India.

## Jeffersonia

Berberidaceae

## Jeffersonia diphylla

twin leaf
A perennial for part shade in humus-rich, well-drained soil. Flowers in spring, white. Grows 10–12 inches (25–30 cm) high, 16 inches (40 cm) wide. Zones 5–8. Eastern North America, Ontario to Alabama.

*Isopyrum thalictrioides,* courtesy of Fritz Kummert

*Jankaea heldreichii,* courtesy of Phil Pearson

*Jasione laevis,* courtesy of Fritz Kummert

*Jasminum parkeri,* courtesy of Fritz Kummert

*Jeffersonia diphylla,* courtesy of Armen Gevjan

*Jeffersonia dubia,* courtesy of Fritz Kummert

## Jeffersonia dubia

synonym, *Plagiorhegma dubium*
A perennial for part shade in humus-rich, well-drained, gritty soil. Flowers in spring, lavender to blue. Grows 8 inches (20 cm) high, 12 inches (30 cm) wide. Zones 5–8. Manchuria and North Korea.

## Jovibarba hirta

Crassulaceae
A perennial succulent for sun or part shade in any well-drained soil. Flowers in summer, greenish white to pale yellow. Grows 8 inches (20 cm) high, 6 inches (15 cm) wide when in flower. Zones 5–10. Central and southeastern Europe.

## Juniperus

juniper
Cupressaceae

A gardener would be hard-pressed to find a genus of evergreen conifers more tolerant of cold, hot, and even dry conditions.

## Juniperus communis

An evergreen shrub for sun in any good, well-drained soil. Zones 3–8. Eurasia.

**Cultivars**. *Juniperus communis* 'Compressa', dwarf Irish juniper, grows 18 inches (45 cm) high, 4 inches (10 cm) wide.

*Juniperus communis* 'Echiniformis', hedgehog juniper, is the only truly cushion-forming juniper, a prickly foliaged gem. A slowly growing shrublet that reaches 12 inches (30 cm) in height and 18 inches (45 cm) in width after several years.

*Juniperus communis* 'Gold Cone' grows 36 inches (90 cm) high, 12 inches (30 cm) wide, eventually much taller.

## Juniperus conferta

shore juniper
An evergreen shrub for sun in any good, well-drained soil. The cultivar 'Silver Mist' grows 12 inches (30 cm) high, 30 inches (75 cm) wide. Zones 5–10. The species is from Japan and Sakhalin.

## Juniperus procumbens

An evergreen shrub for sun in any good, well-drained soil. The cultivar 'Nana' grows 6 inches (15 cm) high, 36 inches (90 cm) wide. Zones 3–9. The species is from Kyushu, Japan.

*Jovibarba hirta,* courtesy of Fritz Kummert

*Juniperus communis* 'Echiniformis'

*Juniperus conferta* 'Silver Mist'

*Juniperus communis* 'Compressa'

*Juniperus communis* 'Gold Cone'

*Juniperus procumbens* 'Nana'

## Juniperus squamata

A low, irregularly shaped cushion of steel blue foliage. An evergreen shrub for sun in any good, well-drained soil. Grows 12 inches (30 cm) high, 18 inches (45 cm) wide. Zones 4–10. The species is from Afghanistan to China.

## Kalmia
Ericaceae

## Kalmia angustifolia
sheep laurel
An evergreen shrub for sun or part shade in moist, humus-rich, acid soil. The cultivar 'Nana', dwarf sheep laurel, flowers in early to midsummer, deep pink. Grows 12–16 inches (30–40 cm) high, 12 inches (30 cm) wide. Zones 2–0. The species is from eastern North America.

## Kalmia polifolia
bog kalmia, bog or swamp laurel
An evergreen shrub for sun or part shade in humus-rich, moist, acid soil. Flowers in late spring, pink or magenta. Grows 12–18 inches (30–45 cm) high, 18 inches (45 cm) wide. Zones 2–8. Southern Alaska to northern California and northeastern Alberta to the Atlantic

coast of Canada, south to Wisconsin, Michigan, and New England. *Kalmia polifolia* var. *microphylla* is a dwarf form from the wild, only about 6 inches (15 cm) high.

## Kalmiopsis leachiana
Ericaceae
synonym, *K. fragrans*
One of the rarest dwarf ericaceous shrubs, an evergreen that many believe to be a relict and a parent of all rhododendrons and azaleas. Native to the Siskiyou Mountains and a few locations near the Umpqua River in the Cascade Range of southern Oregon. Plants from these latter localities, including the cultivar 'Umpqua Valley', are dwarfer and grow more compactly than plants from other localities, such as Curry County, Oregon. Cultivate in sun or part shade in

*Kalmia angustifolia* 'Nana'

fertile, acid, well-drained soil. Flowers in May, often again in October, in light to dark shades of rose red to purplish red. Grows 8–12 inches (20–30 cm) high, 10–18 inches (25–45 cm) wide. Zones 6–8. Southern Oregon.

## Kelseya uniflora
Rosaceae
It is well worth a trip into the northern U.S. Rocky Mountains to see venerable plants clinging to the volcanic and lime-

*Kalmia polifolia,* courtesy of Fritz Kummert

*Kalmiopsis leachiana,* Curry County form

*Kalmiopsis leachiana* 'Umpqua Valley'

*Juniperus squamata* 'Blue Star'

stone cliffs; difficult in cultivation and a challenge to all growers of rare plants. A cushion-forming, evergreen subshrub for sun or part shade in tufa or limestone scree, keeping it dryish in winter, and in the alpine house. Flowers in spring, white, tinged pink. Grows 1–2 inches (2.5–5 cm) high, 6 inches (15 cm) wide, and in the wild to 36 inches (90 cm) wide. Zones 3–7. Mountains of Idaho, Montana, and Wyoming.

 **L**

## *Lagotis stolonifera*
Scrophulariaceae
A perennial for sun or part shade in fertile, well-drained moist soil. Flowers in

late spring to midsummer, blue or purple to mauve-pink. Grows 8 inches (20 cm) high, 12 inches (30 cm) wide. Zones 6–9. Central Asia.

## *Lamium*
dead nettle
Labiatae

## *Lamium armenum*
One of the choicest and most desirable of all lamiums. It is a mat-forming perennial that is not easy to grow and is best attempted in the alpine house. Cultivate in sun or part shade in fertile, well-drained soil, and in the alpine house. Flowers in summer, pale pink to white. Grows 4 inches (10 cm) high, 10 inches (25 cm) wide. Zones 5–8. Turkey.

## *Lamium maculatum*
A stoloniferous perennial for sun or part shade in any good soil. The cultivar 'Pink Pewter' flowers in summer, pink. Grows 6 inches (15 cm) high, 24 inches (60 cm) wide. Zones 3–10. The species is from Europe, northern Africa, and western Asia.

## *Larix laricina*
American larch
Pinaceae
A deciduous, shrubby conifer for sun or part shade in any good, moist soil. The cultivar 'Newport Beauty', dwarf American larch, grows 12 inches (30 cm) high, 18 inches (45 cm) wide. Zones 2–8. The species is from northern North America.

## *Lathyrus vernus*
spring vetch
Leguminosae
synonym, *Orobus vernus*
A perennial for sun or part shade in any good soil. Flowers in late winter and

*Kelseya uniflora*

*Lagotis stolonifera*, courtesy of Fritz Kummert

*Lamium armenum*

*Lamium maculatum* 'Pink Pewter'

*Larix laricina* 'Newport Beauty'

spring, red-violet, aging blue. Grows 12–24 inches (30–60 cm) high, 18 inches (45 cm) wide. Zones 3–9. Europe.

*Lathyrus vernus,* courtesy of Fritz Kummert

*Lavandula angustifolia* 'Hidcote'

## *Lavandula*
lavender
Labiatae

The dwarfer forms of lavender make excellent shrubs for the rock garden. All have deliciously aromatic foliage and flowers, and are heat and drought tolerant.

## *Lavandula angustifolia*
English lavender
synonyms, *L. officinalis, L. spica, L. verna*
The most popular lavender, an evergreen shrub for sun in any good, well-drained soil. The cultivar 'Hidcote' flowers in summer, blue-purple. Grows 12–16 inches (30–40 cm) high and wide, the cultivars 'Nana Atropurpurea' (blue-purple flowers) and 'Nana Alba'

(white flowers) to 12 inches (30 cm) high and wide. Zones 5–10. The species is Mediterranean.

## *Lavandula stoechas*
French or Spanish lavender
An evergreen shrub for sun in any good, well-drained soil. Flowers in summer, purple with darker bracts. Grows 12 inches (30 cm) high, 24 inches (60 cm) wide. Zones 7–10. Mediterranean region and Portugal.

## *Leiophyllum buxifolium*
sand myrtle
Ericaceae
An evergreen shrub for sun or part shade in humus-rich, acid, well-drained soil. Flowers in May and June, white to pale pink. Grows 6–12 inches (15–30 cm) high, 24 inches (60 cm) wide. Zones 5–9. Mountains of the eastern United States in Tennessee, North Carolina, and northern Georgia.

## *Leontopodium alpinum* subsp. *nivale*
edelweiss
Compositae
Not a colorful or showy plant but the clustered flower heads of grayish felt are enchanting. A perennial for sun or part shade in well-drained, but not dry, soil. Flowers in late spring, off-white. *Leontopodium alpinum* subsp. *nivale* is but one of several geographical forms of the legendary alpine wildflower. Grows 6 inches (15 cm) high, 12 inches (30 cm)

*Lavandula stoechas*

*Leiophyllum buxifolium*

*Leontopodium alpinum* subsp. *nivale,* courtesy of Fritz Kummert

wide. Zones 5–8. Central Apennines and mountains of the Balkan Peninsula.

## Leptospermum scoparium
New Zealand tea tree
Myrtaceae

A shrub for sun or part shade in any good, well-drained, moist soil. The cultivar 'Kiwi' has outstanding purple foliage, tiny and almost needle-like. Combining handsome foliage with charming, deep pink flowers from spring into summer, it is a tender plant worth the greenhouse space if one lives in a cold climate zone. Grows 18 inches (45 cm) high and wide. Zones 8–10. The species is from New Zealand and Tasmania.

## Leucogenes grandiceps
New Zealand edelweiss
Compositae

A woody-based, evergreen perennial for sun or shade in humus-rich, gritty soil. Flowers in summer, yellow surrounded by white, woolly bracts. Grows 4–6 inches (10–15 cm) high, 8 inches (20 cm) wide. Zones 7–9. South Island, New Zealand.

## Leucojum
snowflake
Amaryllidaceae

The snowflakes are hardy bulbous perennials, quite similar to snowdrops, *Galanthus*. They are easy to grow in good, deep, well-drained soil and should be left undisturbed for years.

## Leucojum aestivum
summer snowflake

Cultivate in sun or part shade in moist, humus-rich, well-drained soil. The cultivar 'Gravetye Giant' flowers in April and May, white with green tips. Grows 24 inches (60 cm) high, 12 inches (30 cm) wide. Zones 4–10. The species is from central and southern Europe.

## Leucojum autumnale
autumn snowflake

Cultivate in sun or part shade in humus-rich, gritty soil. Flowers in June through

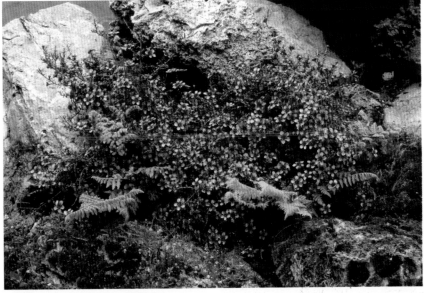

*Leptospermum scoparium* 'Kiwi'

*Leucogenes grandiceps*, courtesy of Franz Hadacek

*Leucojum aestivum* 'Gravetye Giant'

*Leucojum autumnale*, courtesy of Fritz Kummert

August, white. Grows 6 inches (15 cm) high. Zones 4–10. Mediterranean.

## Leucojum vernum
spring snowflake

Cultivate in shade or part shade in humus-rich, moist soil. Flowers in spring, white, tipped green. Grows 6–12 inches (15–30 cm) high. Zones 4–10. Central Europe.

## Lewisia
Portulacaceae

The lewisias are an important genus of western American succulents for any alpine plant collection. They are best grown in scree, on well-drained slopes, in vertical rock garden crevices, in the alpine house, and wherever a drying-off period can be achieved after flowering.

## Lewisia brachycalyx

A deciduous perennial for sun in humus rich, gritty soil, and in the alpine house.

Flowers in early spring, white to pastel pink. Grows 3 inches (7.5 cm) high, 5 inches (12.5 cm) wide. Zones 6–9. Mountains of Arizona and southern California.

## Lewisia columbiana subsp. rupicola

An evergreen perennial for part shade in humus-rich scree. Flowers in May through July, purple-magenta to rose. Grows 6 inches (15 cm) high and wide. Zones 4–9. British Columbia to the Cascade Range of Washington and Oregon.

## Lewisia cotyledon

An evergreen perennial for part shade in humus-rich scree, and in the alpine house. Flowers in March through May, pink, white, orange, or salmon, often bicolored and striped. Grows 12 inches (30 cm) high, 8 inches (20 cm) wide. Zones 5–9. Siskiyou Mountains of northern California and southern Oregon. The

type form of *L. cotyledon* is correctly *L. cotyledon* var. *cotyledon*. Other recognized varieties include *alba*, *heckneri*, and *howellii*. By crossing and selecting from these varieties, innumerable groups and strains have been developed.

**Cultivar**. *Lewisia cotyledon* 'Siskiyou White' includes various seedling forms with white flowers.

## Lewisia leana

Sometimes misspelled *leeana*, *L. leana* is an evergreen perennial for sun or part shade in humus-rich scree with additional grit, and in the alpine house. Flowers in summer, magenta-pink and white with dark veining. Grows 6 inches (15 cm) high, 10 inches (25 cm) wide. Zones 5–9. Mountains of Oregon and California.

## Lewisia longipetala

A deciduous perennial. Cultivate in part shade in humus-rich scree. Flowers in

*Leucojum vernum*, courtesy of Fritz Kummert

*Lewisia columbiana* subsp. *rupicola*, courtesy of Fritz Kummert

*Lewisia cotyledon* close up

*Lewisia brachycalyx*, courtesy of Fritz Kummert

*Lewisia cotyledon* at Alex Hole, Siskiyou Mountains, courtesy of Ted Kipping

*Lewisia cotyledon* 'Siskiyou White'

early summer, white flushed with pink. Grows 6 inches (15 cm) high and wide. Zones 3–9. Sierra Nevada and Crystal Range of California and Nevada.

## Lewisia nevadensis

A deciduous perennial for sun in moist scree. Flowers in early summer, white, veined green, sometimes flushed pink. Grows 2 inches (5 cm) high, 3 inches (7.5 cm) wide. Zones 4–9. Washington east to Colorado, possibly south to Arizona.

## Lewisia 'Pinkie'

An evergreen perennial for part shade in humus-rich scree. Flowers in March through May, pink. Grows 8 inches (20 cm) high and wide. Zones 4–9. A garden hybrid, *L. cotyledon* × *L. longipetala*.

## Lewisia rediviva

bitter root

A beautiful deciduous perennial with relatively huge flowers that is a challenge for most gardeners to cultivate. The quill foliage goes dormant in late spring, at or prior to flowering. Withhold summer irrigation. Foliage appears again after the first fall rains. Cultivate in sun in humus-rich scree, and in the alpine house. Flowers in June and July, pink or white. Grows 2 inches (5 cm) high, 3 inches (7.5 cm) wide. Zones 3–9. British Columbia to California and the Rocky Mountains.

**Cultivar**. *Lewisia rediviva* 'Alba'. Flowers white.

*Lewisia* 'Pinkie'

*Lewisia rediviva*, courtesy of Fritz Kummert

*Lewisia rediviva* 'Alba', courtesy of Ted Kipping

*Lewisia leana*

*Lewisia longipetala*, courtesy of Fritz Kummert

*Lewisia nevadensis*, courtesy of Fritz Kummert

## Lewisia tweedyi

Considered by many to be the most beautiful alpine plant, *L. tweedyi* is an evergreen perennial that must have winter dryness at the crown and is thus easiest to maintain if it is covered for the wet, cold season. Cultivate in part shade in humus-rich scree in a vertical crevice, and in the alpine house. Flowers in spring, normally apricot pink to soft yellow, selections existing that are deep rose or white. Grows 8 inches (20 cm) high and wide. Zones 5–8. Wenatchee Mountains of Washington and Walathian Mountains of British Columbia.

**Cultivar**. *Lewisia tweedyi* 'Alba'. Flowers white.

## Liatris spicata f. montana

dwarf button snakeroot
Compositae

A perennial for sun in any well-drained soil. Flowers in summer, rose purple. Grows 18–24 inches (45–60 cm) high, 18 inches (45 cm) wide. Zones 3–10. Mountains of Virginia and Georgia.

## Lilium

lily
Liliaceae

## Lilium bolanderi

A bulbous perennial for sun in fertile, sharply drained soil. Flowers in summer, brick red to wine red. Grows 12–24 inches (30–60 cm) high. Zones 6–9. Siskiyou Mountains of northern California and southern Oregon.

## Lilium bulbiferum var. croceum

fire or orange lily

A good, dwarf, rock garden lily if grown in poorish scree soil where it will rarely exceed 12 inches (30 cm) in height, as it is seen in rocky soil at high elevations in the wild. A bulbous perennial for sun or part shade in humus-rich, well-drained soil. Flowers in summer, orange. Grows 24–40 inches (60–100 cm) high. Zones 5–9. Pyrenees, central and southern Europe.

Liatris spicata f. montana, courtesy of Fritz Kummert

Lilium bulbiferum var. croceum, courtesy of Fritz Kummert

Lewisia tweedyi 'Alba', courtesy of Sheila Gaquin

Lilium bolanderi

Lilium pumilum, courtesy of Fritz Kummert

## Lilium pumilum

coral lily

synonym, *L. tenuifolium*

A bulbous perennial for sun in any good, well-drained soil. Flowers in summer, scarlet. Grows 18 inches (45 cm) high. Zones 5–9. Mongolia, northern China, North Korea, and Siberia.

## Limonium bellidifolium

marsh rosemary, sea lavender, statice

Plumbaginaceae

There are a few members of *Limonium* that are small enough for the rock garden. These smaller species are neat, evergreen plants that are quite hardy in addition to being heat and drought tolerant. *Limonium bellidifolium* is a perennial with a woody rootstock for sun in any good, well-drained soil. Flowers in June through August, lilac. Grows 10 inches (25 cm) high, 6 inches (15 cm) wide. Zones 5–9. Mediterranean.

## Linaria

spurred snapdragon, toadflax

Scrophulariaceae

## Linaria alpina

A short-lived perennial, sometimes an annual or biennial, for sun in any good, well-drained soil. Flowers in summer, violet to purple with a yellow or orange palate. Grows 6 inches (15 cm) high, 12 inches (30 cm) wide. Zones 4–9. Mountains of central and southern Europe.

## Linaria tristis var. lurida

dull-colored or sad-colored linaria

A perennial for sun in any good, well-drained soil. Flowers in summer, pale yellow with purple veining and a purple lower lip. Grows 8–12 inches (20–30 cm) high, 12 inches (30 cm) wide. Zones 8–10. Southern Spain, Portugal, North Africa and Canary Islands.

## Linnaea borealis

twin flower

Caprifoliaceae

An evergreen woodlander with glossy leaves and creeping, rooting stems, widely distributed in the northern woodlands of the world. Cultivate in shade or part shade in moist, humus-rich, well-drained soil. Flowers in April through June, pale pink. Grows 2 inches (5 cm) high, 12–24 inches (30–60 cm) wide. Zones 2–8. Northern woodlands of the world.

## Linum

flax

Linaceae

## Linum campanulatum

A woody-based perennial for sun in any good, well-drained soil, preferably calcareous. Flowers in summer, yellow. Grows 8–12 inches (20–30 cm) high, 12 inches (30 cm) wide. Zones 6–10. Italy to eastern Spain.

*Limonium bellidifolium*

*Linnaea borealis*

*Linaria alpina,* courtesy of Fritz Kummert

*Linaria tristis* var. *lurida,* courtesy of Fritz Kummert

*Linum campanulatum,* courtesy of Fritz Kummert

## Linum 'Gemmell's Hybrid'

A perennial with a woody rootstock for sun in any good, well-drained soil. Flowers in late spring, rich yellow. Grows 4 inches (10 cm) high, 8 inches (20 cm) wide. Zones 5–8. A garden hybrid, *L. campanulatum* × *L. elegans*.

## Linum perenne subsp. *alpinum*

alpine perennial flax

A woody-based perennial for sun in any good, well-drained soil. Flowers in summer, clear blue. Grows 12 inches (30 cm) high and wide. Zones 5–10. Central and eastern Europe.

## Lithocarpus densiflorus var. echinoides

dwarf tanbark oak

Fagaceae

Although ultimately the smaller oaks (see also *Quercus*) are somewhat large for all but the larger rock garden, they are fairly slow growing and add a wild, rugged look. *Lithocarpus densiflorus* var. *echinoides* is an evergreen shrub for sun in any good, well-drained soil. Flowers in late spring, whitish, acorns following in groups of one to three. Grows 36 inches (90 cm) high and wide in 10 years. Zones 6–9. Oregon and California.

## Lithodora
Boraginaceae

## Lithodora diffusa

Several forms of the species rank as some of the world's most popular rock garden plants. The cultivar 'Picos' is from the Picos de Europa, Spain; the other two popular cultivars are 'Grace Ward' and 'Heavenly Blue'. Admittedly all can be impermanent and not reliably hardy in severe climates but they are worth the trouble. Evergreen subshrubs for sun (provide shade from the hottest sun) or part shade in humus-rich, well-drained, lime-free soil. *Lithodora diffusa* 'Picos' flowers in June to August, gentian blue. Grows 6 inches (15 cm) high, 18 inches (45 cm) wide. Zones 6–9. The species is from southwestern Europe.

## Lithodora oleifolia

An evergreen shrublet for sun or part shade in humus-rich, well-drained, neutral to limy soil. Flowers in summer, with pink buds, opening blue. Grows 6 inches (15 cm) high, 18 inches (45 cm) wide. Zones 5–8. Eastern Pyrenees.

## Lithodora zahnii

An evergreen shrub for sun in any good, well-drained soil. Flowers in early summer, sky blue to white. Grows 12–16 inches (30–40 cm) high, 24 inches (60 cm) wide. Zones 7–10. Southern Greece.

*Linum* 'Gemmell's Hybrid'

*Lithocarpus densiflorus* var. *echinoides*

*Lithodora oleifolia,* courtesy of Fritz Kummert

*Linum perenne* subsp. *alpinum,* courtesy of Fritz Kummert

*Lithodora diffusa* 'Picos', courtesy of Fritz Kummert

*Lithodora zahnii*

## Lithophragma parviflorum
fringe cups, woodland star
Saxifragaceae
A tuberous and bulblet-bearing perennial for part shade in moist, humus-rich, well-drained soil. Flowers in spring and early summer, white or pale pink. Grows 8–14 inches (20–35 cm) high, 12 inches (30 cm) wide. Zones 5–8. British Columbia to California, east to the Rocky Mountains.

## Lithospermum canescens
Indian paint, puccoon
Boraginaceae
A perennial for sun or part shade in humus-rich, limy, well-drained soil. Flowers in late spring, orange-yellow.

Grows 12–16 inches (30–40 cm) high, 24 inches (60 cm) wide. Zones 3–9. Ontario to Texas, east to Georgia.

## Lloydia serotina
alp or Snowdon lily
Liliaceae
So diminutive, a perennial that is best planted as a group of several bulbs. Place it among other small, scree plants to achieve an alpine arrangement with a look of authenticity. Cultivate in part shade in humus-rich, gritty, moist, acid soil. Flowers in summer, white, flushed pink and veined purple. Grows 4–6 inches (10–15 cm) high. Zones 2–8. Mountains of Europe, Asia, and North America.

## Lobelia linnaeoides
Campanulaceae (Lobeliaceae)
A perennial for sun or part shade in moderately moist, humus-rich, well-drained soil. Flowers in summer, pale blue to white. Grows 2–3 inches (5–7.5 cm) high, 12 inches (30 cm) wide. Zones 8–9. New Zealand.

## Loiseleuria procumbens
alpine or mountain azalea
Ericaceae
Not an easily cultivated plant unless placed in a naturally cool location in a garden that is full of good light and air circulation. A mat-forming, evergreen shrub for part shade in humus-rich, gritty, acid soil. Flowers in spring and early summer, rose pink to white, tinted rose. Grows 2–4 inches (5–10 cm) high, 12 inches (30 cm) wide. Zones 2–7. Alpine and subarctic regions of North America, Europe, and Asia.

Lithophragma parviflorum, courtesy of Fritz Kummert

Lobelia linnaeoides, courtesy of Fritz Kummert

Lithospermum canescens

Lloydia serotina, courtesy of Fritz Kummert

Loiseleuria procumbens, courtesy of Fritz Kummert

## *Lotus corniculatus*

bird's-foot trefoil

Leguminosae

A perennial for sun in any good, well-drained soil. Flowers in summer, bright yellow, flushed and streaked red. Grows 3–6 inches (7.5–15 cm) high, 12–24 inches (30–60 cm) wide. Zones 5–9. Europe, Asia, and mountains of northern and eastern Africa.

## *Lupinus lepidus* var. *lobbii*

Leguminosae

More often than not, successfully growing lupines in rock gardens are sown in place and given a 1- to 2-inch (2.5- to 5-cm) layer of stone chips about the crown and under the foliage. Lupines are adversely affected by root disturbance, rarely surviving transplanting. *Lupinus lepidus* var. *lobbii* is a woody-based perennial for sun in well-drained, gritty soil. Flowers in early summer, violet-blue. Grows 4 inches (10 cm) high, 12–18 inches (30–45 cm) wide. Zones 3–8. Northwestern North America to Colorado and Utah.

## *Luzula nivea*

snow rush

Juncaceae

A grass-like perennial for sun in moist, humus-rich, well-drained soil. Flowers in summer in off-white clusters. Grows 12–24 inches (30–60 cm) high, 12 inches (30 cm) wide. Zones 6–9. Central Europe and the Alps.

## *Lychnis*

campion, catchfly

Caryophyllaceae

The campions or catchflies appear similar to *Silene* except that they usually have sticky foliage. They are exceptionally hardy to coldness and prefer a fairly humus-rich soil. They are easily raised from the abundant seed.

## *Lychnis alpina*

synonym, *Viscaria alpina*

A perennial for sun or part shade in any good, well-drained soil. Flowers in summer, rose purple, occasionally white. Grows 2–6 inches (5–15 cm) high, 6 inches (15 cm) wide. Zones 5–8. Mountains of Europe, northeastern North America, and subarctic regions of the northern hemisphere.

*Lotus corniculatus*, courtesy of Fritz Kummert

*Lupinus lepidus* var. *lobbii*, courtesy of Fritz Kummert

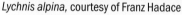

*Lychnis alpina*, courtesy of Franz Hadace

*Luzula nivea,* courtesy of Fritz Kummert

*Lychnis ×arkwrightii*, courtesy of Fritz Kummert

## Lychnis ×arkwrightii

A perennial for sun in any good, well-drained soil. Flowers in summer, brilliant scarlet. Grows 12–16 inches (30–40 cm) high, 12 inches (30 cm) wide. Zones 4–9. A garden hybrid, *L. chalcedonica* × *L. ×haageana*.

## Lychnis flos-jovis

flower of Jove

A perennial for sun in any good, well-drained soil. Flowers in April and May, pink. The cultivar 'Nana' (synonym, 'Minor') grows 8 inches (20 cm) high and wide. Zones 4–9. The species is from the Alps.

## Lychnis viscaria

A perennial for sun in any good, well-drained soil. The cultivar 'Splendens Plena', double-flowered German catchfly, flowers in summer, bright magenta-pink. Grows 12–18 inches (30–45 cm) high, 12 inches (30 cm) wide. Zones 4–9. Europe.

## Lysichiton

skunk cabbage
Araceae

Skunk cabbages are perennials that start out with flowers emerging in a prominent spadix. The plants are short until the huge leaves unfold as the flowers fade. Give skunk cabbages deep, humus-rich, moist or wet soil.

## Lysichiton americanum

Cultivate in part shade in humus-rich, moist soil. Flowers in early spring, yellow. The flowering spike, the spadix, grows to 18 inches (45 cm) high; leaves grow to 48 by 48 inches (120 by 120 cm). Zones 5–9. Western North America.

## Lysichiton camtschatcensis

Asian skunk cabbage

Cultivate in part shade in humus-rich, moist soil. Flowers in early spring, white. The flowering spike, the spadix, grows to 12 inches (30 cm) high; leaves grow to 36 by 36 inches (90 by 90 cm). Zones 5–9. Japan to Siberia.

## Lysimachia japonica

Primulaceae

A mat-forming perennial loosestrife for shade or part shade in moist, humus-rich soil. Flowers in summer, yellow. The cultivar 'Minutissima' grows 1–2 inches (2.5–5 cm) high, 8 inches (20 cm) wide. Zones 6–9. The species is from Eurasia.

## Maianthemum bifolium

false lily of the valley
Liliaceae (Convallariaceae)

A perennial from creeping rhizomes for part shade in humus-rich, moist soil. Flowers in spring, white, followed by red berries in summer. Grows 6–8 inches (15–20 cm) high, 36 inches (90 cm) wide. Zones 3–9. Western Europe to Japan.

Lychnis flos-jovis 'Nana'

Lychnis viscaria 'Splendens Plena', courtesy of Fritz Kummert

Lysichiton americanum

Lysichiton camtschatcensis

Lysimachia japonica 'Minutissima', courtesy of Fritz Kummert

Maianthemum bifolium, courtesy of Fritz Kummert

## Maihuenia poeppigii

Cactaceae

A charming little clump-forming cactus that grows well in lean scree with summer irrigation. Springtime feeding helps to encourage the big silky, yellow blossoms. Cultivate in sun in scree with protection from winter wetness. Flowers in late spring, pale yellow. Grows 3 inches (7.5 cm) high, 8 inches (20 cm) wide. Zones 6–10. Chile and Argentina.

## Mandragora officinarum

devil's apples, mandrake
Solanaceae

A perennial for sun in any well-drained soil. Flowers in winter and spring, greenish white. Grows 6 inches (15 cm)

Maihuenia poeppigii, courtesy of Phyllis Gustafson

Mandragora officinarum, courtesy of Fritz Kummert

high, 24 inches (60 cm) wide. Zones 7–9. Northern Italy and the western Balkan Peninsula.

## Marrubium rotundifolium

Labiatae

A horehound whose flowers are insignificant and are best sheared off to better enjoy the felted, pale green leaves with scalloped edges of woolly white, also backed white. Stems and branchlets of this perennial are woolly white, too. Cultivate in sun in any well-drained soil, even poorish soil. Flowers in early summer, yellowish. Grows 4 inches (10 cm) high, 12–18 inches (30–45 cm) wide. Zones 5–10. Turkey.

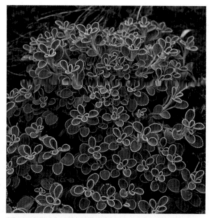

Marrubium rotundifolium

Matthiola fruticulosa subsp. valesiaca with Alyssum in the foreground, courtesy of Fritz Kummert

## Matthiola fruticulosa subsp. valesiaca

gillyflower, stock
Cruciferae

A woody-based perennial with underground runners for sun in any good, extremely well drained soil, preferably alkaline. Flowers in late spring and summer, mauve-purple to red-purple. Grows 10 inches (25 cm) high, 12 inches (30 cm) wide. Zones 6–9. Northern and eastern Spain, Pyrenees, southern Alps, and the Balkan Peninsula.

## Mazus reptans

Scrophulariaceae

A perennial for sun or part shade in humus-rich, moist soil. Flowers in summer, purple-blue marked with white and yellow. Grows 2 inches (5 cm) high, 18 inches (45 cm) wide. Zones 3–9. Himalayas.

Mazus reptans

Meehania urticifolia, courtesy of Sigurd Lock

## *Meehania urticifolia*
Labiatae

A perennial Meehan's mint, creeping by stolons, for part shade in any good soil. Flowers in early summer in one-sided spikes, violet-blue. Grows 4 inches (10 cm) high, 36 inches (90 cm) wide. Zones 6–9. Japan.

## *Mentha*
mint
Labiatae

## *Mentha requienii*
Corsican mint

A tiny, mat-forming perennial with extremely strong, peppermint scented foliage. Some love the plant for the fragrance, some avoid it. Cultivate in part shade in any good, moist soil. Flowers in summer, pale lilac. Grows ½ inch (1 cm) high, 12 inches (30 cm) wide. Zones 6–9. Corsica, Sardinia, and the Italian mainland.

## *Mertensia*
Boraginaceae

## *Mertensia alpina*
A perennial for sun or part shade in scree, keeping it moist in the growing season, drier after flowering. Flowers in early summer, dark blue. Grows 8 inches (20 cm) high, 12 inches (30 cm) wide. Zones 4–8. Rocky Mountains.

## *Mertensia maritima*
oyster plant

A perennial for sun or part shade in sandy scree. Flowers in summer, soft blue from pink buds. Grows 6 inches (15 cm) high, 24 inches (60 cm) wide. Zones 3–7. Alaska and coastal northeastern North America, Greenland and Eurasia.

## *Mertensia pterocarpa*
synonym, *M. yezoensis*

A perennial for sun or part shade in humus-rich, gritty, well-drained soil. Flowers in summer, blue. Grows 12–16 inches (30–40 cm) high, 12 inches (30 cm) wide. Zones 6–8. Hokkaido, Japan, and the Kuriles. Some authorities consider *M. pterocarpa* to be a Far Eastern version of *M. sibirica*, which is native throughout Eurasia.

## *Meum athamanticum*
baldmoney
Umbelliferae

An aromatic, herbaceous perennial grown mainly for its finely dissected foliage. Cultivate in sun or part shade in any good soil. Flowers in summer, white or pink. Grows 12–16 inches (30–40

*Mentha requienii*, courtesy of Franz Hadacek

*Mertensia pterocarpa*

*Mertensia alpina*

*Mertensia maritima*, courtesy of Fritz Kummert

*Meum athamanticum*, courtesy of Fritz Kummert

cm) high, 12 inches (30 cm) wide. Zones 5–8. Europe.

## Microbiota decussata
Cupressaceae

A prostrate, evergreen, coniferous shrub for sun or part shade in any good, well-drained soil. Grows 6 inches (15 cm) high, 36 inches (90 cm) wide. Zones 2–8. Siberia.

## Milium effusum
wood millet
Gramineae

A perennial grass for sun or part shade in any good soil. The cultivar 'Aureum' (synonym, 'Bowle's Golden Grass'), golden wood millet, flowers in late spring in golden panicles. Grows 12–24 inches (30–60 cm) high, 12 inches (30 cm) wide. Zones 6–10. The species is from Eurasia and North America.

## Mimulus
monkeyflower
Scrophulariaceae

## Mimulus 'Andean Nymph'

A curious situation evolved after Martyn Cheese and John Watson collected this perennial in the Chilean Andes in 1973. It was never given a scientific name though it has proven itself to be worthy of species status. It lightly self-sows and comes true from seed. Cultivate in sun or part shade in any good, well-drained, moist soil. Flowers in late spring to early fall, pastel yellow tinged with pink and spotted with red. Grows 6–10 inches (15–25 cm) high, 12 inches (30 cm) wide. Zones 4–10.

## Mimulus cardinalis
scarlet monkeyflower

A perennial for sun or part shade in any good, moist soil. Flowers in June through August, scarlet. Grows 18–24 inches (45–60 cm) high, 18 inches (45 cm) wide. Zones 4–10. Southern Oregon to Mexico, and Nevada.

*Microbiota decussata* in bronze winter color

*Mimulus* 'Andean Nymph'

*Milium effusum* 'Aureum'

*Mimulus cardinalis*

## Mimulus primuloides

A fine dwarf, rhizomatous and mat-forming perennial that does best if kept in cool, gritty soil and is divided and replanted frequently to maintain vigor. Cultivate in sun or part shade in any good, well-drained, moist soil. Flowers in June and July, yellow. Grows 4–6 inches (10–15 cm) high, 12 inches (30 cm) wide. Zones 4–9. California north to Washington and east into the Rocky Mountains.

## Minuartia
sandwort
Caryophyllaceae

Confusion still exists in distinguishing between *Minuartia* and *Arenaria*. Plants of both genera require similar conditions and most have appealing hummock and cushion shapes ideal for the rock garden.

## Minuartia circassica
synonym, *Arenaria pinifolius*
A perennial for sun in scree. Flowers in early summer, white. Grows 8 inches (20 cm) high, 12 inches (30 cm) wide. Zones 5–8. Caucasia.

## Minuartia laricifolia

A woody-based perennial for sun in any good, well-drained soil. Flowers in summer, white. Grows 4–8 inches (10–20 cm) high, 12 inches (30 cm) wide. Zones 5–9. Austrian Alps and the Carpathians.

## Minuartia sedoides

A densely hummock-forming perennial for sun in any good, well-drained soil. Flowers in summer, greenish white or yellowish. Grows 2 inches (5 cm) high, 6–12 inches (15–30 cm) wide. Zones 5–8. Pyrenees, Alps, Carpathians, and Scotland.

## Minuartia verna subsp. *gerardii*

A loosely dome-shaped perennial for sun in any good, well-drained soil. The cultivar 'Plenum', double-flowered sandwort, flowers in summer, white. Grows 4 inches (10 cm) high, 12 inches (30 cm) wide. Zones 3–8. The species is from Europe.

## Mitchella repens
partridge berry, running box, two-eyed berry
Rubiaceae
One of the finest little carpeting plants for shaded areas if provided lime-free,

*Mimulus primuloides*, courtesy of Fritz Kummert

*Minuartia laricifolia*, courtesy of Fritz Kummert

*Minuartia sedoides*, courtesy of Fritz Kummert

*Minuartia circassica*

*Minuartia verna* subsp. *gerardii* 'Plenum', courtesy of Fritz Kummert

peaty soil and a cool location. A woody-based, evergreen perennial for shade or part shade in humus-rich, well-drained, neutral to acid soil. Flowers in spring, pinkish white, followed by shiny red berries. Grows 1 inch (2.5 cm) high, 12–18 inches (30–45 cm) wide. Zones 3–8. Eastern United States and Canada. There is a slower growing, white-berried form, well worth acquiring, *M. repens* f. *leucocarpa*.

## Moltkia suffruticosa
Boraginaceae
A shrublet for sun in any good, well-drained soil. Flowers in summer, blue. Grows 6–10 inches (15–25 cm) high, 18 inches (45 cm) wide. Zones 6–9. Mountains of northern Italy.

*Mitchella repens*, courtesy of Armen Gevjan

*Moltkia suffruticosa*, courtesy of Fritz Kummert

## Morisia monanthos
Cruciferae
A rosette-forming perennial for sun or part shade in well-drained, sandy or gritty soil. Flowers in spring and early summer, golden yellow. Grows 2 inches (5 cm) high, 6 inches (15 cm) wide. Zones 7–9. Corsica and Sardinia.

## Muehlenbeckia axillaris
creeping wire vine
Polygonaceae
A mat-forming shrub for sun or shade in any good, well-drained soil. Flowers in summer, greenish, followed by attractive white fruit. Grows 4 inches (10 cm) high, 18 inches (45 cm) wide. Zones 7–10. New Zealand.

*Morisia monanthos*, courtesy of Fritz Kummert

## Mukdenia rossii
Saxifragaceae
synonym, *Aceriphyllum rossii*
Forming thick, creeping rhizomes, large glossy leaves, and white, *Bergenia*-like flowers, in or out of flower an herbaceous perennial that is a bold-looking addition to a cool, moist site. Cultivate in part shade in humus-rich, moist, neutral to acid soil. Flowers in April and May. Grows 12 inches (30 cm) high, 18 inches (45 cm) wide. Zones 6–9. China.

## Muscari
grape hyacinth
Liliaceae (Hyacinthaceae)

## Muscari armeniacum
A bulbous perennial for sun or part shade in any good, well-drained soil. The cultivar 'Blue Spike' flowers in spring, soft blue, doubled. Grows 6 inches (15 cm) high. Zones 4–9. The species is from southeastern Europe to Caucasia.

*Muehlenbeckia axillaris*, courtesy of Franz Hadacek

*Mukdenia rossii*

## Muscari comosum

tassel hyacinth

synonyms, *Leopoldia comosa, L. tenuiflora*
A bulbous perennial for sun or part
shade in any good, well-drained soil.
Flowers in spring, blue or violet. Grows
8–14 inches (20–35 cm) high. Zones
4–9. Central and southern Europe,
northern Africa, and southwestern Asia.

## Myosotis colensoi

Boraginaceae

synonym, *M. decora*
A perennial forget-me-not for part
shade in humus-rich, well-drained soil.
Flowers in early summer, white. Grows 3

Muscari armeniacum 'Blue Spike', courtesy
of Fritz Kummert

Muscari comosum, courtesy of Fritz Kummert

inches (7.5 cm) high, 8 inches (20 cm)
wide. Zones 7–9. Waimakariri Valley,
South Island, New Zealand.

## Narcissus

daffodil
Amaryllidaceae

There are many fine dwarf and miniature species and cultivars of daffodils for
the rock garden, containers, and the
alpine house, the latter especially for the
winter-flowering species. The best soil
for these bulbous perennials should be
very well drained with humus added,
preferably including leaf mold, and
should remain reasonably moist year-
round.

## Narcissus asturiensis

Cultivate in sun or part shade in humus-
rich, well-drained soil. Flowers in late

Myosotis colensoi, courtesy of Fritz Kummert

Narcissus asturiensis 'Giant'

winter and early spring, yellow. The cultivar 'Giant' grows 4–6 inches (10–15
cm) high. Zones 4–9. The species is from
the Pyrenees, northern Spain, and
northern Portugal.

## Narcissus bulbocodium var. conspicuus

Cultivate in sun or part shade in humus-
rich, well-drained soil. Flowers in late
winter and early spring, golden yellow.
Grows 6 inches (15 cm) high. Zones 5–9.
The species, hoop petticoat daffodil, is
from western France, Spain, Portugal,
and North Africa.

## Narcissus cyclamineus

Cultivate in part shade in humus-rich,
well-drained, moist, acid soil. Flowers in
early spring, deep yellow. Grows 8 inches
(20 cm) high. Zones 5–9. Northern Portugal and northwestern Spain.

## Narcissus jonquilla

jonquil
Cultivate in sun or part shade in humus-
rich, well-drained soil. Zones 4–9.

Narcissus bulbocodium var. conspicuus

Narcissus cyclamineus

Central and northern Portugal and Spain.

**Cultivars**. *Narcissus jonquilla* 'Baby Moon' flowers in spring, yellow. Grows 8 inches (20 cm) high.

*Narcissus jonquilla* 'Sundisc' flowers in spring, pale yellow petals, flat yellow cup. Grows 8–10 inches (20–25 cm) high.

## Narcissus triandrus

angel's tears

Cultivate in sun or part shade in humus-rich, well-drained soil. Flowers in spring, milky white. Grows 12 inches (30 cm) high. Zones 4–9. Portugal, Spain, and northwestern France.

*Narcissus jonquilla* 'Baby Moon'

## Nectaroscordum siculum

Sicilian honey garlic
Liliaceae (Alliaceae)
synonym, *Allium siculum*

A bulbous perennial for sun or shade in any soil, *N. siculum* is a close *Allium* relative, quite tall but elegant when in flower. Flowers in late spring and early summer, greenish white flushed with maroon and with a green stripe. Grows 30–48 inches (75–120 cm) high. Zones 6–9. Western Mediterranean and southern Europe.

## Nepeta phyllochlamys

Labiatae

The catmints benefit from occasional division to encourage new, vigorous growth that in turn makes them hardier

*Narcissus triandrus* var. *triandrus*, courtesy of Fritz Kummert

in severe climates, as does a well-drained soil fairly devoid of nutrients. *Nepeta phyllochlamys* is a perennial for sun in any well-drained soil, even poor soil. Flowers in May and June, pink with red spots. Grows 6 inches (15 cm) high, 24 inches (60 cm) wide. Zones 5–9. Turkey.

*Nectaroscordum siculum*, courtesy of Fritz Kummert

*Nepeta phyllochlamys*

*Nerine bowdenii* 'Mark Fenwick', courtesy of Fritz Kummert

*Narcissus jonquilla* 'Sundisc'

## Nerine bowdenii
Amaryllidaceae

The hardiest species of *Nerine* and a few different color forms exist, ranging from pink to deep rose. These bulbous perennials will continue to flower until December in an alpine house or in mild climates. Cultivate in sun or part shade in humus-rich, well-drained soil. The cultivar 'Mark Fenwick' (synonym, 'Fenwick's Variety') flowers in late summer and fall, cyclamen pink. Grows 18–24 inches (45–24 cm) high. Zones 7–10. The species is from the Drakensberg Mountains of South Africa.

## Nierembergia repens
whitecup
Solanaceae
synonym, *N. rivularis*

A mat-forming perennial for sun or part shade in fertile, well-drained, gritty soil. Flowers in summer, white with a yellow eye. Grows 2 inches (5 cm) high, 12 inches (30 cm) wide. Zones 7–10. Chile, Argentina, and Uruguay.

## Oenothera
evening primrose
Onagraceae

## Oenothera caespitosa subsp. crinita

*Oenothera caespitosa*, fragrant, tufted, or white evening primrose, and its sub-

species are the northern counterparts of the Chilean *O. acaulis*, which consistently has pinnatifid, dandelion-like leaves. *Oenothera caespitosa* is variable in leaf, subspecies *crinita* always having simply sinuate leaves. All are well worth growing but often prove short-lived in cultivation. *Oenothera caespitosa* subsp. *crinita* is a perennial for sun or part shade in any good, well-drained soil. Flowers in summer, white, fading rose pink, closing in bright sunshine. Grows 8–10 inches (20–25 cm) high, 24 inches (60 cm) wide. Zones 4–9. The species is from California north to Washington and east to Utah.

## Oenothera kunthiana

A self-sowing perennial for sun in any well-drained soil. Flowers in summer, deep pink. Grows 4 inches (10 cm) high, 12 inches (30 cm) wide. Zones 7–10. Texas and Mexico.

## Oenothera missouriensis
Ozark sundrops
synonym, *O. macrocarpa*

A perennial for sun or part shade in any soil. Flowers in late spring or summer, yellow. Grows 8 inches (20 cm) high, 30 inches (75 cm) wide. Zones 4–10. Southern central United States.

## Oenothera speciosa
Mexican evening primrose
synonym, *O. berlandieri*

A perennial, spreading by underground rhizomes, for sun in any good, well-drained soil. All forms can be invasive spreaders if not controlled. The cultivar

*Oenothera caespitosa* subsp. *crinita*

*Nierembergia repens,* courtesy of Fritz Kummert

*Oenothera kunthiana*

*Oenothera missouriensis*

'Siskiyou' flowers in June through August, during the day, rose pink. This cultivar was selected from plants purchased from Siskiyou Rare Plant Nursery, Medford, Oregon, and given the nursery's name. It is described as lighter rose pink, more compact, and more nearly everblooming than the species. Grows 8 inches (20 cm) high, 24– 36 inches (60–90 cm) wide. Zones 5–10. The species is from the southwestern United States and Mexico. 'Woodside White' is a taller, white-flowered clone.

## Omphalodes
navelseed, navelwort
Boraginaceae

### Omphalodes cappadocica
A perennial for shade or part shade in moist, humus-rich, well-drained soil.

Flowers in spring, deep blue. Grows 6 inches (15 cm) high, 18 inches (45 cm) wide. Zones 5–8. Black Sea coast of Turkey.

### Omphalodes luciliae
A perennial for sun or part shade in well-drained, limy soil in rock crevices, or in the alpine house. Flowers in summer, sky blue from pink buds. Grows 6–8 inches (15–20 cm) high, 8 inches (20 cm) wide. Zones 6–8. Turkey.

### Omphalodes verna
blue-eyed Mary, creeping forget-me-not
An easy-to-grow, small, perennial ground cover, forming colonies by stolons, which in mild weather will begin blooming in late winter. Cultivate in shade or part shade in humus-rich, moist soil. Flowers in late winter and

early spring, deep, bright blue. Grows 6–8 inches (15–20 cm) high, 24 inches (60 cm) wide. Zones 6–9. Europe. The cultivar 'Alba' is a good, pure white form.

## Onosma
Boraginaceae

### Onosma alborosea
A perennial for sun in fertile scree with protection from winter wetness, or in the alpine house. Flowers in April and May, white flushed with pink. Grows 6 inches (15 cm) high, 12 inches (30 cm) wide. Zones 4–9. Mediterranean and central Asia.

### Onosma taurica
golden drop
A perennial for sun in fertile scree. Flowers in summer, yellow or cream.

Oenothera speciosa 'Siskiyou'

Omphalodes verna

Omphalodes cappadocica

Omphalodes luciliae, courtesy of Franz Hadacek

Onosma alborosea, courtesy of Panayoti Kelaidis

Grows 8–10 inches (20–25 cm) high, 24 inches (60 cm) wide. Zones 6–9. Turkey and southeastern Europe.

## *Ophiopogon japonicus*
Liliaceae (Convallariaceae)
An evergreen perennial for sun or part shade in humus-rich, well-drained soil. The cultivar 'Kyoto Dwarf', miniature Mondo grass, flowers in summer, light lilac, followed by blue fruit. It is a nice, evergreen foil for the alpine house, a miniature ground cover in mild climates and good for bonsai. Grows 2 inches (5 cm) high, 6 inches (15 cm) wide. Zones 7–10. The species is from Japan.

## *Opithandra primuloides*
Gesneriaceae
A perennial for shade or part shade in humus-rich, gritty soil in an alpine house or in a sheltered spot in the rock garden. Flowers in spring, violet-purple. Grows 4 inches (10 cm) high, 8 inches (20 cm) wide. Zones 7–9. Japan.

## *Opuntia polyacantha*
Cactaceae
The prickly pear cacti are primarily native to the western United States and most are very cold hardy. In spite of their dangerously sharp spines, they are very decorative when producing their big silken flowers. *Opuntia polyacantha* is a mat-forming cactus for sun in any well-drained soil. Flowers in early summer, yellow. Grows 6 inches (15 cm) high, 24 inches (60 cm) wide. Zones 5–9. Canada, United States, and northern Mexico.

## *Orchis*
Orchidaceae

## *Orchis mascula*
early purple orchid
A tuberous terrestrial orchid for part shade in humus-rich, well-drained, moist soil. Flowers in late spring, pale to deep purple with a brown hood. Grows 8–24 inches (20–60 cm) high. Zones 5–8. Europe to Caucasia and northern Africa.

## *Orchis spectabilis*
showy orchid
A tuberous terrestrial orchid for part shade in humus-rich, well-drained,

*Opuntia polyacantha,* courtesy of Fritz Kummert

*Orchis mascula,* courtesy of Armen Gevjan

*Onosma taurica*

*Ophiopogon japonicus* 'Kyoto Dwarf'

*Opithandra primuloides*

*Orchis spectabilis,* courtesy of Armen Gevjan

moist soil. Flowers in late spring or early summer, white lip with a rosy purple hood. Grows 4–12 inches (10–30 cm) high. Zones 5–8. Eastern North America.

## *Origanum*
marjoram, oregano
Labiatae

The origanums are ornamental, aromatic herbs, mostly found in the Mediterranean region. Since they benefit from dryish winter conditions, they are appropriate for the alpine house, especially the furry-leaved varieties, which may succumb to winter wetness. All thrive in sun and have showy summer flowers with surrounding bracts for a long season of bloom.

## *Origanum amanum*
A low and spreading subshrub for sun in any good, well-drained, gritty soil. Flowers in summer, lilac pink. Grows 4–6 inches (10–15 cm) high, 10 inches (25 cm) wide. Zones 6–9. Nur (Amanus) Mountains of southern Turkey.

## *Origanum dictamnus*
dittany of Crete, hop marjoram
A subshrub for sun in any good, well-drained, gritty soil with protection from winter wetness, or in the alpine house. Flowers in summer, pink surrounded by reddish purple bracts. Grows 12 inches (30 cm) high, 16 inches (40 cm) wide. Zones 7–9. Crete.

## *Origanum* ×*hybridum*
A perennial subshrub for sun in any good, well-drained, gritty soil. Flowers in June to August, pink with pink-tinged bracts, aging to maroon. Grows 10 inches (25 cm) high, 18 inches (45 cm) wide. Zones 6–10. A garden hybrid, *O. dictamnus* × *O. sipyleum*.

## *Origanum* 'Kent Beauty'
A woody-based perennial for sun in any good, well-drained, gritty soil. Flowers in summer, pink with rich pink bracts. Grows 8 inches (20 cm) high, 18 inches (45 cm) wide. Zones 6–9. A garden hybrid, *O. rotundifolium* × *O. scabrum*.

## *Origanum pulchellum*
synonym, *O. scabrum* subsp. *pulchellum*
A perennial subshrub, spreading underground, for sun in any good, well-drained soil. Flowers in summer, pink from long, hop-like, straw-colored bract clusters. Grows 18 inches (45 cm) high,

*Origanum amanum,* courtesy of Fritz Kummert

*Origanum* 'Kent Beauty'

*Origanum dictamnus,* courtesy of Fritz Kummert

*Origanum* ×*hybridum* with fresh flowers and bracts

*Origanum pulchellum*

24 inches (60 cm) wide. Zones 6–9. Southeastern Europe.

## Origanum scabrum

A woody-based, rhizomatous perennial for sun in any good, well-drained soil. Flowers in summer, lilac with pink to purple bracts. Grows 18 inches (45 cm) high and wide. Zones 7–10. Mountains of Greece.

## Origanum tournefortii

synonym, *O. calcaratum*

A subshrub similar to *O. dictamnus* but a bit less woolly so it seems to handle more winter moisture, an excellent plant. Cultivate in sun in any good, well-drained, gritty soil protected from winter wetness, or in the alpine house.

Flowers in summer, pink surrounded by reddish bracts. Grows 14 inches (35 cm) high, 18 inches (45 cm) wide. Zones 7–10. Crete and the Cyclades.

## Ornithogalum oligophyllum

star of Bethlehem
Liliaceae (Hyacinthaceae)
synonym, *O. balansae*

A bulbous perennial for sun or part shade in any well-drained soil. Flowers in late winter and spring, white from green buds. Grows 6 inches (15 cm) high. Zones 6–9. Balkan Peninsula and western Turkey.

## Orostachys
Crassulaceae

## Orostachys iwarenge

iwa-renge
synonym, *Sedum iwarenge*

A curious but handsome little succulent, which loses only its flowering rosette after it blooms. To promote greater production of offsets on stolons, pinch out the top of the flowering spike before it matures. Cultivate in sun or part shade in any well-drained soil. Flowers in fall, white. Grows 8–12 inches (20–30 cm) high, 8 inches (20 cm) wide. Zones 6–9. China.

## Orostachys spinosa

synonym, *Sedum spinosum*

A monocarpic succulent, producing multiple biennial rosettes, for sun or part shade in any well-drained soil, and in the alpine house. Flowers in summer, greenish yellow in a spike-like panicle. Grows 8–12 inches (20–30 cm) high, 8 inches (20 cm) wide. Zones 4–8. Central and northern Asia.

Origanum scabrum, courtesy of Fritz Kummert

*Orostachys iwarenge,* courtesy of Franz Hadacek

*Origanum tournefortii*

*Ornithogalum oligophyllum,* courtesy of Fritz Kummert

*Orostachys spinosa* with *Veronica spicata* 'Nana'

## *Ourisia*
figwort
Scrophulariaceae

### *Ourisia caespitosa* var. *gracilis*
A mat-forming perennial for part shade in well-drained, moist, peaty soil. Flowers in summer, white. Grows 4 inches (10 cm) high, 10 inches (25 cm) wide. Zones 6–9. Mountains of South Island, New Zealand.

### *Ourisia coccinea*
A mat-forming perennial for part shade in well-drained, moist, peaty soil. Flowers in spring and summer, scarlet. Grows 10 inches (25 cm) high, 12 inches (30 cm) wide. Zones 6–9. Southern Chile.

*Ourisia caespitosa* var. *gracilis*, courtesy of Fritz Kummert

*Ourisia coccinea*, courtesy of Fritz Kummert

## *Oxalis*
shamrock, sorrel
Oxalidaceae

There are some weedy species of *Oxalis* that plague gardens, but do not let the few "bad apples" prevent growing the many worthy ones.

### *Oxalis acetosella*
alleluia, cuckoo bread, European wood sorrel
A rhizomatous perennial for shade or part shade in humus-rich, well-drained soil. Flowers in summer, white with pink veining. Grows 4 inches (10 cm) high, 12 inches (30 cm) wide. Zones 3–8. Europe, central and northern Asia to Japan.

### *Oxalis adenophylla*
sauer klee
A bulbous perennial for sun or part shade in humus-rich scree. Flowers in June through August, veined lilac pink to rose pink with deeper color. Grows 6

*Oxalis acetosella*, courtesy of Fritz Kummert

*Oxalis adenophylla*, courtesy of Fritz Kummert

inches (15 cm) high and wide. Zones 5–9. Alpine areas in Chile and southern Argentina.

### *Oxalis depressa*
synonym, *O. inops*
Only slightly invasive when grown in mild winter climates, otherwise a delightful creeping ground cover that reappears every spring and blooms in summer. A bulbous and rhizomatous perennial for sun or part shade in any good, well-drained soil. Flowers in early summer, rose pink. Grows 4 inches (10 cm) high, 8 inches (20 cm) wide. Zones 5–10. South Africa.

### *Oxalis enneaphylla*
scurvy grass
A rhizomatous perennial for sun or part shade in well-drained, sandy soil rich in leaf mold. Flowers in late spring and summer, white to rosy purple with purplish veins. Grows 2–4 inches (5–10 cm)

*Oxalis depressa*

*Oxalis enneaphylla*, courtesy of Fritz Kummert

high, 6 inches (15 cm) wide. Zones 6–9. Southern tip of South America and the Falkland Islands.

## Oxalis hirta

A bulbous and clump-forming perennial for sun or part shade in any good, well-drained soil. Flowers in fall to early winter, bright rose. Grows 12 inches (30 cm) high, 18 inches (45 cm) wide. Zones 8–10. South Africa.

## Oxalis microphylla

synonym, *O. exigua*

A mat- or hummock-forming perennial for sun or part shade in humus-rich scree. Flowers in summer, yellow. Grows 4–6 inches (10–15 cm) high, 12 inches (30 cm) wide. Zones 6–9. Alpine regions of Chile.

## Oxalis obtusa

From tiny bulblets, a perennial that appears in spring and blooms, goes dormant in summer, resprouts in fall, then goes dormant in winter. Cultivate in sun or part shade in humus-rich scree. Flowers in April and May, coral pink. Grows 4 inches (10 cm) high, 6 inches (15 cm) wide. Zones 7–10. South Africa.

## Oxalis oregana

redwood sorrel

A rhizomatous and colony-forming perennial for cool shade to part shade in humus-rich, well-drained soil. Flowers in late spring and summer, white to pink. Grows 4–8 inches (10–20 cm) high, 18 inches (45 cm) wide. Zones 7–10. Washington south to California.

## Oxyria digyna

mountain sorrel

Polygonaceae

A perennial for sun or part shade in poorish, well-drained, moist soil. Flowers in summer, insignificant and green, followed by bright pink, winged fruit.

Grows 6–12 inches (15–30 cm) high, 12 inches (30 cm) wide, and larger in cultivation. Zones 2–7. Arctic and alpine regions of North America, Europe, and Asia.

## Oxytropis

crazy weed, locoweed, point vetch

Leguminosae

Seed is the best means to acquire members of the genus *Oxytropis*. They are perennials that do not transplant easily. Once established they should be left undisturbed.

## Oxytropis campestris

meadow milkvetch, yellow oxytropis

Cultivate in sun in deep, well-drained soil. Flowers in summer, white, yellow, or violet. Grows 4–8 inches (10–20 cm) high, 12 inches (30 cm) wide. Zones 3–8. Northern Europe and mountains of central and southern Europe.

*Oxalis hirta*

*Oxalis obtusa*

*Oxyria digyna*, courtesy of Fritz Kummert

*Oxalis microphylla*

*Oxalis oregana*

*Oxytropis campestris*, courtesy of Fritz Kummert

## Oxytropis halleri
purple oxytropis

Cultivate in sun in deep, well-drained soil. Flowers in summer, blue to purple with a darker keel. Grows 6–8 inches (15–20 cm) high, 10 inches (25 cm) wide. Zones 6–8. Pyrenees, Alps, Carpathians, and mountains of Scotland and Albania.

## Oxytropis lazica

A perennial with a woody rootstock for sun in deep, well-drained soil. Flowers in late summer, violet to pale blue or white. Grows 6 inches (15 cm) high, 12 inches (30 cm) wide. Zones 5–8. Alpine meadows of Transcaucasia and Turkey.

**P**

## Pachysandra procumbens
Allegheny spurge
Buxaceae

A semi-evergreen perennial for part shade in humus-rich soil. Flowers in early spring, purplish. Grows 8–12 inches (20–30 cm) high, 18 inches (45 cm) wide. Zones 6–9. Southeastern United States.

## Paeonia
peony
Paeoniaceae

The dwarfer peonies are outstanding plants for the large rock garden. Plant in good, deep soil and be patient; they take time to get established and start performing.

## Paeonia cambessedesii

A perennial for sun or part shade in humus-rich soil. Flowers in late spring and early summer, rose pink to red. Grows 18 inches (45 cm) high and wide. Zones 7–9. Balearic Islands, Spain.

## Paeonia tenuifolia

A perennial for sun or part shade in humus-rich soil. Flowers in early summer, dark crimson. Grows 14–20 inches (35–50 cm) high, 24 inches (60 cm) wide. Zones 5–9. Southeastern Europe to Caucasia.

## Pancratium illyricum
Amaryllidaceae

A bulbous perennial for sun in any good, sharply drained soil. Flowers in late spring and early summer, white or cream. Grows 18 inches (45 cm) high and wide. Zones 8–10. Corsica, Sardinia, and Capri.

## Papaver
poppy
Papaveraceae

## Papaver burseri

A perennial with incomparably delicate blossoms. Plants live about 3 years in the garden but are replaced by self-sown seedlings. In hot climates give them good, moist, well-drained soil plus a top-dressing of stone chips. Flowers in summer, white. Grows 6–10 inches (15–25 cm) high, 8 inches (20 cm) wide.

*Oxytropis halleri,* courtesy of Fritz Kummert

*Pachysandra procumbens*

*Paeonia tenuifolia,* courtesy of Fritz Kummert

*Oxytropis lazica,* courtesy of Fritz Kummert

*Paeonia cambessedesii,* courtesy of Fritz Kummert

*Pancratium illyricum,* courtesy of Fritz Kummert

Zones 5–8. Northern Alps, Carpathians, and other mountains of Europe.

## Papaver nudicaule
arctic or Iceland poppy
A perennial for sun in any good, well-drained soil. The cultivar 'Garden

*Papaver burseri*, courtesy of Fritz Kummert

*Papaver nudicaule* 'Garden Gnome', courtesy of Fritz Kummert

*Papaver rhaeticum*, courtesy of Fritz Kummert

Gnome' (synonym, 'Gartenzwerg') flowers in summer in shades of yellow, orange, and pink. Grows 12 inches (30 cm) high, 8 inches (20 cm) wide. Zones 2–8. The species is from Siberia to Mongolia and mountains of central Asia and Afghanistan.

## Papaver rhaeticum
A perennial for sun in any good, well-drained soil. Flowers in summer, bright yellow. Grows 4–6 inches (10–15 cm) high, 6 inches (15 cm) wide. Zones 5–8. Pyrenees and the southwestern and eastern Alps.

## Parahebe catarractae
Scrophulariaceae
A mat-forming subshrub for sun or part shade in any good, well-drained soil. Flowers in summer, white, veins pink or purple. Grows 12 inches (30 cm) high, 18 inches (45 cm) wide. Zones 8–10. New Zealand.

*Parahebe catarractae*

*Paraquilegia anemonoides*, courtesy of Fritz Kummert

## Paraquilegia anemonoides
Ranunculaceae
synonym, *P. grandiflora*
A perennial for part shade in humus-rich, sharply drained, gritty soil, preferably limy, and doing best in an alpine house. Flowers in spring, rich lavender to pale violet-blue. Grows 6–10 inches (15–25 cm) high, 10 inches (25 cm) wide. Zones 5–8. Himalayas from Pakistan to western China and central and northern Asia.

## Parnassia palustris
Saxifragaceae
A perennial grass of Parnassus or bog star for sun or part shade in humus-rich, constantly moist soil. Flowers in summer, white. Grows 4–12 inches (10–30 cm) high. Zones 4–8. Europe, temperate Asia and North America.

## Paronychia argentea
Caryophyllaceae
*Paronychia*—chickweed, nailwort, Whitlowwort—has several fine species that sport papery bracts with a silvery, frosted appearance that lasts all summer. *Paronychia argentea* is a mat-forming perennial for sun in any good, well-drained soil. Flowers in late spring to midsummer, tiny, petalless flowers in

*Parnassia palustris*, courtesy of Fritz Kummert

silvery bracts. Grows 2 inches (5 cm) high, 12–24 inches (30–60 cm) wide. Zones 6–9. Southern Europe, northern Africa, and southwestern Asia.

## Paxistima canbyi
cliff green, mountain lover
Celastraceae
Sometimes misspelled as *Pachistima* or *Pachystima*, *Paxistima canbyi* is an evergreen shrub for sun or part shade in any good soil. Flowers in spring and summer, tiny and reddish. Grows 10–16 inches (25–40 cm) high, 18 inches (45 cm) wide. Zones 4–8. Eastern United States from Ohio to Virginia and Kentucky.

*Paronychia argentea,* courtesy of Fritz Kummert

*Paxistima canbyi,* courtesy of Fritz Kummert

## Pediocactus simpsonii
snowball cactus
Cactaceae
A low-growing, shrubby perennial for sun in any well-drained soil. Flowers in spring, white, pink, magenta, yellow, or yellow-green. Grows 6 inches (15 cm) high and wide. Zones 5–9. Western Kansas west to New Mexico, Montana, and Idaho.

## Pelargonium endlicherianum
Geraniaceae
The hardiest of the pelargoniums or stork's bills, not to be confused with true geraniums. Keep this rhizomatous perennial dryish in winter in order to enjoy the glowing pink flowers that stand out

*Pediocactus simpsonii,* courtesy of Fritz Kummert

*Pelargonium endlicherianum*

in the summer garden. Cultivate in sun or part shade in any good, well-drained soil protected from excess winter wetness, and in the alpine house. Flowers in summer, bright magenta-pink. Grows 8–12 inches (20–30 cm) high, 8 inches (20 cm) wide. Zones 7–9. Turkey and Syria.

## Pellaea breweri
Brewer's cliff brake
Adiantaceae
All pellaeas have unusual, blue-green foliage and will take considerable sun and drought. *Pellaea breweri* is an evergreen perennial fern for sun or part shade in any good, sharply drained soil, preferably alkaline. Grows 6–8 inches (15–20 cm) high, 12 inches (30 cm) wide. Zones 4–8. California north to Washington and east to Utah.

## Pennisetum alopecuroides
fountain grass
Gramineae
A perennial grass for sun or part shade in any good soil. Flowers in summer and fall, greenish white, maturing to a creamy tan. The short, nonaggressive tuffets of the cultivar 'Little Bunny', miniature fountain grass, add a natural look and texture to the rock garden and alpine lawn. Grows 12 inches (30 cm) high, 18 inches (45 cm) wide. Zones 5–9. The species is from eastern Asia to western Australia. More dwarf forms of the large-growing grasses are becoming available for the rock garden. There is a

*Pellaea breweri*

silver-variegated form of 'Little Bunny', 'Little Honey'.

## Penstemon
beard tongue
Scrophulariaceae

Most penstemons for the rock garden are dwarf shrubby types, nearly all native to the western United States. They provide invaluable color for the summer garden. Good, well-drained, rocky soil is best, as is full sun, but avoid parched, hot sites and excessively poor soil.

## Penstemon cardwellii
An evergreen shrublet for sun in fertile, sharply drained soil. Flowers in summer in shades of purple and blue-violet. Grows 4–10 inches (10–25 cm) high, 18 inches (45 cm) wide. Zones 6–9. Mountains of Washington and Oregon.

**Cultivar**. *Penstemon cardwellii* 'Roseus' flowers in summer, rose pink. Grows 6 inches (15 cm) high, 18 inches (45 cm) wide.

## Penstemon davidsonii
A mat-forming, evergreen shrub for sun in fertile, sharply drained soil. Flowers in summer, blue-lavender to purple-violet. Grows 4 inches (10 cm) high, 18 inches (45 cm) wide. Zones 4–9. British Columbia to California, Vancouver Island, the Olympic Mountains, the Cascade Range, and the Sierra Nevada.

## Penstemon eatonii
Eaton's firecracker
A perennial for sun in any good, sharply drained soil. Flowers in midsummer into fall, scarlet. Grows 24–30 inches (60–75 cm) high, 24 inches (60 cm)

*Pennisetum alopecuroides* 'Little Bunny'

*Penstemon cardwellii* 'Roseus'

*Penstemon cardwellii*

*Penstemon davidsonii*

*Penstemon eatonii*

wide. Zones 6–9. Southwestern United States north to Utah.

### Penstemon fruticosus subsp. scouleri

synonym, *P. scouleri*

An evergreen shrub for sun in fertile, sharply drained soil. The cultivar 'Albus' flowers in summer, pure white. Grows 12 inches (30 cm) high, 24 inches (60 cm) wide. Zones 4–8. The subspecies is from mountains of the Washington-Idaho border north to British Columbia.

### Penstemon hirsutus

A self-sowing perennial for sun in any good, well-drained soil. The cultivar 'Pygmaeus' is very pretty with dense clusters of flowers. Weed out taller seedlings that are not pygmy enough for the rock garden. Flowers in June through August, lavender with white tips. Grows 4–6 inches (10–15 cm) high, 12 inches (30 cm) wide. Zones 4–8. The species is

Penstemon fruticosus subsp. scouleri 'Albus'

Penstemon hirsutus 'Pygmaeus'

from Maine to Virginia, east to Wisconsin.

### Penstemon newberryi

mountain pride

An evergreen subshrub for sun in fertile, sharply drained, acid soil. It does best in a rock crevice. Flowers in summer, brilliant rosy red. Grows 12 inches (30 cm) high and wide. Zones 6–8. Alpine areas of northern California and adjacent Nevada.

### Penstemon pinifolius

One of the easiest to grow and showiest of shrubby penstemons. Given humus-rich but well-drained soil, it is an evergreen that will contradict the myth that it is shy about flowering in the garden. Cultivate in sun. Flowers in June through August, scarlet. Grows 6 inches (15 cm) high, 18 inches (45 cm) wide. Zones 4–10. New Mexico to Arizona and Mexico.

**Cultivar**. *Penstemon pinifolius* 'Mersea Yellow' flowers in June through September, yellow.

### Penstemon rupicola

rock penstemon

A mat-forming, evergreen shrublet for sun or part shade in fertile, sharply

Penstemon newberryi, courtesy of Ted Kipping

drained soil. Flowers in summer, rich reddish pink. The cultivar 'Fiddler Mountain' is a Siskiyou Rare Plant Nursery selection from Fiddler Mountain in the Siskiyou Mountains of Oregon, chosen for its superior silver foliage, prostrate habit, and rich red flowers. Grows 6 inches (15 cm) high, 12 inches (30 cm) wide. Zones 4–8. The species is from mountains, mostly, of Washington south to northern California.

### Penstemon 'Six-Hills Hybrid'

An old, woody-based perennial named in honor of a once famous English nursery, remaining one of the finest shrubby penstemons for the rock garden. Cultivate in sun or part shade in fertile, sharply drained soil. Flowers in late spring and early summer, violet. Grows 8 inches (20 cm) high, 18 inches (45 cm) wide. Zones 5–9. A garden hybrid, *P. davidsonii* × *P. eriantherus*.

Penstemon pinifolius

Penstemon pinifolius 'Mersea Yellow'

## Penstemon speciosus subsp. kennedyi

A woody-based perennial for sun in fertile, sharply drained soil. Flowers in summer, bright purple-blue. Grows 4–12 inches (10–30 cm) high, 12 inches (30 cm) wide. Zones 3–7. Sierra Nevada and White Mountains of California.

## Penstemon teucrioides

One of the smallest and finest penstemons, perfect for the rock garden crevice or trough. A mat-forming perennial with a creeping, woody rootstock for sun in fertile, sharply drained soil. Flowers in summer, blue to blue-purple. Grows 2–4 inches (5–10 cm) high, 12–16 inches (30–40 cm) wide. Zones 4–8. Mountains of Colorado.

## Perezia recurvata

Compositae

A good, small candidate for the trough, from exposed, high elevations. A cushion- to mat-forming perennial with deep green, bristly foliage, forming a dense bun. The daisy flower heads resemble chicory blossoms. Cultivate in sun in fertile, well-drained soil. Flowers in June through August, blue. Grows 3 inches (7.5 cm) high, 8 inches (20 cm) wide. Zones 6–9. Southern Chile, southern Argentina, and the Falkland Islands.

## Pernettya tasmanica

Ericaceae

synonym, *Gaultheria tasmanica*

A mat- to cushion-forming, evergreen shrub for sun or part shade in humus-rich, fairly moist, neutral to acid soil. Flowers in spring or early summer, white, followed by white or pinkish fruit. Grows 2–4 inches (5–10 cm) high, 12 inches (30 cm) wide. Zones 6–9. Mountains of Tasmania.

*Penstemon teucrioides*

*Perezia recurvata,* courtesy of Fritz Kummert

*Penstemon rupicola* 'Fiddler Mountain'

*Penstemon* 'Six-Hills Hybrid'

*Penstemon speciosus* subsp. *kennedyi*

*Pernettya tasmanica,* courtesy of Fritz Kummert

## Petrocallis pyrenaica

Cruciferae

synonym, *Draba pyrenaica*

An ideal perennial for the trough or miniature crevice with its diminutive proportions. Cultivate in sun in scree, preferably alkaline. Flowers in early summer, pale lavender (*P. pyrenaica* var. *leucantha*, white flowers), very fragrant. Grows 2 inches (5 cm) high, 6 inches (15 cm) wide. Zones 4–7. Pyrenees, Alps, and Carpathians.

## Petrophytum caespitosum

Rosaceae

A mat-forming, evergreen, subshrubby rock spirea for sun or part shade in neutral to acid scree, in a crevice to provide a cool root run. Flowers in June through August, white. Grows 4 inches (10 cm) high, 12 inches (30 cm) wide. Zones 6–8. Western mountains of the United States. A very similar species is *P. cinerascens* from mountain cliffs in Idaho and Washington. *Petrophytum hendersonii* from the Olympic Mountains in Washington forms low hummocks in cultivation although it is mat-like in the wild.

## Petrorhagia saxifraga

coat flower

Caryophyllaceae

synonyms, *Kohlrauschia saxifraga, Tunica saxifraga*

An alpine, easy to grow and thriving in sun, that produces clouds of small baby's breath (*Gypsophila paniculata*) flowers during the summer season when few other plants are in bloom in the rock garden. A mat-forming perennial for sun in scree. The cultivars 'Rosette' and 'Alba Plena' flower in June through August, pink and white, respectively, doubled. Grow 8 inches (20 cm) high, 18 inches (45 cm) wide. Zones 4–8. The species is from central and southern Europe.

## Phacelia sericea

Hydrophyllaceae

A perennial or biennial scorpion weed from a woody rootstock for sun in scree, and in the alpine house. Flowers in summer, bluish purple to white. Grows 6–18 inches (15–45 cm) high, 6 inches (15 cm) wide. Zones 3–7. Mountains of Oregon to northeastern California, and Arizona to Wyoming.

*Petrocallis pyrenaica,* courtesy of Fritz Kummert

*Petrophytum caespitosum*

*Petrorhagia saxifraga* 'Rosette', left, and *P. saxifraga* 'Alba Plena', right

*Phacelia sericea,* courtesy of Fritz Kummert

*Phlox adsurgens*

## *Phlox*
Polemoniaceae

### *Phlox adsurgens*

*Phlox adsurgens* is a western counterpart to *P. divaricata* and *P. stolonifera*, two woodland species of the eastern United States, and rambles through acid, forest duff in its native habitat. Not always easy to cultivate far from its native region, it is a perennial best grown in a rocky crevice with leaf mold added to the soil. Cultivate in part shade in well-drained, neutral to acid soil. Flowers in late spring and summer, pink, salmon-pink, or lilac with a white eye and darker basal stripe. Grows 6–12 inches (15–30 cm) high, 18 inches (45 cm) wide. Zones 6–9. Woodlands of southern Oregon and northern California.

There is a white form and other variants such as 'Wagon Wheel', which has pink petals uniquely long and narrow.

### *Phlox bifida*
cleft or sand phlox

A perennial for sun in any good, well-drained soil. Flowers in May and June, lavender-blue, sometimes lilac or white. Grows 8 inches (20 cm) high, 12 inches (30 cm) wide. Zones 4–8. Midwestern United States.

**Cultivars**. *Phlox bifida* 'Colvin's White' has white flowers. Grows 4 inches (10 cm) high, 12 inches (30 cm) wide.

*Phlox bifida* 'Starbrite' has little star-shaped flowers, lavender with purple markings. Grows 4 inches (10 cm) high, 12 inches (30 cm) wide.

### *Phlox caespitosa*
synonym, *P. douglasii* var. *caespitosa*

A perennial for sun in any good, well-drained soil. Flowers in spring and summer, lavender, pink, to white. Grows 4 inches (10 cm) high, 8 inches (20 cm) wide. Zones 5–8. Mountains of Colorado, Montana, and Utah to northern California.

### *Phlox divaricata*
wild sweet William

A mat-forming perennial with branches spreading out and rooting at the nodes to form a colony. Cultivate in part shade in humus-rich, well-drained, moist soil. Flowers in spring and early summer, light lavender-blue or lilac. Grows 12 inches (30 cm) high, 18 inches (45 cm)

*Phlox bifida*

*Phlox bifida* 'Colvin's White'

*Phlox caespitosa*, courtesy of Fritz Kummert

*Phlox bifida* 'Starbrite'

*Phlox divaricata*, courtesy of Fritz Kummert

wide. Zones 3–8. Quebec to Michigan, south to Georgia and northern Alabama.

**Cultivar**. *Phlox divaricata* 'Eco Texas Purple' flowers in spring and early summer, purple with a red-violet center. It is one of several fine cultivars of this eastern American woodland phlox.

### Phlox douglasii

Cultivate in sun in any good, well-drained soil. The cultivar 'Crackerjack' flowers in May and June, crimson-red. Grows 4 inches (10 cm) high, 8 inches (20 cm) wide. Zones 4–9. The species is from northeastern Oregon and Washington to northwestern Montana. "*Phlox douglasii*" is the label applied to several excellent cultivars, such as 'Crackerjack', but they are believed to be the result of hybridizing with other species in the garden. All are tufted to mat-forming perennials and flower very freely. Other such cultivars include 'May Snow', white with a purple eye, 'Red Admiral', crimson-rose, and 'Rose Cushion', rose pink.

### Phlox hirsuta

A shrublet for sun in scree, withholding water in summer. Flowers in April and May, purple to pink. Grows 2–4 inches (5–10 cm) high, 6 inches (15 cm) wide. Zones 4–8. Northern California.

### Phlox hoodii

A perennial for any good, well-drained soil. Flowers in spring, white or pale to dark lavender. Grows 2–3 inches (5–7.5 cm) high, 6–12 inches (15–30 cm) wide. Zones 4–8. British Columbia to Manitoba, the Great Plains of the United States, and Colorado and Utah.

### Phlox 'Intensity'

A perennial for sun in any good, well-drained soil. Flowers in spring, lavender-pink, aging paler, with a dark purple basal mark. Grows 2 inches (5 cm) high, 12 inches (30 cm) wide. Zones 3–8.

### Phlox mesoleuca

A perennial for sun in fertile, well-drained, gritty soil. Grows 6 inches (15 cm) high, 18 inches (45 cm) wide. Zones 6–9. The species is from northern central Mexico and adjacent Texas and New Mexico. Species allied to *P. mesoleuca* include *P. mexicana*, *P. nana*, and *P. triovulata*, and much taxonomic confusion exists about them, possibly because all seem capable of crossing with each other.

**Cultivars**. Of the following cultivars, 'Arroyo', 'Chameleon', and 'Mary Maslin' are examples of northern Mexican hybrids that are considered color forms re-

*Phlox hirsuta*

*Phlox divaricata* 'Eco Texas Purple'

*Phlox* 'Intensity'

*Phlox douglasii* 'Crackerjack', courtesy of Fritz Kummert

*Phlox hoodii,* courtesy of Fritz Kummert

*Phlox mesoleuca* 'Arroyo'

sulting from the cross, *P. mesoleuca* var. *lutea* (synonym, *P. lutea*) × *P. mesoleuca* var. *purpurea* (synonym, *P. purpurea*). *Phlox mesoleuca* 'Arroyo' flowers in June through August, bright cerise.

*Phlox mesoleuca* 'Chameleon' flowers in June through August, creamy yellow, fading to near white.

*Phlox mesoleuca* 'Mary Maslin' flowers in June through August, vermilion.

*Phlox mesoleuca* 'Chameleon'

*Phlox mesoleuca* 'Mary Maslin'

*Phlox mesoleuca* 'Paul Maslin'

*Phlox mesoleuca* 'Paul Maslin' (synonyms, *P. lutea* 'Paul Maslin', *P. mesoleuca* var. *lutea* 'Paul Maslin') flowers in June through August, canary yellow.

## Phlox nana

Closely allied to *P. mesoleuca* but of smaller dimensions, *P. nana* is a perennial for sun in fertile, well-drained gritty soil. Flowers in summer and fall, purple, lilac, pink, or white. Grows 4 inches (10 cm) high, 12 inches (30 cm) wide. Zones 6–9. New Mexico and adjacent Mexico, Texas and eastern Arizona.

## Phlox pilosa

prairie phlox

A perennial for sun or part shade in humus-rich, well-drained soil.

**Subspecies and Cultivar**. *Phlox pi-*

*Phlox nana*, courtesy of Fritz Kummert

*losa* subsp. *fulgida* 'Moody Blue' (formerly misnamed *Phlox* 'Chattahoochee') flowers in April and May, blue with a red eye. Grows 8–12 inches (20–30 cm) high, 18 inches (45 cm) wide. Zones 3–9. The subspecies is from Ontario, Canada to Texas, and east to the Atlantic States.

*Phlox pilosa* subsp. *osarkana* (synonym, *P. osarkana*) flowers in late spring, pink. Grows 10–18 inches (25–45 cm) high, 18 inches (45 cm) wide. Zones 5–9. Missouri to eastern Oklahoma and northern Louisiana.

## Phlox ✕procumbens

The variegated cultivar 'Folio-variegata' is a perennial for sun or part shade in any good, well-drained soil. Flowers in spring, pink. Grows 6 inches (15 cm)

*Phlox pilosa* subsp. *fulgida* 'Moody Blue'

*Phlox pilosa* subsp. *osarkana*, courtesy of Armen Gevjan

high, 18 inches (45 cm) wide. Zones 4–9. *Phlox ×procumbens* is a hybrid, *P. stolonifera* × *P. subulata*.

## Phlox 'Sileneflora'

An unusual introduction by H. Lincoln Foster, a perennial making a tight polster of minute foliage for a perfect trough plant. Cultivate in sun or part shade in any good, well-drained soil. Flowers in spring, pinkish white, shaped like the flowers of *Silene acaulis*. Grows 4 inches (10 cm) high, 6 inches (15 cm) wide. Zones 3–8. A hybrid believed to involve *P. subulata*.

## Phlox stolonifera

creeping phlox
A mat-forming perennial for part shade in humus-rich, well-drained, moderately acid soil. Flowers in late spring, rose pink to light lavender and pale pink. Grows 8 inches (20 cm) high, 24 inches (60 cm) wide. Zones 3–8. Penn-

sylvania to Ohio and northern Georgia. Many popular cultivars exist, including 'Alba' (synonym, 'Ariane'), 'Blue Ridge', 'Pink Ridge', and 'Sherwood Purple'.

## Phlox subulata

moss phlox, moss pink, mountain phlox
A perennial for sun in any good, well-drained soil. Northeastern United States and adjacent Canada.

**Cultivars**. The many cultivars of *P. subulata* are valuable, easy-to-grow plants that should be in every rock garden. Innumerable forms are cultivated, including flower colors ranging from white, pink, to bluish. *Phlox subulata* 'Brittonii Rosea' flowers in spring, light pink. Grows 3 inches (7.5 cm) high, 12 inches (30 cm) wide. Zones 3–8.

*Phlox subulata* 'Fort Hill' flowers in spring, deep rose. Grows 6 inches (15 cm) high, 18 inches (45 cm) wide. It is a more southern and slightly less hardy selection. Zones 5–9.

*Phlox subulata* 'Laura', an introduction by H. Lincoln Foster that was named after his granddaughter, is considered by many to be the best, clear pink selection. Flowers in April and May, pastel pink. Grows 4 inches (10 cm) high, 12 inches (30 cm) wide. Zones 3–8.

*Phlox subulata* 'Samson' flowers in spring, strong pink with a reddish eye. Grows 6 inches (15 cm) high, 24 inches (60 cm) wide. Zones 3–8.

*Phlox subulata* 'Schneewittchen', German for snow white, is one of the finest miniature varieties for a special spot in the rock garden or trough. Flowers in spring, white. Grows 3 inches (7.5 cm) high, 10 inches (25 cm) wide. Zones 3–8.

*Phlox subulata* 'Tamanonagalei' is one of a number of rock garden phlox cultivars available with candy-striped flowers. This one was discovered and named by the Woodbank Nursery, Tas-

Phlox ×procumbens 'Folio-variegata', courtesy of Fritz Kummert

Phlox stolonifera

Phlox subulata 'Fort Hill'

Phlox 'Sileneflora'

Phlox subulata 'Brittonii Rosea'

Phlox subulata 'Laura'

mania. Flowers in spring, white with pink candy-striped petals. Grows 6 inches (15 cm) high, 18 inches (45 cm) wide. Zones 3–8.

## ×*Phylliopsis hillieri*
Ericaceae

An evergreen subshrub for part shade in any good, well-drained, moist, neutral to acid soil, and doing well in a peat bed. The cultivar 'Pinocchio' flowers in spring, red-purple. Grows 12 inches (30 cm) high, 18 inches (45 cm) wide. Zones 6–8. The genus is a garden hybrid, believed to be *Phyllodoce breweri* × *Kalmiopsis leachiana*.

## *Phyllodoce*
Ericaceae

Success with phyllodoces depends on lime-free soil and a cool location in the garden.

## *Phyllodoce aleutica*

An evergreen shrublet for part shade in any good, well-drained, moist, neutral

*Phlox subulata* 'Samson'

*Phlox subulata* 'Schneewittchen'

to acid soil, and doing well in a peat bed. Flowers in late spring, light yellow-green to yellowish white. Grows 4–12 inches (10–30 cm) high, 12 inches (30 cm) wide. Zones 2–7. Alpine slopes from Japan to Alaska.

## *Phyllodoce breweri*
Brewer's mountain heather, purple heather

An evergreen shrublet for part shade in any good, well-drained, moist, neutral to acid soil, and doing well in a peat bed. Flowers in early summer, rose purple to pink. Grows 4–12 inches (10–30 cm) high, 18 inches (45 cm) wide. Zones 3–7. Sierra Nevada of California.

## *Phyllodoce empetriformis*
pink mountain heather

An evergreen shrublet for part shade in any good, well-drained, moist, neutral to acid soil, and doing well in a peat bed. Flowers in summer, rose purple to pink. Grows 6–12 inches (15–30 cm) high, 18

*Phlox subulata* 'Tamanonagalei'

×*Phylliopsis hillieri* 'Pinocchio', courtesy of Franz Hadacek

inches (45 cm) wide. Zones 3–7. Alpine and subalpine areas Alaska to California.

## *Phyllodoce* ×*intermedia*

An evergreen shrublet for part shade in any good, well-drained, moist, neutral

*Phyllodoce aleutica*, courtesy of Franz Hadacek

*Phyllodoce breweri*

*Phyllodoce empetriformis*

to acid soil, and doing well in a peat bed. Flowers in spring and summer, bright reddish purple to pale pink. Grows 4–12 inches (10–30 cm) high, 12 inches (30 cm) wide. Zones 3–7. A naturally occurring hybrid, *P. aleutica* subsp. *glanduliflora* × *P. empetriformis*.

## Physaria chambersii
Cruciferae
A perennial bladderpod for sun in scree. Flowers in late spring, yellow, followed by inflated seed pods. Grows 6–8 inches (15–20 cm) high, 10 inches (25 cm) wide. Zones 6–9. California to Nevada and Utah.

*Phyllodoce ×intermedia,* courtesy of Fritz Kummert

*Physaria chambersii,* courtesy of Fritz Kummert

## Physoplexis comosa
horned rampion
Campanulaceae
synonym, *Phyteuma comosum*
An honored celebrity among alpine plants, to be protected from winter wetness and slug and snail attacks. A perennial for part shade in humus-rich, sharply drained soil, preferably alkaline. Flowers in early summer, violet. Grows 4 inches (10 cm) high, 6 inches (15 cm) wide. Zones 6–8. Alps.

## Phyteuma
horned rampion
Campanulaceae

## Phyteuma globulariaefolium
synonym, *P. pauciflorum*
A perennial for sun or part shade in any good, well-drained soil. Flowers in summer, violet-blue. Grows 2–4 inches (5–10 cm) high, 8 inches (20 cm) wide. Zones 6–8. Eastern Alps.

*Physoplexis comosa,* courtesy of Armen Gevjan

*Phyteuma globulariaefolium,* courtesy of Fritz Kummert

## Phyteuma hemisphaericum
A perennial for sun or part shade in any good, well-drained soil. Flowers in late spring and early summer, deep blue. Grows 4–10 inches (10–25 cm) high, 6 inches (15 cm) wide. Zones 6–8. Pyrenees, Alps, and Apennines.

## Picea
spruce
Pinaceae

The spruces are conifers that have many dwarf selections, some tiny enough for trough gardens, others perfect for the small or large rock garden. They have no special soil requirements but perform best in a cool location with ample water.

## Picea abies
Norway spruce
An evergreen conifer for sun or part shade in fertile, well-drained, moist soil. The cultivar 'Little Gem' is a dwarf, an evergreen shrublet growing 8 inches (20 cm) high, 12 inches (30 cm) wide. Zones

*Phyteuma hemisphaericum,* courtesy of Fritz Kummert

*Picea abies* 'Little Gem'

2–8. The species is from central and northern Europe.

## Picea glauca
white spruce

An evergreen conifer for sun or part shade in fertile, well-drained, moist soil. Zones 2–7. Canada and the northeastern United States.

**Cultivars**. *Picea glauca* 'Alberta Globe' is a very slowly growing dwarf mutation of the already dwarf *P. glauca* 'Conica', which is known as dwarf Alberta spruce. Unlike 'Conica', 'Alberta Globe' forms a globular plant instead of a conical tree with a pointed top. Grows 10 inches (25 cm) high and wide.

*Picea glauca* 'Echiniformis' is a dwarf shrublet, growing 8 inches (20 cm) high, 12 inches (30 cm) wide.

*Picea glauca* 'Pixie' is one of the most slowly growing forms of the dwarf Alberta spruce, *P. glauca* 'Conica', and sports a pointed leader like a most miniature Christmas tree. *Picea glauca* 'Pixie'

*Picea glauca* 'Alberta Globe'

*Picea glauca* 'Echiniformis'

is one of the finest dwarf conifers that will not outgrow its welcome even in a small rock garden, a shrublet growing 16 inches (40 cm) high, 8 inches (20 cm) wide.

## Picea mariana
black spruce

An evergreen conifer for sun or part shade in fertile, well-drained, moist soil. The cultivar 'Nana' is a dwarf that grows 6 inches (15 cm) high, 18 inches (45 cm) wide. Zones 3–8. The species is from Alaska to the northern contiguous

*Picea glauca* 'Pixie'

*Picea mariana* 'Nana'

United States, east to mountains of Virginia.

## Pieris japonica
andromeda, lily of the valley bush
Ericaceae

An evergreen, woodland and peat garden shrub that looks good in every season with glossy, evergreen foliage, lush in summer, decorative flower buds that swell all winter until spring flowers open in drooping or upright clusters, followed by brilliant, reddish new foliage. Cultivate in part shade in humus-rich, moist, acid soil, or in a bog or peat bed. Zones 5–9. Japan, Taiwan, and eastern China.

**Cultivars**. *Pieris japonica* 'Bonsai'. Flowers in March and April, white. Grows 12–18 inches (30–45 cm) high, 12 inches (30 cm) wide.

*Pieris japonica* 'Bonsai'

*Pieris japonica* 'Debutante'. Flowers in early spring, pure white. Grows 12 inches (30 cm) high, 18 inches (45 cm) wide.

### Pimelea prostrata
rice flower
Thymelaeaceae
synonym, *P. coarctata*
An evergreen shrublet for sun or part shade in any good, well-drained, moist, neutral to acid soil. Flowers in summer, white, followed by translucent white berries. Grows 3–6 inches (7.5–15 cm) high, 16 inches (40 cm) wide. Zones 8–9. New Zealand, from the lowlands to the subalpine zone.

*Pieris japonica* 'Debutante', courtesy of Fritz Kummert

*Pimelea prostrata* with foliage of *Geranium sessiliflorum* subsp. *novaezelandiae* 'Nigricans', courtesy of Fritz Kummert

### Pinellia ternata
Araceae
A tuberous-rooted perennial for sun or part shade in humus-rich, well-drained, moist soil. Flowers in late spring to mid-summer, green spathe and purple spadix. Grows 8–12 inches (20–30 cm) high. Zones 6–9. Japan, Korea, and China.

### Pinguicula grandiflora
Lentibulariaceae
All butterworts are insectivorous perennials, a few hardy in temperate climate

*Pinellia ternata* with foliage and flowers of *Anemone sylvestris*, courtesy of Fritz Kummert

*Pinguicula grandiflora*, courtesy of Fritz Kummert

gardens and requiring boggy conditions. Cultivate *P. grandiflora* in part shade in moist, peaty soil. Flowers in late spring and summer, violet-purple, sometimes pink. Grows 3–6 inches (7.5–15 cm) high, 4 inches (10 cm) wide. Zones 7–9. Southwestern Ireland to Spain and France.

### Pinus
Pinaceae

### Pinus heldreichii
Bosnian pine
synonym, *P. leucodermis*
An evergreen conifer for sun or part shade in any good, well-drained, neutral to acid soil. The cultivar 'Schmidtii' is a dwarf, growing 48–60 inches (120–150 cm) high, 36 inches (90 cm) wide. Zones 5–9. The species is from the western Balkan Peninsula, southeastern Italy, and the mountains of Greece.

### Pinus mugo
mountain pine
An evergreen conifer for sun or part shade in any good, well-drained soil. The cultivar 'Gordon Bentham' is a Siskiyou Rare Plant Nursery introduction. This fine dwarf pine was given to us by Gordon Bentham, who was a keen plantsman from British Columbia. Grows 6 inches (15 cm) high, 18 inches (45 cm) wide. Zones 3–9. The species is

*Pinus heldreichii* 'Schmidtii', courtesy of Fritz Kummert

from mountains of Spain, central Europe, and the Balkan Peninsula.

## Pinus sylvestris
Scotch or Scots pine
An evergreen conifer for sun or part shade in any good, well-drained soil. The cultivar 'Globosa Viridis' (synonym, 'Viridis Compacta') is a dwarf, growing 36–48 inches (90–120 cm) high, 24 inches (60 cm) wide. Zones 2–8. The species is from Siberia and eastern Asia to Europe.

## Plantago nivalis
Plantaginaceae
A perennial plantain for sun or part shade in any good, well-drained soil. Flowers in summer, brownish. Grows 6 inches (15 cm) high and wide. Zones 6–9. Sierra Nevada of southern Spain.

*Pinus mugo* 'Gordon Bentham'

*Pinus sylvestris* 'Globosa Viridis'

## Platycodon grandiflorus
Campanulaceae
A perennial balloon flower for sun or part shade in any good, well-drained soil. *Platycodon grandiflorus* 'Apoyama' (synonym, *P. grandiflorus* var. *apoyama*) is remarkably reduced in size when grown in sun and confined to a container, where it will be about 3 inches (7.5 cm) tall with full-sized flowers. Flowers in summer, blue. Grows up to 8 inches (20 cm) high and wide. Zones 3–10. A naturally occurring dwarf from Mount Apoi, Hokkaido, Japan.

## Pleione
Indian crocus
Orchidaceae

Pleiones are beautiful Asian terrestrial orchids ideally suited to container cul-

*Plantago nivalis,* courtesy of Fritz Kummert

*Platycodon grandiflorus* 'Apoyama'

ture, where they can easily be given dry winter conditions from November to February. They require plenty of summer moisture.

## Pleione bulbocodioides
A perennial orchid from pseudobulbs for part shade in fertile, well-drained, moist soil with generous amounts of peat or leaf mold, and crushed fir bark. It should be kept dry but not parched during winter dormancy. The cultivar 'Yunnan' flowers in spring, bright magenta with lip spotted dark red and centered white. Grows 6–12 inches (15–30 cm) high. Zones 7–10. The species is from central to western China.

## Pleione formosana
A perennial orchid from pseudobulbs for part shade in fertile, well-drained, moist soil with generous amounts of peat or leaf mold, and crushed fir bark. It should be kept dry but not parched during winter dormancy. Grows 6–12 inches (15–30 cm) high. Zones 7–10. The species is from Taiwan and eastern China.

*Pleione bulbocodioides* 'Yunnan', courtesy of Fritz Kummert

*Pleione formosana* 'Blush of Dawn'

**Cultivars**. *Pleione formosana* 'Blush of Dawn' flowers in spring with sepals light pink, petals white flushed with light pink, and lip spotted yellow and brown.

*Pleione formosana* 'Polar Sun' flowers in spring with white sepals and the tube with lip marked yellow.

### Pleione limprichtii

synonym, *P. bulbocodioides* 'Limprichtii'
A perennial orchid from pseudobulbs for part shade in fertile, well-drained, moist soil with generous amounts of peat or leaf mold, and crushed fir bark. It should be kept dry but not parched during winter dormancy. Flowers in spring, bright rosy magenta with a white throat spotted brick red. Grows 6–12 inches (15–30 cm) high. Zones 7–10. Southwestern China and northern Myanmar (Burma).

### Polemonium
Jacob's ladder
Polemoniaceae

*Pleione formosana* 'Polar Sun'

*Pleione limprichtii*, courtesy of Fritz Kummert

### Polemonium carneum

A perennial for part shade in any good, well-drained soil. Flowers in late spring, flesh color flushed with apricot pink. Grows 12 inches (30 cm) high and wide. Zones 6–8. Siskiyou Mountains and Cascade Range of Oregon and Washington.

### Polemonium viscosum

alpine Jacob's ladder, sky pilot
synonym, *P. confertum*
A perennial requiring considerable sun, and scree with some fertility, in order to grow short and true to its alpine character. Flowers in summer, blue to violet. Grows 4–18 inches (10–45 cm) high, 12 inches (30 cm) wide. Zones 5–8. Rocky Mountains and high peaks of western North America.

### Polygala
milkwort
Polygalaceae

*Polemonium carneum*, courtesy of Fritz Kummert

*Polemonium viscosum*

### Polygala calcarea

A woody-based and mat-forming perennial for sun or part shade in fertile, well-drained soil, preferably alkaline. The cultivar 'Linnet' flowers in late spring and summer, gentian blue. Grows 2 inches (5 cm) high, 6 inches (15 cm) wide. Zones 6–8. The species is from western Europe, including England; the cultivar is a selection from the wild from northeastern Spain.

### Polygala chamaebuxus

An evergreen shrublet with an underground suckering growth habit, allowing it eventually to form a good-sized, spreading mat. Cultivate in part shade in peaty, well-drained soil. *Polygala chamaebuxus* 'Rhodoptera' (synonyms, *P. chamaebuxus* var. *grandiflora*, *P. chamaebuxus* var. *purpurea*) flowers in February through May, wine red and yellow. Grows 6 inches (15 cm) high, 12 inches

*Polygala calcarea* 'Linnet', courtesy of Fritz Kummert

*Polygala chamaebuxus* 'Rhodoptera'

(30 cm) wide. Zones 6–8. Mountains of western Europe.

## Polygala paucifolia
bird-on-the-wing, flowering wintergreen, fringed polygala, gaywings

A rhizomatous and stoloniferous perennial for shade or part shade in humus-rich, well-drained, neutral to acid soil. Flowers in late spring and summer, rose purple with a fringed white lip. Grows 2–4 inches (5–10 cm) high, 12 inches (30 cm) wide. Zones 2–8. Woodlands of eastern Canada to Minnesota and Georgia.

## Polygala vayredae
A suckering, evergreen shrub for sun or part shade in any good, well-drained soil. Flowers in April and May, red-purple with a yellow keel. Grows 4 inches (10 cm) high, 18 inches (45 cm) wide. Zones 6–8. Eastern Pyrenees.

## Polygonatum
Solomon's seal
Liliaceae (Convallariaceae)

*Polygala paucifolia*

*Polygala vayredae*

## Polygonatum hookeri
The only truly alpine Solomon's seal and not easy to cultivate. When doing well it will spread into a dense colony more than 24 inches (60 cm) across. It seems to be most vigorous with a good amount of sun and an alkaline, clay-based soil. A rhizomatous perennial for sun or part shade. Flowers in early summer, purple or lilac pink. Grows 2–4 inches (5–10 cm) high, usually 12–18 inches (30–45 cm) wide. Zones 6–8. Eastern Himalayas and China.

## Polygonum affine
Polygonaceae
synonym, *Persicaria affine*

A mat-forming perennial fleece flower, knotweed, or smartweed for sun or part shade in any good soil. Flowers in late summer and fall, pale to deep pink. Grows 6–8 inches (15–20 cm) high, 36 inches (90 cm) wide. Zones 3–9. Himalayas, Afghanistan to Nepal.

*Polygonatum hookeri,* courtesy of Fritz Kummert

*Polygonum affine*

## Polypodium hesperium
western polypody
Polypodiaceae
synonym, *P. vulgare* var. *columbianum*

Because it is so widespread, it is a very hardy and adaptable small perennial fern with creeping rhizomes. It is a fine plant for a shady nook in the rock garden. Cultivate in part shade in humus-rich, well-drained soil. Grows 6–8 inches (15–20 cm) high, 18 inches (45 cm) wide. Zones 4–9. Alaska and British Columbia to South Dakota, south to New Mexico and Arizona.

## Polystichum
holly fern
Dryopteridaceae

## Polystichum imbricans
imbricated sword fern
synonym, *P. munitum* var. *imbricans*

A densely clump-forming, evergreen perennial for light shade in humus-rich, well-drained soil. It is at home in a rock crevice. Grows 12–14 inches (30–35 cm)

*Polypodium hesperium*

*Polystichum imbricans*

high, 10 inches (25 cm) wide. Zones 6–9. Alaska to Montana and California.

## Polystichum lonchitis

mountain or northern holly fern
An evergreen perennial for shade or part shade in humus-rich, well-drained, moist soil. Grows 12 inches (30 cm) high, 24 inches (60 cm) wide. Zones 4–8. Mountains of North America, Europe, and Asia.

## Polystichum polyblepharum

Japanese tassel fern
An evergreen perennial for shade or part shade in humus-rich, well-drained, moist soil. Grows 18 inches (45 cm) high, 30 inches (75 cm) wide. Zones 5–9. Japan and South Korea.

Polystichum lonchitis

## Polystichum setiferum

soft shield fern
An evergreen perennial for shade or part shade in humus-rich, well-drained, moist soil. The cultivar 'Divisilobum', divided soft shield fern, grows 12 inches (30 cm) high, 30 inches (45 cm) wide. Zones 6–9. The species is from Europe.

## Potentilla

cinquefoil
Rosaceae

## Potentilla alba

A mat-forming perennial for sun or part shade in fertile, well-drained soil. The cultivar 'Snow White' flowers in spring and summer, white. Grows 4 inches (10 cm) high, 18 inches (45 cm) wide. Zones 5–9. The species is from Europe.

Polystichum setiferum 'Divisilobum'

## Potentilla cinerea

A perennial that eventually forms a wide-spreading, flat mat of silvery, strawberry-like foliage, durable enough to take light foot traffic and very hot conditions. Cultivate in sun in any good, well-drained soil. Flowers in spring and summer, yellow. Grows 2 inches (5 cm) high, 24 inches (60 cm) wide. Zones 5–9. Alps.

## Potentilla fruticosa

golden hardhack, shrubby cinquefoil, widdy
A widely distributed and variable deciduous shrub found in many small varieties and cultivars appropriate for the rock garden. It is a valuable, sturdy plant that has a long season of cheerful flowers, including selections with pinkish and red blossoms. Cultivate in sun in well-drained soil, watering only moderately. Flowers in late spring and summer in many shades of yellow to white.

Potentilla alba 'Snow White'

Polystichum polyblepharum, courtesy of Fritz Kummert

Potentilla cinerea

Grows 12–60 inches (30–150 cm) high and wide. Zones 2–9. Northern hemisphere.

## Potentilla tabernaemontani
spring cinquefoil
synonyms, *P. neumanniana, P. verna*
A perennial for sun or part shade in any good, well-drained soil. The cultivar 'Orange Flame' is a form of 'Nana' (synonym, *P. verna* 'Nana') with vivid green leaves and golden flowers, more orange than those of 'Nana'. 'Orange Flame' forms a neat tuft of foliage and flowers for a long season. Flowers in spring and summer, deep gold. Grows 4 inches (10 cm) high, 12 inches (30 cm) wide. Zones 4–9. The species is from Europe.

## Primula
primrose
Primulaceae

*Potentilla fruticosa,* courtesy of Fritz Kummert

*Potentilla tabernaemontani* 'Orange Flame'

## Primula allionii
A perennial for part shade in humus-rich, well-drained, moist soil with protection from winter wetness, or in the alpine house. Flowers in early spring, rosy pink to reddish purple with a white eye, or sometimes white. Grows 3 inches (7.5 cm) high, 4 inches (10 cm) wide. Zones 6–8. French and Italian Maritime Alps.

*Primula allionii,* courtesy of Fritz Kummert

**Cultivar.** *Primula allionii* 'Crowsley Variety' has small gray-green leaves and deep crimson flowers with a white eye.

## Primula auricula
auricula
A perennial, subshrubby with age. Cultivate in part shade in humus-rich, well-drained, moist, neutral to limy soil. Flowers in spring, pale to deep yellow. Many colorful hybrids exist. Grows 8 inches (20 cm) high and wide. Zones 3–8. Alps, Carpathians, and Apennines.

*Primula allionii* 'Crowsley Variety', courtesy of Phil Pearson

*Primula auricula* in the wild near Neuhaus, Austria, courtesy of Fritz Kummert

## Primula ×berninae

A perennial for part shade in humus-rich, well-drained, moist soil. The cultivar 'Windrush', one of the most dwarfed, compact selections, with vivid flowers, flowers in March and April, deep rosy purple. Grows 4 inches (10 cm) high, 6 inches (15 cm) wide. Zones 4–8. A naturally occurring hybrid from the Alps, *P. hirsuta* × *P. latifolia*. The hybrids known as *P.* ×*berninae* come in a variable array of foliage and flower; *P. hirsuta* and *P. latifolia* are known to hybridize freely in the wild in Switzerland and Austria.

## Primula carniolica

A perennial for part shade in humus-rich, well-drained, moist soil. Flowers in spring and summer, rose to purple-pink with a white eye. Grows 6 inches (15 cm)

*Primula* ×*berninae* 'Windrush'

*Primula carniolica,* courtesy of Fritz Kummert

high, 4 inches (10 cm) wide. Zones 6–8. Mountains of Slovenia.

## Primula clarkei

With regular division and replanting immediately after flowering, this little gem will remain in vigorous good health and increase quite rapidly. It is a perennial for part shade in humus-rich, well-drained, moist soil. Flowers in early spring, rose pink with a white and yellow eye. Grows 3 inches (7.5 cm) high, 4 inches (10 cm) wide. Zones 6–8. Kashmir.

## Primula clusiana

A perennial for part shade in humus-rich, well-drained, moist soil. Flowers in early summer, pinkish red, fading to lilac, with a white eye. Grows 4–8 inches (10–20 cm) high, 8 inches (20 cm) wide. Zones 5–8. Northeastern Alps, Austria and Germany.

## Primula daonensis

synonym, *P. oenensis*
A perennial for part shade in humus-

*Primula clarkei,* courtesy of Fritz Kummert

*Primula clusiana,* courtesy of Fritz Kummert

rich, well-drained, moist soil. Flowers in early spring, rose pink. Grows 4 inches (10 cm) high, 6 inches (15 cm) wide. Zones 5–7. Rhaetian Alps.

## Primula denticulata

drumstick primula
A very hardy perennial that performs best in cold winter climates and quite moist, even wet conditions. Cultivate in sun or part shade in humus-rich, moist or even wet soil. Flowers in spring, rose, pink, lavender, and white. Grows 12 inches (30 cm) high and wide. Zones 4–8. Damp alpine meadows, Afghanistan to China. There is a miniature form, not yet named as a cultivar, that grows only half as tall.

## Primula deorum

A perennial for part shade in humus-rich, well-drained, moist soil. Flowers in late spring, violet to crimson-purple. Grows 8 inches (20 cm) high, 6 inches

*Primula daonensis,* courtesy of Fritz Kummert

*Primula denticulata,* courtesy of Fritz Kummer

(15 cm) wide. Zones 5–8. Mountains of southwestern Bulgaria.

## Primula elatior
oxlip

A widespread species with many subspecies with flowers in a wide range of yellow shades and throat colors ranging from greenish to orange. A perennial for part shade in humus-rich, well-drained soil. Flowers in spring in one-sided umbels, all flowers of the umbel leaning to one side, pale yellow, throat marked orange (subspecies *meyeri*, deep pink flowers). Grows 8 inches (20 cm) high and wide. Zones 5–8. The species is from western Europe, including Britain, to Ukraine and Iran.

Primula deorum, courtesy of Fritz Kummert

Primula elatior subsp. *elatior*, courtesy of Fritz Kummert

## Primula glaucescens

A perennial for part shade in humus-rich, well-drained, moist soil. Flowers in spring, pinkish red to lilac. Grows 2–4 inches (5–10 cm) high, 6 inches (15 cm) wide. Zones 6–8. Southern Alps of Italy.

## Primula glutinosa

A beautiful perennial that unfortunately is not easy to cultivate, much less bring into flower in the garden. Cultivate in part shade in well-drained, moist, peaty soil. Flowers in late spring, deep violet, rarely white. Grows 4 inches (10 cm) high, 6 inches (15 cm) wide. Zones 4–8. Austrian Alps to the central Balkan Peninsula.

## Primula ×heerii

A perennial for part shade in fertile scree. Flowers in spring, deep pink.

Primula glaucescens, courtesy of Fritz Kummert

Primula glutinosa, courtesy of Fritz Kummert

Grows 2 inches (5 cm) high, 6 inches (15 cm) wide. Zones 5–8. A naturally occurring hybrid, *P. hirsuta* × *P. integrifolia*.

## Primula hirsuta
synonym, *P. rubra*

A perennial for part shade in fertile scree. Flowers in spring, pale lilac to good clear pink or red, usually with a white center. Grows 2–4 inches (5–10 cm) high, 6 inches (15 cm) wide. Zones 5–8. Central Alps and Pyrenees.

## Primula 'Joan Hughes'

A perennial for part shade in humus-rich, well-drained, moist soil. Flowers in

Primula ×heerii, courtesy of Fritz Kummert

Primula hirsuta, courtesy of Fritz Kummert

Primula 'Joan Hughes', courtesy of Fritz Kummert

spring, magenta-pink. Grows 4 inches (10 cm) high, 6 inches (15 cm) wide. Zones 6–8. A garden hybrid, *Primula* 'Linda Pope' × *P. allionii*.

## Primula 'Johanna'

A hybrid that combines the qualities of its esteemed parents, being both petite and vigorous with handsome, stout-stemmed flowers. A perennial for part shade in humus-rich, well-drained, moist soil. Flowers in spring, bright pink with yellow throat. Grows 5 inches (12.5 cm) high, 6 inches (15 cm) wide. Zones 4–9. A garden hybrid, *P. clarkei* × *P. warshenewskiana*.

## Primula kisoana

A perennial, spreading by underground stolons, for part shade in humus-rich, well-drained soil. Flowers in spring, deep rose, mauve-pink, or occasionally white. Grows 8 inches (20 cm) high, 18 inches (45 cm) wide. Zones 4–9. Japan.

## Primula kitaibeliana

A perennial for part shade in humus-rich, well-drained, moist soil. Flowers in late spring, pink to magenta with a white eye. Grows 6 inches (15 cm) high and wide. Zones 7–9. Central and western Balkan Peninsula.

## Primula latifolia

synonym, *P. viscosa*

A perennial for part shade in humus-rich, well-drained, moist soil. Flowers in late spring, purple to violet. Grows 6 inches (15 cm) high and wide. Zones 5–8. Pyrenees and the central, southern, and western Alps.

*Primula kitaibeliana,* courtesy of Fritz Kummert

## Primula 'Linda Pope'

A perennial, forming woody stems, with a pronounced silver edge to the foliage and fine umbels of large flowers. Cultivate in sun or part shade in humus-rich, gravelly, moist soil. Flowers in spring, mauve-blue with a white farinose eye. Grows 4 inches (10 cm) high, 12 inches (30 cm) wide. Zones 5–8. A hybrid, *P. allionii* × *P. marginata*.

## Primula macrophylla

A Himalayan native often confused with *P. nivalis, P. macrophylla* has long, strap leaves that are farinose beneath and tall stems of many-flowered umbels. A perennial for part shade in humus-rich, well-drained, moist soil. Flowers in late spring, purple, violet, or lilac with a darker eye, or tinged yellow. Grows 12

*Primula* 'Linda Pope'

*Primula* 'Johanna'

*Primula kisoana*

*Primula latifolia,* courtesy of Fritz Kummert

*Primula macrophylla,* courtesy of Fritz Kummert

inches (30 cm) high, 6 inches (15 cm) wide. Zones 6–8. Mountain meadows, Afghanistan to Tibet.

## Primula magellanica

synonym, *P. decipiens*

A perennial for part shade in humus-rich, well-drained, moist soil. Flowers in spring, white or rarely lilac to purple, with a yellow eye. Grows 6 inches (15 cm) high and wide. Zones 6–8. Patagonia to Tierra del Fuego and the Falkland Islands.

## Primula marginata

A perennial, forming woody stems, for sun or part shade in humus-rich, gravelly, moist soil. Flowers in spring, pale lavender or lilac to pink, with a white farinose eye. Grows 3 inches (7.5 cm) high, 12 inches (30 cm) wide. Zones 5–8. Maritime and Cottian Alps of France and Italy.

## Primula megaseifolia

Often misspelled *megasaefolia*, *P. megaseifolia* is a perennial for part shade in humus-rich, well-drained, moist soil. Flowers in early spring, magenta-rose to rose pink. Grows 6–8 inches (15–20 cm) high, 6 inches (15 cm) wide. Zones 7–8. Black Sea coast of northern Turkey.

## Primula minima

A mat-forming perennial for sun or part shade in humus-rich, well-drained, moist soil, keeping it drier in fall. Flowers in spring, bright pink, lilac, or white. Grows 1–2 inches (2.5–5 cm) high, 6 inches (15 cm) wide. Zones 5–8. Mountains of southeastern Europe.

## Primula palinuri

A perennial for sun or part shade in sandy, fertile, well-drained soil. Flowers in spring, deep yellow with a white farinose ring. Grows 6–10 inches (15–25 cm) high, 12 inches (30 cm) wide. Zones 5–8. Southern Italy.

## Primula pedemontana

Like a more compact *P. hirsuta* and having handsome, quite glossy leaves that are round and edged in russet hairs. A perennial for part shade in humus-rich, well-drained, moist soil. Flowers in spring and early summer, pink, purplish pink, to white. Grows 5 inches (12.5 cm) high, 4 inches (10 cm) wide. Zones 6–8. Southwestern Alps, Pyrenees.

## Primula ×pruhoniciana

polyanthus

synonym, *P. ×juliana*

No special care is required, just fertile, well-drained soil and some shade. A popular line of hybrids for part shade in humus-rich, well-drained soil. Zones 4–8. *Primula ×pruhoniciana* is a garden hybrid, *P. juliae* × *P. vulgaris*.

*Primula palinuri*, courtesy of Fritz Kummert

*Primula magellanica*, courtesy of Fritz Kummert

*Primula megaseifolia*, courtesy of Fritz Kummert

*Primula marginata*, courtesy of Fritz Kummert

*Primula minima*, white-flowered form, courtesy of Fritz Kummert

*Primula pedemontana*, courtesy of Fritz Kummert

**Cultivars**. *Primula* ×*pruhoniciana* 'Garryarde Guinevere' is a stoloniferous or mat-forming perennial. Flowers in spring, soft pink. Grows 6 inches (15 cm) high, 12 inches (30 cm) wide.

*Primula* ×*pruhoniciana* 'Juanita' is a more recently introduced cultivar that is a clump-forming perennial with sunshine bright flowers that last for several weeks. Flowers in spring, soft yellow with a golden eye. Grows 8 inches (20 cm) high, 12 inches (30 cm) wide.

*Primula* ×*pruhoniciana* 'Wanda' is a mat-forming perennial. Flowers in spring, claret crimson. Grows 4 inches (10 cm) high, 12 inches (30 cm) wide.

## Primula ×pubescens

A perennial for part shade in humus-rich, well-drained, moist soil. Flowers in spring, selections available in shades of white, yellow, pink, red, or purple. Grows 4–8 inches (10–20 cm) high, 8 inches (20 cm) wide. Zones 4–8. A hybrid, *P. auricula* × *P. hirsuta*.

**Cultivar**. *Primula* ×*pubescens* 'Harlow Car' is one of the loveliest of pastel primroses; the petals are arranged in a tubular "hose-in-hose" fashion. Flowers in spring, white flushed with pink. Grows 4 inches (10 cm) high, 6 inches (15 cm) wide.

## Primula reptans

A stoloniferous perennial for part shade in acid scree, and doing well in the alpine house. Flowers in spring in shades of purple to pink with a white eye. Grows 1 inch (2.5 cm) high, 8 inches (20 cm) wide. Zones 4–8. Alpine regions of Pakistan to Nepal.

## Primula rosea

A perennial for sun or part shade in humus-rich, well-drained, wet soil. Flowers in spring, rose pink to rose red with a yellow eye. Grows 4–10 inches (10–25 cm) high, 6 inches (15 cm) wide. Zones 5–8. Alpine regions of Kashmir to Afghanistan.

## Primula sieboldii

A primrose that is easy to grow and permanent, a rhizomatous perennial in which dormancy occurs in summer when the plant is safe underground, thus tolerating drier conditions better than most primulas. The leaves emerge from spreading rhizomes in early spring, and umbels of up to 10 large flowers follow. Cultivate in shade or part shade in humus-rich, well-drained, moist soil. Flowers in spring and early summer in all shades of pink, cerise, red to lavender, and white. Grows 8 inches

*Primula* ×*pruhoniciana* 'Garryarde Guinevere'

*Primula* ×*pruhoniciana* 'Juanita'

*Primula* ×*pruhoniciana* 'Wanda'

*Primula* ×*pubescens*, courtesy of Fritz Kummert

*Primula* ×*pubescens* 'Harlow Car'

*Primula reptans*, courtesy of Fritz Kummert

*Primula rosea*, courtesy of Fritz Kummert

(20 cm) high and wide. Zones 4–9. Japan and Siberia.

**Cultivars**. There are hundreds of named cultivars, mostly of Japanese origin, exhibiting a wide range of colors

*Primula sieboldii,* courtesy of Fritz Kummert

*Primula sieboldii* 'Musashino'

*Primula sieboldii* 'Yubisugata'

and petal shapes. *Primula sieboldii* 'Musashino' has large flowers of pale rose pink with a darker rose reverse.

*Primula sieboldii* 'Yubisugata' has jagged petaled flowers that are pure white on the back and lavender splashed with white on the front.

### Primula sinopurpurea

A perennial for part shade in humus-rich, well-drained, moist soil. Flowers in summer, purple-violet with a white or gray eye. Grows 8–12 inches (20–30 cm) high, 6 inches (15 cm) wide. Zones 5–8. China.

### Primula spectabilis

A perennial for part shade in humus-rich, well-drained, moist soil. Flowers in

*Primula sinopurpurea,* courtesy of Fritz Kummert

*Primula spectabilis,* courtesy of Fritz Kummert

late spring, pink-red to lilac. Grows 6 inches (15 cm) high and wide. Zones 5–8. Lake Garda region of the Italian Alps.

### Primula tyrolensis

A perennial very much like *P. allionii* although, unfortunately, not as freely flowering in cultivation. Cultivate in part shade in humus-rich, well-drained, moist soil. Flowers in spring, lilac to purplish pink with a white eye. Grows 2 inches (5 cm) high, 4 inches (10 cm) wide. Zones 5–8. Dolomites of the eastern Alps.

### Primula veris subsp. *macrocalyx*

A perennial cowslip for part shade in humus-rich, well-drained, moist soil. Flowers in early spring in one-sided umbels, all flowers of the umbel leaning to one side, yellow with an orange spot at the base. Grows 8 inches (20 cm) high, 12 inches (30 cm) wide. Zones 5–9. All of Asia to eastern Turkey.

*Primula tyrolensis,* courtesy of Fritz Kummert

*Primula veris* subsp. *macrocalyx,* courtesy of Fritz Kummert

### Primula vialii

With tall flower stems emerging from 8-inch- (20-cm-) high foliage, the flower clusters of *P. vialii* remind one of the spikes of red-hot poker *(Knifophia)* in a dwarfer form. The entire plant appears late in spring, flowers in summer, and goes dormant from November to May. A perennial for part shade in humus-rich, well-drained, moist soil with drier conditions during dormancy. Flowers in summer, lavender, topped by vivid crimson buds. Grows 14–18 inches (35–45 cm) high, 8 inches (20 cm) wide. Zones 5–9. China.

### Primula ×vochinensis

A perennial for part shade in humus-rich, well drained, moist soil. Flowers in

*Primula vialii,* courtesy of Ted Kipping

*Primula ×vochinensis,* courtesy of Fritz Kummert

spring in shades of reddish pink to purple-red. Grows 4 inches (10 cm) high, 8 inches (20 cm) wide. Zones 6–9. A naturally occurring hybrid from the eastern Dolomites of the Alps, *P. minima × P. wulfeniana.*

### Primula vulgaris subsp. sibthorpii

A perennial primrose for part shade in humus-rich, well-drained, moist soil. Flowers in spring, clear pink. Grows 6–8 inches (15–20 cm) high, 8 inches (20 cm) wide. Zones 6–8. Greece to Iran.

### Primula warshenewskiana

A perennial for part shade in humus-rich, well-drained, moist soil. Flowers in spring, pink to pinkish red with white markings. Grows 3 inches (7.5 cm) high, 4 inches (10 cm) wide. Zones 6–8. Central Asia to the northern Himalayas.

### Primula wulfeniana

In its best color form, a very attractive perennial with ruby-purple flowers,

*Primula vulgaris* subsp. *sibthorpii,* courtesy of Fritz Kummert

*Primula warshenewskiana,* courtesy of Fritz Kummert

good sized and in umbels of three or more. *Primula wulfeniana* is easy to grow but, sadly, flowers poorly in cultivation. Cultivate in part shade in humus-rich, well-drained, moist soil. Flowers in spring, reddish purple with a white eye. Grows 2–4 inches (5–10 cm) high, 8 inches (20 cm) wide. Zones 5–8. Austrian Alps to the southern Carpathians.

### Prostanthera cuneata
Labiatae

An evergreen shrub, an Australian mint bush for sun in well-drained, moist, acid soil. Flowers in late spring and summer, white or pale mauve. Grows 30–40 inches (75–100 cm) high, 40 inches (100 cm) wide. Zones 9–10. Tasmania and southeastern Australia.

### Prunella grandiflora
Labiatae

A perennial, creeping by runners, a heal-all or self-heal for sun or part shade in any good soil. Flowers in summer,

*Primula wulfeniana,* courtesy of Fritz Kummert

*Prostanthera cuneata,* courtesy of Fritz Kummert

deep violet. Grows 8 inches (20 cm) high, 18 inches (45 cm) wide. Zones 4–9. Europe.

## *Prunus*
cherry, plum
Rosaceae

### *Prunus prostratus*

A deciduous shrub for sun in any good, well-drained soil. Flowers in spring, reddish pink, followed by red fruit. Grows 36 inches (90 cm) high, 48 inches (120 cm) wide. Zones. Southern Europe and northern Africa to Turkey and Syria.

### *Prunus pumila* var. *depressa*

A very hardy, ground-hugging, deciduous shrub with attractive spring bloom, bird-attracting fruit, and brilliant red fall color. A sand cherry for sun in any good, well-drained soil. Flowers in spring, white, followed by dark brownish purple fruit. Grows 12 inches (30 cm) high, 48 inches (120 cm) wide.

*Prunella grandiflora,* courtesy of Fritz Kummert

*Prunus prostratus,* courtesy of Franz Hadacek

Zones 2–8. The species is from eastern North America from Canada to Pennsylvania.

## *Pseudotsuga menziesii*
Douglas fir
Pinaceae
An evergreen conifer for sun or part shade in any good, well-drained soil. Zones 4–8. Subspecies *menziesii* is from British Columbia to central California.

**Cultivars**. *Pseudotsuga menziesii* 'Hillside Pride' is a shrub that grows 24 inches (60 cm) high, 16 inches (40 cm) wide.

*Pseudotsuga menziesii* subsp. *glauca* 'Fletcheri' is a shrub, a cultivar of Colorado Douglas fir, that grows 24 inches (60 cm) high, 36 inches (90 cm) wide.

*Prunus pumila* var. *depressa*

*Pseudotsuga menziesii* subsp. *glauca* 'Fletcheri'

Zones 4–8. The subspecies is from the Rocky Mountains, Alberta to New Mexico.

## *Pterocephalus perennis*
Dipsacaceae
synonym, *P. parnassii*
The dwarf perennial members of the genus *Pterocephalus* are fine, mat-forming plants with pretty pincushion flowers (like those of *Scabiosa*) sitting right on the foliage. *Pterocephalus perennis* is a mat-forming perennial from a woody base for sun in any good, well-drained soil. Flowers in early summer, light pur-

*Pseudotsuga menziesii* 'Hillside Pride'

ple. Grows 3 inches (7.5 cm) high, 18 inches (45 cm) wide. Zones 5–8. Mountains of Greece.

## *Ptilotrichum spinosum*
Cruciferae
synonym, *Alyssum spinosum*

A subshrub for sun in any good, sharply drained soil. The cultivar 'Roseum' flowers in May and June, rich rose pink. Grows 6 inches (15 cm) high, 12–18 inches (30–45 cm) wide. Zones 4–9. The species is from mountains of the Mediterranean.

## *Pulmonaria*
lungwort
Boraginaceae

The lungworts are versatile plants for light to full shade and moist soil. Many feature strikingly colorful foliage. For

added vigor and tidy foliage throughout summer, shear plants back after the first flowering.

## *Pulmonaria angustifolia*
cowslip lungwort
synonym, *P. azurea*

A colony-forming perennial for part shade in any good, well-drained soil. Flowers in March and April, royal blue. Grows 8 inches (20 cm) high, 12 inches (30 cm) wide. Zones 2–9. Pyrenees, Alps, and the western Apennines.

## *Pulmonaria* 'Janet Fisk'

A rhizomatous perennial for part shade in fertile, well-drained soil. Flowers in late winter and early spring, blue and pink. Grows 12 inches (30 cm) high, 18 inches (45 cm) wide. Zones 3–9.

*Pulmonaria angustifolia*

## *Pulmonaria longifolia*
A rhizomatous and clump-forming perennial for part shade in fertile, well-drained soil. Flowers in late winter and early spring, blue. Grows 12 inches (30 cm) high, 18 inches (45 cm) wide. Zones 3–9. Europe.

## *Pulmonaria montana*
synonym, *P. rubra*

A rhizomatous perennial for part shade in fertile, well-drained soil. The cultivar

*Pulmonaria* 'Janet Fisk'

*Pulmonaria longifolia,* courtesy of Fritz Kummert

*Pterocephalus perennis*

*Ptilotrichum spinosum* 'Roseum'

*Pulmonaria montana* 'Red Start'

'Red Start' flowers in late winter and early spring, pinkish orange. Grows 12 inches (30 cm) high, 18 inches (45 cm) wide. Zones 3–9. The species is from Europe.

## Pulmonaria saccharata
Jerusalem sage
A rhizomatous perennial for part shade in fertile, well-drained soil. Grows 12 inches (30 cm) high, 18 inches (45 cm) wide. Zones 3–9. The species is from Europe.

**Cultivars**. *Pulmonaria saccharata* 'Mrs. Moon' is a long-time favorite with heavily marbled green foliage marked with silver-white. Flowers in late winter and early spring, blue from pink buds.

*Pulmonaria saccharata* 'Sissinghurst White' flowers in late winter and early spring, white.

## Pulsatilla
Ranunculaceae

The pulsatillas include some of the finest, large-flowered alpines. Propagation is best from seed as soon as it is ripe. Color selections should be isolated and hand pollinated so that seedlings will be true. Basal shoots taken as cuttings, and root cuttings, are both slow and uncertain methods of propagation.

## Pulsatilla albana
synonym, *Anemone albana*
A perennial for sun or part shade in any good, well-drained soil. Flowers in late spring and early summer, yellow. Grows 8–12 inches (20–30 cm) high, 12 inches (30 cm) wide. Zones 5–9. Caucasia and northeastern Turkey.

## Pulsatilla alpina subsp. apiifolia
alpine pasque flower
synonym, *P. sulphurea*
A perennial for sun or part shade in humus-rich, well-drained, acid soil. Flowers in spring, pale yellow. Grows 8–18 inches (20–45 cm) high, 12 inches (30 cm) wide. Zones 5–9. Central and southern Europe and Caucasia.

## Pulsatilla halleri
*Pulsatilla halleri* and its subspecies are considered the eastern counterparts of the more western European *P. vulgaris*, pasque flower. In *P. halleri* the foliage is more coarsely dissected and the flowers are less deeply bell shaped and appear before the leaves. A perennial for sun or part shade in any good, well-drained soil. Grows 6–18 inches (15–45 cm) high, 12 inches (30 cm) wide. Zones 4–8. Central and southeastern Europe and Crimea.

**Subspecies and Cultivar**. *Pulsatilla halleri* subsp. *grandis* (synonym, *P. vulgaris* subsp. *grandis*) 'Alba' flowers in spring and early summer, white. The subspecies is from central Europe and Ukraine.

*Pulsatilla halleri* subsp. *slavica* flowers in spring and early summer, dark violet. Carpathians.

## Pulsatilla montana
A perennial for sun or part shade in any good, well-drained soil. Flowers in

*Pulmonaria saccharata* 'Mrs. Moon'

*Pulsatilla albana*, courtesy of Fritz Kummert

*Pulsatilla halleri* subsp. *grandis* 'Alba', courtesy of Fritz Kummert

*Pulmonaria saccharata* 'Sissinghurst White'

*Pulsatilla alpina* subsp. *apiifolia*, courtesy of Fritz Kummert

*Pulsatilla halleri* subsp. *slavica*, courtesy of Fritz Kummert

spring, pendant, deep bluish purple to dark violet. Grows 6–18 inches (15–45 cm) high, 12 inches (30 cm) wide. Zones 6–8. Central and eastern Europe.

## Pulsatilla patens
eastern pasque flower

A widespread and variable species with many forms that some authorities regard as subspecies, *P. patens* is a perennial for sun or part shade in any good, well-drained soil. Flowers in spring and early summer, blue-violet to lilac. Grows 6–12 inches (15–30 cm) high, 12 inches (30 cm) wide. Zones 4–8. Northern Europe and Russia.

**Subspecies.** A North American version native from the Mississippi River westward, *Pulsatilla nuttalliana,* is con-

sidered by some to be only a subspecies of *P. patens. Pulsatilla patens* subsp. *flavescens* (synonym, *P. flavescens*) flowers in late spring, yellow, occasionally flushed with blue on the outside. Zones 5–8. Eastern Russia.

## Pulsatilla vulgaris
pasque flower

synonym, *Anemone pulsatilla*

A very variable species often considered to include the subspecies *grandis,* found here under *P. halleri. Pulsatilla vulgaris* is a perennial for sun or part shade in any good, well-drained soil. In cultivation there are many color forms and selections of pasque flower, including the beautiful red forms. The cultivar 'Rubra' flowers in early spring to early summer,

rust red to red-purple. Grows 8–18 inches (20–45 cm) high, 12 inches (30 cm) wide. Zones 4–9. The species is from Great Britain, France to Sweden, east to Ukraine.

## Puschkinia scilloides var. libanotica
Liliaceae (Hyacinthaceae)

A bulbous perennial for sun or part shade in fertile, well-drained soil. Flowers in spring, pale blue with darker stripes. Grows 6 inches (15 cm) high. Zones 4–9. Caucasia, Turkey, Lebanon, Iraq, and Iran.

## Putoria calabrica
Rubiaceae

A mat-forming shrublet for a hot, sunny spot, the flowers are reminiscent of those of *Daphne cneorum*. It is undeservedly neglected, perhaps due to the unpleasant odor if foliage is bruised. Cultivate in sun in any good, well-drained, neutral to alkaline soil. Flowers in summer, pur-

*Pulsatilla montana,* courtesy of Fritz Kummert

*Pulsatilla vulgaris* 'Rubra', courtesy of Fritz Kummert

*Pulsatilla patens,* courtesy of Fritz Kummert

*Pulsatilla patens* subsp. *flavescens,* courtesy of Fritz Kummert

*Puschkinia scilloides* var. *libanotica,* courtesy of Fritz Kummert

plish rose, followed by blackish red berries. Grows 4 inches (10 cm) high, 18–24 inches (45–60 cm) wide. Zones 7–10. Mediterranean.

 **Q**

## Quercus
oak
Fagaceae

The small oaks, in addition to *Lithocarpus densiflorus* var. *echinoides*, are fine, small, slowly growing plants for the rock garden background, lending an appropriate mountain look to the landscape.

## Quercus sadleriana
deer oak
A semi-evergreen shrub for sun or part shade in any good, well-drained soil. Acorns borne in summer. Grows 36 inches (90 cm) high, 48 inches (120 cm) wide. Zones 6–9. Mountains of southwestern Oregon and northern California.

*Putoria calabrica*

*Quercus sadleriana*

## Quercus vaccinifolia
huckleberry oak
An evergreen shrub for sun or part shade in any good, well-drained soil. Acorns borne in summer. Grows 24–48 inches (60–120 cm) high, 48 inches (120 cm) wide. Zones 6–9. Oregon and California.

 **R**

## Ramonda
Gesneriaceae

*Ramonda* is a hardy relative of the African violet *(Saintpaulia)* that is at home in a lightly shaded, vertical rock crevice, where it is easiest to prevent the hairy foliage from resting on moist soil.

*Quercus vaccinifolia,* courtesy of Fritz Kummert

*Ramonda myconi*

## Ramonda myconi
synonym, *R. pyrenaica*
An evergreen perennial for part shade in humus-rich, well-drained soil, and in the alpine house. Flowers in late spring and summer, deep violet. Grows 3–8 inches (7.5–20 cm) high, 8 inches (20 cm) wide. Zones 5–8. Central and eastern Pyrenees.

## Ramonda nathaliae
An evergreen perennial for part shade in humus-rich, well-drained soil, and in the alpine house. Flowers in late spring and summer, lilac to violet with an orange or yellow eye. Grows 6 inches (15 cm) high, 8 inches (20 cm) wide. Zones 6–8. Balkan Mountains of Romania to northern Greece.

## Ranunculus
buttercup, crowfoot
Ranunculaceae

## Ranunculus alpestris
One of the lovely, white-flowered buttercups. Like other alpine species that are

*Ramonda nathaliae,* courtesy of Fritz Kummert

*Ranunculus alpestris,* courtesy of Fritz Kummert

native to wet spots close to melting snows, *R. alpestris* must have good, wet soil during the growing season. A perennial for sun in fertile, well-drained, moist soil. Flowers in spring, white with sepals tinged red-brown. Grows 4–6 inches (10–15 cm) high, 8 inches (20 cm) wide. Zones 5–8. Mountains of Europe, except Scandinavia.

### Ranunculus amplexicaulis

A perennial for sun or part shade in fertile, well-drained, moist soil. Flowers in spring, white, occasionally pink. Grows 6–10 inches (15–25 cm) high, 12 inches (30 cm) wide. Zones 6–8. Central and eastern Pyrenees.

### Ranunculus calandrinioides

A beautiful perennial that does best in the alpine house where its thinly textured, solitary blossoms are protected from winter weather, and where one can easily facilitate a summer dormant pe-

riod. Cultivate in sun or part shade in fertile, well-drained, moist soil. Flowers in late winter and spring, white sometimes flushed with pink. Grows 6 inches (15 cm) high, 12 inches (30 cm) wide. Zones 7–9. Atlas Mountains of Morocco.

### Ranunculus crenatus

A perennial for sun or part shade in fertile, well-drained, moist soil. Flowers in spring, white. Grows 6 inches (15 cm) high, 12 inches (30 cm) wide. Zones 6–8. Eastern Alps, Apennines to the Balkan Peninsula, and the Carpathians.

### Ranunculus eschscholtzii

A perennial for sun or part shade in moist, fertile, well-drained soil. Flowers in spring, yellow. Grows 4–6 inches (10–15 cm) high, 8 inches (20 cm) wide. Zones 4–8. Mountains of the northwestern United States and British Columbia.

### Ranunculus ficaria

lesser celandine, pilewort
The species should not be released in a garden as it spreads invasively by seed

and root tubers. A perennial with a summer dormant period for sun or part shade in any moist soil. Flowers in late winter and spring; flowers of the species bright yellow. Grows 3–6 inches (7.5–15 cm) high, 12 inches (30 cm) wide. Zones 5–9. Europe, northwestern Africa, western Asia, and naturalized in North America.

**Cultivars.** The many garden-worthy color variants spread only modestly and must be propagated by separating the clustered root tubers, though if occasional seed is produced it should be removed and destroyed as seedlings will be the reverted invasive species.

*Ranunculus ficaria* 'Brazen Hussy' has chocolate brown leaves and golden flowers.

*Ranunculus ficaria* 'Cupreus' (synonym, 'Aurantiacus') has bright orange flowers.

*Ranunculus ficaria* 'Eremit' has yellow flowers.

*Ranunculus ficaria* 'Flore Pleno' is smaller in leaf and flower with double, clear yellow blossoms.

*Ranunculus amplexicaulis,* courtesy of Fritz Kumme

*Ranunculus crenatus,* courtesy of Fritz Kummert

*Ranunculus ficaria* 'Brazen Hussy'

*Ranunculus calandrinioides,* courtesy of Fritz Kummert

*Ranunculus eschscholtzii*

*Ranunculus ficaria* 'Cupreus'

*Ranunculus ficaria* 'Eremit', courtesy of Fritz Kummert

*Ranunculus ficaria* 'Flore Pleno'

*Ranunculus glacialis*, courtesy of Fritz Kummert

*Ranunculus gramineus*

### Ranunculus glacialis

A perennial for sun or part shade in humus-rich, gritty, moist soil. It is best grown in the alpine house. Flowers in late spring and summer, white or pink, aging reddish. Grows 4–6 inches (10–15 cm) high, 12 inches (30 cm) wide. Zones 4–8. Mountains of Europe to Greenland.

### Ranunculus gramineus

An easy-to-grow perennial with graceful, grassy foliage and flowers atop wiry stems, lending an airy effect to the garden. Cultivate in sun or part shade in any good, well-drained soil. Flowers in late spring and summer, yellow. Grows 12–18 inches (30–45 cm) high, 6 inches (15 cm) wide. Zones 6–9. Southern Europe and northern Africa.

### Ranunculus muelleri var. brevicaulis

A perennial for sun or part shade in fertile, well-drained, moist soil. Flowers in spring and summer, yellow. Grows 2 inches (5 cm) high, 4 inches (10 cm)

*Ranunculus muelleri* var. *brevicaulis*, courtesy of Fritz Kummert

*Ranunculus parnassifolius*, courtesy of Fritz Kummert

wide. Zones 6–8. Summit of Mount Kosciusko, Australia.

### Ranunculus parnassifolius

A perennial for sun or part shade in fertile, well-drained, moist soil. Flowers in spring and summer, white, sometimes veined or flushed red or pink. Grows 8–10 inches (20–25 cm) high, 12 inches (30 cm) wide. Zones 5–8. Mountains of northern Spain, Pyrenees, and rarely, the Alps.

### Ranunculus pyrenaeus

A perennial for sun or part shade in fertile, well-drained, moist soil. Flowers in spring and summer, white. Grows 6 inches (15 cm) high and wide. Zones 6–8. Pyrenees, mountains of northern Spain, the Alps, and Corsica.

### Ranunculus rupestris

A tuberous-rooted perennial for sun or part shade in fertile, well-drained soil, keeping it dry in summer. Grows 12

*Ranunculus pyrenaeus*, courtesy of Fritz Kummert

*Ranunculus rupestris*

inches (30 cm) high, 6 inches (15 cm) wide. Zones 7–9. Southern Portugal, southern Spain, and Sicily.

### Ranunculus seguieri

A perennial for sun or part shade in fertile, well-drained, moist soil. Flowers in early summer, white. Grows 4–8 inches (10–20 cm) high, 8 inches (20 cm) wide. Zones 5–8. Mountains from Spain to the Balkan Peninsula.

### Raoulia
Compositae

All of the raoulias are appealing ground covers that form dense sheets or mounds of minutely foliaged rosettes, dotted with miniature composite flowers in

*Ranunculus seguieri,* courtesy of Fritz Kummert

spring. Provide scree soil with just enough organic matter to retain moisture in summer when the plants require regular watering. In winter, protect them from excessive wetness with a pane of glass. All grow well in the alpine house, too.

### Raoulia australis
synonym, *R. lutescens*

A mat-forming, evergreen perennial for sun in fertile, well-drained, gritty, moist soil with protection from winter wetness. Flowers in spring, yellow. Grows $^{1}/_{2}$ inch (1 cm) high, 24 inches (60 cm) wide. Zones 7–9. Mountains of North and South Islands, New Zealand.

*Raoulia hookeri* var. *albo-sericea,* courtesy of Fritz Kummert

### Raoulia hookeri

A mat-forming, evergreen perennial for sun in fertile, well-drained, gritty, moist soil with protection from winter wetness. Flowers in spring, yellow.

**Varieties.** *Raoulia hookeri* var. *albo-sericea* grows 1 inch (2.5 cm) high, 18 inches (45 cm) wide. Zones 6–10. North Island, New Zealand.

*Raoulia hookeri* var. *apice-nigra* grows 1 inch (2.5 cm) high, 24 inches (60 cm) wide. Zones 6–9. South Island, New Zealand.

### Raoulia ×loganii

An evergreen perennial for sun or part shade in fertile, well-drained gritty, moist soil. It is best grown in the alpine house. Flowers in spring, yellowish. Grows 3 inches (7.5 cm) high, 8 inches (20 cm) wide. Zones 6–9. Believed to be a naturally occurring hybrid from the mountains of North Island, New Zealand, *R. goyenii* × *R. grandiceps.*

*Raoulia hookeri* var. *apice-nigra*

*Raoulia* ×*loganii,* courtesy of Fritz Kummert

*Raoulia australis,* in flower

## Raoulia mammillaris
vegetable sheep
A cushion-forming, evergreen perennial for sun in moist, fertile, well-drained, gritty soil in the alpine house. Flowers in spring, yellow. Grows 4 inches (10 cm) high, 6 inches (15 cm) wide. Zones 6–9. Mountains of South Island, New Zealand.

## Raoulia tenuicaulis
A carpeter that is remarkably easy to grow, an excellent foil and ground cover for small bulbs. A mat-forming, evergreen perennial for sun in moist, fertile, well-drained, gritty soil. Flowers in spring, white and honey scented. Grows 1 inch (2.5 cm) high, 36 inches (90 cm) wide. Zones 7–10. North and South Islands, New Zealand.

## Rehmania glutinosa
Gesneriaceae
A perennial, spreading by underground stolons to form a wide colony, with unusually colored flowers blooming in spring and continuing well into summer. Rehmania glutinosa performs best in slightly poor, gritty soil with minimal winter moisture. Cultivate in sun or part shade in fertile, well-drained soil. Flowers in early summer, pinkish brown and purple. Grows 12 inches (30 cm) high, 24 inches (60 cm) wide. Zones 6–10. Central China.

## Rhodiola rosea
roseroot
Crassulaceae
synonym, Sedum roseum
A perennial for sun or part shade in any good, well-drained soil. Flowers in early summer, greenish yellow with promi-

Raoulia mammillaris, courtesy of Fritz Kummert

Raoulia tenuicaulis

Rehmania glutinosa, courtesy of Fritz Kummert

Rhodiola rosea, courtesy of Fritz Kummert

nent orange nectaries. Grows 6–14 inches (15–35 cm) high, 12 inches (30 cm) wide. Zones 1–8. Circumpolar in the northern hemisphere and mountains farther south.

## *Rhododendron*
Ericaceae

### *Rhododendron* 'Alexander'
Hardiest of the popular Nakaharae Hybrids, very prostrate with finely textured foliage. An evergreen azalea for sun or part shade in humus-rich, well-drained, acid soil. Flowers in June and July, bright salmon red. Grows 6–10 inches (15–25 cm) high, 24 inches (60 cm) wide. Zones 6–9.

### *Rhododendron* 'Chinzan'
An evergreen azalea for sun or part shade in humus-rich, well-drained, acid soil. Flowers in late spring and early summer, salmon pink. Grows 8 inches (20 cm) high, 18 inches (45 cm) wide. Zones 6–9.

*Rhododendron* 'Alexander'

*Rhododendron* 'Chinzan'

### *Rhododendron keleticum*
synonym, *R. calostrotum* subsp. *keleticum*
One of the smallest species of *Rhododendron* and ideal for the rock garden and troughs, where it forms a hummock of tiny, dark green leaves. The pansy-like flowers are surprisingly large. An evergreen shrublet for sun or part shade in humus-rich, well-drained, acid soil. Flowers in May and June, rosy purple. Grows 6 inches (15 cm) high, 12 inches (30 cm) wide. Zones 5–9. Southeastern Tibet.

### *Rhododendron* 'Purple Gem'
An evergreen shrub for sun or part shade in humus-rich, well-drained, acid soil. Flowers in April, purple-violet. Grows 24 inches (60 cm) high and wide. Zones 4–9.

*Rhododendron keleticum,* courtesy of Fritz Kummert

*Rhododendron* 'Purple Gem'

### *Rhododendron* 'Wildwood Pixie Petticoat'
An evergreen shrub for part shade in humus-rich, well-drained, acid soil. Flowers in early spring, purple-pink. Grows 10 inches (25 cm) high, 24 inches (60 cm) wide. Zones 5–9.

### *Rhododendron yakushimanum*
synonym, *R. degronianum* subsp. *yakushimanum*
An evergreen shrub for sun or part shade in humus-rich, well-drained, acid soil. Flowers in late spring, pink, fading to white. Grows 24–30 inches (60–75 cm) high, 30 inches (75 cm) wide. Zones 6–9. Yaku Shima, an island off southern Kyushu, Japan.

*Rhododendron* 'Wildwood Pixie Petticoat'

## Rhodohypoxis baurii
red star
Hypoxidaceae
Related to the American *Hypoxis,* the tiny *Rhodohypoxis* rates as one of the world's smallest "bulbs," in this case a perennial from a corm-like rhizome. Cultivate in sun or part shade in fertile, well-drained soil, keeping it dry during winter. Flowers in April through September. Grows 6 inches (15 cm) high. Zones 7–10. Eastern South Africa.

**Cultivar.** Selected color forms range from white, pink, to red with some bi-colored selections. *Rhodohypoxis baurii* 'Lily Jean' is an unusual doubled form discovered and introduced by Siskiyou Rare Plant Nursery. Flowers in April through September, soft pink.

## Rhodothamnus chamaecistus
Ericaceae
The lone species of the genus ranks as one of the best alpine shrubs. Although ericaceous, it is native to limestone areas but tolerates slightly acid conditions in

cultivation. A dwarf evergreen shrub for sun or part shade in humus-rich, well-drained, gritty soil. Flowers in spring, light pink. Grows 10 inches (25 cm) high, 12 inches (30 cm) wide. Zones 6–8. Eastern Alps.

## Romanzoffia sitchensis
mist maiden
Hydrophyllaceae
synonym, *R. suksdorfii*
A perennial with swollen, bulb-like, rootstocks, dormant in summer, for shade or part shade in humus-rich, moist soil. Flowers in spring, white. Grows 6–12 inches (15–30 cm) high, 6 inches (15 cm) wide, and is shorter in pooer, drier soils. Zones 3–8. Western North America to central Canada.

## Romulea bulbocodium
Iridaceae
An elegant, though rarely seen, cormous perennial ideally suited to the mild-cli-

mate garden, also easily grown and protected in a bulb frame, or in pots in colder climates. Cultivate in sun in any good, well-drained soil, keeping it dry-ish in summer. Flowers in spring, satiny violet, lilac, pink, yellow, or white. Grows 6–8 inches (15–20 cm) high. Zones 7–10. Mediterranean, Portugal and Spain to Bulgaria.

## Roscoea
Zingiberaceae

Given cool, deep soil and some shade, these small, tropical-looking perennials will delight with hooded "orchid" flowers. Plant deep, about 5 inches (12.5 cm), and be patient; they do not sprout until May or June.

## Roscoea alpina
A tuberous and fleshy-rooted perennial for part shade in humus-rich, well-drained, moist soil. Flowers in summer, purple, pink, or rarely white. Grows 4–8

*Rhododendron yakushimanum,* courtesy of Fritz Kummert

*Rhodohypoxis baurii* 'Lily Jean'

*Romanzoffia sitchensis*

*Rhodohypoxis baurii,* white form

*Rhodothamnus chamaecistus,* courtesy of Fritz Kummert

*Romulea bulbocodium,* courtesy of Fritz Kummert

inches (10–20 cm) high. Zones 5–9. Pakistan to southwestern China.

### Roscoea cautleoides

A tuberous and fleshy-rooted perennial for part shade in humus-rich, well-drained, moist soil. The cultivar 'Kew Beauty' flowers in summer, large and orchid-like, pale yellow. Grows 18 inches (45 cm) high. Zones 5–9. The species is from Yunnan and Sichuan Provinces, China.

### Roscoea purpurea

Grows 12–18 inches (30–45 cm) high. Zones 5–9. Himalayas and Sikkim. A tuberous and fleshy-rooted perennial for part shade in humus-rich, well-drained, moist soil. Flowers in summer and fall, purple or bicolored white and purple.

### Roscoea scillifolia

A tuberous and fleshy-rooted perennial, sometimes erroneously labeled as *R. alpina* in the nursery trade, for part shade in humus-rich, well-drained, moist soil. Flowers in summer, pink, rarely purple or black-purple. Grows 12 inches (30 cm) high. Zones 5–9. Central Nepal.

### Rosmarinus officinalis

rosemary
Labiatae
An evergreen shrub for sun in well-drained soil, preferably limy. It is easy to find a place in the large rock garden for the spreading or mat-forming rosemary cultivars. They tolerate hot sun and any well-drained soil, even poor soil. The cultivar 'Mozart' has deep blue flowers in late winter and spring, usually with a repeat bloom in fall. It grows 12 inches (30 cm) high, 36 inches (90 cm) wide. Zones 7–10, with other cultivars hardy to Zone 6. The species is from the Mediterranean and southern Europe.

### Rosularia chrysantha

Crassulaceae
synonyms, *R. pallida*, *Umbilicus chrysanthus*
Frequently confused with *R. aizoon*, *R. chrysantha* is a perennial succulent for

*Roscoea alpina,* courtesy of Fritz Kummert

*Roscoea purpurea*

*Roscoea scillifolia,* unusual black form, courtesy of Fritz Kummert

*Roscoea cautleoides* 'Kew Beauty', courtesy of Fritz Kummert

*Rosmarinus officinalis* 'Mozart'

sun or part shade in fertile, gritty soil, and in the alpine house. Flowers in early summer, yellowish to white. Grows 4–6 inches (10–15 cm) high, 8 inches (20 cm) wide. Zones 6–9. Turkey.

### *Rubus acaulis*
arctic bramble
Rosaceae
synonym, *R. arcticus* var. *grandiflorus*
Quite an ornamental little blackberry with sweet fruit. A slenderly rhizomatous perennial for sun or part shade in moist, humus-rich, well-drained soil. Flowers in summer, pink, followed by red fruit. Grows 4 inches (10 cm) high, 18 inches (45 cm) wide. Zones 1–8. Eastern Asia to eastern Canada, south to mountains of the northern United States.

### *Ruellia humilis*
Acanthaceae
A perennial for sun or part shade in any well-drained soil. Flowers in summer, violet-blue. Grows 18 inches (45 cm)

high, 24 inches (60 cm) wide. Zones 4–9. Southern Pennsylvania to Nebraska, Texas, and northwestern Florida.

### *Rumex flexuosus*
Polygonaceae
A perennial dock or sorrel for sun in any good, well-drained soil. Flowers in summer, greenish, followed by semiglossy brown fruit. Grows 12–18 inches (30–45 cm) high, 18 inches (45 cm) wide. Zones 7–10. New Zealand.

### *Rupicapnos africana*
Fumariaceae
A perennial forming a rhizome-like rootstock that is not very hardy but may survive mild winters outdoors in a vertical crevice, otherwise perfect for the alpine house. Cultivate in sun or light shade in sharply drained, alkaline soil. Flowers in late spring to fall, white to rose pink with dark purple tips. Grows 4–6 inches (10–15 cm) high, 12 inches

(30 cm) wide. Zones 7–9. Northwestern Africa and southwestern Spain.

### *Ruta graveolens*
herb of grace, rue
Rutaceae
An evergreen shrub for sun in any well-drained soil. The cultivar 'Curly Girl' flowers in summer, yellow. Grows 18 inches (45 cm) high, 24 inches (60 cm) wide. Zones 5–10. The species is from the Balkan Peninsula and southwestern Europe.

### *Sagina boydii*
Caryophyllaceae
Unlike the other pearlworts that spread and smother smaller plants, *S. boydii* forms an attractively domed hummock. An ideal plant for the alpine house and trough, but wherever it is grown, watch

*Rosularia chrysantha*

*Ruellia humilis*

*Rupicapnos africana*

*Rubus acaulis*

*Rumex flexuosus*, courtesy of Fritz Kummert

*Ruta graveolens* 'Curly Girl'

out for attacks by red spider mites. A densely cushion-forming perennial for part shade in well-drained gritty, moist soil, and doing best in the alpine house. Flowers in summer, greenish, inconspicuous. Grows 2 inches (5 cm) high, 4 inches (10 cm) wide. Zones 5–8. Found in Scotland in 1878 but never subsequently rediscovered in the wild.

## *Salix*
willow
Salicaceae

Dwarf willows spread in dense mats or grow erect into twiggy shrubs. Considerable sun and fairly moist soil are best for their growth.

### *Salix* ×*boydii*
A deciduous shrub for sun or part shade in any good, moist soil. Flowers in

*Sagina boydii,* courtesy of Franz Hadacek

*Salix* ×*boydii,* courtesy of Fritz Kummert

spring in silky, pale yellow catkins. Grows 18 inches (45 cm) high, 12 inches (30 cm) wide. Zones 5–8. A naturally occurring hybrid from Great Britain, believed to be *S. lanata* × *S. reticulata.*

### *Salix dodgeana*
A deciduous subshrub for sun or part shade in peaty, well-drained, moist soil. Flowers in spring in purplish catkins. Grows 2 inches (5 cm) high, 8 inches (20 cm) wide. Zones 2–7. Rocky Mountains from Montana to Wyoming.

### *Salix* ×*grahamii*
A deciduous shrub for sun or part shade in well-drained, moist, peaty soil. Flowers in spring in gray catkins. The cultivar 'Moorei' grows 12 inches (30 cm) high, 36 inches (90 cm) wide. Zones 4–8. *Salix* ×*grahamii* is a naturally occurring hybrid from Ireland, *S. aurita* × *S. herbacea* × *S. repens.*

*Salix dodgeana*

*Salix* ×*grahamii* 'Moorei'

### *Salix helvetica*
Swiss willow
A very handsome deciduous shrub with thick, congested branches, and glabrous leaves with the undersurface white tomentose. Cultivate in sun or part shade in well-drained, moist, peaty soil. Flowers in spring in silver catkins, aging yellow. Grows 18–36 inches (45–90 cm) high, 18 inches (45 cm) wide. Zones 6–8. Alps, Tatra Mountains.

### *Salix hylematica*
During the 1970s and 1980s several fine willows were introduced from Nepal. *Salix hylematica* is very similar to *S. fruticulosa* and *S. serpyllum* and some authorities consider them synonymous. *Salix lindleyana* is often mistakenly considered synonymous also, but it is distinct with almost globular, few-flowered catkins. *Salix hylematica* a deciduous, mat-forming shrub for sun or part

*Salix helvetica,* courtesy of Fritz Kummert

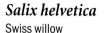

*Salix hylematica,* courtesy of Franz Hadacek

shade in well-drained, moist, peaty soil. Flowers in spring in densely flowered catkins with dark crimson scales. Grows 4 inches (10 cm) high, 24 inches (60 cm) wide. Zones 4–8. Himalayas.

## Salix reticulata

A deciduous, mat-forming shrub for sun or part shade in peaty, well-drained, moist soil. Flowers in spring in brownish catkins. Grows 2 inches (5 cm) high, 12 inches (30 cm) wide. Zones 1–8. Circumpolar: northern Europe, northern Asia, and northern North America.

## Salix yezoalpina

synonym, *S. nakamurana* var. *yezoalpina*
An attractive, large-leaved, large-catkined, deciduous, prostrate shrub with thick, trailing stems of reticulated leaves that emerge in spring covered in silver hairs. Cultivate in sun or part shade in well-drained, moist, peaty soil. Flowers in spring, white. Grows 4 inches (10 cm) high, 36 inches (90 cm) wide. Zones 5–8. Japan.

## Salvia
sage
Labiatae

## Salvia caespitosa

The gem of salvias, which benefits from dryish winter conditions, making it a good alpine house plant in wet and cold winter climates. A woody-based perennial for sun in fertile, well-drained or sandy soil. Flowers in late spring, lilac pink. Grows 6 inches (15 cm) high, 12 inches (30 cm) wide. Zones 6–9. Turkey.

## Salvia jurisicii

A perennial for sun in fertile, well-drained soil. Flowers in summer, white, pink, or violet. Grows 12–18 inches (30–45 cm) high, 12 inches (30 cm) wide. Zones 6–9. Northern Balkan Peninsula.

## Sanguinaria canadensis
Papaveraceae
A perennial bloodroot from rhizomes containing orange-red sap. Cultivate in part shade in humus-rich, well-drained, moist soil. Flowers in spring, white. Grows 6 inches (15 cm) high, 12 inches (30 cm) wide. Zones 3–8. Eastern North America, Quebec to Manitoba south to Kansas and Kentucky.

**Cultivar**. *Sanguinaria canadensis* 'Multiplex', double-flowered bloodroot, is one of the most beautiful forms of any North American wildflower. It is at home in the woodland or in a slightly shaded nook in the rock garden. This doubled, white form is sterile because the stamens have been transformed into petals; flowers last longer than those of

*Salix reticulata*, courtesy of Fritz Kummert

*Salvia caespitosa*, courtesy of Fritz Kummert

*Sanguinaria canadensis*, courtesy of Fritz Kummert

*Salix yezoalpina*

*Salvia jurisicii,* courtesy of Fritz Kummert

*Sanguinaria canadensis* 'Multiplex'

the fertile, single form. Propagation is only by division of the "bloodroot."

### Santolina chamaecyparissus
lavender cotton
Compositae
An evergreen shrublet for sun in any soil that does not stay wet. The cultivar 'Nana', dwarf lavender cotton, flowers in summer in buttons of yellow. Grows 12 inches (30 cm) high, 18 inches (45 cm) wide. Zones 6–9. The species is from the central and western Mediterranean.

### Saponaria
soapwort
Caryophyllaceae

The species and hybrid soapworts are fairly easy to grow and they thrive in sun. They are perennials that smother themselves with flowers in spring and summer.

### Saponaria 'Bressingham Hybrid'
Cultivate in sun in any good, sharply drained soil. Flowers in May and June, deep pink. Grows 3 inches (7.5 cm) high, 8 inches (20 cm) wide. Zones 5–8. A garden hybrid, *S. ocymoides* × *S.* ×*olivana*.

### Saponaria lutea
Cultivate in sun in any good, sharply drained soil. Flowers in early summer, yellow. Grows 6–8 inches (15–20 cm) high, 12 inches (30 cm) wide. Zones 6–9. Southern Alps.

### Saponaria ocymoides
Cultivate in sun in any good, sharply drained soil. The cultivar 'Rubra Compacta' (synonym, 'Compacta') is a miniature form that must be increased by cuttings and is very condensed and tight, with brilliant, deep pink flowers. Beware of seedling impostors, which can be larger growing with paler flowers, which tend to be more similar to the typical form of the species. Flowers in late spring and summer. Grows 3 inches

(7.5 cm) high, 12 inches (30 cm) wide. Zones 4–9. The species is from mountains of southern Europe, Spain to the Balkan Peninsula.

### Saponaria ×olivana
Cultivate in sun in any good, sharply drained soil. Flowers in late spring, pale pink. Grows 2 inches (5 cm) high, 12 inches (30 cm) wide. Zones 5–8. A garden hybrid, *S. caespitosa* × *S. pumilio*.

### Saponaria pumilio
synonyms, *Saponaria pumila*, *S. pulvinaris*, *Silene pumilio*
Cultivate in sun in any good, sharply drained soil. Flowers in late spring and summer, crimson to pale purple, occasionally white. Grows 2–4 inches (5–10 cm) high, 16 inches (40 cm) wide. Zones 5–8. Eastern Alps, southeastern Carpathians.

### Satureja montana subsp. *illyrica*
winter savory
Labiatae
A woody-based perennial for sun in any good, well-drained soil. Flowers in sum-

Santolina chamaecyparissus 'Nana'

Saponaria lutea, courtesy of Fritz Kummert

Saponaria ×olivana

Saponaria 'Bressingham Hybrid'

Saponaria ocymoides 'Rubra Compacta'

Saponaria pumilio, courtesy of Fritz Kummert

mer, pink or purplish. Grows 6 inches (15 cm) high, 12 inches (30 cm) wide. Zones 5–9. Turkey.

## Saussurea
Compositae

*Saussurea* is a genus that includes some fascinating species with unusually bracted flower heads. Most of these interesting perennials are difficult to keep, especially after flowering. Alpine house conditions may help their survival. In addition to the ones treated here, other interesting species include *S. alpina, S. gossypiphora, S. obvallata,* and *S. tridactyla.*

## Saussurea pygmaea
Cultivate in sun in any good, sharply drained, reasonably moist soil. Flowers

*Satureja montana* subsp. *illyrica,* courtesy of Fritz Kummert

*Saussurea pygmaea,* courtesy of Fritz Kummert

in late summer, reddish purple. Grows 8 inches (20 cm) high, 12 inches (30 cm) wide. Zones 3–8. Eastern Alps to Siberia.

## Saussurea stella
Cultivate in sun in any good, sharply drained, reasonably moist soil. Flowers in summer, red-purple. Grows 4 inches (10 cm) high, 12–16 inches (30–40 cm) wide. Zones 6–8. Mountains of China.

## Saxifraga
saxifrage
Saxifragaceae

The substantial genus *Saxifraga* may be divided into sections, some of which may be further divided into subsections and series. The saxifragas represented here may be grouped into the following sections:

Section *Irregulares*—*S. stolonifera*
Section *Porphyrion,* classic alpine plants with tight cushion foliage and colorful, short-stemmed flowers that smother the plant; ruggedly hardy and suited to planting in the rock or crevice garden, miniature enough for trough

*Saussurea stella,* courtesy of Fritz Kummert

*Saxifraga aizoides,* courtesy of Fritz Kummert

and container culture; early bloom, February to April, making them ideal plants for the alpine house—*S. aizoides, S. ×apiculata, S. biflora, S. burseriana, S. corymbosa, S. federici-augusti, S. ×gloriana, S. ×hornibrookii, S. marginata, S. ×megaseiflora, S. oppositifolia, S. ×paulinae, S. retusa, S. scardica, S. sempervivum, S. stribrnyi, S. tombeanensis*

Section *Ligulatae,* "silver" or "encrusted" saxifrages whose foliage in hard mounds of leathery leaves is usually edged with silver beading; lime in the soil improves the silver encrustation but is not essential for good growth—*S. ×burnatii, S. cotyledon, S. crustata, S. paniculata,* and the hybrid, *Saxifraga* 'Whitehills'

Section *Gymnopera*—*S. ×urbium*
Section *Saxifraga*—*S. exarata* and the Mossy Hybrids, *Saxifraga* 'Hardes Zwerg' and *Saxifraga* 'Sir Douglas Haig'

## Saxifraga aizoides
Section *Porphyrion.* A perennial for part shade in fertile, moist soil. It requires cool conditions. Flowers in summer, orange-yellow to copper red. Grows 6–10 inches (15–25 cm) high, 12 inches (30 cm) wide. Zones 4–8. Europe, Asia, and Arctic North America.

## Saxifraga ×apiculata
A garden hybrid, *S. marginata* × *S. sancta,* both section *Porphyrion.* An evergreen perennial for part shade in humus-rich, well-drained soil. The cultivar 'Gregor Mendel', sometimes offered in the nursery trade under the name *S. ×apiculata* only, is vigorous and one of

*Saxifraga ×apiculata* 'Gregor Mendel' with a white *S. ×apiculata* 'Alba' on the right the best saxifrages for easy culture directly in the rock garden. It quickly forms a mound of loose, spiked, rich green foliage. Flowers in March and April, pale yellow. Grows 3 inches (7.5 cm) high, 12–18 inches (30–45 cm) wide. Zones 6–9.

### Saxifraga biflora

Section *Porphyrion*. A woody-based, evergreen perennial, forming a loose cushion or mat, for part shade in humus-rich, gritty soil. Flowers in late spring, dull purple or white. Grows 2 inches (5 cm) high, 6 inches (15 cm) wide. Zones 6–8. Alps.

### Saxifraga ×burnatii

A naturally occurring hybrid, *S. cochlearis* × *S. paniculata*, both section *Ligulatae*. One of the choicest of the silver or encrusted saxifrages, with petite rosettes of small, narrow, blue-green leaves with silver edges. The attractive flower spikes

Saxifraga biflora, courtesy of Fritz Kummert

Saxifraga ×burnatii, top plant on tufa rock

are short, dense, and arching. evergreen perennial for part shade in fertile scree, preferably limy. Flowers in late spring and early summer, white. Grows 6 inches (15 cm) high, 12 inches (30 cm) wide. Zones 5–9. Maritime Alps.

### Saxifraga burseriana

Burser's saxifrage

Section *Porphyrion*. Sometimes misspelled *burserana*, *S. burseriana* is an evergreen perennial for part shade in fertile limestone scree. Flowers in early spring, white. Grows 4 inches (10 cm) high, 8 inches (20 cm) wide. Zones 6–9. Eastern Alps.

### Saxifraga corymbosa

synonym, *S. luteoviridis*

Section *Porphyrion*. An evergreen perennial for part shade in fertile limestone

Saxifraga burseriana, courtesy of Fritz Kummert

Saxifraga cotyledon, courtesy of Fritz Kummert

scree. Flowers in early spring, sepals green and petals yellow. Grows 4 inches (10 cm) high, 6 inches (15 cm) wide. Zones 6–9. Carpathians.

### Saxifraga cotyledon

great alpine rockfoil, greater evergreen saxifrage

Section *Ligulatae*. An evergreen perennial whose flowering rosettes die after flowering. Cultivate in part shade in fertile scree, preferably neutral to acid. Flowers in late spring, white. Grows 12–24 inches (30–60 cm) high, 12 inches (30 cm) wide. Zones 6–9. Scandinavia and Iceland, Pyrenees, and the Alps.

### Saxifraga crustata

Section *Ligulatae*. An evergreen perennial for part shade in fertile scree, preferably limy. Flowers in late spring, yel-

Saxifraga corymbosa, courtesy of Fritz Kummert

lowish white. Grows 6 inches (15 cm) high, 10 inches (25 cm) wide. Zones 6–9. Eastern Alps and mountains of the northern and central Balkan Peninsula.

## *Saxifraga exarata* subsp. *moschata*

synonym, S. *moschata*
Section *Saxifraga*. A perennial for part shade in fertile, well-drained soil. It requires cool conditions. Flowers in spring, dull yellow or greenish. Grows 2 inches (5 cm) high, 8 inches (20 cm) wide. Zones 5–9. The species is from central and southern Europe and Caucasia. *Saxifraga exarata*, furrowed saxifrage, and *S. cespitosa*, *S. granulata*, *S. hypnoides*, and *S. rosacea* have been extensively hybridized to create dozens of cultivars referred to as Mossy Hybrids, for example, *Saxifraga* 'Hardes Zwerg' and *Saxifraga* 'Sir Douglas Haig'. The hybrids surpass the parent plants in ease of cultivation and in production of showy flowers and foliage.

## *Saxifraga federici-augusti* subsp. *grisebachii*

synonym, S. *grisebachii*
Section *Porphyrion*. An outstanding evergreen perennial with large, handsome, symmetrical rosettes of silver leaves. The clusters of colorful flowers unfurl on rather tall, hairy stems. Cultivate in part shade in humus-rich scree. Flowers in spring, dark crimson-purple. Grows 6 inches (15 cm) high and wide. Zones 6–9. Balkan Peninsula.

## *Saxifraga* ×*gloriana*

A garden hybrid, *S. lilacina* × *S. scardica* var. *obtusa*, both section *Porphyrion*. An evergreen perennial for part shade in fertile scree. The cultivar 'Godiva' flowers in spring, soft pink, fading to palest pink. Grows 2 inches (5 cm) high, 8 inches (20 cm) wide. Zones 6–9.

## *Saxifraga* 'Hardes Zwerg'

mossy saxifrage, a Mossy Hybrid
A garden hybrid involving *S. cespitosa*, *S. exarata*, *S. granulata*, *S. hypnoides*, and *S. rosacea*, all section *Saxifraga*. A perennial for part shade in fertile, well-drained soil. Flowers in spring, maroon-red. Grows 6 inches (15 cm) high, 8 inches (20 cm) wide. Zones 5–9.

## *Saxifraga* ×*hornibrookii*

A garden hybrid, *S. lilacina* × *S. stribrnyi*, both section *Porphyrion*. An evergreen perennial with unusually shaped flowers, like small tulips. Cultivate in part shade in fertile limestone scree. The cultivar 'Ariel' flowers in spring, deep wine

*Saxifraga crustata*, courtesy of Fritz Kummert

*Saxifraga* ×*gloriana* 'Godiva'

*Saxifraga exarata* subsp. *moschata*, courtesy of Fritz Kummert

*Saxifraga federici-augusti* subsp. *grisebachii*, courtesy of Fritz Kummert

*Saxifraga* 'Hardes Zwerg', courtesy of Fritz Kummert

red. Grows 3 inches (7.5 cm) high, 4 inches (10 cm) wide. Zones 6–9.

## Saxifraga hostii

Section *Ligulatae*. A vigorous, spreading plant with extremely narrow, leathery leaves that assume a reddish tinge during fall and winter. An evergreen peren-

Saxifraga ×hornibrookii 'Ariel'

Saxifraga hostii, courtesy of Armen Gevjan

Saxifraga marginata var. rocheliana

nial for part shade in fertile limestone scree. Flowers in late spring, milky white, often spotted purple-red. Grows 12 inches (30 cm) high, 10 inches (25 cm) wide. Zones 6–9. Eastern Alps.

## Saxifraga marginata var. rocheliana

Section *Porphyrion*. A fine evergreen perennial with very compact, mat-forming foliage of flattened, leathery green rosettes, and substantial white flowers that are funnel shaped. Cultivate in part shade in fertile limestone scree. Flowers in spring, white. Grows 2 inches (5 cm) high, 6 inches (15 cm) wide. Zones 6–9. Balkan Peninsula and southern Italy.

## Saxifraga ×megaseiflora

A hybrid involving *S. aretioides, S. burseriana, S. lilacina,* and *S. media,* all sec-

Saxifraga ×megaseiflora 'Jupiter'

Saxifraga paniculata 'Brevifolia'

tion *Porphyrion*. Often misspelled *megasaeflora, S. ×megaseiflora* is an evergreen perennial for part shade in fertile scree. The cultivar 'Jupiter' flowers in spring, pale orange-yellow with pinkish veins. Grows 4 inches (10 cm) high, 8 inches (20 cm) wide. Zones 6–9.

## Saxifraga oppositifolia
purple saxifrage

Section *Porphyrion*. A mat- or cushion-forming, evergreen perennial for part shade in humus-rich, gritty soil. The cultivar 'Wetterhorn' flowers in late spring and summer, rose red. Grows 2 inches (5 cm) high, 12 inches (30 cm) wide. Zones 2–8. The species is circumpolar in the northern hemisphere, extending into mountains to the south.

Saxifraga oppositifolia 'Wetterhorn', courtesy of Fritz Kummert

## Saxifraga paniculata

lifelong saxifrage
synonym, *S. aizoon*
Section *Ligulatae*. An evergreen perennial for part shade in fertile scree. The cultivar 'Brevifolia' flowers in early summer, white. Grows 12 inches (30 cm) high, 10 inches (25 cm) wide. Zones 2–9. The species is from central and southern Europe and Arctic regions of Canada, Greenland, Iceland, Norway, and the Faeroe Islands.

## Saxifraga ×paulinae

A hybrid, *S. burseriana* × *S. ferdinandi-coburgi*, both section *Porphyrion*. An evergreen perennial for part shade in fertile scree. Flowers from April into May, deep yellow. The cultivar 'Franzii' forms a neat, symmetrical dome of matte green foliage with hooked tips. It is one of the last saxifrages to bloom in the season. Grows 3 inches (7.5 cm) high, 6 inches (15 cm) wide. Zones 6–9.

*Saxifraga ×paulinae* 'Franzii'

*Saxifraga retusa*, courtesy of Fritz Kummert

## Saxifraga retusa

Section *Porphyrion*. A woody-based, evergreen perennial, forming a dense cushion, for part shade in humus-rich, gritty soil. Flowers in late spring, rose red. Grows 2 inches (5 cm) high, 8 inches (20 cm) wide. Zones 5–8. Mountains of central and southern Europe.

## Saxifraga scardica

Section *Porphyrion*. An evergreen perennial with quite large foliage, forming impressive hummocks. The bicolored flowers are strikingly beautiful. Cultivate in part shade in fertile limestone scree. Flowers in spring, white often tinged pink, aging deep cerise-pink. Grows 5 inches (12.5 cm) high, 10 inches (25 cm) wide. Zones 6–9. Southwestern Balkan Peninsula.

## Saxifraga sempervivum

synonym, *S. porophylla* (of gardens, not
Bertolini) var. *sibthorpiana*
Section *Porphyrion*. A hummock-forming, evergreen perennial for part shade

*Saxifraga scardica*, courtesy of Fritz Kummert

*Saxifraga sempervivum*, courtesy of Fritz Kummert

in fertile limestone scree. Flowers in spring, purplish pink with stems and flowers covered with red, glandular hairs; 7–20 flowers per stem. Grows 3 inches (7.5 cm) high, 8 inches (20 cm) wide. Zones 7–9. Turkey and the Balkan Peninsula, including northeastern Greece.

## Saxifraga 'Sir Douglas Haig'

mossy saxifrage, a Mossy Hybrid
A garden hybrid involving *S. cespitosa*, *S. exarata*, *S. granulata*, *S. hypnoides*, and *S. rosacea*, all section *Saxifraga*. A perennial for part shade in fertile, well-drained soil. Flowers in spring, pink with a white center. Grows 4 inches (10 cm) high, 12 inches (30 cm) wide. Zones 5–9.

## Saxifraga stolonifera

mother of thousands, strawberry begonia,
strawberry geranium
Section *Irregulares*. A perennial, spreading by long, thin, red stolons, for part shade in fertile, well-drained soil. Flow-

*Saxifraga* 'Sir Douglas Haig'

*Saxifraga stolonifera*

ers in spring, white. Grows 6 inches (15 cm) high, 24 inches (60 cm) wide. Zones 5–10. China and Japan.

### Saxifraga stribrnyi

Section *Porphyrion*. A stunning evergreen perennial, forming close, irregular clusters, with silvery, knife-like leaves that give rise to a dramatic floral display. Cultivate in part shade in fertile limestone scree. Flowers in spring, purplish pink with stems and flowers covered with red, glandular hairs; 10–30 flowers per stem. Grows 6–8 inches (15–20 cm) high, 6 inches (15 cm) wide. Zones 6–9. Balkan Peninsula.

### Saxifraga tombeanensis

Section *Porphyrion*. An evergreen perennial, forming a hard mat or hummock, for part shade in fertile limestone scree. Flowers in spring, white. Grows 3 inches (7.5 cm) high, 8 inches (20 cm) wide. Zones 6–9. Southeastern Alps.

### Saxifraga ×urbium

London pride

Both a garden hybrid and a naturally occurring hybrid, *S. spathularis* × *S. umbrosa*, both section *Gymnopera* and found in the Pyrenees. A perennial for shade or part shade in fertile, well-drained soil. Flowers in spring, white with red spots. Grows 10–12 inches (25–30 cm) high, 18 inches (45 cm) wide. Zones 5–9. *Saxifraga ×urbium* has produced variegated leaf forms as well as the popular small-leaved selection, *S. ×urbium* 'Primuloides'. The original 'Primuloides' is said to occur naturally in the Pyrenees. The selection of 'Primuloides' known as *S. ×urbium* 'Clarence Elliott' (synonym, 'Elliott's Variety') is a fine dwarf usually less than 8 inches (20 cm) tall in bloom and with flowers so heavily spotted pink they appear to be rose colored.

### Saxifraga 'Whitehills'

A hybrid, probably *S. cochlearis* × *S. paniculata*, both section *Ligulatae*. A popular evergreen perennial with especially colorful foliage of blue-gray marked conspicuously red on the basal third of each leaf. Cultivate in part shade in fertile scree. Flowers in early summer, creamy white. Grows 6 inches (15 cm) high, 12 inches (30 cm) wide. Zones 4–9.

### Scabiosa

pincushion flower
Dipsacaceae

### Scabiosa graminifolia

A woody-based perennial for sun in any good, well-drained soil. Flowers in summer, lilac to pink. Grows 10–14 inches (25–35 cm) high, 18 inches (45 cm) wide. Zones 4–9. Southern Europe.

*Saxifraga stribrnyi*, courtesy of Fritz Kummert

*Saxifraga* ×*urbium*

*Scabiosa graminifolia*

*Saxifraga tombeanensis*, courtesy of Fritz Kummert

*Saxifraga* 'Whitehills'

*Scabiosa lucida*, courtesy of Fritz Kummert

## Scabiosa lucida

A perennial for sun or part shade in any good, well-drained soil. Flowers in summer and fall, rosy lilac. Grows 8 inches (20 cm) high, 12 inches (30 cm) wide. Zones 4–9. Mountains of central and southern Europe.

## Schizostylis coccinea

crimson flag, Scarlet River lily
Iridaceae
A rhizomatous perennial that is quite evergreen and exceptionally long and late blooming, qualities that make its somewhat invasive, spreading habit more tolerable. Cultivate in sun in any good, moist soil. Flowers in late summer and fall, scarlet-red and selections available in shades of red, pink, and white. Grows 18 inches (45 cm) high, 12 inches (30 cm) wide, but eventually spreading much wider. Zones 6–10. Drakensberg Mountains of South Africa.

## Scilla bifolia

Liliaceae (Hyacinthaceae)
A bulbous perennial squill for sun or part shade in any good soil. Flowers in early spring, blue to purple-blue. Grows

3–6 inches (7.5–15 cm) high. Zones 6–9. Central, southern, and eastern Europe.

## Scleranthus uniflorus

Caryophyllaceae
Few alpines can rival the color of this tiny evergreen perennial when cold turns the olive green, moss-like mound to gold-orange velvet. It is a miniature plant suited for troughs, paving, and the scree garden. Cultivate in sun in any well-drained soil, even poorish soil. Flowers in summer, petalless. Grows 1 inch (2.5 cm) high, 12 inches (30 cm) wide. Zones 6–8. South Island, New Zealand.

Scilla bifolia, courtesy of Fritz Kummert

## Scoliopus bigelovii

fetid adder's tongue, stink pod
Liliaceae (Trilliaceae)
An intriguing little perennial for the collector, requiring same treatment as trilliums. The name comes from scolios, meaning tortuous, and pous, meaning foot, in reference to the shape of the rhizome. Cultivate in part shade in humusrich, well-drained soil or in the peat bed. Flowers in early spring, purple and green. Grows 3–6 inches (7.5–15 cm) high. Zones 7–9. Coast redwood (Sequoia) forests of California.

## Scopolia carniolica

Solanaceae
A perennial for sun or part shade in any good soil. Flowers in spring, brownish

Scoliopus bigelovii

Schizostylis coccinea, courtesy of Fritz Kummert

Scleranthus uniflorus with Edraianthus in the foreground

purple without, brownish yellow to green within. Grows 12 inches (30 cm) high. Zones 5–8. Central and southeastern Europe to Russia.

### Scutellaria orientalis
Labiatae

A woody-based, deciduous perennial helmet flower or skullcap for sun in any good, well-drained soil. The cultivar 'Pinnatifida' flowers in early summer, yellow. Grows 4 inches (10 cm) high, 18 inches (45 cm) wide. Zones 6–9. The species is from Greece to Iran.

### Sedum
stonecrop
Crassulaceae

The alpine and rock garden stonecrops are succulents that will thrive in any well-drained soil when provided with a good deal of sun.

### Sedum acre
wall pepper

A stoloniferous, mat-forming, evergreen perennial for sun in any good, well-drained soil. The cultivar 'Aureum', gold-moss sedum, flowers in summer, yellow. Grows 3 inches (7.5 cm) high, 12 inches (30 cm) wide. Zones 4–10. The species is from Europe, western Asia, and northern Africa.

### Sedum anacampseros
love restorer
synonym, *Hylotelephium anacampseros*

A loosely mat-forming perennial for sun in any good, well-drained soil. Flowers in summer, pale mauve-purple. Grows 4 inches (10 cm) high, 12 inches (30 cm) wide. Zones 4–9. Southwestern Alps, Pyrenees, and Apennines.

### Sedum cauticolum
synonym, *Hylotelephium cauticolum*

A perennial for sun in any good, well-drained soil. Flowers in late summer and fall, crimson. Grows 2 inches (5 cm) high, 12 inches (30 cm) wide. Zones 4–9. Japan.

### Sedum dasyphyllum

A charming cushion- to mat-forming perennial with its powdery, gray-blue foliage, it easily makes a pest of itself if

*Scopolia carniolica,* courtesy of Fritz Kummert

*Sedum acre* 'Aureum'

*Scutellaria orientalis* 'Pinnatifida'

*Sedum anacampseros,* courtesy of Fritz Kummert

not controlled. In some gardens it spreads by seed and broken pieces that quickly take root. Cultivate in sun in any good, well-drained soil. Flowers in summer, white and pink. Grows 2 inches (5 cm) high, 10 inches (25 cm) wide. Zones 4–9. Northern Africa and southern Europe.

*Sedum cauticolum*, courtesy of Franz Hadacek

## Sedum laxum

A perennial for sun or part shade in any good, well-drained, gritty soil. Flowers in summer, pink. Grows 6–10 inches (15–25 cm) high, 6 inches (15 cm) wide. Zones 7–9. Northern California and southern Oregon.

## Sedum pachyclados

A perennial with powdery, blue leaves where the flowers serve as an added bonus. The attractive foliage is toothed and arranged in little rosettes. *Sedum pachyclados* tolerates moist soil better than most stonecrops. Cultivate in sun in any good, well-drained soil. Flowers in summer, white. Grows 2 inches (5 cm) high, 8 inches (20 cm) wide. Zones 5–8. Afghanistan and Pakistan.

## Sedum pilosum

synonym, *Hylotelephium pilosum*
A rosette-forming biennial for sun in any good, well-drained soil. Flowers in

early summer, bright pink. Grows 4–6 inches (10–15 cm) high, 8 inches (20 cm) wide. Zones 5–9. Turkey to Iran.

## Sedum sempervivoides

A biennial, monocarpic, for sun in any good, well-drained soil. Flowers in summer, bright red. Grows 4–8 inches (10–20 cm) high, 6 inches (15 cm) wide. Zones 6–9. Caucasia, Turkey, and Iran.

## Sedum sieboldii

synonym, *Hylotelephium sieboldii*
A perennial from a caudex-like rootstock for part shade in any good, well-drained soil. Flowers in fall, dusty rose pink. Grows 3 inches (7.5 cm) high, 16 inches (40 cm) wide. Zones 6–10. Japan.

## Sedum spathulifolium

A hummock-forming perennial for sun or part shade in any good, well-drained soil. Flowers in early summer, yellow. Although it can grow in mild-climate

*Sedum dasyphyllum*, courtesy of Fritz Kummert

*Sedum pachyclados*, courtesy of Franz Hadacek

*Sedum sempervivoides*, courtesy of Fritz Kummert

*Sedum laxum*, courtesy of Fritz Kummert

*Sedum pilosum*, courtesy of Fritz Kummert

*Sedum sieboldii*

coastal regions, selections made from higher elevations are cold hardy. The foliage of the cultivar 'Purpureum' is purple and silver, turning brilliant red when nipped by winter cold. Grows 2 inches (5 cm) high, 12 inches (30 cm) wide. Zones 5–9. The species is from British Columbia to central California.

## Sedum spurium

A loosely mat-forming perennial for sun or part shade in any good, well-drained soil. The cultivar 'Tricolor' flowers in summer, rose pink. Grows 4 inches (10 cm) high, 12–18 inches (30–45 cm) wide. Zones 3–9. The species is from Caucasia and northern Iran.

## Selaginella
club moss
Selaginellaceae

Relatively few of the selaginellas are hardy garden plants; most are for the greenhouse or alpine house. Those for outdoor growing are neat, nonflowering, spore-producing, moss-like companion plants.

## Selaginella involvens
little club moss

synonym, *S. caulescens*

An evergreen perennial for shade or part shade in humus-rich, lightly moist soil. Grows 6 inches (15 cm) high, 12 inches (30 cm) wide. Zones 6–9. Eastern Asia.

## Selaginella sanguinolenta var. compressa
little club moss

An evergreen perennial for shade or part shade in humus-rich, lightly moist soil. Grows 3–4 inches (7.5–10 cm) high, 8 inches (20 cm) wide. Zones 7–9. Japan.

## Semiaquilegia ecalcarata
Ranunculaceae

synonym, *Aquilegia ecalcarata*

A close columbine relative with delicate, nodding flowers with petals that are not spurred but instead are pouched at the base. A perennial for sun or part shade in any good, well-drained soil. Flowers in early summer, wine red to purple. Grows 12–18 inches (30–45 cm) high, 12 inches (30 cm) wide. Zones 6–9. Mountains of western China.

## Sempervivum
houseleek
Crassulaceae

Houseleeks are some of the toughest, most easily grown plants. They are succulent perennials that spread by "hatching chicks" and form hard pads consisting of many symmetrical rosettes of leaves.

## Sempervivum arachnoideum
cobweb houseleek, spiderweb houseleek

Cultivate in sun or part shade in any well-drained soil. Flowers in summer, rose red. Grows 4–6 inches (10–15 cm)

*Sedum spathulifolium* 'Purpureum'

*Selaginella involvens*, courtesy of Fritz Kummert

*Semiaquilegia ecalcarata*

*Sedum spurium* 'Tricolor'

*Selaginella sanguinolenta* var. *compressa*

*Sempervivum arachnoideum*, courtesy of Fritz Kummert

high, 12 inches (30 cm) wide. Zones 5–10. Mountains from Spain to Austria.

### Sempervivum 'Ashes of Roses'

Cultivate in sun or part shade in any well-drained soil. Flowers in summer, rose red. Grows 4 inches (10 cm) high, 10 inches (25 cm) wide. Zones 5–10.

### Sempervivum calcareum

A large and impressive plant, possibly a hybrid. The relatively big rosettes of green and purple leaves are most handsome. Cultivate in sun or part shade in any well-drained soil. Flowers in summer, pale pink. Grows 10 inches (25 cm) high, 12 inches (30 cm) wide. Zones 5–10. Southwestern Alps.

### Sempervivum wulfenii

Cultivate in sun or part shade in any well-drained soil. Flowers in summer, lemon yellow. Grows 6–10 inches (15–25 cm) high, 12 inches (30 cm) wide.

Sempervivum 'Ashes of Roses', courtesy of Armen Gevjan

Sempervivum calcareum

Zones 5–10. Switzerland, Italy, and Austria.

### Senecio incanus

Compositae

A perennial with a woody rootstock for sun in humus-rich, gritty scree. Flowers in summer, yellow. Grows 4 inches (10 cm) high, 8 inches (20 cm) wide. Zones 5–8. Alps, Apennines, and Carpathians.

**Subspecies**. *Senecio incanus* subsp. *carniolicus* flowers in summer, orange-yellow. Grows 8 inches (20 cm) high, 12 inches (30 cm) wide. Alps, Apennines, and Carpathians.

### Sequoia sempervirens

coast redwood
Cupressaceae (Taxodiaceae)
An evergreen conifer for sun or part

Sempervivum wulfenii, courtesy of Fritz Kummert

shade in any good, well-drained soil. The cultivar 'Prostrata' (synonym, 'Nana Pendula') is a dwarf shrub, particularly intriguing to grow in a rock garden—it is a form of one of the world's largest trees. Grows 12 inches (30 cm) high, 36

Senecio incanus, courtesy of Fritz Kummert

Senecio incanus subsp. *carniolicus*, courtesy of Fritz Kummert

Sequoia sempervirens 'Prostrata'

inches (90 cm) wide. Zones 6–10. The species is from the Coast Ranges of central and northern California to southern Oregon.

## Serratula seoanei

Compositae
synonym, *S. shawii* (of gardens)
A perennial for sun in any good, well-drained soil. Flowers in early to late fall, pinkish purple. Grows 10–12 inches (25–30 cm) high, 18 inches (45 cm) wide. Zones 6–9. Northern Portugal, northwestern Spain, and southwestern France.

## Shortia galacifolia

Oconee bells
Diapensiaceae
*Shortia galacifolia* and the Japanese *S. uniflora*, or Nippon bells, are elite perennials for the acid-soil, shady garden. *Shortia galacifolia* produces dense, evergreen carpets and glorious flowers. Cul-

tivate in shade or part shade in humus-rich soil. Flowers in spring, white, aging pinkish. Grows 6–8 inches (15–20 cm) high, 18 inches (45 cm) wide. Zones 4–8. Appalachian Mountains of North Carolina and Georgia.

## Sibbaldia procumbens

Rosaceae
synonym, *Potentilla sibbaldii*
A perennial with a woody, branched rootstock for sun in fertile, well-drained soil. Flowers in summer, yellow or yellow-green. Grows 8 inches (20 cm) high, 12 inches (30 cm) wide. Zones 1–7. Northern Europe, Asia, and North America.

## Silene

campion, catchfly
Caryophyllaceae

## Silene acaulis

moss campion
An outstanding miniature plant in both foliage and flower, ideal for the crevice

garden and trough. The cultivar 'Floribunda' produces abundant flowers in cultivation, unlike many seedling and collected forms. A densely mat- or cushion-forming perennial for sun or part shade in sharply drained, moderately moist soil. Flowers in summer, abundant and pink. Grows 1 inch (2.5 cm) high, 4–12 inches (10–30 cm) wide. Zones 2–8. The species is circumpolar in the northern hemisphere, extending into mountains farther south.

## Silene alpestris

A colony-forming perennial for sun or part shade in any good, well-drained soil. The cultivar 'Flore Pleno' flowers in early summer, white, doubled. Grows 8 inches (20 cm) high, 18 inches (45 cm) wide. Zones 5–9. The species is from the eastern Alps and mountains of the Balkan Peninsula.

## Silene caroliniana

A perennial for sun or part shade in sharply drained, acid soil. Flowers in

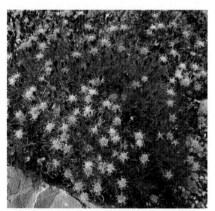

*Serratula seoanei,* courtesy of Fritz Kummert

*Sibbaldia procumbens,* courtesy of Fritz Kummert

*Silene alpestris* 'Flore Pleno'

*Shortia galacifolia*

*Silene acaulis* 'Floribunda', courtesy of Fritz Kummert

*Silene caroliniana*

late spring to midsummer in shades of pink. Grows 4–8 inches (10–20 cm) high, 10 inches (25 cm) wide. Zones 4–8. Central and eastern North America, Pennsylvania to Georgia and west to Oklahoma.

### Silene dinarica

A perennial for sun or part shade in moderately moist, sharply drained soil. Flowers in summer, rich pink. Grows 4 inches (10 cm) high, 6 inches (15 cm) wide. Zones 4–8. Romania, at alpine levels.

### Silene elisabethae

synonym, *Melandrium elisabethae*
A perennial for sun or part shade in sharply drained soil. Flowers in sum-

mer, magenta-crimson. Grows 6–10 inches (15–25 cm) high, 10 inches (25 cm) wide. Zones 7–9. Southern and eastern Alps.

### Silene hookeri

*Silene hookeri,* including subspecies *bolanderi,* and *S. ingramii* are among the most beautiful western U.S. wildflowers, with downy, gray foliage and deeply cleft flowers. *Silene hookeri* is a perennial for sun or part shade in humus-rich, lime-free scree. Flowers in spring, light to dark pink or salmon pink. Grows 3 inches (7.5 cm) high, 10 inches (25 cm) wide. Zones 6–9. Northern California and southern Oregon.

**Subspecies.** *Silene hookeri* subsp. *bolanderi* flowers in spring, white.

Grows 3–4 inches (7.5–10 cm) high, 10 inches (25 cm) wide. Northern California.

### Silene ingramii

Now considered a synonym of *S. hookeri* by most authorities *S. ingramii* remains a distinctive plant in both flower color and distribution. It is a perennial for sun or part shade in humus-rich, lime-free scree. Flowers in spring, cherry red. Grows 6 inches (15 cm) high, 12 inches (30 cm) wide. Zones 6–9. Central western Oregon.

### Silene uniflora

synonym, *S. maritima*
A perennial for sun or part shade in any good, well-drained soil. The cultivar

*Silene dinarica,* courtesy of Fritz Kummert

*Silene hookeri*

*Silene elisabethae,* courtesy of Fritz Kummert

*Silene hookeri* subsp. *bolanderi*

*Silene ingramii,* courtesy of Fritz Kummert

'Flore Pleno' flowers in summer, white, doubled. Grows 8 inches (20 cm) high, 18 inches (45 cm) wide. Zones 3–9. The species is from Atlantic Europe.

## Silene zawadzkii

A perennial for sun or part shade in any good, well-drained soil. Flowers in summer, white. Grows 8 inches (20 cm) high, 12 inches (30 cm) wide. Zones 5–8. Eastern Carpathians.

## Sisyrinchium
Iridaceae

## Sisyrinchium bellum
California blue-eyed grass

A perennial for sun or part shade in any well-drained, moist soil. Flowers in spring, violet-blue and veined purple, or occasionally purple or white. Grows 6–16 inches (15–45 cm) high, 12 inches (30 cm) wide. Zones 6–9. California. The selection shown is a particularly dwarf form that stays consistently short.

It was found around the community of Fort Bragg, Mendocino County, California.

## Sisyrinchium douglasii
grass widow, purple-eyed grass
synonym, *Olsynium douglasii*

A perennial for sun or part shade in any well-drained, moist soil. Flowers in early spring, wine red, purple-pink, or white. Grows 8–12 inches (20–30 cm) high. Zones 4–9. Northern California to British Columbia.

## Sisyrinchium 'E. K. Balls'

A nonreseeding, long-blooming, easy-to-grow hybrid, thus highly recommended. A perennial for sun or part shade in any well-drained, moist soil. Flowers in summer and fall, purple. Grows 6 inches (15 cm) high, 18 inches (45 cm) wide. Zones 5–9.

*Sisyrinchium bellum,* dwarf form

*Sisyrinchium douglasii*

## Sisyrinchium macrocarpon

A perennial for sun or part shade in any well-drained, moist soil. Flowers in summer, golden yellow with a basal, brown, V-shaped band. Grows 8 inches (20 cm) high and wide. Zones 6–10. Argentina.

## Soldanella
Primulaceae

All of the soldanellas are perennials with underground, running stems that will spread and form sizable colonies with attractive, round, leathery leaves. For good flower production, buds, which form in fall, must be protected from excessive freezing and damage by slugs and snails.

## Soldanella alpina

Cultivate in part shade in humus-rich, gritty soil. Flowers in early spring, lavender. Grows 3–6 inches (7.5–15 cm)

*Sisyrinchium* 'E. K. Balls'

*Sisyrinchium macrocarpon,* courtesy of Fritz Kummert

*Silene uniflora* 'Flore Pleno'

*Silene zawadzkii,* courtesy of Fritz Kummert

high, 6 inches (15 cm) wide. Zones 4–8. Pyrenees and Alps.

## Soldanella carpatica

Cultivate in part shade in humus-rich, gritty soil. Flowers in early spring, purple-blue. Grows 6 inches (15 cm) high, 10 inches (25 cm) wide. Zones 4–8. Carpathians, and High and Low Tatra Mountains.

## Soldanella minima

Cultivate in part shade in humus-rich, gritty soil. Flowers in early spring, white or pale lilac blue with violet streaks inside. Grows 3 inches (7.5 cm) high, 6 inches (15 cm) wide. Zones 4–8. Alps.

## Soldanella montana

Perhaps because *S. montana* is so widespread through the mountains of Europe, it is the easiest of the soldanellas to cultivate. It is also the biggest, with leaves up to 2.5 inches (6 cm) across. Cultivate in part shade in humus-rich, gritty soil. Flowers in early spring, blue to lilac. Grows 8 inches (20 cm) high, 12 inches (30 cm) wide. Zones 5–8. Austrian Alps, Carpathians, and the Balkan Peninsula.

## Soldanella pusilla

Cultivate in part shade in humus-rich, gritty soil. Flowers in early spring, pale to reddish violet. Grows 4 inches (10 cm) high, 6 inches (15 cm) wide. Zones

4–8. Alps, Carpathians, Rhodope Mountains of the Balkan Peninsula, and Apennines.

## Solidago virgaurea var. minutissima

Compositae

A perennial goldenrod for sun or part shade in any moderately moist soil. Flowers in summer, deep yellow. Grows 2–4 inches (5–10 cm) high, 6 inches (15 cm) wide. Zones 4–8. Japan. The species is widespread through Europe, northern Africa, and Asia, and except in the cases of dwarf forms it is too large for the rock garden. Subspecies *minuta* is nice and compact with short, dense flower heads, but variety *minutissima* is the smallest.

## Sorbus reducta

Rosaceae

A deciduous, shrubby mountain ash for sun in any good, well-drained soil. Flowers in spring, white, followed by

*Soldanella alpina*, courtesy of Fritz Kummert

*Soldanella minima*, courtesy of Fritz Kummert

*Soldanella pusilla*, courtesy of Fritz Kummert

*Soldanella carpatica*, courtesy of Fritz Kummert

*Soldanella montana*, courtesy of Fritz Kummert

*Solidago virgaurea* var. *minutissima*, courtesy of Fritz Kummert

white, rose, or red berries. Grows 6–18 inches (15–45 cm) high, 24–36 inches (60–90 cm) wide. Zones 6–9. Western China and Myanmar (Burma).

## Spigelia marilandica
Indian pink, pink root, worm grass
Loganiaceae

The showy, unusual flowers make it a perennial worth accommodating. Choose a warm location with sun, humidity, and humus-rich, moist soil for short, floriferous plants. Cultivate in sun or part shade. Flowers in summer, scarlet outside, yellow inside. Grows 12–24 inches (30–60 cm) high, 12 inches (30 cm) wide. Zones 6–9. Southeastern United States, South Carolina to Florida and west to Texas.

Sorbus reducta, courtesy of Fritz Kummert

Spigelia marilandica, courtesy of Armen Gevjan

## Spiraea japonica
Rosaceae
synonym, S. ×bumalda

The cultivar 'Nyewoods' is a deciduous, shrubby bridal wreath or spirea for sun or part shade in any good soil. Flowers in summer, raspberry pink. Grows 12–16 inches (30–40 cm) high, 24–36 inches (60–90 cm) wide. Zones 3–9. The species is from Japan and China.

## Stachys
betony, hedge nettle
Labiatae

### Stachys candida
A woody-based perennial that is an excellent miniature version of S. byzantina, lamb's ears, S. candida has white,

Spiraea japonica 'Nyewoods'

Stachys candida, courtesy of Fritz Kummert

felted leaves that need some protection from excessive winter wetness. It can be easily accommodated in a dry crevice, wall, or alpine house. Cultivate in sun in fertile, sharply drained soil. Flowers in summer, white, heavily veined pink. Grows 3 inches (7.5 cm) high, 12 inches (30 cm) wide. Zones 5–10. Southern Greece.

### Stachys discolor
synonym, S. nivea

A perennial for sun in any good, well-drained soil. Flowers in summer, rose to cream. Grows 8–12 inches (20–30 cm) high, 12 inches (30 cm) wide. Zone 5–9. Caucasus Mountains.

### Stachys lavandulifolia
A woody-based perennial with creeping, rooting stems for sun in any good, well-drained soil. Flowers in summer, pinkish mauve to purple. Grows 6–12 inches (15–30 cm) high, 24 inches (60 cm)

Stachys discolor, courtesy of Fritz Kummert

Stachys lavandulifolia, courtesy of Fritz Kummert

wide. Zones 5–9. Turkey, Iraq, Iran, and Transcaucasia.

## Sternbergia
autumn daffodil
Amaryllidaceae

### Sternbergia clusiana
A bulbous perennial for sun in well-drained soil, keeping it dry during summer dormancy. It does well in the bulb frame or alpine house. Flowers in fall, bright yellow-green. Grows 3 inches (7.5 cm) high when in flower. Zones 6–9. Turkey, Jordan, Israel, and Iran.

### Sternbergia fischeriana
A bulbous perennial for sun in well-drained soil, keeping it dry during summer dormancy. It does well in the bulb frame or alpine house. Flowers in spring, bright yellow. Grows 8 inches (20 cm) high when in flower. Zones 6–9. Turkey, Iran, and Iraq to Kashmir.

*Sternbergia clusiana*, courtesy of Fritz Kummert

*Sternbergia fischeriana*, courtesy of Fritz Kummert

### Sternbergia lutea
The most easily grown species of *Sternbergia*, bringing bright spring color to the fall garden when effectively combined with companions such as *Cyclamen hederifolium*. A bulbous perennial for sun in any good, well-drained soil. Flowers in fall, deep yellow. Grows 6–8 inches (15–20 cm) high when in flower. Zones 6–9. Spain to Iran and central Asia.

### Stylophorum diphyllum
celandine poppy
Papaveraceae
A perennial for part shade in humus-rich, well-drained soil. Flowers in spring, yellow. Grows 12 inches (30 cm) high, 24 inches (60 cm) wide. Zones 4–9. Eastern United States from Wisconsin to Pennsylvania south to Missouri and Virginia.

### Symphyandra wanneri
Campanulaceae
A perennial, or usually biennial, ring bellflower for sun or part shade in humus-rich, well-drained soil. Flowers

*Sternbergia lutea*, courtesy of Fritz Kummert

*Stylophorum diphyllum*, courtesy of Fritz Kummert

in spring, violet-blue. Grows 12 inches (30 cm) high and wide. Zones 6–9. Alps.

## Synthyris
Scrophulariaceae

Synthyrises are western American woodland natives that herald the arrival of spring with dense, *Muscari*-like flower spikes just above the foliage.

### Synthyris missurica
A perennial for sun or part shade in humus-rich, well-drained, moist soil. Flowers in spring, light blue-purple. Grows 12 inches (30 cm) high, 18 inches

*Symphyandra wanneri*, courtesy of Fritz Kummert

*Synthyris missurica*, courtesy of Fritz Kummert

(45 cm) wide. Zones 2–8. Arctic Canada to northeastern California.

### Synthyris stellata
Columbia synthyris
A perennial for sun or part shade in humus-rich, well-drained, moist soil. Flowers in spring, purple. Grows 12 inches (30 cm) high, 8 inches (20 cm) wide. Zones 5–8. Columbia River Gorge of Oregon and Washington.

### Talinum
fameflower
Portulacaceae

### Talinum okanoganense
A perennial for sun in sandy scree with winter protection from cold and wetness. It does well in the alpine house. Flowers in summer, white or palest pink. Grows 2 inches (5 cm) high, 4–8 inches (10–20 cm) wide. Zones 6–9. Washington and British Columbia.

### Talinum spinescens
A perennial for sun in sandy scree with winter protection from cold and wetness. It does well in the alpine house.

Synthyris stellata, courtesy of Fritz Kummert

Flowers in summer, light to deep rose red. Grows 4 inches (10 cm) high, 8 inches (20 cm) wide. Zones 6–9. Washington and Oregon.

### Tanacetum
Dalmatia pyrethrum, pyrethrum
Compositae

### Tanacetum cinerariifolium
synonyms, *Chrysanthemum cinerariifolium, Pyrethrum cinerariifolium*
A perennial for sun or part shade in any good, well-drained soil. Flowers in summer, white. Grows 14–18 inches (35–45 cm) high, 24 inches (60 cm) wide. Zones 6–9. Western Balkan Peninsula.

### Tanacetum densum subsp. amanum
synonym, *Chrysanthemum haradjanii*
A striking perennial grown for its gorgeous, feathered foliage of silvery white and corymbs of substantial, rayless flower heads. *Tanacetum densum* subsp. *amanum* has proven itself remarkably hardy to cold when kept on the dry side in winter. It tolerates some drought once established. Cultivate in sun in any good, well-drained soil. Flowers in summer, bright yellow. Grows 8 inches (20 cm) high, 18 inches (45 cm) wide. Zones 5–9. Turkey.

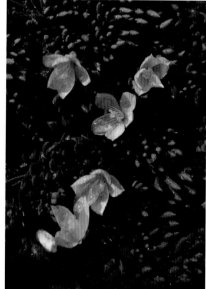

Talinum okanoganense, courtesy of Fritz Kummert

### Tanacetum huronense var. terra-novae
A perennial for sun in any good, well-drained soil. Flowers in summer, gold. Grows 6 inches (15 cm) high, 24 inches (60 cm) wide. Zones 2–9. Western Newfoundland, Canada.

### Tanakea radicans
Saxifragaceae
A rhizomatous and stoloniferous perennial for part shade in humus-rich or

Talinum spinescens, courtesy of Armen Gevjan

Tanacetum cinerariifolium, courtesy of Fritz Kummert

Tanacetum densum subsp. *amanum*

peaty, moist soil. Flowers in spring, white. Grows 6 inches (15 cm) high, 24 inches (60 cm) wide. Zones 6–9. Japan.

## Telesonix jamesii
Saxifragaceae
synonym, *Boykinia jamesii*
A perennial for part shade in humus-rich, well-drained, gritty soil. Flowers in early summer, purplish rose. Grows 6–8 inches (15–20 cm) high, 8 inches (20 cm) wide. Zones 3–8. Mountains of Colorado. *Telesonix jamesii* var. *heucheriformis* (synonyms, *T. heucheriformis, Boykinia heucheriformis*) is similar and the variety is sometimes not recognized as distinct from the species.

## Tellima grandiflora
fringe cups
Saxifragaceae
A perennial for shade or part shade in humus-rich, well-drained, moist soil. Flowers in early summer, white tinged with green to red. Grows 24–30 inches (60–75 cm) high, 12 inches (30 cm)

Tanacetum huronense var. terra-novae

Tanakea radicans

wide. Zones 4–9. Western North America.

## Teucrium
germander, wood sage
Labiatae

The germanders all thrive in sun and flower in the summer. They have aromatic foliage and unusual, attractive flowers.

Telesonix jamesii

Tellima grandiflora, courtesy of Fritz Kummert

## Teucrium aroanium
A mat-forming shrublet for sun in any sharply drained soil. Flowers in summer, bluish white, veined purple. Grows 2 inches (5 cm) high, 12 inches (30 cm) wide. Zones 5–9. Southern Greece.

## Teucrium cossonii
A cushion-forming subshrub for sun in any sharply drained soil. Flowers in summer, purplish red to red. Grows 8 inches (20 cm) high, 18 inches (45 cm) wide. Zones 7–9. Majorca, Spain.

## Teucrium montanum
A subshrub for sun in any sharply drained soil. Flowers in summer, white

Teucrium aroanium, courtesy of Fritz Kummert

Teucrium cossonii

Teucrium montanum, courtesy of Fritz Kummert

to cream. Grows 8 inches (20 cm) high, 18 inches (45 cm) wide. Zones 6–9. Central and southern Europe and northern Africa to western Asia.

### Teucrium polium subsp. *aureum*
synonym, *T. aureum*
A shrublet for sun in any sharply drained soil. Flowers in summer, yellow with chartreuse bracts. Grows 4 inches (10 cm) high, 12 inches (30 cm) wide. Zones 6–9. Turkey and southern Europe.

*Teucrium polium* subsp. *aureum*

*Teucrium pyrenaicum*, courtesy of Fritz Kummert

*Teucrium subspinosum*

### Teucrium pyrenaicum
A mat-forming perennial for sun in any sharply drained soil. Flowers in summer, cream and maroon. Grows 3 inches (7.5 cm) high, 18 inches (45 cm) wide. Zones 5–8. Pyrenees.

### Teucrium subspinosum
A shrublet for sun in any sharply drained soil. Flowers in summer, purple to red-purple. Grows 4 inches (10 cm) high, 12 inches (30 cm) wide. Zones 6–8. Majorca, Spain.

---

### Thalictrum
meadow rue
Ranunculaceae

---

The dwarf meadow rues are delightful plants, thriving in shade, for the cooler

*Thalictrum ichangense*

*Thalictrum kiusianum*, courtesy of Franz Hadacek

parts of the rock garden. They have delicate foliage and a long summer bloom.

### Thalictrum ichangense
synonym, *T. coreanum*
A perennial for part shade in humus-rich, well-drained, moist soil. Flowers in summer and fall, lilac. Grows 8 inches (20 cm) high, 12 inches (30 cm) wide. Zones 4–8. Northern and eastern China.

### Thalictrum kiusianum
A rhizomatous and colony-forming perennial for part shade in humus-rich, well-drained, moist soil. Flowers in summer, pink. Grows 4–6 inches (10–15 cm) high, 12–18 inches (30–45 cm) wide. Zones 5–8. Japan.

*Thlaspi rotundifolium*, courtesy of Fritz Kummert

## *Thlaspi rotundifolium*
Cruciferae
A perennial, forming mats by stolons, for sun in well-drained, gritty soil. Flowers in summer, purple to pink. Grows 2–4 inches (5–10 cm) high, 8 inches (20 cm) wide. Zones 6–8. Alps.

## *Thuja occidentalis*
American arborvitae
Cupressaceae
An evergreen conifer for sun or part shade in humus-rich, well-drained soil. Zones 2–8. Northeastern United States and Canada.

*Thuja occidentalis* 'Recurva Nana'

*Thuja occidentalis* 'Rheingold'

*Thuja occidentalis* 'Tiny Tim'

**Cultivars**. American arborvitae is the source for many fine dwarfs with characteristic flattened branchlets with scale-like foliage. *Thuja occidentalis* 'Recurva Nana' is a shrub, growing 8 inches (20 cm) high, 18 inches (45 cm) wide.

*Thuja occidentalis* 'Rheingold', Rheingold arborvitae, is a shrub, growing 24 inches (60 cm) high, 48 inches (120 cm) wide.

*Thuja occidentalis* 'Tiny Tim' is a shrub, growing 12 inches (30 cm) high, 18 inches (45 cm) wide.

## *Thymus*
thyme
Labiatae

## *Thymus broussonetii*
A beautiful species but unfortunately only half-hardy, especially in damp, cold

*Thymus broussonetii*

*Thymus cilicicus*

conditions. A subshrub for sun in any well-drained soil. Flowers in early summer, red to purple-red. Grows 6–12 inches (15–30 cm) high, 18 inches (45 cm) wide. Zones 7–10. Morocco.

## *Thymus cilicicus*
A subshrub for sun in any well-drained soil. Flowers in summer, lilac pink. Grows 3 inches (7.5 cm) high, 10 inches (25 cm) wide. Zones 5–9. Turkey.

## *Thymus ×citriodorus*
A subshrub for sun in any well-drained soil. The cultivar 'Silver Queen' flowers in summer, pale lilac. Grows 6–8 inches (15–20 cm) high, 18 inches (45 cm) wide. Zones 6–9. *Thymus ×citriodorus* is a naturally occurring hybrid, *T. pulegioides* × *T. vulgaris*.

*Thymus ×citriodorus* 'Silver Queen'

### Thymus membranaceus

A rare beauty with tangled woody stems that form a neat dome of dark foliage, a subshrub for the alpine house or a warm, dry location. Cultivate in sun in any well-drained soil. Flowers in summer, white. Grows 6 inches (15 cm) high, 12 inches (30 cm) wide. Zones 7–10. Southeastern Spain.

### Thymus polytrichus

A mat-forming subshrub for sun in any well-drained soil. The cultivar 'Pink Chintz' flowers in summer, salmon pink. Grows 2 inches (5 cm) high, 18–24 inches (45–60 cm) wide. Zones 4–9. The species is from Europe to Turkey, Caucasia, and Iran.

Thymus membranaceus

Thymus polytrichus 'Pink Chintz'

### Thymus pulegioides

A vigorous, low-growing, mat-forming subshrub with dark, lemon-scented foliage. It is a good addition to an alpine lawn. Cultivate in sun in any well-drained soil. Flowers in summer, mauve-pink. Grows 3 inches (7.5 cm) high, 24 inches (60 cm) wide. Zones 4–9. Europe.

### Tiarella wherryi

Wherry's foam flower
Saxifragaceae
synonym, *T. cordifolia* var. *collina*
A refined, evergreen, clump-forming, woodland perennial whose large, three-lobed leaves turn red in winter. Combine with ferns and primroses. Cultivate in part shade in any good soil. Flowers in late spring and early summer, white or tinted pink. Grows 12 inches (30 cm)

Thymus pulegioides

high, 18 inches (45 cm) wide. Zones 3–8. Appalachians.

### Townsendia

Compositae

*Townsendia* is a genus of small *Aster* relatives that come easily from seed and may prove short-lived in the garden. Dry summer conditions seem to improve their longevity.

### Townsendia exscapa

Easter daisy
A perennial for sun in gritty scree with protection from winter wetness. Flowers in May through July, white to pale pink. Grows 3 inches (7.5 cm) high, 6 inches (15 cm) wide. Zones 3–8. Central Canada to Mexico.

### Townsendia hookeri

Easter daisy
A perennial for sun in gritty scree with protection from winter wetness. Flowers in May through July, white above tinged

Tiarella wherryi

Townsendia exscapa, courtesy of Fritz Kummert

pink beneath. Grows 3 inches (7.5 cm) high, 8 inches (20 cm) wide. Zones 4–8. Central United States to Canada.

## Townsendia parryi

A biennial or short-lived perennial for sun in gritty scree with protection from winter wetness. Flowers in early summer, lavender to purple, white, or pink. Grows 6–12 inches (15–30 cm) high, 8 inches (20 cm) wide. Zones 5–8. Mountains of the northwestern United States and adjacent Canada.

## Trachelium
Campanulaceae

The tracheliums are excellent subjects for the alpine house.

## Trachelium asperuloides

synonym, *Diosphaera asperuloides*
A cushion-forming perennial for part shade in tufa or limestone scree and avoid overhead watering. Flowers in early summer, lilac. Grows 1–2 inches

*Townsendia hookeri,* courtesy of Fritz Kummert

*Townsendia parryi,* courtesy of Armen Gevjan

(2.5–4 cm) high, 6 inches (15 cm) wide. Zones 7–8. Southern Greece.

## Trachelium jaquinii subsp. rumelianum

synonyms, *T. rumelianum, Diosphaera rumelianum*

A clump-forming perennial from a woody rootstock for part shade in tufa or limestone scree. Flowers in summer, blue to lilac. Grows 12 inches (30 cm) high, 16 inches (40 cm) wide. Zones 7–8. Greece and the Aegean Islands.

## Tradescantia longipes
Commelinaceae

The only species of spider lily or spiderwort small enough for the rock garden. It is very charming with late spring blossoms that start on 4-inch (10-cm) stems

*Trachelium asperuloides,* courtesy of Fritz Kummert

*Trachelium jaquinii* subsp. *rumelianum,* courtesy of Fritz Kummert

that elongate as the foliage emerges. A perennial for sun or part shade in slightly fertile scree. Flowers in late spring, pink, purple, or blue. Grows 4 inches (10 cm) high, 12 inches (30 cm) wide. Zones 5–9. Missouri.

## Tricyrtis
toad lily
Liliaceae (Tricyrtidaceae)

*Tricyrtis* is a genus of unusual plants for the shade garden, with exotic flowers, spotted and speckled, and curiously detailed.

## Tricyrtis formosana

A perennial for shade or part shade in humus-rich, moist soil. The species is sometimes made available under the name of the cultivar, *T. formosana*

*Tradescantia longipes,* courtesy of Fritz Kummert

'Stolonifera', which is, however, not distinct from the species. Flowers in late summer and fall, white to pink with dense crimson spotting. Grows 30 inches (75 cm) high, 12 inches (30 cm) wide. Zones 4–9. Taiwan.

## Tricyrtis hirta

A perennial for shade or part shade in humus-rich, moist soil. Flowers in late summer and fall, light lavender, heavily dotted with purple. Grows 18–24 inches (45–60 cm) high, 12 inches (30 cm) wide. Zones 3–8. Japan.

Tricyrtis formosana

Tricyrtis hirta

Tricyrtis macrantha, courtesy of Fritz Kummert

## Tricyrtis macrantha

A perennial for shade or part shade in humus-rich, moist soil. Flowers in late summer and fall, golden yellow, spotted purple-red or chocolate inside. Grows 12–24 inches (30–60 cm) high, 12 inches (30 cm) wide. Zones 5–8. Shikoku, Japan.

## Tricyrtis macranthopsis

synonym, *T. macrantha* var. *macranthopsis*
The showiest toad lily, with glossy green leaves on arching stems that progressively weep as the huge flowers develop. A perennial for shade or part shade in humus-rich, moist soil. Flowers in late summer and fall, yellow, spotted chocolate inside. Grows 18 inches (45 cm) high, 24 inches (60 cm) wide. Zones 4–9. Honshu, Japan.

## Tricyrtis macropoda

A perennial for shade or part shade in humus-rich, moist soil. Flowers in early

Tricyrtis macranthopsis

Tricyrtis macropoda

fall, white, spotted purple. Grows 24 inches (60 cm) high, 12 inches (30 cm) wide. Zones 5–9. Japan, Korea, and China.

## Trientalis latifolia
Primulaceae
synonym, *T. europaea* var. *latifolia*
A rhizomatous perennial chickweed, starflower, or wintergreen for shade or part shade in humus-rich soil. Flowers in summer, pink to rose, occasionally white. Grows 4–8 inches (10–20 cm) high. Zones 3–8. Central California to British Columbia and Alberta.

## Trifolium
clover
Leguminosae

The clovers treated here are not the least bit weedy like the common lawn clovers. These natives of higher mountains and pastures can require care when planting. The best success has come with a scree soil with clayey loam added.

Trientalis latifolia, courtesy of Fritz Kummert

Trifolium alpinum, courtesy of Fritz Kummert

## *Trifolium alpinum*
alpine clover

A perennial for sun in moderately fertile, well-drained soil. Flowers in summer, pink, purple, or cream. Grows 4–8 inches (10–20 cm) high, 12 inches (30 cm) wide. Zones 3–8. Alps, Pyrenees, and Apennines.

## *Trifolium nanum*

A perennial for sun in moderately fertile, well-drained soil. Flowers in summer, purplish red. Grows 4 inches (10 cm) high, 8 inches (20 cm) wide. Zones 4–8. Rocky Mountains.

Trifolium nanum

Trillium albidum

## *Trillium*
wake robin, wood lily
Liliaceae (Trilliaceae)

The trilliums are elegant plants for semishade and humus-rich soil. They are perennials with tuber-like rhizomes and have leaves and flower parts in threes.

## *Trillium albidum*

Cultivate in part shade in humus-rich, well-drained, moist soil. Flowers in spring, white, sometimes flushed with rose pink at the base. Grows 12 inches (30 cm) high. Zones 6–9. Coastal areas of central California north to central Washington.

Trillium chloropetalum

Trillium chloropetalum var. giganteum

## *Trillium chloropetalum*
giant trillium

Cultivate in part shade in humus-rich, well-drained, moist soil. Flowers in spring, green to yellow to purple. Grows 12–24 inches (30–60 cm) high. Zones 5–9. Northern California and southern Oregon.

**Variety**. *Trillium chloropetalum* var. *giganteum* flowers in spring, white, cream, or red-brown. San Francisco Bay area.

## *Trillium decumbens*
decumbent trillium

Cultivate in part shade in humus-rich, well-drained, moist soil. Flowers in spring, deep purple. Grows 6 inches (15 cm) high. Zones 6–9. Southeastern United States, in and around Alabama.

Trillium decumbens

Trillium erectum, courtesy of Fritz Kummert

Trillium grandiflorum, courtesy of Armen Gevjan

Trillium grandiflorum 'Flore Pleno'

## Trillium erectum
red or purple trillium, stinking Benjamin, squaw root, wake robin
Cultivate in part shade in humus-rich, well-drained, moist soil. Flowers in spring, red-maroon, sometimes white, yellow, green, or pink. Grows 8–18 inches (20–45 cm) high. Zones 4–9. Eastern Canada south to Georgia.

## Trillium grandiflorum
great white trillium, white wake robin
Cultivate in part shade in humus-rich, well-drained, moist soil. Flowers in spring, white, sometimes aging pink. Grows 12–18 inches (30–45 cm) high. Zones 4–9. Eastern North America, Quebec to Georgia.
**Cultivar.** Trillium grandiflorum 'Flore Pleno'. Flowers doubled.

## Trillium kurabayashii
Cultivate in part shade in humus-rich, well-drained, moist soil. Flowers in spring, deep purple to red brown. Grows 10–20 inches (25–50 cm) high. Zones 5–9. Siskiyou Mountains on the California-Oregon border east to the foothills of the northern Sierra Nevada.

## Trillium luteum
wax trillium, yellow toad shade or trillium
Cultivate in part shade in humus-rich, well-drained, moist soil. Flowers in spring, bright to chrome yellow. Grows 8–14 inches (20–35 cm) high. Zones 5–9. Eastern Tennessee and just into the bordering states.

Trillium kurabayashii

## Trillium nivale
dwarf white or snow trillium
Cultivate in part shade in humus-rich, well-drained, moist soil. Flowers in early spring, bright white. Grows 6 inches (15 cm) high. Zones 5–8. Western Pennsylvania to Nebraska, Missouri and Kentucky.

## Trillium ovatum
coast or western white trillium
Cultivate in part shade in humus-rich, well-drained, moist soil. Flowers in early

Trillium luteum

Trillium nivale, courtesy of Fritz Kummert

Trillium ovatum

spring, white, fading to purplish pink. Grows 12 inches (30 cm) high. Zones 4–9. Colorado west to British Columbia and south to central California.

## Trillium rivale
brook wake robin
An excellent rock garden trillium or one that grows well as a container plant for the alpine house. Cultivate in part shade in humus-rich, gritty, sharply drained, moist soil. Flowers in spring, white or pale pink with varied intensity of purple spotting inside. Grows 2–6 inches (5–15 cm) high. Zones 5–9. Siskiyou Mountains and Coast Ranges of southern Oregon and northern California. Beautiful forms have been found in the wild, including richly colored pink forms and one called 'Purple Heart', with purple basal spots forming a central eye.

## Trillium sessile
sessile trillium, toad shade, toad trillium
The sessile trilliums of eastern North

Trillium rivale

Trillium sessile, courtesy of Fritz Kummert

America, especially *T. cuneatum* and *T. sessile,* can be very difficult to distinguish from one another. *Trillium sessile* is rare in cultivation and, more often than not, much shorter than *T. cuneatum,* which can be 8–18 inches (20–45 cm) high. Cultivate *T. sessile* in part shade in humus-rich, well-drained soil. Flowers in spring, maroon to purplish brown, green, or yellow-green. Grows 4–12 inches (10–30 cm) high. Zones 5–9. Mississippi to eastern New York and North Carolina.

## Trillium undulatum
painted lady, painted trillium, striped wake robin
Cultivate in part shade in humus-rich, well-drained soil. Flowers in spring, pink to white, marked with magenta. Grows 6–12 inches (15–30 cm) high. Zones 4–8. Eastern North America from Nova Scotia to the highest elevations of the Carolinas and Georgia.

## Trollius
globe flower
Ranunculaceae

The smaller globe flowers are brightly flowered candidates for the cool and moist parts of the shaded rock garden.

## Trollius acaulis
A perennial for sun or part shade in fertile, moist soil. Flowers in early summer, deep yellow. Grows 4–8 inches (10–20

Trillium undulatum

cm) high, 12 inches (30 cm) wide. Zones 5–9. Pakistan to Nepal.

### Trollius pumilus
A perennial for sun or part shade in fertile, moist soil. Flowers in early summer, golden yellow. Grows 8–12 inches (20–30 cm) high, 6 inches (15 cm) wide. Zones 5–9. Himalayas and eastern Tibet.

### Tropaeolum polyphyllum
Tropaeolaceae
A beautiful, deeply rooted nasturtium or Indian cress that needs to be planted 12 inches (30 cm) deep in a sunny wall where it will trail down and effectively display its silver leaves and richly colored flowers. A tuberous and nonclimbing perennial for sun in fertile, sharply drained soil. Flowers in summer, yellow from pink-gray buds. Grows 8 inches (20 cm) high, 36 inches (90 cm) wide. Zones 7–9. Alpine areas of Chile and Argentina.

Trollius acaulis, courtesy of Fritz Kummert

Trollius pumilus, courtesy of Panayoti Kelaidis

### Tsuga canadensis
hemlock
Pinaceae
An evergreen conifer for part shade in any good, well-drained soil. Zones 4–8. North America, east of the Rocky Mountains.

**Cultivars**. The dwarf hemlocks are hardy and elegant little trees that thrive in a cool setting with acid-rich soil.

*Tsuga canadensis* 'Cole's Prostrate' (synonym, 'Cole') is a shrublet, growing 4 inches (10 cm) high, 18 inches (45 cm) wide.

*Tsuga canadensis* 'Jeddeloh' is a shrublet, growing 18 inches (45 cm) high, 30 inches (75 cm) wide.

Tropaeolum polyphyllum, courtesy of Reuben Hatch

Tsuga canadensis 'Cole's Prostrate'

### Tulipa
tulip
Liliaceae

### Tulipa batalinii
Some authorities consider *T. batalinii* to be only a form of *T. linifolia*. All forms serve to constitute a fine group of popular rock garden tulips. *Tulipa batalinii* is a bulbous perennial for sun in any good, well-drained soil. Flowers in midspring. Grows 6 inches (15 cm) high. Zones 3–8. Central Asia.

**Cultivars**. *Tulipa batalinii* 'Bright Gem'. Flowers sulfur yellow flushed with orange.

*Tulipa batalinii* 'Red Jewel'. Flowers bright red.

### Tulipa fosteriana
A bulbous perennial for sun in any good, well-drained soil. Flowers in spring, vivid red with a black basal

Tsuga canadensis 'Jeddeloh', courtesy of Fritz Kummert

Tulipa batalinii 'Bright Gem'

blotch. Grows 8–16 inches (20–40 cm) high. Zones 5–8. Central Asia.

## Tulipa pulchella

A bulbous perennial for sun in any good, well-drained soil. Flowers in late winter and spring, mauve or pink to rosy purple. Grows 4 inches (10 cm) high. Zones 3–7. Turkey. There are several cultivars of this early-blooming species, including 'Eastern Star', rose pink with a

*Tulipa batalinii* 'Red Jewel'

*Tulipa fosteriana*, courtesy of Fritz Kummert

*Tulipa pulchella*, courtesy of Fritz Kummert

yellow base; 'Lilliput', a dwarf with brilliant red flowers; 'Odalisque', pale purple; and 'Persian Pearl', magenta-rose.

## Tulipa saxatilis

Candia tulip

A bulbous perennial for sun in any good, well-drained soil. Flowers in spring, lilac pink with a white-edged, yellow center. Grows 6–14 inches (15–40 cm) high. Zones 5–9. Crete and western Turkey.

## Tulipa sprengeri

Elegant and stately, the latest-flowering tulip species, coming into bloom in late spring and early summer. It is one of the few species that thrives in part shade. A bulbous perennial for part shade in any

*Tulipa saxatilis*, courtesy of Fritz Kummert

*Tulipa sprengeri*

good, well-drained soil. Flowers red to orange-red. Grows 12–18 inches (30–45 cm) high. Zones 5–9. Turkey.

## Tulipa tarda

synonym, *T. dasystemon* (of gardens)

A bulbous perennial for sun or part shade in any good, well-drained soil. Flowers in spring, golden center and white-tipped segments backed purplish green. Grows 4–6 inches (10–15 cm) high. Zones 4–9. Central Asia.

## Ulmus parvifolia

Ulmaceae

A semi-evergreen to deciduous tree for sun or part shade in any good soil. The cultivar 'Hokkaido', miniature Chinese elm, is doubtless one of the smallest known sports of any tree. It forms a corky trunk with minute, serrated leaves. Nonflowering. Grows 12 inches (30 cm) high, 8 inches (20 cm) wide.

*Tulipa tarda*

*Ulmus parvifolia* 'Hokkaido'

Zones 5–9. The species is from China and Korea.

## Uvularia grandiflora
great bellwort, merrybells, or wild oats
Liliaceae (Uvulariaceae)

A rhizomatous perennial for part shade in humus-rich, well-drained, moist soil. Flowers in spring, yellow. Grows 12–18 inches (30–45 cm) high. Zones 3–9. Quebec to North Dakota, south to Georgia and Oklahoma.

## Vaccinium
Ericaceae

Vacciniums produce many of our berries, including blueberries, cowberries, cranberries, huckleberries, and lingonberries. Besides producing edible fruit, many are fine plants for the peat and woodland gardens.

Uvularia grandiflora

Vaccinium macrocarpon, courtesy of Fritz Kummert

## Vaccinium macrocarpon
American cranberry
synonym, Oxycoccus macrocarpus

A mat-forming, evergreen shrub for sun or part shade in any good, moist, acid soil. Flowers in early summer, pinkish white, followed by red fruit. Grows 6 inches (15 cm) high, 24–36 inches (60–90 cm) wide. Zones 2–8. Northeastern North America.

## Vaccinium nummularifolium
An evergreen shrub for part shade in any good, moist, acid soil. Flowers in late spring and early summer, white, tipped rose red, followed by red fruit, turning black. Grows 12 inches (30 cm) high, 18 inches (45 cm) wide. Zones 7–9. Himalayas to Myanmar (Burma).

## Vaccinium vitis-idaea
cowberry

An evergreen shrub for part shade in any good, moist, acid soil. The cultivar

Vaccinium nummularifolium

Vaccinium vitis-idaea 'Koralle', courtesy of Fritz Kummert

'Koralle' flowers in late spring, white tinged with pink, followed by bright red fruit. Grows 12 inches (30 cm) high, 18 inches (45 cm) wide. Zones 5–8. The species is from northern Eurasia, Japan, and northern North America.

## Valeriana
valerian
Valerianaceae

## Valeriana saxatilis
A perennial from creeping, branched rhizomes for sun or part shade in any fertile, well-drained soil. Flowers in summer, white. Grows 4–8 inches (10–20 cm) high, 8 inches (20 cm) wide. Zones 5–8. Alps, Apennines, and mountains of Albania.

## Valeriana supina
A perennial from creeping, branched rhizomes for sun or part shade in any fertile, well-drained soil. Flowers in summer, pink. Grows 4 inches (10 cm) high, 12 inches (30 cm) wide. Zones 5–8. Central and eastern Alps.

Valeriana saxatilis, courtesy of Fritz Kummert

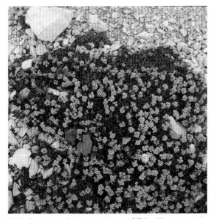
*Valeriana supina*, courtesy of Fritz Kummert

*Vancouveria chrysantha*, courtesy of Fritz Kummert

## Vancouveria
inside-out flower
Berberidaceae

*Vancouveria* is a genus of three species, closely related to *Epimedium*, from California north to Washington.

### Vancouveria chrysantha
The choicest vancouveria, from the foothills of the Siskiyou Mountains, doing best with only a little shade along with rocky, acid soil. An evergreen perennial, forming colonies through creeping rhizomes. Flowers in spring, yellow. Grows 10 inches (25 cm) high, 12 inches (30 cm) wide. Zones 6–9. Southwestern Oregon and northern California.

### Vancouveria hexandra
A deciduous perennial, forming colonies through creeping rhizomes, for part shade in humus-rich, well-drained soil. Flowers in spring, white. Grows 8–12 inches (20–30 cm) high, 24 inches (60 cm) wide. Zones 5–9. Washington south to California.

### Vella spinosa
Cruciferae
A shrub for sun in well-drained, gritty, neutral to alkaline soil, and in the alpine house. Flowers in summer, yellow. Grows 12 inches (30 cm) high, 18 inches (45 cm) wide. Zones 6–9. Mountains of southern and southeastern Spain.

## Verbascum
mullein
Scrophulariaceae

### Verbascum acaule
synonym, *Celsia acaulis*
The genus *Celsia* has been merged with *Verbascum*. Those mulleins that are compact perennials and subshrubs are fine, summer-flowering plants for the sunny rock garden. *Verbascum acaule* is a perennial for sun in any sharply drained soil in a vertical crevice or wall, and in the alpine house. Flowers in summer, lemon yellow. Grows 12 inches (30 cm) high and wide. Zones 5–9. Southern Greece.

*Vella spinosa*, courtesy of Fritz Kummert

*Verbascum acaule*, courtesy of Fritz Kummert

*Vancouveria hexandra*, courtesy of Fritz Kummert

## Verbascum dumulosum

A perennial with distinctive soft, hairy leaves, gray-white on both sides. Cultivate in sun in any sharply drained soil, and in the alpine house. Flowers in summer, yellow with a darker eye. Grows 12 inches (30 cm) high, 12–18 inches (30–45 cm) wide. Zones 6–10. Turkey.

## Verbascum 'Golden Wings'

synonym, ×*Celsioverbascum* 'Golden Wings'

A perennial for sun in any sharply drained soil, and in the alpine house. Flowers in spring and summer, bright yellow with orange anthers. Grows 10 inches (25 cm) high, 18 inches (45 cm) wide. Zones 5–9. A garden hybrid, *V. acaule* × *V. spinosum*.

## Verbascum 'Letitia'

A wonderful chance hybrid discovered at the Royal Horticultural Society's Wisley Garden, England, with deeply lobed, velvety, blue-green leaves. A perennial for sun in any sharply drained soil, and in the alpine house. Flowers in summer, yellow. Grows 12 inches (30 cm) high and wide. Zones 6–10. A garden hybrid, *V. dumulosum* × *V. spinosum*.

## Verbena
Verbenaceae

## Verbena peruviana

A mat-forming perennial for sun in any well-drained soil with protection from winter wetness, and in the alpine house. Flowers in summer, bright crimson. Grows 2–4 inches (5–10 cm) high, 24 inches (60 cm) wide. Zones 6–10. Argentina and southern Brazil.

## Verbena tenuisecta

With many color forms, in the wild *V. tenuisecta* can be blue, purple, red-purple, lilac, or white. For all the South American verbenas, it is best to withhold water in the fall to harden the plants for winter. *Verbena tenuisecta* is a perennial for sun in any well-drained soil with protection from winter wetness, and in the alpine house. The cultivar 'Tatted Lace' flowers in spring and summer, white. Grows 3–4 inches (7.5–10 cm) high, 48 inches (120 cm) wide. Zones 7–10. The species is from southern South America.

## Veronica
bird's eye, speedwell
Scrophulariaceae

Verbascum 'Letitia'

Verbascum dumulosum, courtesy of Fritz Kummert

Verbascum 'Golden Wings'

Verbena peruviana

Verbena tenuisecta 'Tatted Lace'

## Veronica armena

One of many fine, blue-flowering veronicas, well suited to the rock garden. A perennial for sun or part shade in any good, well-drained soil. Flowers in summer, blue. Grows 4 inches (10 cm) high, 12 inches (30 cm) wide. Zones 4–8. Southwestern Asia.

## Veronica caespitosa

A cushion-forming perennial for sun or part shade in fertile, well-drained gritty soil, and in the alpine house. Flowers in early to late summer, sky blue to purple-blue. Grows 3 inches (7.5 cm) high, 8–12 inches (20–30 cm) wide. Zones 5–8. Lebanon and Turkey.

## Veronica gentianoides

A mat-forming perennial for sun or part shade in any good, well-drained soil. The cultivar 'Nana' is a neat, clean, herbaceous plant with shiny, green basal leaves like those of the spring gentian, *Gentiana verna*. Flowers in May and June, pale blue. Grows 12 inches (30 cm) high, 18 inches (45 cm) wide. Zones 4–9. The species is from Turkey, Caucasia, and Iran.

## Veronica incana

silver speedwell

synonym, *V. spicata subsp. incana*

A perennial with ground-hugging stems with glossy, round leaves less than 1 inch (2.5 cm) high, making a neat carpet. Cultivate in sun in any good, well-drained soil. Flowers in early summer, lavender-blue. Grows 12–18 inches (30–45 cm) high, 24 inches (60 cm) wide. Zones 3–8. Eastern Europe.

## Veronica liwanensis

A perennial, woody at the base, for sun or part shade in any good, well-drained soil. An introduction from the James MacPhail and John Watson Turkish expedition of 1977. Flowers in May and June, blue. Grows 2 inches (5 cm) high, 18 inches (45 cm) wide. Zones 4–9. Turkey and Caucasia.

## Veronica orientalis

A perennial, woody at the base, for sun in any good, well-drained soil. Subspecies *orientalis* flowers in April through June, blue. Grows 4 inches (10 cm) high, 12–18 inches (30–45 cm) wide. Zones 5–8. Eastern Mediterranean to Caucasia.

## Veronica peduncularis

A perennial for sun in any good, well-drained soil. The cultivar 'Georgia Blue' is an introduction by Roy Lancaster from the mountains of the Republic of

*Veronica liwanensis*

*Veronica orientalis* subsp. *orientalis*

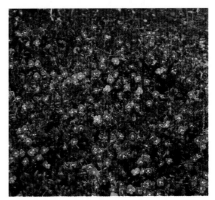

*Veronica peduncularis* 'Georgia Blue'

*Veronica gentianoides* 'Nana'

*Veronica incana*, courtesy of Fritz Kummert

*Veronica armena*

*Veronica caespitosa*, courtesy of Fritz Kummert

Georgia. Its dark green foliage turns bronze in fall. Flowers in March and April and at intervals all summer, cobalt blue. Grows 6 inches (15 cm) high, 18 inches (45 cm) wide. Zones 6–9. The species is from Turkey and Caucasia.

## Veronica petraea

A perennial for sun or part shade in any good, well-drained soil. Flowers in late spring, blue or pink. Grows 4 inches (10 cm) high, 10 inches (25 cm) wide. Zones 5–8. Caucasus Mountains.

Veronica petraea, courtesy of Fritz Kummert

Veronica prostrata

Veronica prostrata 'Alba'

## Veronica prostrata

A veronica that has passed the test of time as a reliable and easy-to-grow carpeter, with a burst of brilliant flowers. A perennial for sun or part shade in any good, well-drained soil. Flowers in spring and early summer, rich blue, pink, to white. Grows 3–4 inches (7.5–10 cm) high, 18 inches (45 cm) wide. Zones 4–8. Europe

**Cultivars**. Many named clones are available.

*Veronica prostrata* 'Alba' has white flowers.

*Veronica prostrata* 'Rosea' has pink flowers.

## Veronica spicata

A perennial for sun or part shade in any good, well-drained soil. The cultivar 'Nana' flowers in summer, deep blue.

Veronica prostrata 'Rosea'

Viola aetolica

Grows 4 inches (10 cm) high, 18 inches (45 cm) wide. Zones 4–9. See under *Orostachys spinosa* for another photograph. The species is from Europe.

## Viola
violet
Violaceae

## Viola aetolica

A perennial for part shade in any good, well-drained, moist soil. Flowers in summer, yellow. Grows 4–6 inches (10–15 cm) high, 12 inches (30 cm) wide. Zones 6–8. Southwestern Balkan Peninsula.

## Viola alpina

A perennial for part shade in any good, well-drained, moist soil. Flowers in early summer, blue-purple with a white eye

Veronica spicata 'Nana'

and darker veining. Grows 4 inches (10 cm) high, 8 inches (20 cm) wide. Zones 6–8. Northeastern Alps and Carpathians.

## Viola beckwithii
Great Basin violet
A challenging perennial that benefits from a dry summer-fall dormancy period. Depending on rainfall and garden conditions, grow these plants either in sandy scree that receives only enough summer moisture to prevent parching, or in a fairly humus-rich, well-drained soil that receives little or no summer or fall water. Cultivate in sun. Flowers in spring, deep purple and pale violet. Grows 3 inches (7.5 cm) high, 6 inches (15 cm) wide. Zones 5–8. Eastern and northern California to Utah and north to Oregon and Idaho.

## Viola biflora
A perennial for sun or part shade in any good, well-drained, moist soil. Flowers in spring, yellow with purple-black lines. Grows 2–4 inches (5–10 cm) high,

6 inches (15 cm) wide. Zones 4–8. Europe to northern Asia, Alaska, and the Rocky Mountains.

## Viola calcarata
A prolific, self-sowing colony maker that only stops flowering when frosty fall weather begins. A perennial for sun or part shade in any good, well-drained, moist soil. Flowers in spring and summer in shades of violet, blue, or yellow. Grows 4 inches (10 cm) high, 12 inches (30 cm) wide. Zones 5–9. Alps and the western Balkan Peninsula.

## Viola cazorlensis
One of the trinity of shrubby violas that are sought after and difficult in cultivation; the other two are *V. delphinantha* from Bulgaria and Greece, and *V. kosaninii* from Albania. Woody-based perennials for sun or part shade in a limestone-scree-filled crevice, in tufa, and in the alpine house. *Viola cazorlensis* flowers in summer, pink to purplish pink. Grows 4–6 inches (10–15 cm) high, 6 inches (15 cm) wide. Zones 6–8. Sierra Cazorla in southeastern Spain.

## Viola cuneata
wedge-leaved violet
Like *V. beckwithii*, a western U.S. dryland species, requiring the same cultivation techniques, *V. cuneata* is a perennial for sun or part shade in any good, well-drained gritty, moist soil, kept dryish in summer. Flowers in spring, white with purple spots and veining, purple backed. Grows 4–8 inches (10–20 cm) high, 8 inches (20 cm) wide. Zones 5–9. California and Oregon.

## Viola delphinantha
A woody-based perennial for sun or part shade in a limestone-scree-filled crevice,

*Viola cazorlensis,* courtesy of Fritz Kummert

*Viola alpina,* courtesy of Fritz Kummert

*Viola biflora,* courtesy of Fritz Kummert

*Viola cuneata*

*Viola beckwithii*

*Viola calcarata,* courtesy of Fritz Kummert

*Viola delphinantha,* courtesy of Fritz Kummert

in tufa, and in the alpine house. Flowers in summer, rose pink. Grows 4 inches (10 cm) high, 6 inches (15 cm) wide. Zones 6–8. Bulgaria and northern Greece.

## *Viola flettii*
Olympic violet, rock violet
A perennial for part shade in fertile scree. Flowers in summer, purplish violet with a yellow eye. Grows 4–6 inches (10–15 cm) high, 8 inches (20 cm) wide. Zones 5–8. Olympic Mountains of Washington.

## *Viola gracilis*
A perennial for sun or part shade in any good, well-drained soil. Flowers in summer, violet or yellow. Grows 8 inches (20 cm) high, 12 inches (30 cm) wide. Zones 6–9. Balkan Peninsula.

## *Viola odorata*
English, garden, or sweet violet
A perennial, spreading by stolons, for sun or part shade in any good, well-

*Viola flettii*

*Viola gracilis,* courtesy of Fritz Kummert

drained, moist soil. Flowers in winter and spring, blue-purple, deep violet, bluish rose, or white. Grows 4–6 inches (10–15 cm) high, 12 inches (30 cm) wide. Zones 5–10. Europe except the north, and Turkey, Caucasia, Syria, and northern Africa.

*Viola odorata,* courtesy of Fritz Kummert

*Viola odorata* 'Rosina', courtesy of Fritz Kummert

*Viola sororia* 'Immaculata', courtesy of Fritz Kummert

**Cultivar**. *Viola odorata* 'Rosina' has dusty rose flowers.

## *Viola pedata*
bird's-foot, crow's-foot, or pansy violet
A violet with unusual cultivation requirements, it is a perennial that thrives

*Viola pedata* 'Bicolor' (of gardens)

*Viola pedata* 'Concolor'

in more sun than most, or very light shade, and the soil needs to be sandy or rocky or both, fertile, and acid. Flowers in spring and summer in shades of lavender or lilac purple, often with the upper two petals dark violet, also occasionally all white or pinkish. Grows 4–6 inches (10–15 cm) high, 6 inches (15 cm) wide. Zones 4–8. Widespread in the eastern United States and occurring west to Wisconsin.

**Cultivars**. *Viola pedata* 'Bicolor' (of gardens) has two-toned flowers with the upper two petals always darker.

*Viola pedata* 'Concolor' has petals all the same color, usually lavender or lilac purple.

## Viola sororia
woolly blue violet
A perennial for shade or part shade in any good, well-drained, moist soil. The cultivar 'Immaculata' flowers in spring

*Viola variegata* var. *nipponica*, courtesy of Fritz Kummert

*Vitaliana primuliflora*, courtesy of Fritz Kummert

and summer, white. Grows 4 inches (10 cm) high, 12 inches (30 cm) wide. Zones 4–9. The species is from eastern North America.

## Viola variegata var. nipponica
synonym, *V. koreana*
A perennial for shade or part shade in any good, well-drained, moist soil. Flowers in spring, pinkish to pale purple. Grows 2–4 inches (5–10 cm) high, 6 inches (15 cm) wide. Zones 6–9. Japan.

## Vitaliana primuliflora
Primulaceae
synonyms, *Androsace vitaliana, Douglasia vitaliana*
A choice little alpine but easy to grow in the trough or rock garden. A cushion- to

*Waldsteinia fragarioides*, courtesy of Fritz Kummert

*Waldsteinia geoides*, courtesy of Fritz Kummert

mat-forming perennial for sun in fertile, well-drained, gritty soil. Flowers in summer, yellow. Grows 2 inches (5 cm) high, 6–10 inches (15–25 cm) wide. Zones 4–8. Mountains of Europe.

## Waldsteinia
Rosaceae

## Waldsteinia fragarioides
barren strawberry
An evergreen perennial for sun or shade or part shade in humus-rich, moist soil, but it is tolerant of dry conditions. Flowers in spring and early summer, yellow. Grows 8 inches (20 cm) high, 12 inches (30 cm) wide. Zones 3–9. Mountain woods of the eastern United States.

## Waldsteinia geoides
golden strawberry
A perennial for sun or shade or part shade in humus-rich, moist soil, but it is tolerant of dry conditions. Flowers in spring and early summer, yellow. Grows 10 inches (25 cm) high, 12–18 inches (30–45 cm) wide. Zones 5–9. Mountain woods of central Europe to southern Russia.

### Weldenia candida
Commelinaceae
A perennial with a tuberous root for sun in moderately fertile, gritty soil, keeping it on the dry side during winter dormancy. Flowers in spring to fall, brilliant white. Grows 4 inches (10 cm) high, 12 inches (30 cm) wide. Zones 7–8. Guatemala and Mexico.

### Woodsia oregana
Oregon woodsia
Woodsiaceae
A perennial fern for part shade in humus-rich, well-drained, gritty soil. Grows 12 inches (30 cm) high and wide. Zones 4–9. Quebec to British Columbia south to New Mexico and California.

### Wulfenia orientalis
Scrophulariaceae
An evergreen perennial for sun or part shade in fertile, well-drained, moist soil. Protect from winter moisture, thus doing well in the alpine house. Flowers in early summer, violet-blue. Grows 6–12 inches (15–30 cm) high, 12 inches (30 cm) wide. Zones 5–8. Turkey and Lebanon.

### Xerophyllum tenax
bear grass, elk grass, Indian basket grass
Liliaceae (Melanthiaceae)
A spectacular lily relative from high forests and meadows, needing humus-rich soil that is rocky and quickly draining, it is not necessarily difficult to grow but is reluctant to flower in cultivation.

*Wulfenia orientalis*, courtesy of Fritz Kummert

A perennial with a woody rootstock for sun or part shade. Flowers in summer, creamy white. Grows 24–36 inches (60–90 cm) high, 24 inches (60 cm) wide, and to 48 inches (120 cm) high when in flower. Zones 3–8. Rocky Mountains westward, British Columbia to central California.

### Zaluzianskya ovata
Scrophulariaceae
An introduction by Panayoti Kelaidis of the Denver Botanic Gardens, who brought this fine plant into wide cultivation after finding it during the 1994 South African expedition sponsored by the North American Rock Garden Society. A perennial for sun or part shade in humus-rich, well-drained soil. Flowers in spring, white backed with red, from red buds. Grows 6 inches (15 cm) high, 12 inches (30 cm) wide. Zones 7–9. South Africa.

*Weldenia candida*, courtesy of Fritz Kummert

*Woodsia oregana*

*Xerophyllum tenax*

*Zaluzianskya ovata*

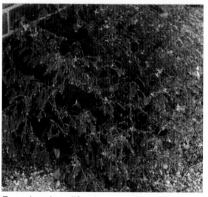

*Zauschneria californica*, courtesy of Fritz Kummert

## *Zauschneria californica*
California fuchsia, hummingbird flower
Onagraceae
synonym, *Epilobium canum*

Zauschnerias are heat- and drought-tolerant plants that put on a spectacular floral display for many months. Spreading is accomplished by underground stems so placement should be among equally aggressive, spreading plants. Waiting till spring to remove the former year's spent growth seems to improve winter hardiness. *Zauschneria californica* is a woody-based and rhizomatous perennial for sun in any well-drained soil. Flowers in summer and fall, scarlet to white. Grows 8–18 inches (20–45 cm) high, 30 inches (75 cm) wide. Zones 7–10. California and southern Oregon.

**Cultivars**. *Zauschneria californica* 'Alba'. Flowers white.

*Zauschneria californica* 'Etteri' has a low, spreading habit, growing less than 8 inches (20 cm) high, 30 inches (75 cm) wide, and eventually twice that. Flowers extra large, scarlet.

*Zauschneria californica* 'Solidarity Pink' has pastel, shell pink flowers. Grows 12 inches (30 cm) high, 24 inches (60 cm) wide.

## *Zinnia grandiflora*
Compositae

An unusual, hardy species that will slowly colonize by runners and needs little or no water once established. If some moisture is given, blooming will occur from spring through fall. A woody-based perennial for sun in any good, well-drained soil. Flowers in summer, yellow with an orange eye. Grows 4–10 inches (10–25 cm) high, 12 inches (30 cm) wide. Zones 4–10. Northern Mexico and the southwestern United States to Colorado and Kansas.

*Zauschneria californica* 'Alba' with typical *Z. californica*

*Zauschneria californica* 'Etteri'

*Zauschneria californica* 'Solidarity Pink'

*Zinnia grandiflora*

# FAMILIES OF ROCK GARDEN PLANTS

Related plant genera are grouped into families, and families included in this book are listed alphabetically below. In addition to flowering plants, families for ferns (Adiantaceae, Aspleniaceae, Blechnaceae, Dryopteridaceae, Polypodiaceae, Pteridaceae, Woodsiaceae), spike mosses (Selaginellaceae), and gymnosperms (Cupressaceae, Ephedraceae, Pinaceae) are listed. Some families such as Liliaceae may be divided into smaller ones, and cross-references for the different family names are given.

Acanthaceae
  *Ruellia*
Acoraceae (Araceae)
  *Acorus*
Adiantaceae
  *Adiantum*
  *Cheilanthes*
  *Pellaea*
Agavaceae
  *Agave*
Aizoaceae
  *Delosperma*
Alliaceae (Liliaceae)
  *Allium*
  *Bloomeria*
  *Ipheion*
  *Nectaroscordum*
Alstroemeriaceae
  *Alstroemeria*
Amaryllidaceae
  *Galanthus*
  *Leucojum*
  *Narcissus*
  *Nerine*
  *Pancratium*
  *Sternbergia*
Aphyllanthaceae (Liliaceae)
  *Aphyllanthes*
Apiaceae, see Umbelliferae
Araceae, including Acoraceae
  *Acorus*
  *Arisaema*
  *Arum*

*Biarum*
  *Lysichiton*
  *Pinellia*
Araliaceae
  *Hedera*
Aristolochiaceae
  *Asarum*
Asphodelaceae (Liliaceae)
  *Asphodelus*
Aspleniaceae
  *Asplenium*
Asteraceae, see Compositae
Begoniaceae
  *Begonia*
Berberidaceae
  *Berberis*
  *Epimedium*
  *Gymnospermium*
  *Jeffersonia*
  *Vancouveria*
Betulaceae
  *Betula*
Bignoniaceae
  *Incarvillea*
Blechnaceae
  *Blechnum*
Boraginaceae
  *Alkanna*
  *Anchusa*
  *Arnebia*
  *Brunnera*
  *Buglossoides*
  *Eritrichium*

*Lithodora*
  *Lithospermum*
  *Mertensia*
  *Moltkia*
  *Myosotis*
  *Omphalodes*
  *Onosma*
  *Pulmonaria*
Brassicaceae, see Cruciferae
Buxaceae
  *Buxus*
  *Pachysandra*
Cactaceae
  *Echinocereus*
  *Escobaria*
  *Maihuenia*
  *Opuntia*
  *Pediocactus*
Calochortaceae (Liliaceae)
  *Calochortus*
Campanulaceae, including
Lobeliaceae
  *Campanula*
  *Codonopsis*
  *Cyananthus*
  *Edraianthus*
  *Jasione*
  *Lobelia*
  *Physoplexis*
  *Phyteuma*
  *Platycodon*
  *Symphyandra*
  *Trachelium*

Caprifoliaceae
  *Linnaea*
Caryophyllaceae
  *Arenaria*
  *Cerastium*
  *Dianthus*
  *Gypsophila*
  *Lychnis*
  *Minuartia*
  *Paronychia*
  *Petrorhagia*
  *Sagina*
  *Saponaria*
  *Scleranthus*
  *Silene*
Celastraceae
  *Euonymus*
  *Paxistima*
Cistaceae
  *Cistus*
  *×Halimiocistus*
  *Halimium*
  *Helianthemum*
Colchicaceae (Liliaceae)
  *Bulbocodium*
  *Colchicum*
  *Disporum*
Commelinaceae
  *Commelina*
  *Tradescantia*
  *Weldenia*
Compositae
  *Achillea*

Compositae, continued
  *Anacyclus*
  *Anaphalis*
  *Andryala*
  *Antennaria*
  *Anthemis*
  *Arnica*
  *Artemisia*
  *Aster*
  *Balsamorhiza*
  *Bellis*
  *Bellium*
  *Berardia*
  *Brachycome*
  *Carduncellus*
  *Carlina*
  *Catananche*
  *Celmisia*
  *Centaurea*
  *Chamaemelum*
  *Chrysanthemum*
  *Chrysogonum*
  *Cirsium*
  *Coreopsis*
  *Cotula*
  *Craspedia*
  *Crepis*
  *Doronicum*
  *Erigeron*
  *Eriophyllum*
  *Euryops*
  *Haplocarpha*
  *Haplopappus*
  *Helichrysum*
  *Hymenoxys*
  *Inula*
  *Leontopodium*
  *Leucogenes*
  *Liatris*
  *Perezia*
  *Raoulia*
  *Santolina*
  *Saussurea*
  *Senecio*
  *Serratula*
  *Solidago*
  *Tanacetum*
  *Townsendia*
  *Zinnia*
Convallariaceae (Liliaceae)
  *Clintonia*
  *Maianthemum*
  *Ophiopogon*
  *Polygonatum*

Convolvulaceae
  *Convolvulus*
Cornaceae
  *Cornus*
Crassulaceae
  *Chiastophyllum*
  *Jovibarba*
  *Orostachys*
  *Rhodiola*
  *Rosularia*
  *Sedum*
  *Sempervivum*
Cruciferae
  *Aethionema*
  *Alyssum*
  *Arabis*
  *Aubrieta*
  *Aurinia*
  *Biscutella*
  *Cardamine*
  *Degenia*
  *Draba*
  *Erysimum*
  *Hutchinsia*
  *Iberis*
  *Matthiola*
  *Morisia*
  *Petrocallis*
  *Physaria*
  *Ptilotrichum*
  *Thlaspi*
  *Vella*
Cupressaceae, including Taxodiaceae
  *Chamaecyparis*
  *Cryptomeria*
  *Juniperus*
  *Microbiota*
  *Sequoia*
  *Thuja*
Cyperaceae
  *Carex*
  *Eriophorum*
Cryptogrammataceae (Pteridaceae)
  *Cryptogramma*
Diapensiaceae
  *Shortia*
Dipsacaceae
  *Pterocephalus*
  *Scabiosa*
Dryopteridaceae
  *Dryopteris*
  *Polystichum*

Ephedraceae
  *Ephedra*
Ericaceae
  *Andromeda*
  *Arctostaphylos*
  *Bruckenthalia*
  *Calluna*
  *Cassiope*
  *Daboecia*
  *Erica*
  *Gaultheria*
  *Kalmia*
  *Kalmiopsis*
  *Leiophyllum*
  *Loiseleuria*
  *Pernettya*
  *×Phylliopsis*
  *Phyllodoce*
  *Pieris*
  *Rhododendron*
  *Rhodothamnus*
  *Vaccinium*
Euphorbiaceae
  *Euphorbia*
Fabaceae, see Leguminosae
Fagaceae
  *Lithocarpus*
  *Quercus*
Frankeniaceae
  *Frankenia*
Fumariaceae
  *Dicentra*
  *Rupicapnos*
Gentianaceae
  *Gentiana*
Geraniaceae
  *Erodium*
  *Geranium*
  *Pelargonium*
Gesneriaceae
  *Conandron*
  *Haberlea*
  *Jankaea*
  *Opithandra*
  *Ramonda*
  *Rehmania*
Globulariaceae
  *Globularia*
Gramineae
  *Alopecurus*
  *Deschampsia*
  *Festuca*
  *Hakonechloa*
  *Imperata*

  *Milium*
  *Pennisetum*
Hyacinthaceae (Liliaceae)
  *Albuca*
  *Chionodoxa*
  *Muscari*
  *Ornithogalum*
  *Puschkinia*
  *Scilla*
Hydrangeaceae
  *Deutzia*
  *Hydrangea*
Hydrophyllaceae
  *Hesperochiron*
  *Phacelia*
  *Romanzoffia*
Hypericaceae
  *Hypericum*
Hypoxidaceae
  *Hypoxis*
  *Rhodohypoxis*
Iridaceae
  *Anomatheca*
  *Crocus*
  *Diplarrhena*
  *Gladiolus*
  *Hermodactylus*
  *Iris*
  *Romulea*
  *Schizostylis*
  *Sisyrinchium*
Juncaceae
  *Luzula*
Labiatae
  *Acinos*
  *Ajuga*
  *Calamintha*
  *Dracocephalum*
  *Horminum*
  *Lamium*
  *Lavandula*
  *Marrubium*
  *Meehania*
  *Mentha*
  *Nepeta*
  *Origanum*
  *Prostanthera*
  *Prunella*
  *Rosmarinus*
  *Salvia*
  *Satureja*
  *Scutellaria*
  *Stachys*
  *Teucrium*
  *Thymus*

Lamiaceae, see Labiatae
Leguminosae
  *Anthyllis*
  *Astragalus*
  *Carmichaelia*
  *Chamaecytisus*
  *Coronilla*
  *Cytisus*
  *Dorycnium*
  *Erinacea*
  *Genista*
  *Hippocrepis*
  *Indigofera*
  *Lathyrus*
  *Lotus*
  *Lupinus*
  *Oxytropis*
  *Trifolium*
Lentibulariaceae
  *Pinguicula*
Liliaceae, including Alliaceae,
Aphyllanthaceae, Asphodelaceae,
Calochortaceae, Colchicaceae,
Convallariaceae, Hyacinthaceae,
Melanthiaceae, Tricyrtidaceae,
Trilliaceae, and Uvulariaceae
  *Albuca*
  *Allium*
  *Anthericum*
  *Aphyllanthes*
  *Asphodelus*
  *Bloomeria*
  *Bulbocodium*
  *Calochortus*
  *Chionodoxa*
  *Clintonia*
  *Colchicum*
  *Disporum*
  *Erythronium*
  *Fritillaria*
  *Hosta*
  *Ipheion*
  *Lilium*
  *Lloydia*
  *Maianthemum*
  *Muscari*
  *Nectaroscordum*
  *Ophiopogon*
  *Ornithogalum*
  *Polygonatum*
  *Puschkinia*
  *Scilla*
  *Scoliopus*
  *Tricyrtis*
  *Trillium*

  *Tulipa*
  *Uvularia*
  *Xerophyllum*
Linaceae
  *Linum*
Lobeliaceae (Campanulaceae)
  *Lobelia*
Loganiaceae
  *Spigelia*
Malvaceae
  *Callirhoe*
Melanthiaceae (Liliaceae)
  *Xerophyllum*
Myrtaceae
  *Leptospermum*
Oleaceae
  *Jasminum*
Onagraceae
  *Calylophus*
  *Epilobium*
  *Gaura*
  *Oenothera*
  *Zauschneria*
Orchidaceae
  *Amitostigma*
  *Bletilla*
  *Calanthe*
  *Cypripedium*
  *Dactylorhiza*
  *Epipactus*
  *Goodyera*
  *Orchis*
  *Pleione*
Oxalidaceae
  *Oxalis*
Paeoniaceae
  *Paeonia*
Papaveraceae
  *Corydalis*
  *Hylomecon*
  *Papaver*
  *Sanguinaria*
  *Stylophorum*
Pinaceae
  *Abies*
  *Cedrus*
  *Larix*
  *Picea*
  *Pinus*
  *Pseudotsuga*
  *Tsuga*
Plantaginaceae
  *Plantago*
Plumbaginaceae
  *Acantholimon*

  *Armeria*
  *Limonium*
Poaceae, see Gramineae
Polemoniaceae
  *Collomia*
  *Ipomopsis*
  *Phlox*
  *Polemonium*
Polygalaceae
  *Polygala*
Polygonaceae
  *Eriogonum*
  *Muehlenbeckia*
  *Oxyria*
  *Polygonum*
  *Rumex*
Polypodiaceae
  *Polypodium*
Portulacaceae
  *Calandrinia*
  *Calyptridium*
  *Claytonia*
  *Lewisia*
  *Talinum*
Primulaceae
  *Anagallis*
  *Androsace*
  *Cortusa*
  *Cyclamen*
  *Dionysia*
  *Dodecatheon*
  *Douglasia*
  *Lysimachia*
  *Primula*
  *Soldanella*
  *Trientalis*
  *Vitaliana*
Pteridaceae, including Crypto-
grammataceae
  *Cryptogramma*
Ranunculaceae
  *Adonis*
  *Anemone*
  *Anemonella*
  *Aquilegia*
  *Callianthemum*
  *Caltha*
  *Clematis*
  *Coptis*
  *Delphinium*
  *Eranthis*
  *Glaucidium*
  *Helleborus*
  *Hepatica*
  *Isopyrum*

  *Paraquilegia*
  *Pulsatilla*
  *Ranunculus*
  *Semiaquilegia*
  *Thalictrum*
  *Trollius*
Rhamnaceae
  *Ceanothus*
Rosaceae
  *Acaena*
  *Alchemilla*
  *Aruncus*
  *Cotoneaster*
  *Dryas*
  *Geum*
  *Kelseya*
  *Petrophytum*
  *Potentilla*
  *Prunus*
  *Rubus*
  *Sibbaldia*
  *Sorbus*
  *Spiraea*
  *Waldsteinia*
Rubiaceae
  *Asperula*
  *Houstonia*
  *Mitchella*
  *Putoria*
Rutaceae
  *Ruta*
Salicaceae
  *Salix*
Saxifragaceae
  *Astilbe*
  *Bergenia*
  *Heuchera*
  *Lithophragma*
  *Mukdenia*
  *Parnassia*
  *Saxifraga*
  *Tanakea*
  *Telesonix*
  *Tellima*
  *Tiarella*
Scrophulariaceae
  *Antirrhinum*
  *Asarina*
  *Calceolaria*
  *Chaenorrhinum*
  *Chionohebe*
  *Cymbalaria*
  *Diascia*
  *Erinus*
  *Hebe*

Scrophulariaceae, continued
  *Lagotis*
  *Linaria*
  *Mazus*
  *Mimulus*
  *Ourisia*
  *Parahebe*
  *Penstemon*
  *Synthyris*
  *Verbascum*
  *Veronica*
  *Wulfenia*
  *Zaluzianskya*
Selaginellaceae
  *Selaginella*

Solanaceae
  *Mandragora*
  *Nierembergia*
  *Scopolia*
Taxodiaceae (Cupressaceae)
  *Cryptomeria*
  *Sequoia*
Thymelaeaceae
  *Daphne*
  *Pimelea*
Tricyrtidaceae (Liliaceae)
  *Tricyrtis*
Trilliaceae (Liliaceae)
  *Scoliopus*
  *Trillium*

Tropaeolaceae
  *Tropaeolum*
Ulmaceae
  *Ulmus*
Umbelliferae
  *Aciphylla*
  *Anisotome*
  *Athamanta*
  *Bolax*
  *Bupleurum*
  *Eryngium*
  *Hacquetia*
  *Meum*
Uvulariaceae (Liliaceae)
  *Uvularia*

Valerianaceae
  *Patrinia*
  *Valeriana*
Verbenaceae
  *Verbena*
Violaceae
  *Viola*
Woodsiaceae
  *Athyrium*
  *Gymnocarpium*
  *Woodsia*
Zingiberaceae
  *Roscoea*

# ROCK GARDEN PLANTS FOR SPECIFIC PURPOSES AND LOCATIONS

Here are lists of rock garden plants to help choose plants for your wants, needs, and special growing conditions. The entries in each list are limited to those plants that I believe are most appropriate to each category. By doing this I may have failed to include plants that many would have deemed appropriate, and indeed, I hope the reader will use these lists only as general guides and expand upon the suggestions. Choosing from plants in a list will depend on concerns such as size, exposure, hardiness, and so on; see the individual plant descriptions. Additional information on choosing plants appears in the introductory chapters. When only the genus is given in a list below, all species and cultivars of that genus are appropriate even if not described in this book.

## Alpine Houses and Frames

Alpine houses, cold frames, and bulb frames are structures that are used by the dedicated gardener to successfully grow the more demanding and difficult rock garden plants in adverse climates by creating artificial conditions. Alpine houses are well-ventilated, cool greenhouses needing supplementary heat only when the temperatures drop below 10°F (about −12°C). Frames are structures built on the ground that are just tall enough to grow plants in pots and allow some air space between the pots and the glass or plastic cover. In such structures one can better grow plants that require protection from extreme winter conditions such as cold, wind, rain, and snow. Plants can flower earlier and longer without being battered by poor weather. The structures are particularly useful for keeping plants dry during wet weather. The alpine house allows the gardener to work with the plants inside. Cold frames and bulb frames serve the same purpose though the gardener must work outside. Many books are available that discuss the building and use of such structures. Tiny alpine species and plants with intricate flower details are best enjoyed from the tabletop-high bench in an alpine house. Other plants are chosen for alpine houses because they blossom or have rich foliage during the fall, winter, and early spring when much of the outdoor garden is dormant. The plants range from tiny bulbs to dwarf coniferous trees.

Acantholimon
Adiantum aleuticum
Adiantum venustum
Adonis
Aethionema
Albuca humilis
Alkanna
Allium
Amitostigma kieskii
Anacyclus pyrethrum var. depressus
Anagallis monellii
Anchusa caespitosa
Andromeda polifolia
Androsace
Andryala aghardii
Anemonella thalictroides

Anomatheca laxa
Anthemis punctata subsp. cupaniana
Antirrhinum
Aphyllanthes monspeliensis
Aquilegia
Arabis, smaller types
Arenaria, smaller types
Arisaema
Arum
Asarum, smaller types
Asperula
Asphodelus acaulis
Asplenium
Astilbe
Athamanta cretensis
Begonia sutherlandii

Bellium bellidioides
Berardia subacaulis
Berberis ×stenophylla
Biarum
Blechnum
Bletilla
Bloomeria crocea
Bolax gummifera
Brachycome nivalis
Bulbocodium vernum
Calandrinia umbellata
Calanthe
Calceolaria uniflora
Calochortus
Calyptridium umbellatum
Campanula cenisia
Campanula formanekiana

Campanula hawkinsiana
Campanula 'Joe Elliott'
Campanula mirabilis
Campanula morettiana
Campanula piperi
Campanula raineri
Campanula zoysii
Carduncellus
Carex firma
Carmichaelia enysii
Catananche caespitosa
Cedrus deodara 'Pygmaea'
Chamaecyparis, dwarf cultivars
Cheilanthes
Chionohebe pulvinaris
Chrysanthemum hosmariense
Claytonia megarhiza

*Clematis* ×*cartmanii* 'Joe'
*Codonopsis*
*Colchicum hungaricum*
*Colchicum kesselringii*
*Colchicum luteum*
*Collomia debilis*
*Conandron ramondioides*
*Convolvulus*
*Coronilla*
*Corydalis popovii*
*Corydalis wilsonii*
*Craspedia minor*
*Crocus reticulatus* subsp. *reticulatus*
*Cryptogramma crispa*
*Cryptomeria japonica*, dwarf cultivars
*Cyclamen*
*Daphne*, smaller types
*Degenia velebitica*
*Delosperma*
*Dianthus*
*Dicentra peregrina*
*Dionysia*
*Diplarrhena moraea*
*Douglasia*
*Draba*
*Dryopteris affinis*, dwarf cultivars
*Dryopteris erythrosora*
*Echinocereus fendleri* var. *fendleri*
*Epilobium rigidum*
*Eranthis hyemalis*
*Erigeron*, dwarf types
*Erinacea anthyllis*
*Eriogonum*
*Eritrichium*
*Erodium reichardii*
*Escobaria*
*Euryops acraeus*
*Frankenia thymifolia*
*Fritillaria*, smaller species
*Gladiolus*, smaller species
*Goodyera oblongifolia*
*Gymnospermium albertii*

*Gypsophila aretioides*
*Haberlea ferdinandi-coburgii*
*Hakonechloa macra*
*Hebe*
*Helichrysum*
*Hepatica*
*Hesperochiron*
*Ipheion uniflorum*
*Ipomopsis congesta*
*Iris acutiloba* subsp. *lineolata*
*Iris kolpakowskyana*
*Iris nicolai*
*Jankaea heldreichii*
*Jeffersonia*
*Jovibarba*
*Juniperus*, dwarf cultivars
*Kalmia*
*Kalmiopsis leachiana*
*Kelseya uniflora*
*Lamium armenum*
*Leptospermum scoparium*
*Leucogenes grandiceps*
*Lewisia*
*Lilium*, dwarf types
*Linnaea borealis*
*Linum*
*Lithodora*
*Lobelia linnaeoides*
*Loiseleuria procumbens*
*Lupinus*
*Maihuenia poeppigii*
*Mazus reptans*
*Minuartia*
*Moltkia*
*Morisia monanthos*
*Muscari*
*Myosotis colensoi*
*Narcissus*, smaller types
*Nerine bowdenii*
*Omphalodes luciliae*
*Onosma alborosea*
*Ophiopogon japonicus*
*Opithandra primuloides*
*Origanum*
*Ornithogalum oligophyllum*
*Orostachys*

*Ourisia*
*Oxalis*
*Pancratium illyricum*
*Parahebe*
*Paraquilegia anemonoides*
*Paronychia*
*Pelargonium endlicherianum*
*Perezia recurvata*
*Pernettya tasmanica*
*Petrophytum caespitosum*
*Phacelia sericea*
*Phlox adsurgens*
*Phlox mesoleuca*
*Phlox nana*
*Physoplexis comosa*
*Pimelea prostrata*
*Pinellia ternata*
*Pinguicula grandiflora*
*Pinus*, dwarf cultivars
*Pleione*
*Polemonium carneum*
*Polemonium viscosum*
*Polygala*
*Polypodium*, smaller types
*Polystichum*, smaller types
*Primula*, many
*Prostanthera cuneata*
*Ptilotrichum spinosum*
*Pulsatilla*
*Puschkinia scilloides* var. *libanotica*
*Ramonda*
*Ranunculus calandrinioides*
*Ranunculus glacialis*
*Ranunculus rupestris*
*Raoulia*
*Rehmania glutinosa*
*Rhodohypoxis baurii*
*Rhodothamnus chamaecistus*
*Romanzoffia sitchensis*
*Romulea bulbocodium*
*Rosularia*
*Rupicapnos africana*
*Sagina boydii*
*Salvia caespitosa*
*Saponaria*, smaller types

*Saussurea*
*Saxifraga*, species and cultivars of sections *Porphyrion* and *Ligulatae*
*Scilla bifolia*
*Scoliopus bigelovii*
*Scutellaria*, smaller types
*Selaginella*
*Semiaquilegia ecalcarata*
*Sempervivum*
*Senecio incanus*
*Silene hookeri*
*Silene ingramii*
*Soldanella*
*Stachys candida*
*Sternbergia clusiana*
*Sternbergia fischeriana*
*Talinum*
*Tanacetum*
*Telesonix jamesii*
*Teucrium*
*Thlaspi rotundifolium*
*Thuja*, dwarf cultivars
*Thymus broussonetii*
*Thymus membranaceus*
*Townsendia*
*Trachelium asperuloides*
*Trachelium jaquinii* subsp. *rumelianum*
*Tradescantia longipes*
*Trillium*
*Tropaeolum polyphyllum*
*Tsuga canadensis*, dwarf cultivars
*Tulipa*, smaller types
*Vaccinium nummularifolium*
*Vella spinosa*
*Verbascum*, smaller types
*Verbena*
*Veronica caespitosa*
*Viola cazorlensis*
*Viola delphinantha*
*Weldenia candida*
*Woodsia*
*Wulfenia orientalis*
*Zaluzianskya ovata*

## Troughs and Containers

Plants are usually called trough plants if they are traditionally planted in troughs, sizable trays or box-like containers in which a miniature rock garden landscape can be created. These miniature plants can be effectively grown individually in containers such as clay pots as well. They grow and mature slowly and are content in a container for a long time. Because containers are movable, one can adjust the exposure for different seasons and even display plants at tabletop level. The carved stone troughs of yesteryear, originally used as animal feed receptacles, made perfect planters for alpines. Today we fabricate troughs from a lightweight mixture of cement, perlite, and peat moss, usually making them into shallow rectangular or free-form planters. The largest trough is rarely more than 3 × 2 feet (90 × 60 cm) and can accommodate a couple dozen small plants. The following miniature plants are recommended for troughs and containers.

Abies balsamea 'Nana'
Acantholimon
Acorus gramineus 'Pusillus Aureus Minimus' and 'Pusillus Variegatus'
Aethionema, smaller types
Alyssum, smaller types
Amitostigma kieskii
Anacyclus pyrethrum var. depressus
Androsace, smaller types
Andryala aghardii
Antennaria, smaller types
Aquilegia, smaller types
Arabis, smaller types
Arenaria balearica
Arenaria tetraquetra
Armeria caespitosa
Artemisia pedemontana
Asperula, smaller types
Asplenium ceterach
Asplenium trichomanes
Astilbe, smaller types
Aubrieta gracilis
Bellium bellidioides
Bolax gummifera
Buxus microphylla 'Kingsville'
Calluna vulgaris, smaller types

Campanula, smaller types
Carex firma
Cedrus deodara 'Pygmaea'
Chamaecyparis, smallest cultivars
Claytonia megarhiza
Clematis ×cartmanii 'Joe'
Convolvulus boissieri
Daphne, smaller types
Delosperma cf. congestum
Dianthus, smaller types
Dionysia
Douglasia
Draba
Edraianthus pumilio
Erica cinerea, smaller types
Erigeron, smaller types
Erinus alpinus
Eriogonum
Eritrichium
Erodium reichardii
Genista, smaller types
Gentiana, smaller types
Globularia repens
Gypsophila aretioides
Gypsophila briquetiana
Haberlea ferdinandi-coburgii
Hebe buchananii 'Minor'

Helichrysum milfordiae
Helichrysum selago
Hesperochiron
Juniperus, smaller cultivars
Kelseya uniflora
Lewisia
Linum, smaller types
Lysimachia japonica 'Minutissima'
Maihuenia poeppigii
Minuartia
Morisia monanthos
Omphalodes luciliae
Ophiopogon japonicus 'Kyoto Dwarf'
Orostachys
Penstemon, smaller types
Perezia recurvata
Petrocallis pyrenaica
Petrophytum
Phlox, smaller types
Physoplexis comosa
Picea, smaller cultivars
Plantago nivalis
Platycodon grandiflorus 'Apoyama'
Pleione

Polygala calcarea 'Linnet'
Primula, smaller types
Raoulia species
Rhododendron keleticum
Sagina boydii
Salix, smaller types
Saponaria
Saxifraga, smaller types
Scleranthus uniflorus
Sedum, smaller types
Selaginella
Sempervivum
Silene acaulis
Stachys candida
Talinum okanoganense
Talinum spinescens
Teucrium, smaller types
Thalictrum kiusianum
Thymus cilicicus
Townsendia
Trachelium asperuloides
Tsuga canadensis, smaller cultivars
Ulmus parvifolia 'Hokkaido'
Veronica caespitosa
Viola, smallest types
Vitaliana primuliflora

## Stone Walls

A stone wall is essentially an unmortared retaining wall with fertile soil between the layers of rock. The alpine and other saxatile plants recommended below are at home in these narrow crevices with their roots growing deeply into the well-drained soil behind the wall. Their crowns rest on the rock surface and the foliage and flowers are able to splay out to best advantage, close to the eye of the viewer. Plants suggested for walls are frequently vigorous plants that often root as they spread behind the rock, and many have pendulous flowers best displayed against walls. Many rock garden reference books give advice on building and planting a stone wall.

Acantholimon
Achillea
Adiantum venustum
Aethionema
Alyssum
Androsace sarmentosa
Arabis
Arenaria montana
Arenaria tetraquetra
Artemisia
Asarina procumbens
Asplenium
Aster alpinus

Astragalus
Aubrieta
Bergenia
Campanula betulifolia
Campanula carpatica
Campanula cochleariifolia
Campanula formanekiana
Campanula garganica
Campanula portenschlagiana
Campanula tommasiniana
Cerastium
Cheilanthes
Chiastophyllum oppositifolium

Chrysanthemum weyrichii
Chrysogonum virginianum
Clematis
Corydalis lutea
Corydalis ochroleuca
Cotoneaster
Cymbalaria
Cytisus
Daphne arbuscula
Daphne cneorum
Daphne jasminea, Delphi form
Daphne petraea
Delosperma

Dianthus, many
Draba bruniifolia
Draba ussuriensis
Dryas
Edraianthus
Erinus alpinus
Erodium
Erysimum
Euphorbia myrsinites
Euryops acraeus
Geranium dalmaticum
Geranium sessiliflorum and hybrids

Globularia
Gypsophila repens 'Rosea'
Haberlea ferdinandi-coburgii
Hedera
Helianthemum
Hypericum
Iberis
Jasione laevis
Jovibarba
Lavandula, smaller types
Lewisia
Marrubium rotundifolium
Minuartia

Moltkia suffruticosa
Nepeta phyllochlamys
Oenothera
Onosma
Pelargonium endlicherianum
Petrophytum
Petrorhagia saxifraga
Phlox, most
Physoplexis comosa
Phyteuma
Polypodium
Polystichum imbricans
Primula auricula

Primula marginata
Pterocephalus
Ramonda
Santolina chamaecyparissus
Saxifraga, many
Scabiosa graminifolia
Sedum
Sempervivum
Spiraea japonica 'Nyewoods'
Stachys
Tanacetum densum subsp.
    amanum

Trachelium jaquinii subsp.
    rumelianum
Tropaeolum polyphyllum
Verbascum acaule
Veronica orientalis subsp. orientalis
Veronica peduncularis 'Georgia Blue'
Veronica petraea
Zauschneria
Zinnia grandiflora

## Moist Soil and Bogs

The following plants tolerate or grow best in soil that is constantly moist. By reading the individual descriptions, one will see that many are recommended for humus-rich, moist (or moisture-retentive) soil. Often the same plants recommended for moist soil also require well-drained soil; these plants do not suffer dry conditions but they will not survive stagnant, wet conditions either. The moisture in the soil must continually drain away from their roots. Only the plants indicated with an asterisk will grow in constantly wet, bog-like, or poorly drained soil.

The soil in a bog usually consists simply of peat; sometimes a small amount of sand is added. An ideal location for a bog in the rock garden is at the base of the moraine garden, described under Scree in the section on Soil and Drainage in the chapter, About the Descriptions. Another appropriate spot for a bog is in the lowest point in a garden where water would naturally settle, though it may be necessary to irrigate the bog to keep it constantly wet during dry periods.

*Acorus gramineus
Adiantum
Ajuga
Andromeda
Anemonella thalictroides
Arenaria balearica
Arnica
Astilbe
Athyrium
Bergenia
Betula nana
Brunnera
Calluna vulgaris
Caltha introloba
*Caltha leptosepala
*Caltha palustris
Carex fraseri
Carex oshimensis
Chamaecyparis thyoides
Clematis alpina
Clematis ×cartmanii 'Joe'
Clematis douglasii var. scottii
Coreopsis rosea
Cornus canadensis
Cortusa matthioli
Cryptomeria japonica
Daboecia
Dicentra canadensis

Dicentra cucullaria
Dodecatheon alpinum
Dodecatheon meadia
Dracocephalum austriacum
Dryopteris
*Epipactus gigantea
Epipactus palustris
*Eriophorum
Fritillaria meleagris
Galanthus reginae-olgae
Gaultheria
Gentiana calycosa
Gentiana newberryi
Gentiana sino-ornata
Gentiana verna
Geranium himalayense
Glaucidium palmatum
Gymnocarpium
Hakonechloa macra
Hosta
Houstonia
Hylomecon japonicum
Iris cristata
Iris lacustris
Isopyrum thalictroides
Kalmia
Lagotis stolonifera
Larix laricina

Leucojum aestivum
Leucojum vernum
Linnaea borealis
Lithophragma parviflorum
Lloydia serotina
Lobelia linnaeoides
Luzula nivea
*Lysichiton
Lysimachia japonica
Maianthemum bifolium
Mazus
Mentha requienii
Mertensia alpina
Mimulus
Mukdenia rossii
Narcissus
Nierembergia repens
Omphalodes verna
Orchis
Ourisia
Oxyria digyna
*Parnassia palustris
Pernettya tasmanica
Phlox divaricata
×Phylliopsis hillieri
Phyllodoce
Picea
Pieris

Pimelea
Pinellia
Pinguicula
Polygonum
Polystichum
Primula, most
*Primula denticulata
*Primula rosea
Ranunculus, most
Romanzoffia sitchensis
Roscoea
Rubus
Sagina boydii
Salix
Sanguinaria canadensis
Saxifraga aizoides
Saxifraga exarata subsp.
    moschata
Saxifraga, Mossy Hybrids, e.g.,
    Saxifraga 'Hardes Zwerg' and
    'Sir Douglas Haig'
Saxifraga stolonifera
Saxifraga ×urbium
Schizostylis coccinea
Selaginella
Sisyrinchium
Spigelia
Synthyris

| | | | |
|---|---|---|---|
| *Tanakea radicans* | *Trillium* | *Viola aetolica* | *Viola odorata* |
| *Tellima grandiflora* | *Trollius* | *Viola alpina* | *Viola sororia* |
| *Thalictrum* | *Uvularia* | *Viola biflora* | *Viola variegata* var. *nipponica* |
| *Tricyrtis* | *Vaccinium* | *Viola calcarata* | *Waldsteinia* |

## Sandy Soil

Sand is defined in the dictionary as fine debris of rocks, consisting of small, loose grains, often of quartz. Because sand is often quite devoid of nutrients it supports little vegetation, which in turn produces little in the way of organic matter to die, decompose, and enrich the sandy conditions. Loose and porous, sand lets organic matter leach out rather than retaining it. Sandy soil is not to be confused with scree soil. Scree is less homogeneous, containing a variety of sizes of rock pieces from sand to gravel as well as some degree of trapped organic matter.

The following list of plants includes those native to areas with sandy soil and those that are not, though the latter grow well in sandy soil once they are brought into cultivation. A select group of plants are native to areas with sand. These are plants that have adapted to grow in fast-draining soil low in organic matter and nutrients.

There are many rock garden plants not native to areas with sandy soils that grow better in this medium under some garden conditions. These conditions often include increased humidity, irrigation, and high temperatures, which combine to increase the growth of harmful organisms in the soil such as molds, fungi, and bacteria. The growth of these organisms is reduced in sterile, low-nutrient, quick-drying sand. During prolonged periods without rainfall, some irrigation may be necessary.

For the gardener who possesses land of a sandy nature or who wishes to garden in artificially created sand beds, the following plants may be used provided the sand is not from the seaside, thus containing salts. Build a dry sand bed with pure builder's sand, the kind used to make concrete. The bed should consist of 8 to 12 inches (20–30 cm) of sand over ordinary garden soil.

| | | | |
|---|---|---|---|
| *Acantholimon* | *Erica*, with compost added | *Gypsophila aretioides* | *Primula palinuri* |
| *Achillea* | *Erigeron*, all that require scree | *Lewisia* | *Ptilotrichum spinosum* |
| *Aciphylla*, most species | *Eriogonum* | *Maihuenia poeppigii* | *Salvia caespitosa* |
| *Agave* | *Eryngium maritimum* | *Matthiola fruticulosa* subsp. | *Santolina* |
| *Andryala aghardii* | *Festuca* | *valesiaca* | *Scleranthus uniflorus* |
| *Arenaria*, all that require scree | *Frankenia thymifolia* | *Mertensia maritima* | *Talinum* |
| *Callirhoe involucrata* | *Fritillaria gentneri* | *Morisia monanthos* | *Teucrium* |
| *Calyptridium umbellatum* | *Fritillaria pudica* | *Nepeta* | *Townsendia* |
| *Campanula punctata* | *Fritillaria recurva* | *Paronychia* | *Viola beckwithii* |
| *Daphne cneorum* | *Genista* | *Penstemon*, many species | *Viola cuneata* |
| *Dianthus*, all that require scree | *Globularia* | *Petrophytum* | *Viola pedata* |
| *Ephedra minima* | *Gymnospermium albertii* | *Physaria* | *Zauschneria* |
| *Epilobium rigidum* | | | |

## The Woodland Rock Garden

Many rock garden plants are native to shady habitats. In this book many plants are recommended for part shade and full shade, where they will not lose their compact character. They are useful candidates to fill that dimly lighted portion of the rock garden that falls under the shadows of trees or structures. The individual plant descriptions reveal which plants require partial shade and which will tolerate still shadier conditions.

| | | | |
|---|---|---|---|
| *Adiantum* | *Anemonella thalictroides* | *Blechnum* | *Cornus canadensis* |
| *Ajuga* | *Arenaria balearica* | *Bletilla* | *Corydalis*, most |
| *Alchemilla* | *Arisaema* | *Brunnera macrophylla* | *Cryptogramma crispa* |
| *Anemone apennina* | *Asarina procumbens* | *Buglossoides purpureocaeruleum* | *Dryopteris* |
| *Anemone blanda* | *Asarum* | *Carex fraseri* | *Epimedium* |
| *Anemone nemorosa* | *Asplenium* | *Chamaecyparis* | *Erythronium* |
| *Anemone ranunculoides* | *Astilbe* | *Clintonia* | *Gentiana*, many |
| *Anemone* ×*seemannii* | *Athyrium* | *Conandron ramondioides* | *Glaucidium palmatum* |
| *Anemone sylvestris* | *Bergenia* | *Coptis* | *Goodyera oblongifolia* |

Gymnocarpium
Haberlea
Hakonechloa macra
Helleborus
Hepatica
Hosta
Hylomecon japonicum
Isopyrum
Lamium maculatum
Leucogenes
Leucojum vernum
Linnaea borealis

Lysimachia japonica 'Minutissima'
Mitchella repens
Muehlenbeckia axillaris
Nectaroscordum
Omphalodes cappadocica
Oxalis, some
Phlox adsurgens
Phlox divaricata
Pieris japonica
Pleione
Polygala paucifolia

Polystichum
Primula, most
Pulmonaria
Romanzoffia
Sanguinaria canadensis
Saxifraga stolonifera
Saxifraga ×urbium
Selaginella
Shortia
Synthyris
Tanakea radicans
Tellima

Thalictrum
Tiarella
Tricyrtis
Trientalis
Trillium
Tsuga canadensis
Tulipa sprengeri
Uvularia
Vaccinium
Vancouveria hexandra
Viola, many
Waldsteinia

## The Peat Garden

All lime-hating, humus-loving plants will grow well in a garden peat bed, with its acidic conditions. Best situated to avoid the direct midday sun, the peat bed should be filled with peat, acid humus, and a little lime-free loam and never be allowed to dry out entirely. Avoid planting near trees whose roots can penetrate the peat bed and constantly drink up all the moisture; one can create a vertical underground barrier with material such as strong plastic to prevent this from happening.

Adiantum
Andromeda
Androsace pyrenaica
Androsace wulfeniana
Aquilegia
Arctostaphylos
Astilbe
Betula
Blechnum
Bruckenthalia spiculifolia
Calluna vulgaris
Carex fraseri
Cassiope
Celmisia
Codonopsis
Coptis
Cornus canadensis
Corydalis ambigua
Corydalis cashmeriana
Cyananthus
Cypripedium, most
Daboecia
Dicentra canadensis

Dicentra cucullaria
Dicentra eximia
Dicentra formosa
Diplarrhena moraea
Epimedium
Erica
Fritillaria meleagris
Fritillaria pallidiflora
Gaultheria
Gentiana sino-ornata
Glaucidium palmatum
Goodyera
Haberlea
Houstonia caerulea
Iris gracilipes
Jeffersonia
Kalmia angustifolia
Kalmia polifolia
Kalmiopsis leachiana
Leiophyllum buxifolium
Lilium
Linnaea borealis

Lloydia serotina
Loiseleuria procumbens
Mazus reptans
Mitchella repens
Mukdenia rossii
Narcissus cyclamineus
Parnassia palustris
Paxistima canbyi
Pernettya
Phlox adsurgens
Phlox stolonifera
×Phylliopsis hillieri
Phyllodoce
Pieris
Pimelea prostrata
Pinellia
Pinguicula
Polygala chamaebuxus
Polygala paucifolia
Polypodium
Polystichum setiferum
Primula

Prostanthera cuneata
Ramonda
Ranunculus amplexicaulis
Ranunculus crenatus
Rhododendron
Rhodothamnus chamaecistus
Roscoea
Rubus acaulis
Salix
Sanguinaria canadensis
Saxifraga cotyledon
Saxifraga ×urbium
Scoliopus bigelovii
Senecio incanus
Shortia
Soldanella montana
Tanakea radicans
Thalictrum
Tiarella
Tsuga
Vaccinium
Vancouveria

## For Limy Soil

Most of the following plants will grow best in nonacidic soil, one with a pH value greater than or equal to 7.0. Gardeners who live in lime-rich areas will do best by selecting from those plants that tolerate or require soil that is neutral to alkaline. An increased pH value indicates an increase in the lime content of the soil. Those plants that require limy soil, indicated with an asterisk, need a soil that has a pH value greater than 7.5. If soil is poor in lime, it is not difficult to supplement the soil with lime and increase its pH value.

Acantholimon
Achillea

Acinos alpinus
Adonis vernalis

Aethionema
Ajuga

Alopecurus lanatus
Alyssum

Androsace chamaejasme
Androsace hausmannii
Anemone sylvestris
Anthemis
Asarum europaeum
Asperula
Asplenium
Aster alpinus
Aubrieta
Aurinia saxatilis
Calamintha
Callianthemum anemonoides
Campanula carpatica
Campanula cochlearifolia
Campanula garganica
Campanula glomerata
*Campanula morettiana
Campanula persicifolia
Campanula portenschlagiana
*Campanula raineri
*Campanula zoysii
Carduncellus
Carex firma
Carlina
Catananche caespitosa
Cerastium
Chaenorrhinum origanifolium
Cheilanthes
Chiastophyllum oppositifolium

Cistus
*Clematis tenuiloba
Convolvulus
Corydalis lutea
Corydalis ochroleuca
Cyclamen
Cypripedium calceolus
Dactylorhiza maculata
Daphne
Dianthus, most
Dorycnium hirsutum
Draba
Dryas
Epipactus palustris
Erica carnea
Erica erigena
Erinacea anthyllis
Erysimum
Euphorbia myrsinites
*Fritillaria crassifolia subsp.
    crassifolia
*Fritillaria graeca
Geranium cinereum
Geranium dalmaticum
Geranium sanguineum
Globularia
Gypsophila
Haberlea ferdinandi-coburgii
Hacquetia epipactus

Helianthemum
Helleborus
Hepatica
Hermodactylus tuberosus
Hippocrepis comosa
Horminum pyrenaicum
Hutchinsia alpina
Hypericum olympicum
Iberis
Inula
*Jankaea heldreichii
*Kelseya uniflora
Leontopodium
Limonium
Linaria
Linum
Lithodora oleifolia
*Lithospermum canescens
Marrubium rotundifolium
Matthiola
Origanum
Pancratium illyricum
Pellaea breweri
Petrocallis pyrenaica
Phlox subulata
Physoplexis comosa
Polygala calcarea
Polygonatum

Primula auricula
Primula clusiana
Primula marginata
Primula veris
Ptilotrichum spinosum
Pulsatilla species, except P. ver-
    nalis
Putoria calabrica
Santolina
Saxifraga, especially those of
    sections Porphyrion and
    Ligulatae, with some excep-
    tions
Scabiosa graminifolia
Scabiosa lucida
Silene acaulis
Silene alpestris
Silene caroliniana
Silene dinarica
Silene elisabethae
Silene uniflora
Silene zawadzkii
Soldanella alpina
Teucrium
Trachelium
Vella spinosa
*Viola cazorlensis
*Viola delphinantha

## For Heat and Drought

There are rock garden plants that thrive in full sun and dryish conditions. The following list of plants will live through dry spells with little or no irrigation once they are established in the garden. Most of these plants will not survive in soils that stay moist or do not drain well.

Achillea
Aethionema
Agave
Antennaria
Arctostaphylos
Artemisia
Calylophus
Ceanothus
Cistus
Cytisus
Delosperma

Ephedra
Eriogonum
Euphorbia, most
Euryops acraeus
Festuca
Gaura lindheimeri
Genista
×Halimiocistus
Halimium
Helianthemum
Iris pumila

Juniperus
Lavandula
Limonium
Linum perenne
Lithocarpus densiflorus var. echi-
    noides
Oenothera
Penstemon, many
Quercus sadleriana
Quercus vaccinifolia
Rosmarinus officinalis

Salvia caespitosa
Sedum, many
Tanacetum densum subsp.
    amanum
Teucrium
Thymus
Verbascum
Verbena
Zauschneria
Zinnia grandiflora

## For Heat and High Humidity

Growing plants native to regions with short growing seasons, constant breezes, low humidity, and fast-draining soil can be difficult in some lowland climates. Rock gardeners in areas with lots of heat, rain, and humidity in the summer must choose their rock garden plants carefully. In just such gardens around the United States the plants in the list below have proven mostly successful, but not always. Hundreds of more plants deserve to be tested. Positioning the rock garden away from the hottest sun in an open location with the maximum air circulation and providing exceptionally well drained soil and rocky mulch are the suggested steps to success. Growing in a sand bed is recommended; see the list, Plants for Sandy Soil. Mulching is vital around the crown of many plants, which helps keep the basal foliage dry and assists in reduc-

ing the danger of rotting foliage brought on by mildew and other fungal diseases. Dusting with sulfur and other fungicides may help, but proper siting and choice of soil are most important. Some of the plants listed here require climates with sufficient winter cold to induce dormancy. For gardeners who live in areas with a mild winter climate it is recommended that this list be used in conjunction with the one, Plants for Rock Gardens in Mild Climates.

*Aethionema*
*Ajuga pyramidalis*
*Allium*
*Anemone nemorosa*
*Anemone ranunculoides*
*Anemone* ×*seemannii*
*Anemonella thalictroides*
*Anthemis*
*Arenaria montana*
*Armeria*
*Arum*
*Asplenium platyneuron*
*Aster novi-belgii*
*Astilbe*
*Aubrieta*
*Begonia grandis*
*Begonia sutherlandii*
*Bergenia*
*Bletilla*
*Bolax gummifera*
*Buxus microphylla* 'Kingsville'
*Calanthe*
*Calluna vulgaris*
*Caltha palustris*
*Campanula portenschlagiana*
*Campanula punctata*
*Carex*
*Celmisia*
*Chamaecyparis*
*Cheilanthes lanosa*
*Chrysogonum virginianum*

*Coreopsis rosea*
*Cryptomeria japonica*
*Cyclamen*
*Cymbalaria*
*Daphne* ×*mantensiana*
*Delosperma*
*Dianthus*, some
*Dryas*
*Epimedium*
*Eranthus hyemalis*
*Erica carnea*
*Erigeron aureus*
*Erigeron compositus*
*Erinus alpinus*
*Genista*
*Gentiana acaulis*
*Gentiana paradoxa*
*Gentiana scabra*
*Gentiana septemfida*
*Gentiana sino-ornata*
*Geranium*, many
*Gypsophila*
*Hedera helix*
*Helleborus*
*Hepatica*
*Heuchera*
*Hosta*
*Hydrangea macrophylla*
*Hylomecon japonicum*
*Hypoxis hirsuta*
*Iberis*

*Imperata cylindrica* 'Red Baron'
*Ipheion uniflorum*
*Iris cristata*
*Iris douglasiana*
*Iris gracilipes*
*Iris lacustris*
*Jeffersonia*
*Juniperus*
*Lamium maculatum*
*Leucojum autumnale*
*Lysimachia japonica* 'Minutissima'
*Mazus reptans*
*Muehlenbeckia axillaris*
*Muscari*
*Narcissus*
*Oenothera*
*Ophiopogon japonicus*
*Origanum* ×*hybridum*
*Origanum* 'Kent Beauty'
*Origanum scabrum*
*Ornithogalum oligophyllum*
*Orostachys*
*Oxalis*
*Paxistima canbyi*
*Penstemon hirsutus* 'Pygmaeus'
*Phlox bifida*
*Phlox divaricata*
*Phlox douglasii*
*Phlox subulata*
*Pieris japonica*

*Platycodon grandiflorus*
*Pleione*
*Primula kisoana*
*Primula sieboldii*
*Primula veris*
*Pulmonaria*
*Pulsatilla*
*Rhododendron*, evergreen azaleas
*Sanguinaria canadensis*
*Scabiosa lucida*
*Scilla*
*Sedum*
*Selaginella*
*Sempervivum*
*Solidago virgaurea* var. *minutissima*
*Thalictrum*
*Thuja*
*Thymus*
*Tiarella wherryi*
*Tricyrtis*
*Trillium*
*Tulipa batalinii*
*Tulipa saxatilis*
*Ulmus parvifolia* 'Hokkaido'
*Uvularia grandiflora*
*Verbena*
*Veronica*
*Viola calcarata*
*Viola pedata*

## For Dry Winters

The following plants would be difficult to grow outdoors without protection from winter wetness unless one gardens in a climate with low winter rainfall and humidity. Many alpine and rock garden plants that require minimum winter moisture or that do not thrive with wet foliage at that time of year are also some of the most beautiful and sought after by collectors. The enthusiast who

wants the challenge of growing these somewhat demanding plants may protect them in a well-ventilated alpine house, a covered frame, or a covered garden area such as under a house overhang, or by covering individual plants under panes of glass or Plexiglas supported above the plant.

*Anchusa caespitosa*
*Androsace*, many
*Andryala aghardii*
*Anthemis*
*Antirrhinum*

*Aphyllanthes monspeliensis*
*Asperula*
*Calceolaria*
*Calyptridium umbellatum*
*Campanula cenisia*

*Campanula formanekiana*
*Campanula hawkinsiana*
*Campanula* 'Joe Elliott'
*Campanula mirabilis*
*Campanula morettiana*

*Campanula raineri*
*Cheilanthes*
*Cistus*
*Claytonia megarhiza*
*Conandron ramondioides*

*Crocus serotinus* subsp. *clusii*
*Cyclamen libanoticum*
*Cyclamen pseudibericum*
*Delosperma*
*Dianthus*, cushion formers
*Dionysia*
*Draba*
*Gaura lindheimeri*
*Gypsophila aretioides*
×*Halimiocistus wintonensis*
*Halimium ocymoides*
*Helianthemum*

*Helichrysum*
*Incarvillea*, acaulescent group,
    e.g., *I. mairei*
*Inula rhizocephala*
*Iris attica*
*Jankaea heldreichii*
*Jasione laevis*
*Kelseya uniflora*
*Lewisia tweedyi*
*Maihuenia poeppigii*
*Onosma alborosea*

*Origanum*
*Oxalis obtusa*
*Pancratium illyricum*
*Pelargonium endlicherianum*
*Physoplexis comosa*
*Pleione*
*Primula allionii*
*Ranunculus calandrinioides*
*Raoulia*
*Rehmania glutinosa*
*Rhodohypoxis baurii*

*Salvia caespitosa*
*Stachys candida*
*Talinum*
*Tanacetum*
*Thymus broussonetii*
*Thymus membranaceus*
*Townsendia*
*Verbascum*
*Verbena*
*Weldenia candida*
*Wulfenia orientalis*

## For Dry Summers

The plants listed below are native to regions that have little or no summer rainfall. Most of these enter a period of dormancy during the summer, and rain or irrigation would seriously harm their root systems or the foliage. In the garden it is necessary to re-create this season of dryness to keep the plants healthy. In climates that receive little or no summer rainfall this can be accomplished in a nonirrigated part of the garden. In summer-rainfall regions keep the plants dry in an alpine house, a covered frame, or under protective panes of glass or Plexiglas.

*Allium siskiyouense*
*Bloomeria crocea*
*Ceanothus*
*Claytonia megarhiza*
*Corydalis popovii*
*Cyclamen graecum*
*Dodecatheon*

*Fritillaria*
*Gymnospermium albertii*
*Hermodactylus tuberosus*
*Hesperochiron*
*Iris chrysophylla*
*Iris innominata*

*Lewisia*
*Oxalis obtusa*
*Ranunculus calandrinioides*
*Ranunculus rupestris*
*Romulea bulbocodium*
*Sisyrinchium douglasii*

*Sternbergia clusiana*
*Sternbergia fischeriana*
*Townsendia*
*Tulipa*
*Viola beckwithii*
*Viola cuneata*

## For Mild Climates

The following plants are recommended for the rock gardener planting in a climate that receives little or no freezing weather during winter. Most of these plants are not true alpines but come from regions of lower elevation such as the Mediterranean. Many are plants that can survive in warm, dry climates. It is often the case in such climates that the seasons of hot weather are extended and include higher temperatures. For some of these plants it may be necessary to provide some shade and irrigation during the hottest periods.

*Achillea chrysocoma*
*Acorus gramineus*
*Aethionema grandiflorum*
*Aethionema* 'Warley Rose'
*Agave*
*Ajuga*
*Alyssum*
*Amitostigma kieskii*
*Anacyclus pyrethrum* var. *depressus*
*Anagallis monellii*
*Anomatheca laxa*
*Anthemis*
*Anthyllis hermanniae*
*Antirrhinum*
*Aphyllanthes monspeliensis*
*Arabis sturii*

*Arenaria balearica*
*Arisaema ringens*
*Asarina procumbens*
*Asarum caudatum*
*Asphodelus acaulis*
*Aurinia saxatilis*
*Begonia grandis*
*Begonia sutherlandii*
*Bellis perennis*
*Berberis* ×*stenophylla*
*Betula pendula* 'Trost's Dwarf'
*Biscutella laevigata*
*Bletilla striata*
*Bloomeria crocea*
*Brunnera macrophylla*
*Buxus microphylla* 'Kingsville'
*Calamintha*

*Callirhoe involucrata*
*Caltha palustris*
*Carex flagellifera*
*Carmichaelia enysii*
*Cedrus deodara* 'Pygmaea'
*Cerastium tomentosum* var. *columnae*
*Chrysanthemum hosmariense*
*Cistus*
*Convolvulus*
*Coreopsis rosea*
*Coronilla valentina*
*Cotoneaster apiculatus* 'Tom Thumb'
*Cotula pyrethrifolia*
*Craspedia minor*
*Cymbalaria*

*Daboecia*
*Delosperma*
*Diascia*
*Dicentra eximia*
*Dicentra formosa*
*Dorycnium hirsutum*
*Ephedra*
*Erica carnea*
*Erigeron glaucus*
*Erinus alpinus*
*Erodium reichardii*
*Eryngium*
*Euphorbia*
*Festuca ovina*
*Frankenia thymifolia*
*Gaura lindheimeri*
*Genista tinctoria*

*Geranium cinereum*
*Geranium sessiliflorum*
*Globularia repens*
*Globularia trichosantha*
*Goodyera oblongifolia*
×*Halimiocistus wintonensis*
*Halimium ocymoides*
*Haplocarpha rueppellii*
*Hebe*
*Hedera helix*
*Helianthemum*
*Helichrysum*, most
*Imperata cylindrica* 'Red Baron'
*Ipheion uniflorum*
*Iris douglasiana*
*Iris innominata*
*Jasminum parkeri*
*Jovibarba hirta*

*Juniperus*
*Lamium maculatum*
*Lavandula*
*Leptospermum*
*Leucojum*
*Liatris spicata* f. *montana*
*Linaria*
*Linum campanulatum*
*Linum perenne* subsp. *alpinum*
*Lithodora zahnii*
*Maihuenia poeppigii*
*Marrubium rotundifolium*
*Milium effusum*
*Mimulus*
*Muehlenbeckia axillaris*
*Nerine bowdenii*
*Nierembergia repens*
*Oenothera*

*Ophiopogon japonicus*
*Origanum*
*Oxalis depressa*
*Oxalis hirta*
*Oxalis obtusa*
*Oxalis oregana*
*Pancratium illyricum*
*Parahebe catarractae*
*Penstemon pinifolius*
*Platycodon grandiflorus*
*Pleione*
*Prostanthera cuneata*
*Putoria calabrica*
*Raoulia*
*Rehmania glutinosa*
*Rhodohypoxis baurii*
*Romulea bulbocodium*

*Rosmarinus officinalis*
*Rumex flexuosus*
*Ruta graveolens*
*Saxifraga stolonifera*
*Schizostylis coccinea*
*Sedum acre*
*Sedum sieboldii*
*Sempervivum*
*Sequoia sempervirens* 'Prostrata'
*Sisyrinchium macrocarpon*
*Stachys*
*Thymus*
*Verbascum*
*Verbena*
*Viola odorata*
*Zauschneria*
*Zinnia grandiflora*

## Easy-to-Grow Plants

The following list includes plants that are easy to grow given any good, well-drained soil and sun. They are moderately spreading plants that when properly spaced will not outgrow their welcome. The individual descriptions show that some will also grow in part shade. The plants listed here will thrive in most hardiness zones. Larger rocks arranged to create a naturalistic rock garden setting are not necessary for the health of these plants but will enhance the aesthetic effect.

*Achillea*, dwarf types
*Aethionema grandiflorum*
*Aethionema* 'Warley Rose'
*Ajuga pyramidalis*, dwarfest types
*Alchemilla alpina*
*Androsace lanuginosa*
*Anemone sylvestris*
*Aquilegia discolor*
*Aquilegia flabellata*
*Arabis caucasica*
*Arenaria montana*
*Armeria maritima*
*Aster alpinus*
*Aster novi-belgii*, dwarf types
*Aubrieta* ×*cultorum*
*Aurinia saxatilis*
*Campanula carpatica*
*Campanula cochlearifolia*
*Campanula elatines* var. *fenestrellata*
*Campanula garganica*
*Campanula glomerata*

*Campanula portenschlagiana*
*Cerastium alpinum* subsp. *lanatum*
*Cerastium tomentosum* var. *columnae*
*Chamaecyparis*, dwarf cultivars
*Chrysanthemum weyrichii*
*Cotoneaster apiculatus* 'Tom Thumb'
*Crocus*
*Cymbalaria muralis* 'Nana Alba'
*Delosperma* cf. *nubigenum* 'Lesotho'
*Delphinium grandiflorum*
*Dianthus deltoides*
*Dianthus petraeus* subsp. *noeanus*
*Dianthus* 'Pike's Pink'
*Dianthus* 'Tiny Rubies'
*Dicentra eximia*
*Dicentra formosa* 'Sweetheart'
*Doronicum columnae*
*Draba ussuriensis*

*Dryas octopetala*
*Erigeron glaucus*
*Erysimum helveticum*
*Euphorbia myrsinites*
*Euphorbia polychroma*
*Galanthus*
*Gentiana septemfida*
*Geranium*
*Globularia*
*Gypsophila repens*
*Heuchera*
*Hypericum olympicum*
*Iberis*
*Iris pumila*
*Juniperus*, dwarf cultivars
*Leucojum*
*Lychnis*
*Muscari*
*Narcissus*
*Papaver nudicaule*
*Penstemon hirsutus* 'Pygmaeus'
*Petrorhagia saxifraga*
*Phlox douglasii*

*Phlox subulata*
*Picea abies*, dwarf cultivars
*Picea glauca*, dwarf cultivars
*Potentilla alba*
*Potentilla fruticosa*
*Potentilla tabernaemontani*
*Primula* ×*pruhoniciana*
*Ranunculus gramineus*
*Saponaria*
*Saxifraga*, Mossy Hybrids, e.g., *Saxifraga* 'Hardes Zwerg' and 'Sir Douglas Haig'
*Scabiosa lucida*
*Sedum*
*Sempervivum*
*Silene alpestris*
*Sisyrinchium* 'E. K. Balls'
*Sternbergia lutea*
*Thymus* ×*citriodorus*
*Thymus polytrichus*
*Thymus pulegioides*
*Veronica*, most
*Viola calcarata*

## Cushion Plants

Cushion plants come in a wide variety of foliage and flower; some are easy to grow, others challenge the expert grower. All cushion plants have in common a mound shape composed of densely packed foliage. The flowers of some species rest directly on the cushion; others extend on taller stems. Whether due to rocky soil and drought or harsh exposure to wind, sun, ice, or snow, cushion plants have evolved to survive adverse conditions. Viewing a collection of cushion plants immediately brings to mind the harsh native environments from which they hail. Cushion plants are found from sea level to alpine peak, and from desert to tundra. Their charm is irresistible to many collectors of miniature plants and alpines. When selecting plants from this list, read the individual descriptions carefully as some genera include both cushion- and non-cushion-forming species and cultivars.

*Acantholimon*
*Aethionema oppositifolium*
*Androsace*, many
*Arabis*, some
*Arenaria tetraquetra*
*Armeria caespitosa*
*Bolax gummifera*
*Chamaecyparis*, smallest cultivars, e.g., *C. obtusa* 'Golden Sprite'
*Chionohebe pulvinaris*
*Dianthus*, many
*Dionysia*
*Draba*, most
*Edraianthus pumilio*
*Eriogonum*, most
*Eritrichium*
*Gypsophila aretioides*
*Gypsophila briquetiana*
*Helichrysum frigidum*
*Juniperus communis* 'Echiniformis'
*Kelseya uniflora*
*Minuartia*
*Myosotis colensoi*
*Perezia recurvata*
*Pernettya tasmanica*
*Petrocallis pyrenaica*
*Phlox caespitosa*
*Phlox douglasii*
*Phlox* 'Sileneflora'
*Primula allionii*
*Raoulia* ×*loganii*
*Raoulia mammillaris*
*Sagina boydii*
*Saxifraga*, many
*Sedum dasyphyllum*
*Selaginella sanguinolenta* var. *compressa*
*Silene acaulis*
*Teucrium cossonii*
*Trachelium asperuloides*
*Veronica caespitosa*
*Vitaliana primuliflora*

## Late-Flowering Plants

The majority of plants found in temperate gardens flower in spring and early summer. Without giving it much thought, the average gardener will find he or she has abundant flowers in springtime. It takes a bit of effort to have an equally abundant show of flowers later in the year, midsummer into fall. Fortunately for rock gardeners there are many appropriate plants that put on their best flower display in the later, warm-weather seasons. Carefully choosing plants from the following list will help extend the flowering season in your rock garden.

*Achillea chrysocoma*
*Allium cyaneum*
*Alopecurus lanatus*
*Alyssum propinquum*
*Anagallis monellii*
*Anaphalis triplinervis*
*Androsace lanuginosa*
*Andryala aghardii*
*Anemone narcissiflora*
*Anomatheca laxa*
*Anthemis*
*Anthyllis hermanniae*
*Anthyllis montana*
*Antirrhinum*
*Armeria caespitosa*
*Armeria maritima*
*Asarina procumbens*
*Asperula*
*Aster novi-belgii*
*Astilbe chinensis*
*Astilbe simplicifolia*
*Astragalus angustifolius*
*Astragalus exscapus*
*Begonia grandis*
*Begonia sutherlandii*
*Bellium bellidioides*
*Berardia subacaulis*
*Bletilla striata*
*Brachycome nivalis*
*Buglossoides purpureocaeruleum*
*Calamintha*
*Calceolaria falklandica*
*Calceolaria uniflora*
*Callirhoe involucrata*
*Calluna vulgaris*
*Calylophus*
*Calyptridium umbellatum*
*Campanula*, most species
*Carduncellus*
*Carlina acaulis*
*Catananche caespitosa*
*Celmisia*
*Centaurea uniflora*
*Cerastium alpinum*
*Chaenorrhinum origanifolium*
*Chamaemelum nobile*
*Chrysanthemum*
*Cirsium acaule*
*Cistus ladanifer*
*Cistus* ×*purpureus*
*Clematis integrifolia*
*Codonopsis*
*Colchicum autumnale*
*Colchicum speciosum*
*Colchicum* 'Waterlily'
*Collomia debilis*
*Commelina dianthifolia*
*Conandron ramondioides*
*Convolvulus*
*Coreopsis rosea*
*Cornus canadensis*
*Corydalis lutea*
*Corydalis ochroleuca*
*Cotula pyrethrifolia*
*Craspedia minor*
*Crepis aurea*
*Crocus medius*
*Crocus serotinus* subsp. *clusii*
*Cyananthus*
*Cyclamen cilicium*
*Cyclamen graecum*
*Cyclamen hederifolium*
*Cyclamen mirabile*
*Cyclamen purpurascens*
*Cymbalaria*
*Cypripedium calceolus*
*Daboecia*
*Daphne caucasica*
*Daphne collina*
*Daphne jasminea*, Delphi form
*Daphne* ×*mantensiana*
*Daphne* ×*napolitana*
*Delosperma* cf. *congestum*
*Delosperma cooperi*
*Delphinium oxysepalum*
*Delphinium uliginosum*
*Deschampsia flexuosa*
*Dianthus*, most
*Diascia*
*Dicentra eximia*
*Dicentra formosa*
*Dorycnium hirsutum*

Dracocephalum
Epilobium
Epipactus gigantea
Erica cinerea
Erica tetralix
Erica vagans
Erigeron aureus
Erigeron chrysopsidis 'Grand
    Ridge'
Erigeron compositus
Erigeron glaucus
Erinacea anthyllis
Eriogonum
Eriophorum vaginatum
Eriophyllum lanatum
Erodium
Eryngium
Euphorbia seguieriana subsp.
    niciciana
Festuca ovina
Frankenia thymifolia
Galanthus reginae-olgae
Gaultheria nummularioides
Gaultheria procumbens
Gaura lindheimeri
Genista tinctoria
Gentiana, many
Geranium, most
Gladiolus
Gypsophila, most
×Halimiocistus wintonensis
Haplopappus glutinosus
Hebe, flowering types
Helianthemum
Helichrysum, most
Horminum pyrenaicum
Hosta
Hydrangea macrophylla
Hymenoxys grandiflora
Hypericum, most
Hypoxis hirsuta
Iberis sempervirens 'Autumn
    Snow'

Indigofera decora
Inula
Iris sintenisii
Jasione laevis
Jasminum parkeri
Jovibarba hirta
Lamium
Lavandula
Leucogenes grandiceps
Leucojum autumnale
Lewisia columbiana subsp. rupi-
    cola
Lewisia leana
Lewisia rediviva
Liatris spicata f. montana
Lilium bolanderi
Lilium bulbiferum var. croceum
Lilium pumilum
Limonium
Linaria
Linum campanulatum
Linum perenne subsp. alpinum
Lithodora diffusa
Lithodora oleifolia
Lloydia serotina
Lobelia linnaeoides
Lotus corniculatus
Lychnis, most
Lysimachia japonica 'Minutis-
    sima'
Mazus reptans
Mertensia maritima
Mertensia pterocarpa
Mimulus
Minuartia, most
Moltkia suffruticosa
Nerine bowdenii
Nierembergia repens
Oenothera
Onosma taurica
Ourisia caespitosa var. gracilis
Ourisia coccinea

Oxalis, many
Oxyria digyna
Oxytropis
Papaver
Parahebe catarractae
Parnassia palustris
Paronychia argentea
Pelargonium endlicherianum
Penstemon, most
Petrophytum caespitosum
Petrorhagia saxifraga
Phacelia sericea
Phlox mesoleuca
Phlox nana
Phyteuma globulariaefolium
Phyteuma hemisphaericum
Pimelea prostrata
Platycodon grandiflorus
Polemonium viscosum
Polygonum affine
Potentilla fruticosa
Primula sinopurpurea
Primula vialii
Prunella grandiflora
Putoria calabrica
Rehmannia glutinosa
Rhododendron 'Alexander'
Rhodohypoxis baurii
Roscoea
Rubus acaulis
Ruellia humilis
Rupicapnos africana
Salvia jurisicii
Santolina chamaecyparissus
Satureja montana subsp. illyrica
Saussurea
Scabiosa
Schizostylis coccinea
Sedum
Sempervivum
Senecio incanus
Sibbaldia procumbens

Silene, most
Sisyrinchium 'E. K. Balls'
Sisyrinchium macrocarpon
Solidago virgaurea var. minutis-
    sima
Spigelia marilandica
Spiraea japonica 'Nyewoods'
Stachys
Sternbergia clusiana
Sternbergia lutea
Talinum
Tanacetum
Teucrium
Thalictrum
Thlaspi rotundifolium
Thymus, most
Townsendia
Trachelium jaquinii subsp.
    rumelianum
Tricyrtis
Trientalis latifolia
Trifolium
Tropaeolum polyphyllum
Valeriana
Vella spinosa
Verbascum
Verbena
Veronica armena
Veronica caespitosa
Veronica peduncularis
Veronica spicata
Viola aetolica
Viola calcarata
Viola cazorlensis
Viola delphinantha
Viola flettii
Viola gracilis
Vitaliana primuliflora
Weldenia candida
Zauschneria californica
Zinnia grandiflora

# HARDINESS ZONE MAPS

Please see the discussion of zone guidelines for rock garden plants under Hardiness Zones in the chapter, About the Descriptions.

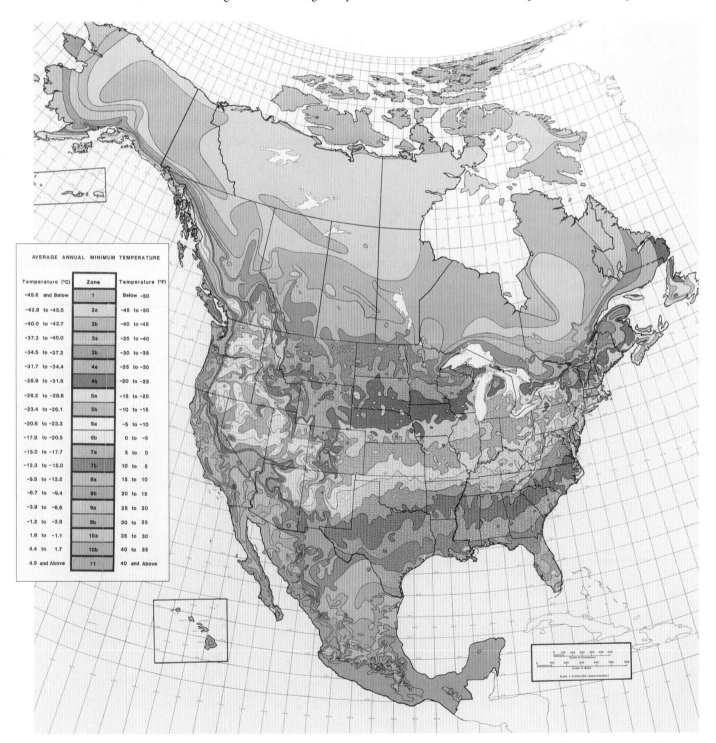

AVERAGE ANNUAL MINIMUM TEMPERATURE

| Temperature (°C) | Zone | Temperature (°F) |
|---|---|---|
| -45.6 and Below | 1 | Below -50 |
| -42.8 to -45.5 | 2a | -45 to -50 |
| -40.0 to -42.7 | 2b | -40 to -45 |
| -37.3 to -40.0 | 3a | -35 to -40 |
| -34.5 to -37.2 | 3b | -30 to -35 |
| -31.7 to -34.4 | 4a | -25 to -30 |
| -28.9 to -31.6 | 4b | -20 to -25 |
| -26.2 to -28.8 | 5a | -15 to -20 |
| -23.4 to -26.1 | 5b | -10 to -15 |
| -20.6 to -23.3 | 6a | -5 to -10 |
| -17.8 to -20.5 | 6b | 0 to -5 |
| -15.0 to -17.7 | 7a | 5 to 0 |
| -12.3 to -15.0 | 7b | 10 to 5 |
| -9.5 to -12.2 | 8a | 15 to 10 |
| -6.7 to -9.4 | 8b | 20 to 15 |
| -3.9 to -6.6 | 9a | 25 to 20 |
| -1.2 to -3.8 | 9b | 30 to 25 |
| 1.6 to -1.1 | 10a | 35 to 30 |
| 4.4 to 1.7 | 10b | 40 to 35 |
| 4.5 and Above | 11 | 40 and Above |

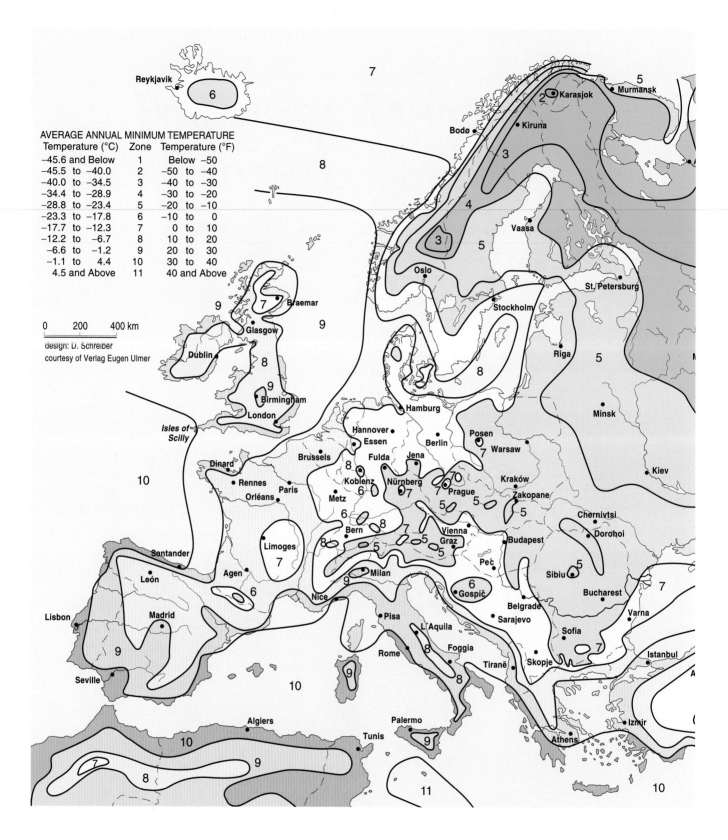

AVERAGE ANNUAL MINIMUM TEMPERATURE

| Temperature (°C) | Zone | Temperature (°F) |
|---|---|---|
| −45.6 and Below | 1 | Below −50 |
| −45.5 to −40.0 | 2 | −50 to −40 |
| −40.0 to −34.5 | 3 | −40 to −30 |
| −34.4 to −28.9 | 4 | −30 to −20 |
| −28.8 to −23.4 | 5 | −20 to −10 |
| −23.3 to −17.8 | 6 | −10 to 0 |
| −17.7 to −12.3 | 7 | 0 to 10 |
| −12.2 to −6.7 | 8 | 10 to 20 |
| −6.6 to −1.2 | 9 | 20 to 30 |
| −1.1 to 4.4 | 10 | 30 to 40 |
| 4.5 and Above | 11 | 40 and Above |

0    200    400 km

design: D. Schreiber
courtesy of Verlag Eugen Ulmer

# INDEX OF COMMON NAMES AND SYNONYMS

Plant entries in the encyclopedia are organized alphabetically and are thus self-indexed. This index includes cross-references from common names and synonyms to the accepted names in the encyclopedia. Some additional cross-references are also included so that no information in the encyclopedia is overlooked. For suggestions on choosing plants for gardens, see the appendix, Rock Garden Plants for Specific Purposes and Locations.

*Acantholimon androsaceum*, see *A. ulicinum*
*Aceriphyllum rossii*, see *Mukdenia rossii*
aconite, winter, see *Eranthis hyemalis*
*Actinella scaposa*, see *Hymenoxys scaposa*
adder's tongue, fetid, see *Scoliopus bigelovii*
*Adiantum pedatum*, see *A. aleuticum*
*Adonis*, Amur, see *A. amurensis*
*Aethionema armenum* 'Warley Rose', see *Aethionema* 'Warley Rose'
African violet, see *Saintpaulia* under *Ramonda*
*Ajuga*, spinach, see *A. pyramidalis*
alleluia, see *Oxalis acetosella*
*Allium*
    *falcifolium*, see under *A. siskiyouense*
    *insubricum*, see under *A. narcissiflorum*
    *siculum*, see *Nectaroscordum siculum*
alumroot, see *Heuchera*
*Alyssum*, see also under *Matthiola fruticulosa* subsp. *valesiaca*
    *saxatile*, see *Aurinia saxatilis*
    *spinosum*, see *Ptilotrichum spinosum*
*Anacyclus depressus*, see *A. pyrethrum* var. *depressus*
andromeda, see *Pieris japonica*
*Androsace*, see also under *Douglasia*
    *carnea* var. *halleri*, see *A. carnea* subsp. *rosea*
    *imbricata*, see *A. vandellii*
    *primuloides*, see *A. sarmentosa*
    *pyrenaica*, see also under *A. vandellii*
    *vitaliana*, see *Vitaliana primuliflora*
*Anemone*, see also rue anemone
    *albana*, see *Pulsatilla albana*

European wood, see *A. nemorosa*, *A. ranunculoides*
    hepatica, see *Hepatica nobilis*
    ×*lipsiensis*, see *A.* ×*seemannii*
    nemorosa, see also under *Buglossoides purpureocaeruleum*
    pulsatilla, see *Pulsatilla vulgaris*
    ranunculoides, see also under *Buglossoides purpureocaeruleum*
    sylvestris, see also under *Pinellia ternata*
angel's tears, see *Narcissus triandrus*
*Anomatheca cruenta*, see *A. laxa*
*Anthemis*
    biebersteiniana, see *A. marschalliana*
    cretica subsp. carpatica, see *A. carpatica*
*Antirrhinum asarina*, see *Asarina procumbens*
*Aquilegia*
    ecalcarata, see *Semiaquilegia ecalcarata*
    jonesii, see also under *A. scopulorum*
*Arabis*
    androsacea, see under *Arabis*
    bryoides, see under *Arabis*
    caucasica 'Monte Rosa', see *A.* ×*arendsii* 'Monte Rosa'
arborvitae
    American, see *Thuja occidentalis*
    Rheingold, see *Thuja occidentalis* 'Rheingold'
*Arctanthemum arcticum*, see *Chrysanthemum arcticum*
*Arctous alpina*, see *Arctostaphylos alpina*
*Arenaria*, see also under *Minuartia*
    pinifolius, see *Minuartia circassica*
*Arisaema serratum*, see *A. japonicum*

*Armeria juniperifolia*, see *A. caespitosa*
*Arnebia echioides*, see *A. pulchra*
*Artemisia*
    assoana, see *A. pedemontana*
    caucasica, see *A. pedemontana*
*Arum italicum* 'Pictum', see under *Daphne mezereum*
asarabacca, see *Asarum*, *A. europaeum*
ash, mountain, see *Sorbus*
asphodel, see *Asphodelus*
aster, beach, see *Erigeron glaucus*
*Astilbe japonica* var. *terrestris*, see *A. glaberrima* 'Saxatilis'
aubretia, see *Aubrieta*
    variegated, see *Aubrieta* ×*cultorum* 'Variegata'
*Aubrieta deltoidea*, see under *A.* ×*cultorum*
auricula, see *Primula auricula*
Australian mint bush, see *Prostanthera*
avens, see *Geum*
    alpine, see *Geum montanum*
    creeping, see *Geum reptans*
    mountain, see *Dryas*
azalea
    alpine, see *Loiseleuria procumbens*
    mountain, see *Loiseleuria procumbens*
bachelor's buttons, see *Craspedia*; see also under *Pterocephalus perennis*
baldmoney, see *Meum athamanticum*
balloon flower, see *Platycodon*
balsam, alpine, see *Erinus alpinus*
balsam root, see *Balsamorhiza*
barberry, coral, see *Berberis* ×*stenophylla* 'Corallina Compacta'